YELLOWSTONE TO GLACIER NATIONAL PARK

Road Trip

CARTER G. WALKER

CONTENTS

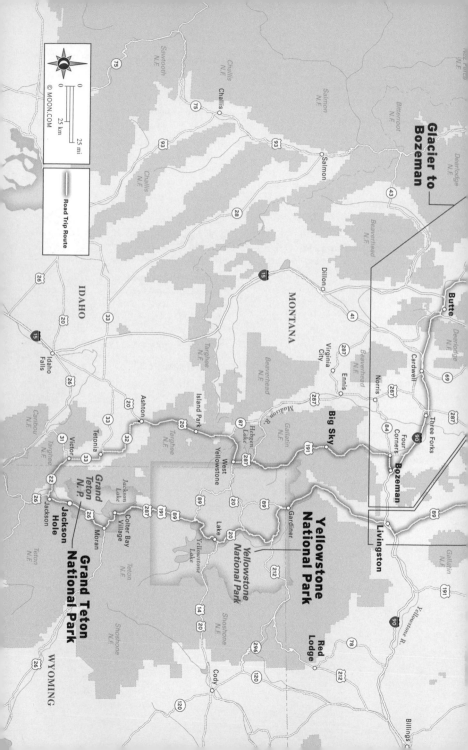

YELLOWSTONE TO GLACIER ROAD TRIP

Glacier National Park

Rocky Mountain Front

First Peoples Buffalo Jump State Park

NATIONAL BISON RANGE

MONTANA

CANADA

Missoula
Philipsburg
Plains
Polson
St Ignatius
Bigfork
Kalispell
Whitefish
West Glacier
East Glacier
St. Mary
Browning
Shelby
Eureka
Augusta
Choteau
Helena
White Sulphur Springs
Great Falls
Fort Benton
Havre
Lewistown
Garrison
Condon

Flathead Lake
Swan Lake
Seeley Lake
Hungry Horse Reservoir
Tiber Reservoir
Flathead R.
Missouri R.

Lolo N.F.
Clearwater N.F.
Kootenai N.F.
Flathead N.F.
Lewis and Clark N.F.
Louis and Clark N.F.
Helena N.F.
Louis and Clark N.F.

DISCOVER THE
Yellowstone to Glacier Road Trip

There is something quintessentially American about a road trip out West.

Amid long stretches of highway and wide-open country, with no evidence of civilization besides a far-off fence line, there's something about being out here that reminds us how a day works: the way the sun moves across the sky, the way your body gets tired when it takes you to the top of a mountain, the taste of a juicy burger. Things are simpler here—but they are also beautiful beyond words.

Yellowstone, Grand Teton, and Glacier National Parks are the jewels in this humble crown. They are ineffable in their beauty and unknowable in their vastness and scale, from soaring mountainscapes and hulking grizzly bears to the tiniest wild orchid, purple against green. There is wildness here. You can feel it.

But there is civilization, too. And culture. There are Native American reservations where you can experience the aural and visual feast of a powwow. There are little towns that feel untouched by time. There are big towns, too, with museums and restaurants and art galleries. You can be comfortable when you travel out here—a big bed, a good meal—but you'll find yourself humbled at being part of something so much larger than any of us dare to imagine. Come out West, to these parks, to this landscape. This place will change you.

PLANNING YOUR TRIP

Where to Go

Yellowstone National Park

This magnificent and dynamic place was the world's first national park. A natural wonderland, Yellowstone offers a rare and up-close view into one of the **last large intact ecosystems** in the Northern Hemisphere. See abundant wildlife, including **bison, elk, bears, and wolves;** marvel at geothermal features like **Old Faithful,** or swim in them at the **Boiling River;** hike the peaks, **Mount Washburn** for starters; and stay in historic lodges like the **Old Faithful Inn** and the rambling **Lake Yellowstone Hotel.** Perimeter communities, including **West Yellowstone, Gardiner,** and remote **Cooke City,** should not be missed.

Grand Teton National Park

Grand Teton packs a punch, particularly when it comes to **mountain splendor.** Twelve peaks in the Teton Range soar above 12,000 feet (3,658 m). While there are only 100 miles (161 km) of roads in the park, there are twice as many **miles of trails,** leaving hikers endless options for adventure at breathtaking spots like **Hidden Falls** and **Inspiration Point.** Favorite landmarks include picturesque **Jenny Lake,** vast **Jackson Lake,** drive-to-the-summit **Signal Mountain,** and serene **Oxbow Bend;** favorite ways to enjoy the beauty of the region include **hiking, biking,** and **rafting.** Just south of the park, the gateway community of **Jackson Hole** offers **ritzy accommodations** and a thriving culinary scene.

ocky Mountain Front

vast plains erupt into **soaring peaks** g the **Rocky Mountain Front.** Tiny s like **Choteau** and **Augusta** offer a charming sense of community, along with fascinating sites like dinosaur mecca **Egg Mountain** and **quaint old hotels.** Straddling the division between mountains and plains, **Great Falls** boasts two of the state's best museums: the **C. M. Russell Museum** and **Lewis and Clark National Historic Trail Interpretive Center.**

History comes to life in the heart of **Helena,** in **Last Chance Gulch** and **Reeder's Alley.** Along the winding roads, there's **fishing** to be done, **bird-watching** opportunities, and an outstanding place to learn about **Blackfeet history and culture** where you can sleep in a **tipi village.**

Glacier National Park

Known as the "Crown of the Continent," **Glacier National Park** embodies the Montana you've always imagined: **rugged mountains** piercing the sky, **crystalline lakes** and **plunging waterfalls, abundant wildlife,** gravity-defying roads, and miles upon miles of trails. For now, the park still lays claim to **25 glaciers** and offers excellent viewing opportunities for such wildlife as **mountain goats, bighorn sheep,** and even **grizzly bears.** There are an infinite number of ways to explore and enjoy this stunning landscape, including **hiking the Highline Trail** to **Granite Park Chalet,** picking **huckleberries** in season, **swimming** or **boating** on **Lake McDonald, biking** the twists and turns of the **Going-to-the-Sun Road,** or just relaxing porch-side in **Many Glacier.**

Glacier to Bozeman

One of the best things about road trips out West is that the journey truly is just as worthwhile as the destination. This six-hour drive from Glacier to Bozeman offers up abundant natural beauty—**Jewel Basin, Flathead Lake,** and the **National Bison Range** for starters—plus access to important cultural hubs, including **Missoula** and **Bozeman,** where the **arts** flourish and excellent restaurants and hotels abound.

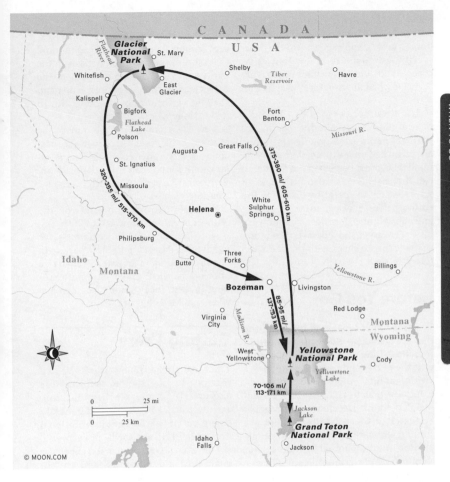

There are wonderful places to get your fill of **mining history,** including **Butte** and **Philipsburg,** and the living **ghost towns** of **Virginia City** and **Nevada City.** Another route down **single-lane highways** takes visitors through **towering forests** to timeless **waterside resorts** at **Holland Lake** and **Seeley Lake.**

When to Go

Summer is the easiest and busiest time to travel the roads, both into and out of the national parks. The roads are mostly open—save for rogue snowstorms that can happen at high elevations—but travel can be slowed by **traffic, animal jams** (particularly in Yellowstone), and **construction.**

Winter road travel can be challenging because of the inevitable storms and possible closures. With the exception of the road in Yellowstone between Gardiner and Cooke City, which stays open year-round for the residents of Cooke City, most of the roads in the three national parks are closed in winter. In Grand Teton National Park, the roads between Jackson and Flagg Ranch (U.S. 89/191 and U.S. 26/287) are plowed and open year-round. Winter travel in Glacier is limited to skis, snowshoes, and the occasional dogsled tour. In Yellowstone, snow coaches and guided snowmobile tours are available when the roads are covered with snow.

The **shoulder seasons** can be a delightful time to travel in this region. The **national parks** are heavenly and much less crowded in **autumn,** but keep in mind that winter comes very early at high elevations. There are also little-known ways to enjoy the parks by bicycle in the **spring,** before they open to cars. Opening and closing times for the parks can vary by year (weather and federal budget, too), so make sure to check with the parks before you travel.

Before You Go

When it comes to staying in any of the three parks, advance planning is critical. In **Yellowstone,** nearly 1 million people visit the park in July, with slightly fewer visiting in June, August, and September. Compare that to right around 20,000 people in both December and March. Statistics in **Glacier National Park** are similar, with more than 1 million people visiting in July, followed by August, and then June. Winter numbers in Glacier range from around 13,000 visitors in December to nearly 20,000 in March. Statistical trends vary in **Grand Teton National Park,** with some 740,000 visitors in July, slightly fewer in June and August, and around 50,000 visitors per month in winter. As such, thoughtful planning and **advance reservations,** particularly for hotels and campgrounds, are essential in summer months. Even in perimeter communities, hotel rooms can be hard to find during peak summer months, especially around local events such as the Fourth of July celebration in Livingston or the Fall Arts Festival in Jackson Hole.

Rates for accommodations are generally lower and rooms more available when snow is on the ground—except around ski areas—but keep in mind that most of the accommodations in the parks are closed during the winter. The exceptions are the Mammoth Hotel and the Old Faithful Snow Lodge, both in Yellowstone.

Very few **campgrounds** in any of the parks can be reserved. Most are first come, first served; in peak season, popular campgrounds can fill up before 8am. Plan to arrive at the site early, and have a backup plan.

For now, there are no limits on the number of visitors allowed into the parks, so you do not need to order **park passes** in advance. Passes for all three parks can be purchased upon arrival. If you arrive after hours, when rangers are not manning the entrance stations, you can pay when you leave the park.

Getting There

The most time-efficient way to see all three parks is to fly into **Jackson Hole Airport** (JAC) and see Grand Teton, Yellowstone, and then Glacier before flying out of **Glacier Park International Airport** (GPI) in Kalispell—or vice versa.

However, it's often much less expensive to fly into and out of the same city. In this case, you will have to cover some of the same ground twice. That's not a bad thing out here. You can build a fantastic itinerary around whatever city offers the best airfare.

Besides Jackson Hole and Kalispell, the airports closest to Yellowstone are **Bozeman Yellowstone International Airport** (BZN) and **Billings Logan International Airport** (BIL). **Great Falls International Airport** (GTF) is closest to Glacier. **Missoula International Airport** (MSO) is about midway between Glacier and Yellowstone. **Helena Regional Airport** (HLN) is about 3 hours from Yellowstone and 3.5 hours from Glacier.

Clockwise from top left: summer powwow; Lower Falls of the Yellowstone; a common sight in this region, the cowboy boot.

Driving Guide

Because the distances between the parks and towns are vast, you will need a private vehicle unless you book an all-inclusive tour. **Rental cars** are available at all of the major airports, with some additional rental agencies having off-airport offices in larger towns. In the busier airports, rental cars can sell out during holidays and peak vacation weeks, so be sure to book ahead. **All-wheel-drive vehicles** are recommended for back-road driving where higher clearance can come in handy. In the winter, all-wheel drive is practically mandatory at high elevations. **RVs** can be rented in most of the major towns including Bozeman, Billings, Missoula, Great Falls, and Kalispell, with both Bozeman and Missoula offering RV rentals from the airports.

While most of the interstates and highways across the region are in good shape, there is often **construction** happening in the snow-free months. Many of the smaller roads into recreation areas are dirt and gravel. There can be significant potholes any time of year, and roads can flood during spring runoff. Always carry a map and emergency supplies of food, water, and winter gear. Drivers should watch for wildlife, particularly at twilight and dark. For Wyoming road conditions, the **Wyoming Department of Transportation** (888/996-7623, www.wyoroad.info) has a wealth of information. Montana information can be found through the **Montana Department of Transportation** (800/226-7623, www.mdt.mt.gov/travinfo).

While most towns have taxi service, only the larger cities have public transportation. If you are planning to travel between cities by bus, check this book's individual town sections for information and consider making arrangements in advance. In Montana, train service is only available across the northern section of the state, known as the Hi-Line.

HIT THE ROAD

The 14-Day Yellowstone to Glacier Road Trip

This ambitious two-week, 1,150-mile (1,852-km) itinerary starts and ends in Bozeman, Montana, taking you through Yellowstone, Grand Teton, and Glacier National Parks. Most days require only 100 miles or fewer of driving, so you can see and experience this breathtaking region without getting stuck behind the wheel. For detailed driving directions for each leg of the trip, see the beginning of each chapter.

Day 1
BOZEMAN
Start your trip in Bozeman, Montana, equal parts college town and mountain town. Fit in a trip to the **Museum of the Rockies** to see where dinosaur guru Jack Horner did much of his work. Throw in a hike up the **M,** just northeast of town, and end with a shopping stroll on historic **Main Street.** Enjoy a game of pool, a local brew, and an excellent meal at the popular **Montana Ale Works.** After a pre-bed ice-cream cone from the **Genuine Ice Cream** truck, bed down for the night at **The Lark,** a hip and artsy hotel.

Day 2
BOZEMAN TO OLD FAITHFUL
120 miles (193 km), 3 hours
Start your morning with a hearty breakfast at **Feed Café** before you head into the **Gallatin Canyon,** toward **Big Sky Resort.** Adrenaline junkies can **raft the Gallatin** with **Montana Whitewater.** Grab lunch at Big Sky's **Bugaboo Café** before continuing on to **West Yellowstone** to check out the critters at the **Grizzly and Wolf Discovery Center.**

Continue into **Yellowstone National Park** and, on a warm day, stop to swim in the geothermally heated water of the **Firehole River.** Leave time to walk around the **Midway and Lower Geyser Basins**—don't miss the colorful **Grand Prismatic Spring**—before arriving at the **Old Faithful Inn** for the night. Make sure to see at least one eruption of its namesake geyser, and check out the **Old Faithful Visitor Education Center** before you enjoy a meal in the hotel's lovely dining room and settle in for the night.

Day 3
OLD FAITHFUL TO JACKSON HOLE
100 miles (161 km), 3 hours
After breakfast and perhaps one more eruption of Old Faithful, head south toward **Yellowstone Lake,** stopping to explore the thermal features at **West Thumb Geyser Basin.** Take your time, cruising south through Yellowstone and into **Grand Teton National Park.** Dip your toes in the water, or just enjoy the scenery at various pull-outs.

You could have lunch at Colter Bay and visit the **Colter Bay Indian Arts Museum.** Stretch your legs with a two-mile loop on the **Colter Bay Lakeshore Trail.** Continue on through Moran and down to Moose, where you'll want to get an overview of the park at the **Craig Thomas Discovery and Visitor Center.**

Settle in for three nights at the **Alpine House** in Jackson. You're within walking distance to all of downtown and to **Hatch Taqueria & Tequilas,** where you can get a delicious elk taco and a margarita.

Days 4-5
JACKSON HOLE
With three nights in Jackson and two full days, you'll have time to pack in both culture and adventure. Make sure to visit **Town Square** for shopping, dining, or the **Jackson Hole Shootout.** Perhaps the first morning you could explore the **National**

Where the Wild Things Are

The most obvious choice for prime wildlife-viewing is Yellowstone National Park, where animals have the right-of-way; just try telling a herd of rutting bison that you have to be somewhere. Grand Teton and Glacier National Parks are also great bets, although the restricted roads and dense forests can limit visibility. Still, this is the Wild West, and there are excellent opportunities to see wildlife almost anywhere.

Yellowstone National Park

♦ The **Lamar Valley** is known as the Little Serengeti, and for good reason. Time it right and you could see bison, elk, coyotes, foxes, wolves, bears, and even the occasional moose in this grassy, wide-open valley.

♦ In summer, the **Hayden Valley** is the gorgeous green stomping ground for hundreds, maybe thousands of bison. Seeing such big herds is an unforgettable sight.

Grand Teton National Park

♦ **Oxbow Bend,** between **Moran Junction** and **Jackson Lake Junction,** is an excellent place to look for moose, deer, birdlife, and the occasional bear. Dusk and dawn are the best times of day to see wildlife.

♦ Just outside **Jackson,** and south of the park, the **National Elk Refuge** is home to 6,000-7,000 elk or more throughout the winter months.

♦ In **Dubois,** the **National Bighorn Sheep Interpretive Center** offers winter tours of the nearby **Whiskey Mountain Habitat Area.** Self-guided tours take visitors into prime sheep country, where raptors and moose can often be seen.

Rocky Mountain Front

♦ Seeing hundreds of thousands of migrating birds at **Freezeout Lake** during early spring, near **Augusta,** is an unforgettable experience.

♦ **Wolf Creek Canyon,** off of I-15 south of **Great Falls,** is a great place to look for bighorn sheep—Lewis and Clark saw their first specimens here—and eagles.

Glacier National Park

♦ The trails to **Avalanche Lake** and **Iceberg Lake** are among the best spots in Glacier to look for grizzly bears in May and June. Mountain goats can also be spotted.

♦ Hikers on the **Grinnell Glacier Trail** often get a chance to see bighorn sheep, mountain goats, and the occasional moose.

Glacier to Bozeman

♦ In **Moiese,** the **National Bison Range** is home to around 400 bison, along with white-tailed and mule deer, bighorn sheep, pronghorn antelope, and elk.

♦ In the **Jewel Basin,** there are 17 species of raptors. Hikers often see mountain goats and even grizzlies, especially during huckleberry season.

Clockwise from top left: Mammoth Hot Springs Terraces; canoeing at Jenny Lake; Yellowstone's Grand Prismatic Spring.

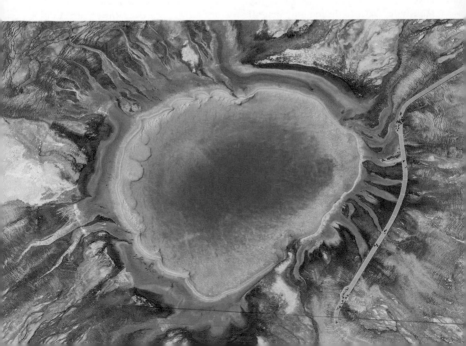

Museum of Wildlife Art before embarking on a white-water rafting adventure on the Snake River or taking the gondola up the mountain at Teton Village to hike the Cirque Trail. Save just enough energy for another excellent meal in Jackson at Wild Sage if you're feeling fancy, or The Merry Piglets if you're not.

The next morning, pick up a picnic lunch at Persephone Bakery and plan to spend your second day back in Grand Teton National Park. Visit the Chapel of the Transfiguration and the historic buildings at Menors Ferry before you head to Jenny Lake for a picnic and a hike to Hidden Falls and Inspiration Point. Before you return to Jackson for another night on the town, you could take a tour of the Murie Ranch or visit the Laurance S. Rockefeller Preserve.

Day 6
JACKSON HOLE TO LAKE LODGE
65 miles (105 km), 2 hours

You can hit The Bunnery on your way out of town, heading north past Antelope Flats and Mormon Row to Signal Mountain. Drive to the top for a magnificent view or hike it if you want. Make a stop at Oxbow Bend to look for wildlife.

For a real treat, plan a lunch cruise from Colter Bay Marina to Elk Island, and then keep heading north and back into Yellowstone. From the Bridge Bay Marina, hike the 2.6 miles round-trip to Natural Bridge, but keep an eye open for grizzlies. Settle in for the night at Lake Lodge and enjoy dinner in the beautiful dining room overlooking the lake.

Day 7
LAKE LODGE TO PARADISE VALLEY
55 miles (89 km), 2 hours

After breakfast, make your way to the Fishing Bridge Visitor Center for a great exhibit on Yellowstone Lake's geology. Take a picture of the old bridge itself, which used to be one of the best fishing spots in the park. Head north into the wide-open Hayden Valley, where hundreds of bison can congregate in summer. Keep driving to the Grand Canyon of the Yellowstone and take in the scenic views. From there, plan on lunch and maybe an afternoon trail ride at Roosevelt Lodge.

From Roosevelt, continue north to Mammoth Hot Springs for a stroll around the boardwalks. When you exit the park, head for Chico Hot Springs for the night where you can soak, dine, and sleep to your heart's content.

Day 8
PARADISE VALLEY TO GREAT FALLS
205 miles (330 km), 3.5 hours

After a big breakfast and a morning dip at Chico, drive north to the hip, artsy town of Livingston, where you can browse galleries and shop until you work up an appetite for lunch at Gil's Goods. From there, continue north on U.S. 89 through ranch country, including Wilsall and White Sulphur Springs.

After you make it through the Kings Hill Scenic Byway and the Little Belt Mountains, consider a hike in the rugged beauty of Sluice Boxes State Park and stop for an outstanding beer in Belt at the Harvest Moon Brewing Company. Before your head hits the pillow in Great Falls at the historic Hotel Arvon, watch the mermaid show at the Sip 'n Dip, and enjoy a local pie at Howard's Pizza.

Day 9
GREAT FALLS TO BROWNING
125 miles (201 km), 2 hours

Decide between art and history when you choose a morning at either the C. M. Russell Museum or the Lewis and Clark National Historic Trail Interpretive Center—you can't go wrong at either place. From Great Falls, make your way northwest on U.S. 89 past Freezeout Lake and Choteau. There's a great little rock shop next to a dinosaur museum in Bynum.

Arrive in Browning in time for a

Blackfeet Cultural History Tour, which can include a visit to the Museum of the Plains Indian. Settle in for a gourmet dinner and a tipi under the stars at the Lodge Pole Gallery and Tipi Village.

Day 10
BROWNING TO MANY GLACIER
45 miles (72 km), 1 hour
Break camp and head to East Glacier for a big breakfast at the Two Medicine Grill. It's worth ambling the grounds of the stately Glacier Park Lodge. As you head toward the park, you could stop for some recreation in the isolated Two Medicine Valley: Consider taking a 45-minute cruise on Two Medicine Lake, cutting 6 miles (9.7 km) off the hike to Twin Falls. Or continue farther north to St. Mary where cruises and cruise-hike combos are also available. You'll end up at the storied Many Glacier Hotel where you can have bison tenderloin or the wild mushroom stroganoff in the Ptarmigan Dining Room.

Day 11
MANY GLACIER
Plan to spend the day adventuring around Many Glacier. Possible activities include an endless number of hiking trails and canoeing, kayaking, or cruising on Swiftcurrent Lake. One option is to combine a scenic cruise with a hike to Grinnell Glacier. The Swiftcurrent Valley and Lookout hike is a favorite and can last as long as your legs do. Other options include ranger-led hikes and Red Bus Tours.

Day 12
MANY GLACIER TO LAKE MCDONALD
65 miles (105 km), 3 hours
You'll head out of the park at Many Glacier and back in again at St. Mary to go up and over the magnificent Going-to-the-Sun Road, the drive you've been waiting for the entire trip, and maybe your whole life. Take the time to park at Logan

Pass and take a hike—the Highline Trail is extraordinary.

Head down the pass for a refreshing dip at Lake McDonald and have a late lunch at Russell's Fireside Dining Room at Lake McDonald Lodge. In the afternoon, consider another short hike—Rocky Point is good, so is Trail of the Cedars and Avalanche Lake—or take a sunset cocktail cruise in a historic wooden boat. You've earned your time to relax and enjoy this place. If you have the energy to leave your hotel, a gourmet dinner at Belton Chalet will not disappoint.

Day 13
LAKE MCDONALD TO WHITEFISH
50 miles (81 km), 1 hour
Take your time getting out of the park—you're going to miss this place. Take a morning hike or a dip in the lake. It's okay to backtrack here and repeat your favorite hike. When it's time, travel through West Glacier and on to Whitefish, where you can do a little shopping and settle in for the night at the Garden Wall Inn after dinner in town at Latitude 48 Bistro.

Day 14
WHITEFISH TO BOZEMAN
320 miles (515 km), 6 hours
The longest day by far, there is a lot of ground to cover between Whitefish and Bozeman. Whatever your plan, you'll want to fuel up with pie for breakfast from Loula's Café. Head south to Big Fork and have a picnic on one of the lovely beaches that line Flathead Lake.

Drive through the beautiful National Bison Range en route to Missoula, where you can stretch your legs on the riverside trail and grab lunch at Caffé Dolce. From here, it's all highway driving east through Butte and on to Bozeman. You might stop in Three Forks for a hike at Madison Buffalo Jump State Park. By the time you roll into Bozeman, you'll be ready for a last big steak at Open Range and a comfy bed for the night at The Lark.

Best Hikes

The best way to see the parks, and to really know them, is to get out and hike. Explore the wilderness. Climb the mountains. Run your fingertips along the bark of trees. Feel the whisper of high grasses on your legs. Earn the best view you've ever seen.

Hidden Lake Overlook Trail

Yellowstone National Park

♦ The 5.1-mile (8-km) round-trip hike on the **South Rim Trail to Point Sublime** offers multiple overlooks of the Grand Canyon of the Yellowstone, including stunning vistas of both the Upper and Lower Falls. The trails winds through forest, down (and back up!) the strenuous Uncle Tom's Trail, and along an exposed section to Point Sublime.

♦ Overlooking the vast Lamar Valley, **Specimen Ridge** is a strenuous 3-mile (5-km) round-trip trail that leads hikers to one of the largest petrified forests in the world, with fossils dating back 50 million years. It's a steep climb, but the views of the valley from the top are well worth the effort, particularly when there are bison in residence.

Grand Teton National Park

♦ The **Taggart Lake-Bradley Lake Loop** takes hikers to two glacially formed lakes at the base of the Tetons. With only 585 feet (178 m) of elevation gained over 5.5 miles (8.9 km), this moderate trail along water and through forest offers views of Nez Perce Peak, Middle and Grand Tetons, and Teewinot Mountain.

♦ **Hidden Falls Trail** offers the best of the park—access to Jenny Lake, pristine conifer forests, rushing creeks, soaring alpine views, and a chance to encounter wildlife. The moderately challenging trail is 4.9 miles (7.9 km), but can be shortened to 1 mile (1.6 km) by taking the shuttle across Jenny Lake.

Glacier National Park

♦ The **Highline Trail** is popular for good reason. Best in midsummer when the wildflowers explode with color, the shorter version of this strenuous hike climbs a total of 1,950 feet (594 m) over 11.8 miles (19 km) and offers outstanding scenery, including a stretch along the Garden Wall, a ledge that will delight thrill seekers.

♦ A short and easy hike through alpine meadows known as the Hanging Gardens, the **Hidden Lake Overlook Trail,** also known as the Hidden Lake Nature Trail, offers extraordinary views of Clements Mountain, the Garden Wall, and Mount Oberlin. The 2.7-mile (4.3-km) round-trip trail crosses the Continental Divide and is often snow-covered, even in midsummer.

Clockwise from top left: dancer performing at a powwow; bison in Yellowstone in the winter; Grinnell Lake.

Clockwise from top left: Old Faithful; Roosevelt Arch at the north entrance to Yellowstone; one of Yellowstone's boardwalks at sunset.

Native American Heritage

The culture and history of indigenous peoples have powerfully defined the identities of both Montana and Wyoming. There are eight reservations between the two states, but only two of them lie close to the parks. The **Blackfeet Reservation** is just east of Glacier, and the **Flathead Reservation** is southwest of Glacier. But you don't have to be on a reservation to be exposed to Native American history and culture here. This region offers tremendous opportunities for those interested in learning about and experiencing Native history, traditions, and contemporary culture. Here are just a few of the ways to engage with Native American culture.

National Park Attractions and Programs

In Grand Teton, the **Colter Bay Indian Arts Museum** is home to important Native American artifacts that belonged to tribes across the country. The David T. Vernon Collection—which comprises more than 1,000 objects including dolls, shields, pipes, weapons, and photography—was donated by the Rockefeller family with the provision that it be displayed permanently in Grand Teton National Park. In 2012, almost the entire collection was sent to a conservation facility; it is slowly being returned to the park, at both the Colter Bay and Craig Thomas Visitor Centers. At various times throughout summer, Native American artisans practice their crafts in the museum and a number of prominent lecturers and daily educational events are scheduled on-site.

One of the most noteworthy programs in Glacier National Park is **Native America Speaks,** where members from the Blackfeet, Salish, Kootenai, and Pend d'Oreille tribes provide campfire talks about their life, culture, and influence in Glacier. The speakers range from artists and musicians to historians who intersperse their talks with personal stories and Native American legends. These talks are given at the Apgar, Many Glacier, Two Medicine, and Rising Sun Campgrounds. During July-August, the St. Mary Visitor Center also hosts weekly Native American dance troupes.

Buffalo Jumps

Used by Native Americans for more than 5,000 years, buffalo jumps are rocky cliffs over which entire herds of bison were driven, causing mortal injury to the animals and providing the hunters with ample meat, fur, and bones to make into weapons, tools, and decorative objects. The jumps have become significant archaeological sites, with discoveries of bones and tools guiding scientists to a better understanding of the various cultures of the people who hunted in this way. They can also be places of quiet contemplation.

Two of the most well-known buffalo jumps in the region can be found outside Bozeman and Great Falls. The **First Peoples Buffalo Jump State Park** in Ulm was used for more than 1,000 years before Lewis and Clark arrived in the area. The site, a mile-long sandstone cliff, is magnificent. Various buildings interpret the history and culture around the jump itself. Overlooking the Madison River between Bozeman and Three Forks, the **Madison Buffalo Jump State Park** was in use 2,000 years ago, and as recently as 200 years ago. Not nearly as large as the jump in Ulm, and with only a small outdoor interpretive display, this site boasts original tipi rings and the remains of eagle-catching pits. Both sites are beautiful and meaningful places to spend an afternoon.

Guided Tours

A fascinating way to learn about Blackfeet culture is by traveling with local Native guides who can interpret Native history and culture and the ways

Best Non-Hikes

Because your legs can only take you so far, and there is a lot of ground (and water) to cover in these national parks, here are the top ways to spend an afternoon without putting miles on your boots.

Yellowstone National Park

♦ No organization in the park helps people understand the wonder of nature better than the **Yellowstone Forever Institute,** where you can go on expert-led excursions. **Yellowstone Day Adventures** are a great choice for scoping out wildlife in the Lamar Valley.

Red Bus Tour

♦ Of the park's thousands of thermal features, only two are swimmable. The **Boiling River** is a worthy adventure year-round, and the **Firehole River** near Madison Junction is an ideal place to spend a warm summer afternoon.

♦ The **Old West Dinner Cookout** takes diners by horseback or covered wagon into Yellowstone's wilderness for a steak-and-potato dinner with all the fixings.

Grand Teton National Park

♦ Whether it's a scenic sunrise float or a white-knuckle ride through such rapids as Lunch Counter and the Big Kahuna, there are many ways to get on the **Snake River.**

♦ Leaving from Colter Bay Marina, the three-hour **meal cruises** are a relaxing way to get out on the water and explore **Elk Island.**

♦ The best way to get out and see wildlife is to go with someone who knows, and no one knows better than the **Wildlife Expeditions** guides from **Teton Science Schools.** The half-day, full-day, or multiday trips are guided by wildlife biologists.

Glacier National Park

♦ Glacier's famed **Red Bus Tours** are the best way to see the park from the road without worrying about the driving.

♦ No matter what interests you—wolves, birds of prey, wildflowers, fly-fishing, photography—the **Glacier Institute** probably offers a class on it. There are amazing offerings for both kids and adults.

♦ Between late May and mid-September, **horseback rides** are available from the corrals at **Apgar, Lake McDonald,** and **Many Glacier.** Trail rides are an excellent way to get up into the high country.

they have shaped and influenced the region. **Blackfeet Tours** offer guided tours around Great Falls—including the First People's Buffalo Jump—in the Badger-Two Medicine National Forest, on the Blackfeet Reservation, and in Glacier. From a fancy, air-conditioned bus to a trusty steed, from half-day to multiday, there are options aplenty.

Another excellent way to learn about Blackfeet culture in the region is by booking a tour and even a night in a tipi camp with Darryl Norman of **Blackfeet Cultural History Tours** out of Browning. These tours focus on the reservation and can be combined with hikes and fishing.

A unique way to see Glacier on a comfortable coach tour is with **Sun Tours.** Its guides are all lifetime residents of the Blackfeet Reservation and provide outstanding narratives on everything from park history and wildlife information to medicinal plants and Blackfeet spiritual perspectives.

Museums

The best Native American museum in the region is the **Museum of the Plains Indian,** in Browning, on the Blackfeet Reservation. The museum exhibits the arts and crafts of the Northern Plains Indians. The permanent collection highlights the diversity of tribal arts and displays artifacts from everyday life, including clothing, weapons, toys, and household implements. Two galleries are dedicated to showcasing contemporary Native American artists. During summer, painted tipis are assembled on the grounds. Although

it is not dedicated to Native American culture and history, the **Lewis and Clark National Historic Trail Interpretive Center** does a good job of portraying the importance of Native Americans to the westward journey.

Native American Reservations

One way to experience the reservations firsthand is by attending traditional celebrations open to the public. On the Flathead Reservation, annual events include the **Arlee 4th of July Celebration** and the **Standing Arrow Powwow,** which happens in mid-July at the Elmo Powwow Grounds in Elmo, Montana. In Pablo, Montana, **The People's Center** is a museum and gift shop where visitors can experience the cultural heritage of the Salish, Pend d'Oreille, and Kootenai tribes. Also on the Flathead Reservation, the **St. Ignatius Mission** tells a much darker story of abuse and betrayal of Native children taken from their families to be educated at the mission.

On the Blackfeet Reservation, annual powwow celebrations include the **North American Indian Days,** held in Browning the second week in July for four days, and the **Heart Butte Society Celebration,** held over four days the second week of August in Heart Butte, 26 miles (42 km) south of Browning. Both events are open to the public and include contest dancing and drumming, games, sporting events, ceremonies, and plenty of food. Also on the reservation is the important **Museum of the Plains Indian,** which should not be missed by anyone interested in Native American culture and history.

Yellowstone
National
Park

Yellowstone National Park

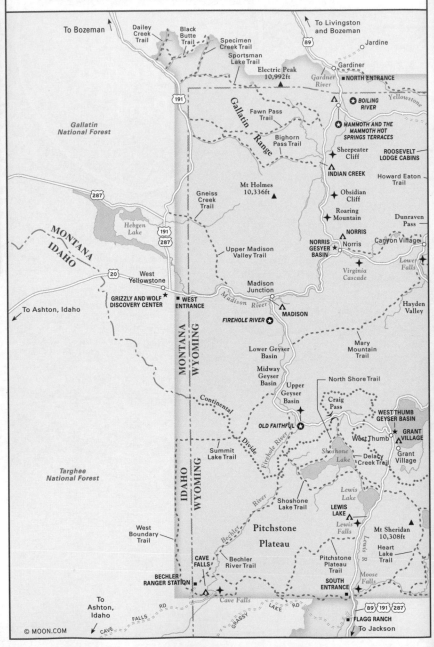

© MOON.COM

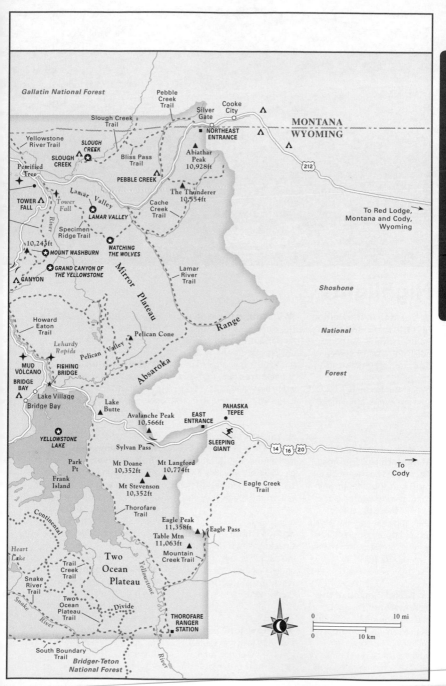

Gallatin National Forest

Pebble Creek Trail

Cooke City

Silver Gate

MONTANA
WYOMING

Slough Creek Trail

NORTHEAST ENTRANCE

212

Yellowstone River Trail

SLOUGH CREEK

SLOUGH CREEK

Bliss Pass Trail

Abiathar Peak 10,928ft

Petrified Tree

PEBBLE CREEK

The Thunderer 10,554ft

To Red Lodge, Montana and Cody, Wyoming

Lamar Valley

TOWER FALL

Tower Fall

Cache Creek Trail

LAMAR VALLEY

Specimen Ridge Trail

10,243ft

MOUNT WASHBURN

WATCHING THE WOLVES

GRAND CANYON OF THE YELLOWSTONE

CANYON

Mirror Plateau

Lamar River Trail

Shoshone

Howard Eaton Trail

Lehardy Rapids

Pelican Valley

Pelican Cone

National

Absaroka

Range

Forest

MUD VOLCANO

FISHING BRIDGE

BRIDGE BAY

Lake Village

Bridge Bay

Lake Butte

Avalanche Peak 10,566ft

EAST ENTRANCE

PAHASKA TEPEE

YELLOWSTONE LAKE

Sylvan Pass

SLEEPING GIANT

14 16 20

Park Pt

Mt Doane 10,352ft

Mt Langford 10,774ft

To Cody

Frank Island

Mt Stevenson 10,352ft

Eagle Creek Trail

Thorofare Trail

Continental

Eagle Peak 11,358ft

Eagle Pass

Heart Lake

Table Mtn 11,063ft

Mountain Creek Trail

Two Ocean Plateau

Trail Creek Trail

Snake River Trail

Two Ocean Plateau Trail

Divide

Snake River

THOROFARE RANGER STATION

South Boundary Trail

Bridger-Teton National Forest

Yellowstone River

0   10 mi

0   10 km

Highlights

★ **Soaking in the Boiling River:** In a stretch of the Gardner River at the park's north entrance, hot water flows over waterfalls and via springs, mixing with the river water to create a perfect soaking temperature (page 36).

★ **Mammoth and the Mammoth Hot Springs Terraces:** The travertine terraces here look like an enormous cream-colored confection. Because the springs shift and change daily, a walk around the colorful terraces is never the same experience twice (page 37).

★ **Grand Canyon of the Yellowstone:** The sheer cliffs and dramatic coloring of this canyon have inspired millions of visitors. In the summer, get a rare bird's-eye view of several osprey nests (page 39).

★ **Watching the Wolves:** The wolves put on a spectacular show—with at least one reported sighting daily since 2001. The sagas of the 11 packs are dramatic, heart-wrenching, and captivating (page 42).

★ **Lamar Valley:** Known as the "Little Serengeti of North America," this scenic, glacially carved valley offers spectacular wildlife-watching year-round (page 43).

★ **Fly Fishing in Slough Creek:** Yellowstone is a fishing paradise. Join other eager anglers as they cast dry flys for cutthroat trout in Slough Creek (page 45).

★ **Yellowstone Lake:** This beautiful lake was touted by early mountain men as perhaps the only place where you could catch a fish and

cook it without ever taking it off the line (page 47).

★ **Old Faithful:** If you see just one thing in Yellowstone, make it this world-famous geyser that erupts every 45-90 minutes (page 49).

★ **Swimming the Firehole River:** This river offers a stunning, heated swimming area surrounded by cliffs. The twists and turns of the cascading canyon are worth seeing even if you don't get wet (page 50).

★ **Hiking Mount Washburn:** Take one of two trails to reach the lookout tower at the summit of Mount Washburn. The views along the way and from the top are worth every step (page 54).

Yellowstone National Park is at the heart of our country's relationship with wilderness. It's also the largest intact ecosystem in the Lower 48— many of the species that have roamed this plateau are still (or once again) in residence.

Yellowstone was our nation's first national park. Signed into being by President Ulysses S. Grant after a series of important and legendary scouting expeditions through the area, the region's history is lengthy and very much alive, from its prehistoric supervolcanic eruptions, to its occupation by the U.S. Army in the 1880s, to the controversial reintroduction of wolves in the 1990s and the more recent snowmobile usage, bison, and grizzly delisting quagmires. The stories, both far-fetched and true, and characters that have emerged from the park are as colorful and compelling as the landscape itself.

A vast 2.2 million acres, Yellowstone is indeed a wonderland, filled with steaming geysers and boiling mud pots, packed with diverse and healthy populations of wildlife, and crisscrossed by hundreds of miles of hiking and skiing trails. A stretch of the park called the Lamar Valley is known as the "Little Serengeti of North America," and for good reason: At certain times of the year, in a single day, visitors can spot grizzly and black bears, moose, wolves, bison, elk, coyotes, bald eagles, and the occasional bighorn sheep or mountain goat. In fact, the opportunities for viewing wildlife in the park are unparalleled anywhere in the United States, and although Yellowstone may not be as picturesque as Glacier or the Tetons, it is magnificent in its wildness and uniquely American.

Seeing Yellowstone from the back of a cramped station wagon—or these days, a decked-out Winnebago—is almost a rite of passage in this country. What parent doesn't dream of hauling their children to see Old Faithful erupt or to catch a glimpse of a grizzly bear? And what kid doesn't want to swim in the Boiling River or lie awake in a sleeping bag, listening to the howl of coyotes? It is not exactly the last frontier it once was—there are convenience stores, beautiful old hotels, and even places to get a decent latte—but Yellowstone still occupies its own corner of our national imagination; classified somewhere between American wilderness and family vacations, it conjures foggy but perfect memories.

Getting to Yellowstone National Park

Keep in mind that while distances through the park may seem short in actual mileage, your drive time is often extended by lower speed limits, traffic congestion, and animal jams. In addition, most of the park roads are **closed in winter.**

Driving from Bozeman
North Entrance: 85 miles (137 km); 1.5 hours
From Bozeman to the park's north entrance at Gardiner is 85 miles (137 km) east on I-90 and south on U.S. 89, a 90-minute drive.

West Entrance: 95 miles (153 km); 2 hours
It takes just under two hours to drive the 95 miles (153 km) south from Bozeman to the west entrance at West Yellowstone on the winding, two-lane U.S. 191.

Driving from Jackson, Wyoming
50 miles (81 km); 1 hour
From the **Jackson Hole airport,** Yellowstone's south entrance, which borders Grand Teton National Park, is 50

Two Days in Yellowstone

Day 1

Start your whirlwind tour at the park's north entrance with a sunrise swim in **Boiling River** before the crowds descend. Then, on your way to the famed **Lamar Valley,** stop at the **Mammoth Visitors Center** for a quick park history lesson and a chance to find out from rangers about recent wildlife sightings. Wind your way through the Lamar, known as the "Little Serengeti of North America" for its abundant and diverse wildlife. Stretch your legs on a short but beautiful hike at **Trout Lake.**

Watch for bears, wolves, bighorn sheep, and mountain goats as you continue on to **Cooke City,** just outside the park's northeast entrance. Stop for lunch at the **Beartooth Café.** After lunch, retrace your route through the Lamar to Tower Junction, where you'll head south through the broad Hayden Valley to the **Grand Canyon of the Yellowstone.** Stop for ice cream and a fascinating exhibit on the Yellowstone supervolcano at the **Canyon Visitors Center** before you hit one of the trails for an outstanding view of the canyon.

After your hike, make your way south to Fishing Bridge and settle in for the night at **Lake Hotel** with a cocktail on the porch and a gourmet dinner in the dining room.

Day 2

After a big breakfast, plan a **scenic cruise** or guided **kayak tour** on **Yellowstone Lake** before you hit the road for **West Thumb Geyser Basin.** Give yourself at least thirty minutes to stroll around the boardwalks and see the unique geothermal features. From there, make your way up the west side of the park to **Old Faithful,** where you can have lunch in the historic **Old Faithful Inn Dining Room** and walk through the geyser basin while you wait for one of the famed eruptions.

After lunch, head north to the **Firehole River** for a swim in the rocky canyon. Then continue north to explore both **Norris Geyser Basin** and the **Mammoth Hot Springs Terraces** before exiting the park at Gardiner and settling in for the night at **Chico Hot Springs.**

---

miles (81 km) north on U.S. 191, a one-hour drive.

Driving from Glacier National Park
375-420 miles (605 km); 6-7.5 hours
The fastest route from Glacier Park's east entrance at **St. Mary** to **Gardiner,** the north entrance of Yellowstone, travels south on U.S. 89 and U.S. 287 for 375 miles (605 km) and should take just over six hours. The drive goes along the Rocky Mountain Front through Choteau, Augusta, Helena, and Bozeman. Just a few miles longer, the southbound route through Great Falls, White Sulphur Springs, and Livingston on U.S. 89 is 380 miles (610 km), and should be a six-hour, 20-minute drive. This route also takes you to Gardiner.

From **West Glacier,** you can drive to Gardiner via U.S. 93 South and I-90 East. The drive is roughly 420 miles (675 km) and will take approximately 7.5 hours without stops. The route takes you through Kalispell, Polson, Missoula, Butte, Bozeman, and Livingston.

From the west side of Glacier, it's also possible to take a route through the **Seeley-Swan Valley** to reach Gardiner. The drive follows MT-83 South (southeast of Kalispell), MT-141, U.S. 12 East, U.S. 287 South, I-90 East, and then U.S. 89 South for a total of 395 miles (635 km) and will take roughly seven hours.

Driving from Billings
125-175 miles (280 km); 3-3.5 hours
From the airport in Billings to the park's north entrance at **Gardiner** is 175 miles

Best Restaurants

★ **Old West Dinner Cookout, Northern Loop:** Departing from the Roosevelt Lodge by either horseback or covered wagon, this steak-and-potatoes dinner in the wilds of Yellowstone is an unforgettable experience (page 66).

★ **Lake Yellowstone Hotel Dining Room, Southern Loop:** The dining room at Lake Yellowstone Hotel dishes up specialties like brown butter lobster sliders and grilled quail in an elegant setting—and the views make everything taste even better (page 66).

★ **Wild West Corral, Gardiner:** The menu is small, the seating sparse, and the line often long, but the huge beef, bison, and elk burgers here are out of this world (page 67).

★ **Beartooth Café, Cooke City:** Housed in a beautiful old log cabin with a sprawling deck, this spot serves up delicious hand-cut steaks, burgers, pasta, salads, and more (page 68).

★ **Café Madriz, West Yellowstone:** Authentic Spanish food—including paella, hot and cold tapas, and plenty of choices for vegetarians—is a delicious surprise in this cozy little West Yellowstone bistro (page 68).

★ **Taqueria Las Palmitas, West Yellowstone:** Located in a converted white school bus parked in an alley, the "Taco Bus" serves authentic and outstanding Mexican street food—soft tacos, enchiladas, and burritos (page 69).

★ **Café Regis, Red Lodge:** A grocery store and restaurant known for organic fare, with fruits and vegetables grown in the back garden, Café Regis serves up hearty portions for reasonable prices (page 82).

★ **Buck's T-4, Big Sky:** An old standard in Gallatin Canyon and known for its extensive menu of wild game and hand-cut steaks, Buck's T-4 offers fine dining year-round (page 86).

★ **Lone Mountain Ranch, Big Sky:** The restaurant here serves seasonal farm-to-table fare—think coffee-rubbed elk chop, crispy-skin Montana trout, and pork belly—with lovely, rustic ambience (page 86).

(280 km) southwest on I-90 West and U.S. 89 South, a three-hour drive.

The 125-mile (201-km), 3.5-hour drive from Billings through Red Lodge and over the **Beartooth Scenic Highway** (only open in summer), to the park's northeast entrance just beyond Cooke City travels via I-90 West and U.S. 212 West.

Bus and Shuttle

Shuttle service with **Karst Stage** (800/845-2778, www.karststage.com) is available from Bozeman to West Yellowstone in winter ($98 pp one-way, $178 pp round-trip). In the summer, Karst offers day trips to Yellowstone for $149 per person with a four-person minimum. Private coaches (10-11 passengers, from $510/day) can also be arranged through Karst.

Air

The **Yellowstone Airport** (WYS, 607 Airport Rd., West Yellowstone, www.yellowstoneairport.org, 406/646-7631) is served by Delta with regular service to

Best Accommodations

★ **Roosevelt Lodge Cabins, Northern Loop:** Among the smallest and most rustic accommodations in the park, these tiny cabins are simple, charming, and set in the trees away from the madding crowds (page 69).

★ **Lake Yellowstone Hotel, Southern Loop:** With a variety of refurbished cabins and cottages and the grand historic hotel, the accommodations at Lake Yellowstone range from rustic to luxe, and the waterside setting is arguably the best in the park (page 70).

★ **Old Faithful Inn, Southern Loop:** This classic beauty is the most popular lodging in the park for its historic log-and-stone architecture, not to mention its location just steps from the famous geyser (page 70).

★ **Gardiner Guest House, Gardiner:** A sweet little bed-and-breakfast just outside the park's north entrance, this guesthouse is long on Victorian charm and Montana hospitality (page 71).

★ **Silver Gate Lodging, Cooke City:** Located just outside the park's northeast entrance, at the foot of the Beartooth Highway, this spot offers several pet-friendly cabins, motel rooms, and a big lodge (page 72).

★ **Yellowstone Under Canvas, West Yellowstone:** There's something about sleeping under the Big Sky, especially when your tent includes a king-size bed, a freestanding tub, Persian rugs, and a woodstove (page 75).

★ **The Pollard Hotel, Red Lodge:** A historic railroad lodging in downtown Red Lodge, this charming redbrick hotel offers cozy accommodations, excellent dining, and an ideal location (page 82).

★ **Yodeler Motel, Red Lodge:** Touting themselves as groovy and noncorporate, this budget- and pet-friendly motel in downtown Red Lodge is run by two former guides who will point you to all the best places (page 82).

Salt Lake City, and is only open late May to late September.

Visiting Yellowstone National Park

Planning Your Time

One could quite literally spend a lifetime in Yellowstone without being able to cover every last corner of this magnificent wilderness, but the reality is that most visitors only have a couple of days, at best, to explore the park. Something like 98 percent of visitors never get more than a mile from the road, but doing so is easier than you might think—and incredibly worthwhile. Three days in the park is ideal, but if you have less time, there are ways to maximize every minute.

One important consideration in planning your time in Yellowstone is to know the season in which you'll be traveling. Summer offers magnificent scenery, usually good weather, and the inevitable "bear jam," when drivers hit the brakes as soon as someone spots anything resembling a brown furry creature. Summer visitors to Yellowstone need to plan for traffic and often for road construction delays. Fall and spring are fantastic times to see wildlife, but the weather can change in a heartbeat—at Yellowstone's high elevation, blizzards can strike nearly any month of the year. Winter is a magical time in the park, but cars are only permitted on one road in the northeast corner. All other travel is done via snow coach, guided snowmobile tour, or on skis and snowshoes. There is no wrong time to visit the park, but knowing the advantages and disadvantages of the various seasons will help you manage your expectations.

Assuming you'll be in Yellowstone when the roads are open to car traffic, there are five entrances and exits to the park, making loop trips relatively easy. From Montana, you can enter or exit the park from the northeast at Cooke City, from the north at Gardiner, or from the west at West Yellowstone. From Wyoming, you can enter the park from the east entrance nearest Cody or from the south through Grand Teton National Park. If you're going from one state to the next, there is no more spectacular route than that through the heart of Yellowstone.

If time won't permit even one night in the park, it is still well worth driving through, just to get a sense of this tremendously diverse place. Consider choosing one feature and pursuing it. To give yourself the best chance of seeing wolves, traveling between the north and northeast entrances is an excellent route during non-summer months. Geothermal aficionados will have no shortage of choices for seeing the park's impressive features, but to swim in them, try the **Boiling River,** a stretch of the Gardner River near Mammoth, which is swimmable year-round except during spring and early summer runoff. The **Firehole River** also offers excellent summer swimming not far from Old Faithful. Landlubbers might prefer a short hike into a less-famous geyser such as **Lone Star,** just a few flat miles from Old Faithful.

The best advice is this: Get off the road, get out of your car, be smart, and come prepared to give yourself the opportunity to see and understand what makes Yellowstone America's first wonderland.

Entrances

Yellowstone National Park is open 365 days a year, 24 hours a day. There are five entrance stations, three in Montana and two in Wyoming.

- The **North Entrance,** at Gardiner, Montana, is the only one open year-round to wheeled vehicles.

- The **Northeast Entrance** is near the small communities of Cooke City and Silver Gate, Montana, and generally open late May to mid-October, depending upon weather and road conditions.

- The **West Entrance,** in West Yellowstone, Montana, is open to wheeled vehicles generally from the third Friday in April until the first Sunday in November.

- The **South Entrance,** 50 miles (81 km) north of Jackson, Wyoming, at the border between Grand Teton National Park and Yellowstone, is open to wheeled vehicles typically the second Friday in May through the first Sunday in November, and to snow coaches and snowmobiles mid-December to mid-March.

- The **East Entrance,** 53 miles (85 km) west of Cody, Wyoming, is generally open to wheeled vehicles from the first Friday in May to the first Sunday in November.

All entrances can be closed at any time due to weather and unscheduled changes. Visit www.nps.gov/yell before your trip for up-to-date road information, or call 307/344-2117 for recorded road and weather information.

Park Fees and Passes

Admission to the park is $35 per vehicle for seven days, $30 for motorcycles, and $20 for hikers and bicyclists. In 2019, entrance fees to the park were waived on five days, including Martin Luther King Jr. Day, April 20 to celebrate the start of National Park Week, September 28 for National Public Lands Day, and Veterans Day. Check the Yellowstone website before you travel to see if any fee-free days are on the horizon. The park is open year-round, but during the winter, cars can only access the park through the north and northeast entrances.

Visitors Centers

There are 10 visitors centers in and around the park. Their days and hours vary seasonally, so it's a good idea to check the website (www.nps.gov/yell) before you go into the park.

The **Albright Visitor Center at Mammoth Hot Springs** (307/344-2263, 8am-6pm daily) is open year-round and houses a bookstore, wildlife and history exhibits, and films on the park and its early visitors. Free Wi-Fi is available.

The **Canyon Visitor Education Center** (307/344-2550, 8am-6pm daily mid-Apr.-early Nov.) offers the best overview of the park's geology, including phenomenal supervolcano exhibits and a dynamic film. During the season, the bathrooms remain open 24 hours a day.

The **Fishing Bridge Visitor Center** (307/344-2450, 8am-7pm daily late May-early Oct.) is home to a bookstore, bird and wildlife exhibits, plus information on the lake's geology.

The **Grant Village Visitor Center** (307/344-2650, 8am-7pm daily late May-early Oct.) offers information on fire in Yellowstone.

The **Madison Information Station and Trailside Museum** (307/344-2821, 9am-5pm daily late May-early Oct.) at Madison Junction provides a bookstore as well as detailed information on the **Junior Ranger** program.

The **Museum of the National Park Ranger** (307/344-7353, 9am-5pm daily late May-late Sept.) is located 1 mile (1.6 km) north of Norris Geyser Basin and gives a good history of the park ranger profession.

The **Norris Geyser Basin Museum & Information Station** (307/344-2812, 9am-6pm daily late May-early Oct.) offers visitors an excellent overview of the hydrothermal features in the park.

The **Old Faithful Visitor Education Center** (307/344-2751, 8am-8pm daily mid-Apr.-early Nov.) includes exhibits, information, films, a bookstore, and geyser eruption predictions.

The **West Thumb Information Center** (307/344-2876, 9am-5pm daily late May-early Oct.) offers information about West Thumb Geyser Basin on the shore of Yellowstone Lake.

In West Yellowstone, the **West Yellowstone Visitor Information Center** (307/344-2876, 8am-8pm daily May-Sept., 8am-8pm Mon.-Fri. Oct.-Apr.) hosts a National Park Service desk, plus information and publications.

Services

Yellowstone National Park Lodges (307/344-7901, www.yellowstonenationalparklodges.com) is the official concessionaire of Yellowstone, and all reservations for lodging, dining, and special activities in the park can be made through them.

If you encounter an **emergency** when traveling through the park, dial 911, but be aware that cell coverage is spotty. Emergency medical services are attended to by rangers.

There are three **urgent care facilities** inside Yellowstone. The clinic at **Mammoth** (307/344-7965, 8:30am-5pm Mon.-Fri. June-late Sept., 8:30am-5pm Mon.-Thurs, 8:30am-1pm Fri. late Sept.-May) is open year-round. The clinics at **Lake** (307/242-7241, 8:30am-8:30pm daily mid-May-mid-Sept., 10am-6:30pm daily mid-Sept.-late Sept.) and **Old Faithful** (307/344-7325, 7am-7pm daily mid-May-mid-Sept., 8:30am-5pm mid-Sept.-early Oct.) are open in prime visiting season.

Getting Around

A cursory glance at a Yellowstone map will reveal the main roads, which form a figure eight in the heart of the park, and the access roads leading to and from the entrances. The majority of the park's big-name highlights—**Old Faithful, West Thumb Geyser Basin, Fishing Bridge, Grand Canyon of the Yellowstone, Norris and Mammoth Geyser Basins**—are accessible from the main loops.

It's important to note that there is **no public transportation** in Yellowstone the way there is in many other national parks. You'll need a car, or to be part of an organized tour group, to get around Yellowstone's roads.

Private Vehicles

Your best bet to see the park on your own terms is to go by car. The nearest car-rental agencies are **Budget, Avis,** and **Big Sky Car Rentals** (800/231-5991), available in West Yellowstone. Cars can also be rented from airports in Billings, Bozeman, Cody, and Jackson Hole.

When planning your drive through Yellowstone, it is best to fill up your tank outside the park. Once inside, the gas prices you'll encounter tend to be extremely high, and options are quite limited. Gas stations are located within the park at Canyon, Fishing Bridge, Grant Village, Mammoth, Upper and Lower Old Faithful, and Tower Junction. They are generally open late spring-early fall.

One of the things that makes Yellowstone so wild and enchanting is its utter unpredictability—something that relates to wildlife, weather, and, unfortunately, road conditions. A 20-year, $300-million plan is currently afoot to address the structural deficiencies of Yellowstone's roads. Keep a close watch on road closures and delays that can happen at any time of year because of construction, bad weather, or even fire. For a 24-hour road report, check **Road Construction Delays and Closures** (307/344-2117, www.nps.gov/

yell). Information on state roads is available from the **Montana Department of Transportation** (800/226-7623, www.mdt511.com) and **Wyoming Department of Transportation** (888/996-7623, www.wyoroad.info). **National Weather Service** (www.crh.noaa.gov) reports are available for Yellowstone and Grand Teton National Parks.

Depending on your time and your plan for accommodations, you could easily spend a full day driving each of the park's two loops.

Tours

Xanterra/Yellowstone National Park Lodges (307/344-7311, www.yellowstonenationalparklodges.com) offers a variety of different bus tours of the park during the summer, including historic Yellow Bus tours that range 1-12 hours. The **Yellowstone In A Day** ($121-128 adults, $60.50-64 kids 3-11) departs daily from Gardiner, Mammoth, and the Old Faithful Inn and covers the entire park in one day. Other options include early-morning or evening wildlife tours, lake sunset tours, geyser-gazing, Lamar Valley wildlife expeditions, photo safaris, boat tours, fishing trips, and custom guided tours.

Depending upon your particular interests, there are a range of companies outside the park that offer specialized tours of Yellowstone. The only one inside the park, and an outstanding option, is the **Yellowstone Forever Institute** (406/848-2400, www.yellowstone.org). Courses are broken into summer and winter semesters, and single-day course fees begin around $139. Multiday tours are also available. The courses are engaging and are taught by experts in their fields. Using Yellowstone as their classroom, the instructors concentrate on "individual aspects of the ecosystem." During the summer, you can take the "Introduction to Wolf Management and Ecology" course led by a wolf biologist or "Mammal Signs: Interpreting

Tracks, Scat, and Hair" with an animal tracker. There's also a three-week naturalist guide certificate program offered. Courses such as "The Art of Wildflower Identification" focus on flora; other options include "Yellowstone's Geoecosystem" and "Wilderness First Aid." The institute can provide unique (and inexpensive) lodging in its two field campuses, in Gardiner and the Lamar Valley, or it can include standard hotel lodging at park hotels.

A newer offering for Yellowstone Forever is **Yellowstone Day Adventures** (May 30-Aug., $79 adults, $49 children), in which guests are picked up at dawn, whisked to the Lamar Valley with a wildlife expert for the chance to see elk, pronghorn, bison, and maybe bears and wolves, and returned by day's end to Gardiner. Tours are offered Wednesdays and Fridays during peak summer season and include breakfast, hot beverages, expert instruction, all transportation, use of scopes, binoculars and digiscoping equipment. If you browse the course catalog, you will likely find something geared to your interests. Any of the Yellowstone Forever Institute tours are among the best ways to get an in-depth insider's view of Yellowstone.

Other tour operators that offer a range of excursions in the park include **Yellowstone Tour & Travel** (800/221-1151, www.yellowstone-travel.com), a full-service travel agency in West Yellowstone that can book everything from accommodations and tours to complete packages, and **Yellowstone Alpen Guides** (555 Yellowstone Ave., 406/646-9591 or 800/858-3502, www.yellowstoneguides.com, from $95 adults, $90 seniors, $85 children under 16), also in West Yellowstone, which offers a fantastic array of naturalist-guided tours year-round.

Alltrans (307/733-3135 or 800/443-6133, www.jacksonholealltrans.com) offers **full-day tours** (Mon., Wed., and Fri. late May-late Sept., starting at $285

for adults) of Yellowstone out of Jackson Hole.

Sights

The Northern Loop

With striking panoramas, wonderful thermals, plentiful wildlife, and year-round vehicle access between the north and northeast entrances, this is one of the most underappreciated parts of the park. The accommodations and dining are not as fancy as elsewhere, but the crowds are more manageable, and the experience is just as good or better. Phenomenal highlights include the Boiling River, Mammoth Hot Springs, the Lamar Valley, Tower Fall, Dunraven Pass, the Grand Canyon of the Yellowstone, and Norris Geyser Basin.

★ Boiling River

Halfway between Gardiner and Mammoth Hot Springs, straddling the Montana-Wyoming border and the 45th parallel—the halfway point between the equator and the North Pole—is the Boiling River, one of only two swimmable thermal features in Yellowstone. From the clearly marked parking area, visitors amble upstream along a 0.5-mile (0.8-km) rocky path running parallel to the Gardner River. Where the trail ends and the steam envelops almost everything, a gushing hot spring called the Boiling River flows into the otherwise icy Gardner River. The hot and cold waters mix to a perfect temperature that can be enjoyed year-round. The area is open during daylight hours only, and all swimmers must wear a bathing suit. The Boiling River is closed each year during spring and early summer runoff, when temperature fluctuations and rushing water put swimmers at risk. Alcohol is not permitted.

Kids and adults alike marvel at the floating Day-Glo green algae found here (the water should not be ingested). Bison and elk frequent the area, and despite the regular crowds of people (note that 20 people constitute a crowd in this part of the West), this is a unique and unforgettable way to enjoy a few hours in Yellowstone.

★ Mammoth and the Mammoth Hot Springs Terraces

Just 5 miles (8 km) into the park and up the road from Gardiner, Mammoth is the primary northern hub of Yellowstone National Park. It is also an interesting little community in its own right, with a small medical center, the most beautiful post office in the West, and a magnificent stone church. The town of Mammoth, once known as Fort Yellowstone, was essentially built by the U.S. Army during its 1886-1918 occupation. Thinking they were on a temporary assignment, the soldiers erected canvas wall tents and lived in them through five harsh winters. In 1890, Congress set aside $50,000 for the construction of a permanent post, a stately collection of stone colonial revival-style buildings, most of which are still in use today.

The recently renovated **Albright Visitor Center** (307/344-2263, 8am-7pm daily late May-Sept., 9am-5pm daily Oct.-late May) is a must-see. There are films, history and wildlife exhibits, and a small but excellent selection of books and videos in the shop run by **Yellowstone Forever** (406/848-2400, www.yellowstone.org). While at the center, don't miss seeing some of the artwork produced during the 1871 Hayden Geological Survey of the park, including quality reproductions of painter Thomas Moran's famous watercolor sketches and original photographs by William Henry Jackson. Rangers on staff can usually give you up-to-date animal sightings and activity reports. The

Top to bottom: elk on a lawn around Mammoth Hot Springs; Canary Spring and Terrace; bison in the Lamar Valley.

The Northern Loop

MADISON

Madison Junction

Mt Holmes 10,336ft

Electric Peak 10,992ft

Gardner River

To Livingston and Bozeman

89

Gardiner

NORTH ENTRANCE

Fawn Pass Trail

Bighorn Pass Trail

INDIAN CREEK

MAMMOTH AND THE MAMMOTH HOT SPRINGS TERRACES

UPPER GRAND LOOP ROAD

BOILING RIVER

Jardine

NORRIS GEYSER BASIN

NORRIS

Norris

Roaring Mountain

Obsidian Cliff

Sheepeater Cliff

Gardner River

Bunsen Peak

Osprey Falls

Undine Falls

Wraith Falls

Mt Everts 7841ft

Black Canyon of the Yellowstone

Yellowstone River Trail

Virginia Cascade

Yellowstone National Park

FORCES OF THE NORTHERN RANGE

Blacktail Deer Creek Trail

BLACKTAIL PLATEAU DR.

Yellowstone River Trail

Custer-Gallatin National Forest

Petrified Tree

ROOSEVELT LODGE/ OLD WEST DINNER COOKOUT

Garnet Hill Trail

MONTANA WYOMING

Hayden Valley

Canyon Village

CANYON

Canyon of the Yellowstone

Lower Falls

Dunraven Pass

CHITTENDEN ROAD

UPPER GRAND LOOP ROAD

TOWER FALL

MOUNT WASHBURN 10,243ft

Tower Fall

SLOUGH CREEK

SLOUGH CREEK

Slough Creek

Slough Creek Trail

Grand Canyon of the Yellowstone

River

GRAND CANYON OF THE YELLOWSTONE

Grand Canyon

Mirror Plateau

Specimen Ridge Trail

WATCHING THE WOLVES

Specimen Ridge Trail

Lamar Valley

YELLOWSTONE INSTITUTE

PEBBLE CREEK

Bliss Pass Trail

Baronette Peak 10,404ft

Pebble Creek Trail

Slough Creek Trail

Howard Eaton Trail

Pelican Valley

Pelican Cone

Lamar River Trail

Cache Creek

Soda Butte Creek

The Thunderer 10,554ft

212

Abiathar Peak 10,928ft

Silver Gate

NORTHEAST ENTRANCE

To Red Lodge, Beartooth Hwy, and Cody

Cooke City

Shoshone National Forest

0   5 km
0   5 mi

© MOON.COM

flush toilets downstairs are the last on this route for a while.

The primary ecological attraction in Mammoth (other than the elk often seen lounging around and nibbling on the green grass) can be found on the **Mammoth Hot Springs Terraces.** Since the days of the earliest stagecoach trails into the park, they have been a visual and olfactory marvel for visitors. The Hayden Expedition named the area White Mountain Hot Spring for the cream-colored, step-like travertine terraces.

Beneath the ground, the Norris-Mammoth fault carries superheated water rich in dissolved calcium and bicarbonate. As the water emerges through cracks in the surface, carbon dioxide is released as a gas, and the carbonate combines with calcium to form travertine. The mountain is continuously growing as travertine is deposited and then shifted as the cracks are sealed and the mineral-laden water emerges somewhere else. For frequent visitors to the park, vast changes are noticeable from one trip to the next. In addition to changes in shape and water flow, the colors at Mammoth can vary dramatically by the day. Not only does travertine morph from bright white when it is new to cream and then gray as it is exposed to the elements, the cyanobacteria create fabulous color shifts too—from turquoise to green and yellow to red and brown, depending on water temperatures, available sunlight, and pH levels.

Liberty Cap, at the base of the terraces, is an excellent example of a dormant spring, where all but the core cone has been eroded away. **Minerva** and **Canary Spring and Terrace** are two other springs worth seeing. Their temperatures average around 160°F, and when they are flowing, they often put on marvelous color displays.

Tower Fall

Eighteen scenic miles (29 km) down the road from Mammoth Hot Springs— past **Undine Falls** and **Blacktail Plateau,** where you can see deer, elk, and bison along with some impressive lookouts— is **Tower Junction** and the breathtaking Tower Fall. The waterfall itself cascades 132 feet (40.2 m) from volcanic basalt. A popular spot with visitors and just steps from the parking lot, this is not the ideal place for solitude, but it is lovely to see.

Dunraven Pass

Between Tower and the dramatic Grand Canyon of the Yellowstone is one of the most nerve-racking and perhaps most beautiful drives in the park. Climbing up the flanks of **Mount Washburn,** Dunraven Pass has the highest road elevation in the park. The spectacular summit tops out at 8,859 feet (2,700 m) and offers impressive views of Yellowstone's caldera rim. Eagle eyes can also spot the nearby Grand Canyon of the Yellowstone. Hikers will have no shortage of trailheads to start from. The whitebark pines that grow along the road are a critical and dwindling food source for grizzly bears, so keep your eyes open. Because of its extreme altitude and relative exposure, Dunraven Pass is one of the last roads to open in the spring and one of the first to close when bad weather hits. For current road information, call 307/344-2117.

★ Grand Canyon of the Yellowstone

Yellowstone's most recent volcanic explosion, some 600,000 years ago, created a massive caldera and subsequent lava flows, one of which was called the Canyon Rhyolite flow, in the area that is now known as the Grand Canyon of the Yellowstone. This particular lava flow was impacted by a thermal basin, which altered the rhyolite and created the beautiful palette of colors in the rock through constant heating and cooling. Over time, lakes, rivers, and glaciers formed in the region, and the relatively soft rhyolite was easily carved away. Roughly 10,000 years ago, the last of the area's glaciers melted, causing a rush of water to carve the canyon into the form it has today. The 20-mile-long (32-km) canyon is still growing thanks to the forces of erosion, including water, wind, and earthquakes. A number of terrific lookouts are on both the North and South Rims of the canyon.

Before setting out for the canyon itself, visitors are advised to visit the **Canyon Visitor Education Center** (307/344-2550, 8am-8pm daily late May-early Sept., 8am-6pm daily early Sept.-late Sept., 9am-5pm daily early Oct.-early Nov.), which has an outstanding and vast exhibit on Yellowstone's supervolcano, geothermal activity, and other natural history. In fact, this should be a mandatory stop for every visitor who might otherwise have no appreciation for the region's fascinating geology.

On the **North Rim,** don't miss **Inspiration Point,** a natural viewing platform that gives a bird's-eye view both up and down the river. Nathaniel Langford, who would go on to be the park's first superintendent, stood in the same spot with the Washburn Expedition in 1870. He wrote:

> Standing there or rather lying there for greater safety, I thought how utterly impossible it would be to describe to another the sensations inspired by such a presence. As I took in the scene, I realized my own littleness, my helplessness, my dread exposure to destruction, my inability to cope with or even comprehend the mighty architecture of nature.

Look down, if you dare, among the nooks and crannies of rock to try to spot nesting ospreys.

Another phenomenal viewing platform can be found at **Lookout Point,** where visitors can gaze from afar at the thundering Lower Falls of the Yellowstone. Visitors who want to get closer to the spray of the falls and don't mind a long hike down, and back up again, can head toward the base of the falls at **Red Rock Point.** It's a 0.5-mile (0.8-km) trip one-way that drops more than 500 vertical feet (152.4

m). There is another platform at the top of the 308-foot (94-m) falls aptly named the **Brink of the Lower Falls.** This lookout also involves a 0.5-mile (0.8-km) hike and a 600-foot (183-m) elevation loss. The **Upper Falls** are just over one-third the size of the Lower Falls, at 109 feet (33.2 m), but they are worth a gander and can be easily accessed at the **Brink of the Upper Falls.** Mountain man Jim Bridger purportedly regaled friends with tales of the Upper Falls as early as 1846 and urged them to see it for themselves.

From the **South Rim,** visitors can see the Upper Falls from the **Upper Falls Viewpoint.** A trail that dates back to 1898, **Uncle Tom's Trail** still takes hardy hikers to the base of the **Lower Falls.** The trail down loses 500 vertical feet (152.4 m) through a series of 300 stairs and paved inclines, but what goes down must come up again. From **Artist Point,** one of the largest and most inspiring lookouts, visitors get a glorious view of the distant Lower Falls and the river as it snakes down the pinkish canyon. It was long thought that Artist Point was where painter Thomas Moran made sketches for his 7-by-12-foot (2.1-by-3.7-m) masterpiece *Grand Canyon of the Yellowstone.* More likely, say historians, he painted from a spot on the North Rim now called **Moran Point.**

Norris Geyser Basin

Both the hottest and the most unpredictable geyser basin in the park, Norris Geyser Basin is a fascinating collection of bubbling and colorful geothermal features. A 2.3-mile (3.7-km) web of boardwalks and trails leads visitors through this remarkable basin. From the **Norris Geyser Basin Museum** (307/344-2812, 9am-6pm daily mid-Apr.-Sept., 9am-5pm daily Oct.-early Nov., free), which carefully unravels the geothermal mysteries of the region, there are two loop trails guiding visitors safely through the basin. The 1930s log-and-stone building that houses the museum

Norris Geyser Basin

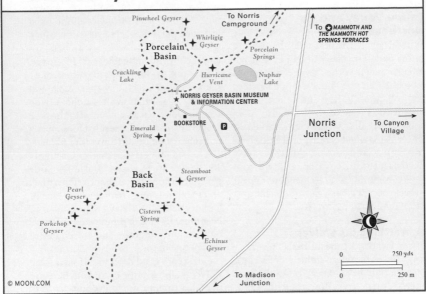

has been designated a National Historic Landmark. There is also an information desk and a Yellowstone Association bookstore inside the building.

Porcelain Basin is a stark, barren setting with a palette of pink, red, orange, and yellow mineral oxides. Some of the features of note include **Africa Geyser,** which had been a hot spring in the shape of its namesake continent and started erupting in 1971. When it is active, **Whirligig Geyser,** named in 1904 by the Hague Party, erupts in a swirling pattern for a few minutes at irregular periods with a roar and hiss. The hottest steam vent in the hottest geothermal basin in the park is **Black Growler,** which has measured 280°F. The second-largest geyser in Norris, **Ledge Geyser** erupts irregularly to heights up to 125 feet (38.1 m).

In Norris's **Back Basin** you'll find the world's tallest geyser, **Steamboat Geyser,** which can erupt more than 300 feet (91.4 m) in the air. Minor eruptions of 10-40 feet (3-12.2 m) in height are more common. The eruptions can last 3-40 minutes and be separated by days or decades (in the past, Steamboat has gone more than 50 years without an eruption, but in 1964, it erupted 29 times). A major eruption in September 2014 happened at 11pm and was witnessed by a park ranger. Prior to that, the last major eruption occurred in 2013, and before that in 2005. In 2018, Steamboat entered an active phase with a record-breaking 30 eruptions starting in March (after more than three years of silence). Just down the boardwalk, **Cistern Spring** is linked to Steamboat Geyser and drains in advance of a major eruption. The color is a beautiful blue, enhanced by as much as 0.5 inch of gray sinter deposited annually. By comparison, Old Faithful only deposits 0.5-1 inch of sinter every century. **Echinus Geyser** is the world's largest acid geyser and is almost as acidic as vinegar. Eruptions since 2007 have been rare and unpredictable, typically lasting about four minutes, but large ones have been known to reach heights of 80-125 feet (24.4-38.1 m).

Lamar Valley and the Northeast Corner

With arguably the best wildlife-viewing in the park, especially in winter, this region is known as the "Little Serengeti of North America." The wide-open spaces of the Lamar Valley and much of the northeast corner of the park also offer some pretty dramatic mountain vistas. There is excellent fishing and hiking in the region, and just outside the park's northeast entrance is Cooke City, a cool little community with tremendous appeal to backcountry skiers, snowmobilers, and other outdoors enthusiasts.

★ Watching the Wolves

When visitors list the animals they most want to see in Yellowstone, wolves rank second, right behind grizzly bears. Since their return to Yellowstone in 1995, wolves have surprised park-goers and wildlife experts alike by being much more visible than anyone anticipated. In fact, since their reintroduction, wolves have been spotted in Yellowstone by at least one person nearly every day. Much of that is thanks to wolf researchers, including the indefatigable Rick McIntyre, who is out in the field an average of 11 hours per day seven days per week, and the ever-passionate wolf watchers (who tend to follow Rick), armed with massive scopes and camera lenses that look strong enough to spot wildlife on other planets.

The bad news is that there are roughly 104 wolves in 11 packs, plus a few lone wolves, roaming throughout Yellowstone, an area that is approximately the size of Connecticut. It's always a good idea to bear those figures in mind when you have only a couple of hours and a keen desire to spot one of these majestic canines.

But there's good news too. If seeing the wolves is a high priority for you, here are five ways to improve your odds:

- **Visit in winter.** Wolves are most active

Porcelain Basin is part of the Norris Geyser Basin.

and most visible (nearest to the roads and against a white backdrop) in the winter when they have significant advantages over their prey, including elk and bison. Spring and fall can offer viewing opportunities as well, but summer visitors are at a disadvantage because the wolves are often way up in the high country, far from roads. Whenever you go, don't forget your binoculars or a scope if you have one.

- **Do your homework or hire a guide.** Stop at the visitors center in Mammoth in winter (or any of the visitors centers at other times of year) and inquire about recent activity. Rangers can often tell you where packs have been spotted, if kills have recently occurred, and so forth. You could also consider hiring a guide that specializes in wolf-watching. **Yellowstone Wolf Tracker** (406/223-0173, www.wolftracker.com, $630/day for 1 person, $660/2 people, $700/4 people) offers 6- to 8-hour tours led by wildlife biologists. The **Yellowstone Forever Institute** (406/848-2400, www.yellowstone.org) offers a variety of courses that focus on wolves.

- **Visit the Lamar Valley.** The only road open to car traffic year-round, the stretch of asphalt that winds through the Lamar Valley takes visitors through the heart of some of the park's best winter wolf terrain. There are numerous pullouts along the road for viewing, but be sure to park safely out of traffic without blocking other visitors. In the summer, along the stretch of road near the confluence of the Lamar River and Soda Butte Creek, the road is often closed to stopping thanks to a wolf-denning site not far from the pavement. Your chances of seeing a wolf—even pups—are good.

- **Wake up early.** Like most wildlife, wolves are most active at the edges of day. Putting yourself in the heart of the Lamar Valley before sunrise greatly improves your odds of seeing the wolves. The same is true at sunset. In this game, patience pays.

- **Watch for the wolf watchers.** They often have significant advantages, including radio telemeters that allow them to track collared wolves. These people know much about the wolves and can regale you with dramatic sagas of individual animals and entire packs. Don't be shy about pulling over when you see them; they are often willing to let you peer through their scopes. But do be safe and courteous; turn off your engine and remain quiet.

★ Lamar Valley

One of my favorite corners of the park, the **Lamar Valley** is stunningly beautiful with wide valleys carved by rivers and glaciers as well as views to the high rugged peaks around Cooke City. Generally uncrowded (save for the ever-growing number of bespectacled and bescoped wolf watchers), some of the best hiking, fishing, and camping can be had at

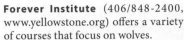

Cinderella: The Real-Life Fairy Tale of Wolf 42

In 1926 the last known wolf in Yellowstone was killed, bringing to a conclusion a decades-long campaign to rid the region of an animal widely considered a worthless pest. The murderous eviction was a tragic end to a noble creature. It took nearly 70 years for wolves to be seen not only for their intrinsic worth but their value in making the Yellowstone ecosystem whole again. This was their home, after all, and they had been unnaturally removed. Thirty-one Canadian gray wolves—*Canis lupus*—were re-introduced to the park in 1995-1996 to loud cheers and simultaneous objections.

Among the wolves brought into the park from Canada was a female who would come to be known as wolf number 42. Her sister, wolf 40, was the alpha female of the Druid Peak pack and known to rule the pack with an iron paw. She was suspected of running off her mother, number 39, and her sister, number 41. Number 42, the pack's beta female, managed to stay in the group, likely as a result of her unmatched speed and excellent hunting ability, but she could not get into her sister's good graces. The two fought constantly for four years. Both bred with wolf 21, the pack's alpha male, and wolf 40 reportedly killed her sister's first litter of pups in 1999. Wolf watchers nicknamed 42 "Cinderella" and flocked to the Lamar Valley to watch the drama unfold. Much of Cinderella's life was captured on film by Bob Landis for two *National Geographic* specials.

In a story that plays out like a fairy tale, wolf 42 got her nieces to den with her in 2000 when she had another litter of pups with 21, and after researchers saw wolf 40 approaching the den just before the pups were weaned, ostensibly to kill this second litter of pups, 42 and her nieces attacked. Wolf 40 was found dying of her wounds, and 42 not only rose to alpha status overnight, paired for life with wolf 21, but also moved into 40's den and adopted her dead sister's seven pups as her own. That year 42 and 21 raised 20 pups.

Over the course of her life—eight years, more than double the average lifespan of wolves—she birthed 32 pups and held her alpha-female status over the Druid Pack, which climbed to 37 members in 2000, becoming one of the largest wolf packs ever recorded. She was known for her faithful and patient parenting, even coaching younger wolves in the middle of an elk hunt. When she was killed by another pack in February 2004, wolf watchers noted wolf 21, her constant companion, atop a ridgeline howling for two days straight. The wolf watchers mourned along with him.

After receiving a mortality signal from 42's radio collar, chief park wolf biologist Doug Smith hiked up the 9,000-foot (2,743-m) Specimen Ridge on a blustery winter day. There he found Cinderella dead. She was the last remaining member of the 31 wolves imported from Canada, but her legacy and story will be forever entwined with the Yellowstone wilderness and the saga of *Canis lupus* finally coming home.

Slough Creek. And the wolf-watching, particularly in the winter, is unrivaled anywhere else in the world. There are also grizzlies, black bears, mountain lions, coyotes, red foxes, elk, bison, bighorn sheep, and pronghorn in the area. In early summer, on occasion, there can be as many as 2,000 bison dotting the wide green expanse; it's a miraculous sight.

Lamar Buffalo Ranch

The **Lamar Buffalo Ranch Field Campus** of the **Yellowstone Forever Institute** (406/848-2400, www.yellowstone.org) is located away from the large crowds (of two-legged creatures, anyway) in the idyllic Lamar Valley. The institute offers field seminars at this private and unique campus year-round. If you bring your own sleeping bag and pillow, you can stay at the ranch in one of its log cabins ($50-75 pp shared cabin in summer, $150 for 1-person private cabin, sleeping bag and pillow rental $20). Propane heaters, a communal bathhouse with individual showers, and a fully equipped kitchen are housed in the common building. It's quite comfortable but not fancy. The best part is waking up each morning in the Lamar Valley, an opportunity very few people have. You can also stay in a nearby campsite or hotel while taking a course at the ranch. Field seminars also take place at hotels throughout the park. The institute holds rooms in various lodges until 30 days before the course.

★ Slough Creek

A 25-mile-long (40-km) tributary of the Lamar River, **Slough Creek** flows from high in Montana's Absaroka-Beartooth Wilderness and into Wyoming and the park, where it converges with the Lamar River near Tower Junction. The creek winds through fir forests, sage flats, and grassland, making it prime habitat for a variety of animals, ranging from bison to coyotes to wolves to grizzly bears. A **campground** and 11 miles (17.7 km) of maintained and relatively flat trails provide excellent access to both hikers and anglers.

Slough Creek is known for its **dry-fly fishing,** with abundant cutthroat trout being the prize. Within the park, the creek flows through big meadows and a few pocketwater areas in small canyons. Only the top portion of Lower Meadow is accessible by car. The rest is earned with a hike. From the campground, anglers walk 1.5 miles to VIP Pool at the end of Lower Meadow, where cutt-bows and rainbow trout are present and can be as big as 22-25 inches. It's 2.5 miles (4 km) to the First Meadow, 4 miles (6.4 km) to the Second Meadow, and 6 miles (9.7 km) to the Third Meadow. In each of these meadows, 14- to 16-inchers are common, with some fish up to 20 inches. The farther you go, the lower the fishing pressure, meaning less company for you and easier catching.

The Southern Loop

Some of the park's biggest highlights are found in the southern loop, along with a significant number of visitors and plentiful wildlife. There are a lot of trees, many of them burned, and not as much dimension to the land as elsewhere, but the southern loop is what many people picture when they think of Yellowstone. From the sweeping Hayden Valley and the otherworldliness of West Thumb Geyser Basin to the sheer size of Yellowstone Lake and the well-deserved hubbub around Old Faithful, this section of the park has an abundance of dynamic features—some world-famous, others hidden gems.

Hayden Valley

South of Canyon is the expansive and beautiful Hayden Valley, a sweep of grassland carved by massive glaciers and named for the famed leader of the 1871 Hayden Expedition. It is occupied by a copious amount of wildlife that includes grizzly bears, wolves, and, in summer, thundering herds of bison. The Yellowstone River weaves quietly through the valley, and because the soil supports grasses and wildflowers instead of trees, this is one of the most scenic drives in the park, especially during the bison rut and migration in late summer. Besides driving, hiking is an excellent way to explore the valley, either on your own (pay very close attention for signs of bear activity) or with a ranger on weekly **guided hikes** (4-5 hours, early July-late Aug., free). The hikes are limited to 15 people, and reservations must be made in advance at the **Canyon Visitor Education Center** (307/344-2550, daily late May-mid-Oct.) in Canyon Village.

Fishing Bridge

What was once the epicenter of Yellowstone fishing is today a relic of the past and a touchstone for the ongoing struggle between nature and human meddling. Fishing Bridge was built in

The Brucellosis Problem

Yellowstone is the only place in the continental United States where bison have existed since prehistoric times. Current policy mandates that the animals stay within the park's unfenced boundaries, and how best to enforce this is a matter of constant debate.

The park's management of the bison has changed throughout the years, just as bison numbers have fluctuated. Prior to 1967, park authorities would trap and reduce the herd to keep it manageable. After 1967, however, the guiding philosophy changed, and the bison were managed by nature alone. By 1996 the number of bison in the park had grown to 3,500. The size of the herd, coupled with winters that brought significant snowfall, led many of the bison to migrate out of the park in order to find better grazing and calving grounds. This led to the problem of brucellosis being played out on the national stage.

Brucellosis is a bacterial infection present in the bison and elk in the Greater Yellowstone area. The disease can cause spontaneous abortions, infertility, and lowered milk production in the infected animal, but the Yellowstone elk and bison populations seem relatively unscathed by the disease, despite the number of animals infected. The same tolerance for the disease is not common among cattle, however. The overwhelming fear is that bison exiting Yellowstone could infect neighboring cattle; this would be gravely detrimental to Montana, Wyoming, and Idaho beef production. Brucellosis cannot be treated in cattle and can be passed on to humans in the form of undulant fever. The government created a fairly simple inoculation program to eradicate the disease in cattle as early as 1934, but brucellosis has never been eliminated from wildlife.

Starting in the 1980s, when more than 50 percent of the park's bison tested positive for the disease, the park's approach was to control the borders with hazing to limit the number of bison that left the park. When hazing was unsuccessful, the bison were shot. The winter of 1996-1997 brought record cold and snow, and bison left the park in large numbers to forage for food; 1,079 bison were shot and another 1,300 starved to death inside the park's boundaries. This incident magnified the problem of maintaining a healthy herd while preventing the spread of brucellosis.

The National Park Service, the U.S. Department of Agriculture, and Montana, Wyoming, and Idaho are working together to see how brucellosis can be eliminated and free-roaming bison protected. A vaccination program has been implemented, with a 65 percent success rate, and the use of quarantine has proven fairly successful. Local bison rancher and wildlife advocate Ted Turner has agreed to accept some of the quarantined bison on his property. A small and highly regulated hunting season on bison is carried out each winter just outside the park boundaries.

But while there are no easy or obvious solutions, there are questions: What about elk, which also carry the disease and have been identified as the source of brucellosis outbreaks among horses in Wyoming and cattle in Idaho? No efforts to limit their natural migration in and out of the park have ever been attempted. Why are bull bison—who can carry the disease but cannot spread it through milk or birthing fluids as females do—quarantined and killed? For now, it seems, we watch, wait, and hope for a healthy, wild, and free-roaming bison population.

1937 and was for years considered the best place to throw a line for native cutthroat trout. Humans were not the only ones fishing in the area, and human-grizzly encounters led to 16 grizzly bear deaths. To protect the bears and the fish, fishing in the vicinity was banned in 1973. Today, because of the sharp decline of cutthroat as a direct result of the introduction of nonnative lake trout, grizzlies are not seen as often fishing in the river.

There are some services—an RV park,

The Southern Loop

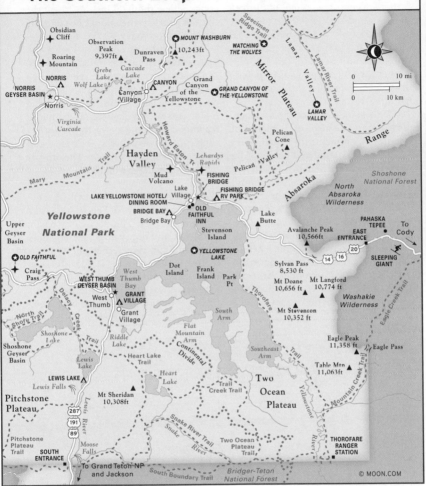

a gas station, and a general store—and a 1931 log-and-stone structure that serves as the **Fishing Bridge Visitor Center** (307/242-2450, 8am-7pm daily late May-Sept., 9am-5pm daily early Oct.). Listed in the National Register of Historic Places, the visitors center has a collection of stuffed bird specimens worth seeing and an exhibit on the lake's geology, including a relief map of the lake bottom.

★ Yellowstone Lake

Covering 136 square miles, Yellowstone Lake is North America's largest freshwater lake above 7,000 feet (2,134 m). In addition to being spectacularly scenic—both when it is placid and when the waves form whitecaps—the lake is a fascinating study in underwater geothermal activity. Beneath the water—or ice, much of the year—the lake bed is littered with faults, hot springs, craters, and the miraculous life-forms that can thrive in such conditions. There is also a rather large bulge, some 2,000 feet (610 m) long, that rises 100 feet (30.5 m) above the rest of the lake bottom. The uplift is related to the ever-present geothermal activity beneath Yellowstone. Whether the bulge is gaseous or potentially volcanic in nature is the subject of ongoing research.

Aside from its geological significance, Yellowstone Lake also offers plenty of recreational opportunities, primarily in the form of boating and fishing. The water is bitter cold, though, typically 40-50°F, and not suitable for swimming. Outboards ($57/hour) can be rented mid-June-early September at **Bridge Bay Marina** (307/344-7311 or 866/439-7375), just south of Lake Village or 21 miles (34 km) north of West Thumb. There is great fishing for native cutthroat trout as well. It's worth mentioning that early visitors to the park loved to tell stories about catching fish at the edge of the lake

and then dipping their catch in the hot springs at West Thumb Geyser Basin to cook them without taking the fish off the line—a practice that would be seriously frowned upon today.

The rambling pale-yellow **Lake Yellowstone Hotel** was built in 1891 and is an elegant reminder of Yellowstone's bygone era. The lobby and deck, which overlook the lake, are worth seeing, even if you are not staying here. Grab an iced tea and soak in the views; this is a stunning spot. If you can, stay for a meal and enjoy the live piano music. The crowds will fade as you gaze on the scenery.

West Thumb Geyser Basin

On the western edge of Yellowstone Lake is the eerie West Thumb Geyser Basin, a collection of hot springs, geysers, mud pots, and fumaroles that dump a collective 3,100 gallons (11,735 liters) of hot water into the lake daily. An excellent boardwalk system guides visitors through the area, but there have been

Old Faithful

injury-causing bison and bear encounters on the boardwalk, so keep your eyes open.

Abyss Pool is a sensational spring, some 53 feet (16.2 m) deep, that transforms in color from turquoise to emerald green to brown and back, depending on a variety of factors. Similarly beautiful, **Black Pool** is no longer black because the particular thermophiles that caused the dark coloration were killed in 1991 when the water temperature rose. **Big Cone** and **Fishing Cone,** surrounded by lake water, are the features that led to the stories of fishing and cooking the catch in a single cast. Called "Mud Puffs" by the 1871 Hayden Expedition, **Thumb Paint Pots** are like miniature reddish mud volcanoes (depending on rainfall, after which they can get soupier) and are an excellent example of mud pots. Throughout the last several years, the mud pots have been particularly active, forming new mud cones and even throwing mud into the air. **Surging Spring** is fun to watch as the dome of water forms and overflows, unleashing a torrent of water on the lake.

Grant Village

On the West Thumb of Yellowstone Lake, Grant Village is a fairly controversial development dating to the 1970s and built in the heart of grizzly bear habitat and among several cutthroat spawning streams. The architecture is ugly, and the location is better suited to wildlife than visitors. In addition to the **Grant Village Visitor Center** (307/344-2650, 8am-7pm daily June-Sept., 9am-5pm daily late May and early Oct.), which houses an exhibit dedicated to fire in the Yellowstone ecosystem, accommodations, a campground, and food services are available.

★ Old Faithful

Though often crowded, the **Old Faithful** complex brings together so many of the phenomena—both natural and human-made—that make Yellowstone so special: the landmark geyser and the incredible assortment of geothermal features surrounding it, the wildlife, the grand old park architecture of the Old Faithful Inn, and even the mass of people from around the world who come to witness the famous geyser.

An obvious stop at the Old Faithful complex is the **Old Faithful Visitor Education Center** (307/545-2750, 8am-8pm daily Memorial Day-Sept., 9am-5pm daily Oct.-early Nov., 9am-6pm mid-Apr.-late May), which showcases Yellowstone's hydrothermal features. The $27 million facility hosts 2.6 million visitors annually. Efficient travelers (who are fighting an uphill battle here most of the time) can call ahead for a recorded message about daily geyser eruption predictions (307/344-2751).

Known as the **Upper Geyser Basin,** the area surrounding Old Faithful is the largest concentration of geysers anywhere in the world. By far the most famous is Old Faithful because of its combination of height (although it is not the tallest) and regularity (although it is not the most frequent or most regular). Intervals between eruptions are generally between 60-110 minutes and can be predicted according to duration of previous eruptions. Eruptions can last anywhere from 90 seconds to five minutes. It spouts 3,700-8,400 gallons (14,006-31,797 liters) of hot water at heights of 106-184 feet (32.3-56.1 m). Signs inside the nearby hotel lobbies and the visitors center, and a Twitter feed (@GeyserNPS), keep visitors apprised of the next expected eruptions, of which there are an average of 17 in any 24-hour period. Keep in mind that Old Faithful doesn't stop being predictable just because people go to bed or the weather turns cold—some of the most magical eruption viewings can happen without crowds. Choose a full-moon night, any time of year, and be willing to get up in the middle of the night. The vision of Old Faithful erupting in winter with snow and ice, frost, and steam in every direction is unforgettable.

If you come to Yellowstone to see Old Faithful, take the time—an hour or more is ideal—to walk through the other marvelous features of the Upper Geyser Basin. **Giantess Geyser** can erupt up to 200 feet (61 m) high in several bursts. The irregular eruptions happen 2-6 times each year and can occur twice hourly, continuing 4-48 hours, and changing the behavior of many of the other geysers in the region. **Doublet Pool,** a colorful hot spring with numerous ledges, is lovely and convoluted. You can actually hear Doublet vibrating and collapsing beneath the surface. Looking something like a fire hose shooting 130-190 feet (39.6-57.9 m) in the air, **Beehive Geyser** typically erupts twice daily, each eruption lasting 4-5 minutes. **Grand Geyser** is the world's tallest predictable geyser, erupting every 7-15 hours, lasting 9-12 minutes, and reaching heights up to 200 feet (61 m). Visible from the road into the Old Faithful complex if you look back over your shoulder, **Castle Geyser** is thought

to be the park's oldest. It generally erupts every 10-12 hours, reaches 90 feet (27.4 m) in height, and lasts roughly 20 minutes. A 30- to 40-minute noisy steam phase follows the eruptions.

★ Firehole River

Because swimming in Yellowstone Lake is not an option unless you are a trained member of the polar bear club, a dip in the heated (but far from hot!) waters of the Firehole River is one of the nicest ways to spend an afternoon. The designated and somewhat popular swimming area is surrounded by high cliffs and some fast-moving rapids both upstream and downstream, so the area is not recommended for new or young swimmers. The water temperature averages 80°F (26.7°C), but this avid swimmer would argue that the temperatures feel more like the 70s (about 23.9°C). Though quite limited, parking is accessible from Firehole Canyon Drive, which leaves the main road south of Madison Junction, less than 1,000 feet (305 m) after crossing the river. There is a toilet available but no lifeguards, so you will be swimming entirely at your own risk.

Midway and Lower Geyser Basins

Between Old Faithful and Madison Junction, along the pastoral Firehole River, are the Midway and Lower Geyser Basins, technically considered part of the same basin. In 1889, Rudyard Kipling dubbed Midway Geyser Basin "hell's half-acre" for its massive hot springs and geysers. Among the most significant features at Midway is **Grand Prismatic Spring,** a colorful and photogenic spring that was immortalized by painter Thomas Moran on the Hayden Expedition. It releases some 560 gallons (2,120 liters) of water into the Firehole River every minute. At 250 by 380 feet (76.2 by 115.8 m), Grand Prismatic is the third-largest hot spring in the world and the largest in Yellowstone. Now dormant, **Excelsior Geyser Crater** was once

Midway and Lower Geyser Basins

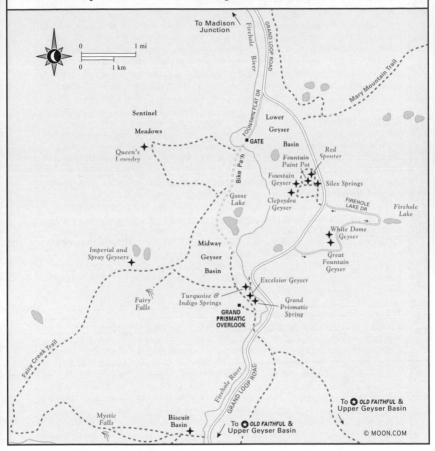

the largest geyser in the world, soaring up to 300 feet (91.4 m) high. Major eruptions in the 1880s led to a dormancy that lasted more than a century. In 1985, Excelsior erupted continuously for two days but never topped 80 feet (24.4 m). Today, acting as a spring, it discharges more than 4,000 gallons (15,142 liters) of heated water every minute.

Compared to the much smaller Midway Geyser Basin, the Lower Geyser Basin is enormous, spanning 12 square miles and including several clusters of thermal features. Among them are the notable **Fountain Geyser,** a placid blue pool that erupts on average every 4.5-7 hours for 25-50 minutes and sprays up to 50 feet (15.2 m) high; the temperamental **White Dome Geyser;** the almost-constant **Clepsydra;** and the **Pocket Basin Mud Pots,** which are the largest collection of mud pots in the park. **Great Fountain Geyser** in the Firehole Lake area is the only predictable geyser in the Lower Geyser Basin and erupts every 10 hours and 45 minutes, give or take two hours, for up to an hour, reaching heights of 70-200 feet (21.3-61 m).

Yellowstone's Supervolcano: Waiting for the Big One?

It's always interesting to watch visitors' expressions when you tell them that in Yellowstone they are standing atop one of the world's largest active supervolcanoes … and that it is overdue for an apocalyptic eruption. While these facts are true, the reality is much less threatening. Indeed, there have been three phenomenal eruptions over the course of the last two million years, and the patterns indicate that the volcano is overdue to erupt. But scientists agree that the chances of a massive eruption in the next 1,000 or even 10,000 years are very slight.

A Super History

The first supervolcanic eruption 2.1 million years ago was 6,000 times more powerful than the 1980 eruption of Mount St. Helens, spouting rock and ash in every direction from Texas to Canada, Missouri to California. The eruption caused a massive sinking of the earth, known as a caldera, within the confines of what is now the park. Small lava flows filled in the perimeter of the Huckleberry Ridge Caldera over the course of hundreds of thousands of years.

The second major eruption occurred 1.3 million years ago and created the Henry's Fork Caldera. The most recent massive eruption took place roughly 640,000 years ago and created the Yellowstone Caldera, which is 30 by 45 miles. The perimeter of the Yellowstone Caldera is still visible in places throughout the park. Hike up Mount Washburn on Dunraven Pass between Canyon and Tower, look south, and you will see the vast caldera. The caldera rim is also visible at Gibbon Falls, Lewis Falls, and Lake Butte. As you drive between Mammoth and Gardiner, look at Mount Everts to the east and you will see layers of ash from the various eruptions.

Today's Earthquakes Are Hints

But volcanic activity is not a thing of the past in Yellowstone. The magma, which some scientists think is just 5 miles (8 km) beneath the surface of the park in places as opposed to the typical 40, has created two enormous bulges, known as resurgent domes, near Sour Creek and Mallard Lake. The Sour Creek Dome is growing at an impressive rate of 1.5 inches per year, causing Yellowstone Lake to tip southward, leaving docks on the north side completely out of the water and flooding the forested shore of the south side. In addition, there are roughly 2,000 earthquakes every year centered in Yellowstone, most of which cannot be felt. In 2014, however, a 4.8-magnitude quake occurred 4 miles (6.4 km) from Norris Geyser Basin. The earthquakes shift geothermal activity in the park and keep the natural plumbing system that feeds the geyser basins flowing. They also suggest volcanic activity. In early 2010, a series of more than 3,200 small earthquakes (the largest registered 3.8 on the Richter scale) rocked the park, with 16 quakes registering a magnitude greater than 3.0. A 1985 swarm recorded more than 3,000 earthquakes over three months, with the largest registering at 4.9 on the Richter scale.

Don't Worry!

Still, the scientists at the Yellowstone Volcano Observatory have no reason to suspect that an eruption, or even a lava flow, is imminent. Scientists have been monitoring the region for precursors to eruptions—earthquake swarms, rapid ground deformation, gas releases, and lava flows—and although there is activity, none of it suggests anything immediately foreboding. Current real-time monitoring data, including earthquake activity and deformation, are available online at http://volcanoes.usgs.gov. The volcano is real and active, but certainly not a threat in the immediate future, and not a reason to stay away from this awe-inspiring place.

Adventure and Recreation

Hiking
The Northern Loop
Bunsen Peak and Osprey Falls

Distance: 4.2 miles (6.8 km) round-trip or
6.6-11.6-mile (10.6-18.7 km) loop

Duration: 3-7 hours

Elevation change: 1,278-2,058 feet (390-627 m)

Effort: strenuous

Trailhead: Old Bunsen Peak Road Trailhead, 4.8 miles (7.7 km) south of Mammoth on the east side of Grand Loop Road

The peak, a volcanic cone named for Robert Bunsen, who invented the Bunsen burner, contains a summit weather station; the building and its connecting power lines are a minor disruption to the wilderness feel. In summer, go early to nab a parking spot at the popular trailhead.

Starting in a sagebrush meadow, the trail climbs through steep forests, meadows, and 1988 burns to the 8,564-foot summit. Shortly after starting the climb, spot the Golden Gate from above along with Glen Creek Canyon hoodoos. The trail winds back and forth around the mountain, passing **Cathedral Rock** at 1.4 miles, where views plunge to Mammoth Hot Springs. Steep switchbacks then lead across talus slopes to the summit. The reward is the view of Electric Peak in the Gallatin Range and Gardners Hole. For the shortest hike, retrace your route back down. Or, for an alternative, drop eastward 1.4 steep miles through a burn zone to the **Old Bunsen Peak Road,** turning right to circle three gentle miles (shared by bikers) around the south flank of **Bunsen Peak** (6.6 miles total).

Strong hikers can lengthen the loop with a descent and return climb to see 150-foot **Osprey Falls** on the Gardner River. Descend eastward from the peak to the Old Bunsen Peak Road, then turn left to find the Osprey Falls Trailhead. From the trailhead, a 1.4-mile trail traverses the edge of Sheepeater Canyon with the basalt-columned Sheepeater Cliffs visible on the opposite side. Drop down steep, narrow, sunny switchbacks into the ravine below the falls. After climbing the 780 feet back up, follow the old road south around Bunsen Peak to return to your vehicle. Those wanting to avoid the Bunsen Peak climb can hike out and back on the old road to see Osprey Falls (8.8 miles, 780 feet elevation gain).

Wraith Falls

Distance: 0.8 mile (1.3 km) round-trip

Duration: 45 minutes

Elevation change: 74 feet (23 m)

Effort: easy

Trailhead: a pullout on the south side of Grand Loop Road, 0.5 mile east of Lava Creek Picnic Area east of Mammoth

Launch onto this trail by walking through a sagebrush-scented meadow blooming with columbine and buckwheat in early summer. An intermittent **boardwalk** crosses small streams and marshes. The route tucks in between coniferous tree islands, crosses Lupine Creek, and climbs one switchback to reach the viewing platform. The 79-foot **Wraith Falls** cascades down a wide-angled rock face squeezed into a canyon. In June, the flow fills the full width, but by September, the water thins to appear like two parallel falls.

Ice Lake

Distance: 0.6 mile (1 km) round-trip

Duration: 30 minutes

Elevation change: 22 feet (6.7 m)

Effort: easy

Trailhead: Norris-Canyon Road, 3.5 miles east of Norris

Ice Lake is a narrow lake tucked amid thick lodgepole pine forest regrowth after the 1988 fires. The lake is less than a mile long and is rimmed with downed timber and pines with only a few small beach areas.

From the trailhead, hike 0.2 mile up the trail to a **junction.** Take the right fork for the quickest access. The left fork heads farther to the northwest corner of the lake and at 0.5 mile reaches a junction with the **Howard Eaton Trail.** The trail westward reaches **Norris Campground** in 4.1 miles, an alternate trailhead. The trail right goes along the north shore of **Ice Lake** to **Wolf Lake, Grebe Lake** (an excellent place to fish for rare Arctic grayling), and **Cascade Lake.**

★ Mount Washburn

Distance: 5.4-6.4 miles (8.7-10.3 km) round-trip
Duration: 4 hours
Elevation change: 1,400-1,483 feet (427-452 m)
Effort: easy grade, but strenuous by elevation
Trailheads: For the south trail: Dunraven Pass Trailhead parking area on the east side of Grand Loop Road, 5.4 miles north of Canyon Junction. For the north trail: 10.3 miles north of Canyon Junction, drive 1.3 miles up Chittenden Road to reach the parking area.

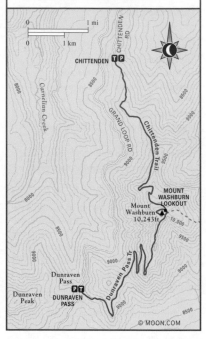

At 10,243 feet, the Mount Washburn Lookout yields a 360-degree panorama with big views. On a clear day, hikers can see the Grand Canyon of the Yellowstone, Yellowstone Lake, and even the Tetons. The Chittenden Trail is steeper and has a bit more elevation gain than the Dunraven Pass Trail, but both high-elevation trails climb switchbacks in a steady plod on former roads.

The **Dunraven Pass Trail** (6.4 miles, hikers only) traverses a southern slope before swinging north at 9,100 feet. It then makes four switchbacks up a west slope to crest a long ridge for a scenic walk that finishes with a 360-degree circle to Mount Washburn Lookout. Bighorn sheep can sometimes be seen in the upper-elevation cliffs and meadows.

The steeper **Chittenden Trail** (5.4 miles, bicycles allowed) ascends just below a ridge with a few switchbacks thrown in to work up the slope. On the final ridge, the trail swings east and then switchbacks west for the last steps to the summit of Mount Washburn.

At the summit, **Mount Washburn Lookout** is an ugly three-story cement block covered in radio equipment. Visitors can access only two levels: an observation room with windows on three sides, interpretive displays, and a viewing scope; and a deck above. Restrooms are available.

Slopes may be **snow-covered in June** but burst with alpine wildflowers by July. Due to afternoon thunderstorms, plan to **descend before early afternoon.** Even though the treeless trail looks hot, **bring warm clothing;** the alpine tundra summit is often windy and cold. Due to the trail's popularity, you'll have company at the lookout.

North Rim of Grand Canyon of the Yellowstone

Distance: 3.8-6.6 miles (6.1-10.6 km) one-way
Duration: 3-4 hours
Elevation change: 250-1,500 feet (76-457 m)
Effort: easy to strenuous

Grand Canyon of the Yellowstone Trails

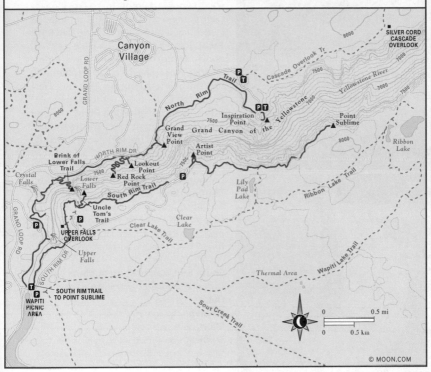

Trailheads: Wapiti Lake Trailhead on South Rim Drive, on the west side of the bridge over the Yellowstone River

Directions: Park at Wapiti Picnic Area on the east side of South Rim Drive. Walk back across the Chittenden Bridge over the Yellowstone River to find the trailhead heading north.

This trail is not about backcountry solitude, but rather tremendous views of the Grand Canyon of the Yellowstone. A combination of paved and dirt trails link multiple overlooks. You can start at either the north or south end to hike the entire trail, or shorten the distance by driving some segments. (In several places, the trail pops out to cross parking lots on North Rim Drive.) At several overlooks, spur trails drop down switchbacks and steep stairways to viewing platforms; all require climbing back up. Completing all the spurs adds a climb of nearly 1,500 feet in elevation and two more miles.

To start at the **south end** of the North Rim Trail, cross Chittenden Bridge to follow the Yellowstone River downstream (heading north). In 0.4 mile, the trail reaches the first viewpoint at **Brink of the Upper Falls.** A spur trail drops 42 feet to an overlook of the 109-foot falls. Continue north, passing the parking lot for Brink of the Upper Falls, to the 130-foot **Crystal Falls** as it spews from a slot in the North Rim cliffs. Heading northeast now, the 308-foot **Lower Falls** comes into view; follow the trail to a junction where a spur plummets 600 feet down switchbacks and stairs to the **Brink of the Lower Falls.** Climb back up the spur

and continue east to the **Lookout Point Trailhead,** where a short trail climbs 25 feet to **Lookout Point.** Just west, a longer trail plunges 500 feet in 0.4 mile down switchbacks and steep stairs to **Red Rock Point.** Returning to the North Rim Trail, continue north to **Grand View Point,** where a short paved trail drops about 150 feet to the viewpoint. Past Grand View Point, the trail curls northeast about 1.3 miles to the **Inspiration Point** parking lot. Walk through the parking lot and descend 50 feet in elevation in 0.1 mile to the classic viewpoint.

To hike the trail in reverse, start at the **north end** by parking at Inspiration Point parking lot. For the 3.8-mile one-way hike, leave a car shuttle at either the Inspiration Point or Wapiti Picnic Area parking lots. Or return the way you came for a 7.6-mile out-and-back hike.

South Rim Trail to Point Sublime
Distance: 5.1 miles (8.2 km) round-trip
Duration: 3 hours
Elevation change: 250-750 feet (76-229 m)
Effort: easy to strenuous
Trailheads: South trailhead: Wapiti Picnic Area on South Rim Drive, on the east side of the bridge over the Yellowstone River. North Trailhead: Artist Point parking lot at terminus of South Rim Drive

The South Rim Trail has multiple overlooks of the Grand Canyon of the Yellowstone. From the Wapiti Picnic Area, a 0.4-mile forested walk heads north following the Yellowstone River to the first viewpoint at the **Upper Falls.** A spur trail drops 15 feet to the viewpoint. After circling north on the bluff for snippets of views, the strenuous **Uncle Tom's Trail** plunges 500 feet down paved switchbacks and 328 metal stairsteps (that you have to climb back up) to an overlook. Skip this if you want the easy walk.

Past Uncle Tom's Trail, the route continues east through the forest with several viewpoints along the canyon rim

Top to bottom: bison in the Lamar Valley; Lower Falls of the Yellowstone; Trout Lake.

until reaching the Artist Point parking lot. Walk northeast through the parking lot to reach the **Artist Point Trailhead** and continue 0.1 mile to the scenic point. From Artist Point, the dirt trail continues east 0.75 mile to **Point Sublime.** On this section, exposed overlooks (no railings) require caution as you take in the depth of the canyon. The Lower Falls drops out of view, but the canyon walls and hoodoos become far more colorful with smears of reds and pinks above the frothy blue water. The trail dead-ends at Point Sublime at a log railing where the forest claims the canyon.

Lamar Valley and the Northeast Corner
Narrows of the Yellowstone River
Distance: 4 miles (6.4 km) round-trip
Duration: 2.5 hours
Elevation change: 393 feet (120 m)
Effort: easy
Trailhead: Yellowstone River Picnic Area Trailhead, 1.2 miles east of Tower Junction on the Northeast Entrance Road

A steep grunt uphill through sagebrush meadows with pink sticky geranium and arrowleaf balsamroot leads to the east rim of the Narrows of the Yellowstone River. The trail saunters along the rim above the deep canyon with several viewpoints. In one mile, the trail overlooks **Calcite Springs.** As it traverses a ridge 500 feet above the Yellowstone River, the route affords spectacular views of the narrows, sculpted minarets, and columnar basalt. It's also a good place to spot bighorn sheep, osprey, and peregrine falcons. Pronghorn cross the ridge, and marmots live in the rocks. In two miles, you'll reach a **four-way trail junction,** which is where most hikers turn around. Those with gumption add a 0.8-mile drop to the Yellowstone River and back on the spur trail that plunges steeply 0.4 mile to the historic **Bannock Indian Ford.**

Specimen Ridge
Distance: 3 miles (4.8 km) round-trip
Duration: 3-4 hours
Elevation change: 1,024 feet (312 m)
Effort: strenuous
Trailhead: Look for a hiker symbol at a pullout 4.5 miles east of Tower Junction on the Northeast Entrance Road just before the Lamar River Bridge

The route up Specimen Ridge goes to a fossil zone, part of the largest group of petrified trees in the world. Most of the fossils come from 50 million years ago, and some are species that no longer grow in the park. One toppled petrified tree stretches 20 feet long and 8 feet in diameter. Do not confuse this unmaintained route with the Specimen Ridge Trail from Yellowstone River Picnic Area, which does not go to the fossils.

Starting off on an **old faint road** and veering off to the right, the route tromps through sage meadows, disappearing frequently in wet seeps. Aim for the trail grunting straight uphill. It will cross multiple wildlife paths before reaching a small forest. The trail switchbacks through the trees to reach an **open ridge.** A rock outcropping marks the **petrified redwood tree trunks** area, and sweeping views span the bison herds in Lamar Valley and the Absaroka Mountains.

Trout Lake Trail
Distance: 1.2 miles (1.9 km) round-trip
Duration: 1 hour
Elevation change: 220 feet (67 m)
Effort: easy
Trailhead: a small pullout with limited parking on the Northeast Entrance Road, 3 miles north of Soda Butte Trailhead and 1.5 miles south of Pebble Creek Campground

An idyllic little lake sitting at about 7,000 feet in elevation, **Trout Lake** is actually the largest of three small lakes tucked near the Northeast Entrance Road in the **Absaroka Mountains.** From the trailhead, the path catapults vertically through a Douglas fir forest to the lake. About 0.3 mile up the trail, the **route splits** to circle the lake. Go either way. The trail circles the shoreline, which is semi-forested on the east shore and open meadows on the west shore. In early summer, phlox blankets the hillsides, cutthroat trout spawn in the inlet stream, and osprey hang around to fish. Short unmaintained trails connect with Shrimp and Buck Lakes. Ambling around the lake in June and early July, when the trout are spawning, is a pretty unforgettable experience.

The Southern Loop
Observation Point
Distance: 2.1 miles (3.4 km) round-trip
Duration: 1 hour
Elevation change: 237 feet (72 m)
Effort: moderate
Trailhead: Old Faithful Visitor Education Center

Most hikers coordinate the walk up to Observation Point with an eruption of Old Faithful Geyser. From the overlook, you can look down on the masses of people surrounding the geyser and watch it blow, but the steam plume sometimes occludes the water spouting, depending on wind direction. In winter, when the ground is snow-covered, wear snowshoes or boot cleats (rent from the Bear's Den in the Snow Lodge). While hiking time is short, the wait for Old Faithful to erupt may be long.

From the Old Faithful Visitor Education Center, circle the east side of Old Faithful Geyser heading toward **Geyser Hill** and cross the Firehole River. After crossing the bridge, turn right at the sign for **Observation Point.** The trail switchbacks uphill for 0.5 mile, making a small loop at the top. At the point, claim your spot in the trees to watch Old Faithful erupt. In winter, you may be the only one there, but in summer, you'll join a crowd. To descend, walk down the loop and continue westward on the trail through the forest to **Solitary Geyser.** From the geyser, a dirt trail connects south with the boardwalk on Geyser Hill near Aurum Geyser. Go east on the boardwalk to retrace your route across the Firehole River and back to Old Faithful.

Lone Star Geyser
Distance: 4.8-8.2 miles (7.7-13.2 km) round-trip
Duration: 3-5 hours
Elevation change: 65-243 feet (20-74 m)
Effort: easy
Trailhead: Lone Star Geyser Trailhead or the adjacent Kepler Cascades parking area (park at either), 2.5 miles east of Old Faithful or Old Faithful Lodge.

From the Lone Star Geyser Trailhead, walk south along the old **asphalt service road** through conifers along the meandering Firehole River. The route passes a large meadow (scout for wildlife) before ascending a gentle hill to the geyser basin. **Lone Star Geyser,** a 12-foot-tall pink and gray sinter cone, sits tucked away, hidden from the hubbub of the Upper Geyser Basin. Spouting up to 40 feet in the air, the geyser erupts about every three hours with spurts lasting 30 minutes. If you see the geyser go off, add the date and time to the logbook in the old interpretive stand.

Hiking the trail **from Old Faithful Lodge** almost doubles the mileage. From the southeast corner of the Old Faithful cabin complex, hop onto the **Mallard Lake Trail.** After crossing the Firehole River, turn right to follow the signage to **Kepler Cascades.** The trail climbs through forest and meadows until it parallels Grand Loop Road, then crosses to the Kepler Cascades parking lot. Locate the Lone Star Geyser Trailhead just south of the cascades. For an alternate return, take the Howard Eaton Trail 2.9 miles north back to Old Faithful.

Natural Bridge
Distance: 2.6 miles (4.2 km) round-trip
Duration: 2 hours
Elevation change: 181 feet (55 m)
Effort: easy
Trailhead: Bridge Bay Marina parking lot near the entrance to the campground

This scenic loop tours Natural Bridge, a 51-foot-high sculpture of rhyolite rock that has been eroded through by Bridge Creek. The bridge is impressive, although much smaller than Utah's famed arches. Note that this trail is **closed late**

Lone Star Geyser

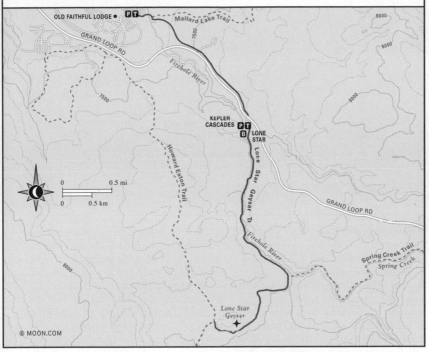

© MOON.COM

spring-early summer due to grizzlies feeding on spawning trout in Bridge Creek. A bicycle route also begins south of the bridge from a separate trailhead.

From the parking lot, the trail cuts west through the forest for 0.7 mile before joining an old **paved road.** The route continues working westward for 0.4 mile, turning right at all junctions to reach an **interpretive exhibit** at the base of the loop trail. From the exhibit, a short, steep path switchbacks 0.2 mile up to the top of **Natural Bridge;** cross the creek behind the bridge to loop back down the other side. (The top of the bridge is closed in order to protect the fragile rock, but you'll see marmots run across it.)

Yellowstone Lake Overlook

Distance: 2 miles (3.2 km) round-trip
Duration: 1.5 hours

Elevation change: 194 feet (59 m)
Effort: moderate
Trailhead: west side of the West Thumb Geyser Basin parking lot

The Lake Overlook Trail climbs from the start, beginning in a meadow and entering a forest. In 0.3 mile, the trail crosses the **South Entrance Road** and reaches a **fork.** Turn left and continue hiking south up to a meadow with red paintbrush and yellow buckwheat in early summer; panoramic views of Yellowstone Lake and the Absaroka Mountains unfold. There is a **bench** to enjoy the view; a **short spur** behind the bench climbs about 30 feet for a peekaboo view of the Tetons. Complete the loop to return to the parking lot.

Duck Lake

Distance: 1 mile (1.6 km) round-trip
Duration: 30 minutes

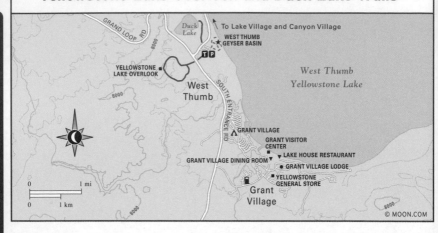

Yellowstone Lake Overlook and Duck Lake Trails

Elevation change: 200 feet (61 m)

Effort: easy

Trailhead: Duck Lake Trailhead at the north end of the West Thumb Geyser Basin parking lot

A short hike through a loose forest leads to 0.3-mile-long **Duck Lake,** a good destination for families with young kids. From the trailhead, the path crosses the road and climbs uphill. At the top of the hill, the trail crosses a power line before dropping down to the lake. The eastern lakeshore has a long **beach** with room to spread out. Wind-protected Duck Lake is often warmer for **swimming** than Yellowstone Lake.

Fishing and Boating
The Southern Loop

Some 80,000 anglers are lured to Yellowstone each year by the promise of elusive trout, and they are seldom disappointed by the offerings at Yellowstone Lake. In addition to the prized native cutthroat, the lake is home to a population of nonnative lake trout that is devastating the cutthroat trout population and endangering all the animals that eat the cutthroat trout. Introduced in 1890 into Lewis and Shoshone Lakes by the U.S. Fish Commission, the lake trout were first documented in Yellowstone Lake

in the mid-1990s; scientists believe they were illegally introduced from a nearby lake in the 1980s. The average lake trout lives and spawns in deep waters, feeding on as many as 40 cutthroat each year. By comparison, cutthroat trout spawn in the shallow tributaries of the lake, making them an important food source for a variety of creatures that include eagles and bears. Because the lake trout have no enemies in the deep waters of Yellowstone Lake, they are creating a serious food shortage by devouring the cutthroat. As a result, the eagles are having to eat other birds—including rare trumpeter swans, American white pelicans, Caspian terns, and double-crested cormorants—instead of fish, and Yellowstone is facing the complete elimination of some nesting bird species. In 2018, biologist Doug Smith described the ecological crisis as "an expanding picture of avian collapse." All lake trout caught in Yellowstone Lake must be killed. Pick up your **fishing permit** at one of the visitors centers along with a copy of the Yellowstone fishing regulations.

There are a number of ways to see Yellowstone Lake by boat. Scenic or fishing boat tours as well as outboard motor rentals ($57/hour) are available from **Bridge Bay Marina,** south of Lake Village or 21 miles (34 km) northeast of West Thumb. Hour-long cruises ($18 adults, $10.50 children 3-11, free for children under 3) depart regularly from the marina mid-June-mid-September. Reservations can be made through **Xanterra** (307/344-7311 or 866/439-7375, www.yellowstonenationalparklodges. com).

Gardiner

The Yellowstone is the longest free-flowing river in the Lower 48, and as such it offers excellent boating and fishing opportunities. With the river plunging through town on its way to Yankee Jim Canyon, Gardiner is home to several outfitters that can whet your appetite for adventure, trout, or both. The **Flying Pig Adventure Company** (511 Scott St., 888/792-9193, www.flyingpigrafting. com, May-Sept., 2 hour raft trip $43 adults, $33 children 12 and under) is a full-service outfitter offering guided white-water rafting, horseback rides, wildlife safaris, and cowboy cookouts. **Yellowstone Raft Company** (111 2nd St., 406/848-7777 or 800/858-7781, www. yellowstoneraft.com, May-Sept., half-day raft trip $43 adults, $33 children 6-12) was established in 1978 and has an excellent reputation for experienced guides and top-of-the-line equipment. For adrenaline junkies, Yellowstone Raft Company offers sit-on-top kayak instruction and adventures.

For anglers eager to wet a line in or out of the park in search of native cutthroats or brown trout, **Park's Fly Shop** (202 2nd St. S., 406/848-7314, www.parksflyshop. com, 8am-6pm daily summer, 9am-5pm Mon.-Sat., 10am-4pm Sun. fall-spring) is the best place to start. This is an old-school shop with a 1920s cash register—nothing fancy here. It offers half-day trips for two people starting around $425, and full-day trips for two from $525. Anglers can pick up their licenses and any supplies in the retail shop, which stays open

year-round. And because Park's has been serving the area since 1953, its guides are keenly aware of the spots where the fish outnumber the anglers.

Cooke City

Combine hiking and fishing 1.8 miles (2.9 km) west of the Pebble Creek Campground at **Trout Lake.** The hike itself is short and steep, just 1.2 miles (1.9 km) round-trip, and leaves from the Trout Lake Trailhead on the north side of the road. Anglers can bring a rod after July 15 when it opens to catch-and-release fishing for native cutthroats. In late spring-early summer, trout can be seen spawning in the inches-deep inlet, a fairly miraculous sight. There is an excellent trail around the 12-acre lake and shallow inlet and a decent chance of spotting playful otters, but hikers should take great care not to disturb the fish, especially during spawning. Bear awareness and a can of bear spray are necessary, as the bruins like fish too.

Another great place to combine fishing, hiking, and wildlife-watching—perhaps the perfect Yellowstone trifecta—is along the trail at **Slough Creek.** East of Tower Junction 5.8 miles (9.3 km) or west of the northeast entrance is an unpaved road on the north side of the road leading to Slough Creek Campground. The trailhead is 1.5 miles (2.4 km) down the road on the right side, just before the campground. The trail itself is a double-rutted wagon trail that leads to Silver Tip Ranch, a legendary private ranch just outside the park. The trail is maintained for 11 miles (17.7 km) one-way and only gains 400 feet (122 m) in elevation. All along the trail there is world-class fishing in slow-moving Slough Creek, home to a healthy population of native cutthroat trout. You may meet elk, bison, wolves, and even grizzlies along the trail, so be prepared and be safe.

West Yellowstone

The fishing around West tends to be as

plentiful as it is phenomenal. In addition to the big-name rivers like the **Madison, Firehole, Yellowstone,** and the nearby **Henry's Fork** across the border in Idaho, there are all sorts of small streams and beautiful lakes of all sizes. **Hebgen Lake** and **Quake Lake** are two favorites for year-round fishing.

You won't have any difficulty finding guides and gear in the town of West Yellowstone. Among the best is **Big Sky Anglers** (formerly Bud Lilly's Trout Shop, 39 Madison Ave., 406/646-7801, www.bigskyanglers.com, 7am-10pm daily during the season), which has been outfitting and guiding anglers for 60 years. Another pretty famous name among anglers is Bob Jacklin of **Jacklin's Fly Shop** (105 Yellowstone Ave., 406/646-7336, www.jacklinsflyshop.com, 8am-8pm daily summer, $550 full-day guided float for 2 people; $450 half-day guided walk/wade for 2 people). Both outfitters are licensed to guide in and out of Yellowstone National Park, and both carry an excellent assortment of top-of-the-line gear. Jacklin's Fly Shop also hosts free flycasting lessons every Sunday evening in summer 7pm-8pm. Anglers do not need state fishing licenses in Yellowstone, but a Yellowstone fishing permit—available at any of the visitors centers in the park—is required.

Winter Recreation
Cooke City

With an average of 500 inches of snowfall each year, mountainous terrain with elevation that ranges 7,000-10,000 feet (2,134-3,048 m), and a nearly interminable winter, Cooke City is a snow sports mecca with 60 miles (97 km) of groomed snowmobile trails and endless acres of ungroomed terrain for skiing and snowmobiling. Some favorite trails are **Daisy Pass, Lulu Pass,** and **Round Creek Trail.**

A number of places in town rent snowmobiles and all the necessary gear. Most important, you'll need to talk with experts about local conditions, trail closures, and avalanche dangers. **Cooke City Motorsports** (203 Eaton St., 406/838-2231, www.cookecitymotorsports.com, snowmobiles from $205/day) and **Cooke City Exxon** (204 Main St., 406/838-2244, www.cookecityexxon.com, snowmobiles from $220/day) are obvious choices in town. When the snow melts, you can rent ATVs from **Bearclaw Sales and Service** (309 E. Main St., 406/838-2244, www.bearclawsalesandservice.com, single ATVs from $35/hour, $100/half day, $160/full day, and side-by-side ATVs from $75/hour, $200/half day, $275/full day) as another way to get out and cover a lot of ground.

West Yellowstone

Sandwiched between Yellowstone and the Gallatin National Forest on a high plateau, West Yellowstone offers excellent terrain for mountain biking. Because of its high altitude and location at the top of a reasonably flat plateau, West Yellowstone is also known for its cross-country ski trails. The town's excellent **Rendezvous Ski Trails** (look for the archway at the south end of Geyser St., www.skirunbikemt.com) offer roughly 22 miles (35 km) of gently rolling terrain, groomed for both skate and classic skiers, which easily converts to a single-track for mountain bikers and trail runners when the snow melts. Athletes from around the world come to train in West thanks in large part to this trail system. And it should be noted that the proximity to Yellowstone opens up a whole new world of opportunity for both mountain bikers and skiers.

The best bike and ski shop in town—which also has surprisingly stylish clothes, great gear, a Pilates studio, and killer coffee—is the **Freeheel & Wheel** (33 Yellowstone Ave., 406/646-7744, www.freeheelandwheel.com, 9am-7pm Mon.-Sat., 9am-6pm Sun.). It rents, sells, and services bikes and skis and can offer any advice you could possibly need on the region's best rides and trails. Front

Be Safe and Smart in the Backcountry

Hiking and camping in the Yellowstone backcountry is undoubtedly the best way to understand and appreciate this magnificently wild place. But with this opportunity comes the responsibility to keep yourself safe, protect the animals from human-caused altercations, and preserve this pristine environment.

When hiking, prevent erosion and trail degradation by hiking single file and always staying on the trail. Don't take shortcuts or cut corners on switchbacks. If you do have to leave the trail, disperse your group so that you don't inadvertently trample the vegetation and create a new, unwanted trail.

Chances are good that you will encounter some kind of wildlife in the backcountry, so you need to be prepared to react. Never approach an animal: Remember to always stay at least 25 yards (22.9 m) away from all wildlife, and at least 100 yards (91.4 m) away from predators, including bears. Make noise as you hike along to give animals the opportunity to depart before an encounter. Do not hike at the edges of day—dawn or dusk—or at night, as these are the most active times for bears and other predators. Always be aware of your surroundings. Look for overturned rocks and logs, dug-out areas, and, of course, carcasses, all of which suggest bear activity.

If you do encounter a bear, know what to do. If there is some distance between you and the bear, give the bear an opportunity to leave, or take the opportunity to redirect your own party. If you run into a bear at close range, be as nonthreatening as possible. Talk calmly and back away. Never turn your back, and never run. Make sure you have your bear spray accessible. If the bear charges, stand your ground. Bears will often bluff charge to determine whether you will run and are thus prey. If the bear does attack, keep your pack on, fall to the ground on your belly, protect your head and neck with your arms, and play dead. When the bear leaves, get up and retreat. In the very uncommon circumstance that a bear provokes an attack or enters a tent, fight the bear with every resource you have.

Go to great lengths to avoid attracting bears by hanging all food, cooking utensils, and scented items (toothpaste, deodorant, other toiletries, and trash) in a bear bag in a tree or atop a bear pole. Designate a separate cooking and eating area away from the sleeping tents. Dispose of your trash and personal waste properly.

You need to plan your trip carefully and secure all permits and backcountry campsites through any one of nine backcountry permit offices: Bechler Ranger Station, Canyon Visitor Center, Grant Village Visitor Center, Bridge Bay Ranger Station, Mammoth Visitor Center, Old Faithful Ranger Station, South Entrance Ranger Station, Tower Ranger Station, and the West Yellowstone Visitor Information Center (307/344-2160, www.nps.gov/yell, permits available 8am-4:30pm daily June-Aug., $25 annual backcountry pass, $3 pp over 9 years old per night). Some of Yellowstone's roughly 300 backcountry campsites can be reserved in advance either in person, by fax, or through the mail. Backcountry use permits are required for all overnight stays and can only be attained in person no more than 48 hours before your trip. A park booklet titled *Beyond Road's End* is available online and will help familiarize you with the backcountry regulations and restrictions.

suspension kid and adult mountain bikes ($10/hour, $35/day) and road bikes ($10/hour, $40/day) can be rented and come with a helmet and water bottle.

Although snowmobiling inside the park has shifted with the four-stroke engine and guide requirements along with daily entry limits, West Yellowstone is still considered the snowmobile capital of the world for its proximity to the 200 miles (320 km) of groomed trails in the park as well as hundreds of miles of groomed terrain in the national forests surrounding West.

There are numerous places in town to rent a snowmobile, and because the

Spring Biking Through the Park

For a few magical weeks between the end of the snowmobile season and the onset of the summer car traffic, Yellowstone's roads are open exclusively to nonmotorized users. This means that bicyclists, walkers, runners, in-line skaters, and roller skiers can cruise through the park in near silence with eyes focused on bison traffic as opposed to wide Winnebagos. Depending on the seasonal snow, the road between the west entrance and Mammoth Hot Springs typically opens the last Friday in March and stays open to nonmotorized users until the third Thursday in April. Opening can be delayed in heavy snow years due to the need for plowing.

Sometime in May there is normally a brief period of bicycle-only traffic permitted from the east entrance to the east end of Sylvan Pass, and from the south entrance to West Thumb Junction. The roads between Madison Junction and Old Faithful, and Norris Junction to Canyon, remain closed to all traffic during this spring season for human safety and bear management.

There is something spellbinding about being on the open road in the park, the wind whistling through your helmet. The relative silence allows some unrivaled wildlife-viewing and necessitates great care. As nerve-racking as it can be to get engulfed by a herd of bison while driving in your car, coming across them on your bike is an entirely different scenario. Still, if you are cautious and respectful, being on your bike can allow you to feel somewhat less like an intruder and more like a resident. You can fall into sync with the flow of the rivers, the movement of the breeze, and the calls of the animals. It is an unforgettable way to experience the park.

With that said: Respect, restraint, and absolute caution are of vital importance to your safety and the well-being of the animals. Keep a good distance from all wildlife—25 yards (22.9 m) from ungulates and 100 yards (91.4 m) from predators. Remember that bison can run at speeds topping 30 mph (48.3 kph), and they can jump a 6-foot (1.8-m) fence. Harbor no illusions about your immunity from an attack. The fact that you have approached silently allows for more of a startle factor for the animals and increases the likelihood of a conflict. Wear a helmet, and dress in layers: Yellowstone in spring can go from blue skies to blizzard conditions in a staggeringly short period of time. Be prepared for anything, and understand that there are no services in the park at this time. Enjoy this unique opportunity to savor the park up close. For specific information about road conditions, call 307/344-2109 from 8am to 4:30pm on weekdays.

park mandates that all snowmobilers within park boundaries use a guide, several outfits also offer guiding services both in and outside of the park. **Two Top Snowmobile Rental** (645 Gibbon Ave., 800/646-7802, www.twotopsnowmobile.com) has rentals for self-guided tours outside the park from $129 per day and guided tours into the park from $219. It also has licensed guides, Yellowstone-mandated four-stroke engines, and other rental equipment. Another full-service rental outfit in West is **Rendezvous Snowmobile Rentals** (415 Yellowstone Ave., 406/646-9564 or 800/426-7669, www.yeloowstonevacations.com), renting snowmobiles at $129-225 per day for travel outside the park or $225 for a single/double snowmobile on a guided trip to Old Faithful. For deep-powder backcountry touring options outside the park, **Hi Country Snowmobile Rentals** (229 Hayden St., 406/646-7541 or 800/624-5291, www.hicountrysnowmobile.com) is an excellent bet, with snowmobile rentals from its entirely new fleet each year, guided trail rides, and guided backcountry tours. Rates vary throughout the year, so call for information.

For those who want to explore the backcountry outside Yellowstone National Park in a slightly quieter

West Yellowstone

WASHBURN AVE

To Bar N Ranch,
Hebgen Lake,
Big Sky, and
Bozeman

191

Yellowstone

FOREST
SERVICE OFFICE

▼ CAFÉ
MADRIZ

TWO TOP
SNOWMOBILE
■ RENTAL

WAGON WHEEL RV
CAMPGROUND & CABINS

GIBBON AVE

BEST WESTERN
WESTON INN

*City
Park*

Nat'l

20 191

● — PINE SHADOWS
■   MOTEL & CONDOS

HI COUNTRY
SNOWMOBILE
RENTALS

FAITHFUL ST

ELECTRIC ST

DUNRAVEN ST

CANYON ST

BOUNDARY ST

To Rodeo Grounds
Island Park, Super 8,
Yellowstone
Under Canvas, Bar N Ranch
and Ashton, ID

FIREHOLE   AVE

▼ ERNIE'S BAKERY & DELI

BRANDIN
IRON INN

Park

IRIS ST

HAYDEN ST

GEYSER ST

PETE'S ROCKY MOUNTAIN
PIZZA AND PASTA ▼

SERENITY ▼
BISTRO

BUCKAROO BILL'S
ICE CREAM

BIG SKY
ANGLERS

MADISON AVE

▼ RUNNING BEAR
PANCAKE HOUSE

● DAYS INN
WEST YELLOWSTONE

ALPINE
MOTEL ●

LIBRARY

TAQUERIA
LAS PALMITAS
▼

To
Madison
Junction

YELLOWSTONE
ALPEN GUIDES
■

RENDEZVOUS
SNOWMOBILE
RENTALS

HOLIDAY INN
WEST
YELLOWSTONE

THREE BEAR
LODGE

CANYON ●
STREET GRILL

TIMBERLINE
CAFÉ ▼

AL'S
WESTWARD HO ●
MOTEL

■ FREEHEEL
& WHEEL

20

YELLOWSTONE AVE

MEDICAL
■ CLINIC

JACKLIN'S
FLY SHOP

VISITOR
CENTER

WEST
ENTRANCE

OBSIDIAN AVE

🚻
RENDEZVOUS
SKI TRAILS

● YELLOWSTONE
KELLY INN

★ YELLOWSTONE
GIANT SCREEEN
THEATER

POST
■ OFFICE

GRIZZLY AVE

GRIZZLY AND WOLF
DISCOVERY CENTER

ELECTRIC ST

GRAY WOLF AVE

CANYON ST

0   200 yds

0   200 m

© MOON.COM

way, dogsledding might be the perfect choice. **Yellowstone Dog Sled Adventures** (406/223-5134, www.yellowstonedogsledadventures.com) offers half-day "Learn to Mush" tours ($235 adults, $150 children 5-12) where guests get to drive their own sled, which are appropriate for ages 5 and up. Other offerings allow guests to cuddle up in a sled while an experienced musher does the driving.

Another amazing way to see the park is on a guided snow coach tour. There are numerous providers, but **Yellowstone Alpen Guides** (555 Yellowstone Ave., 406/646-9591 or 800/858-3502, www.yellowstoneguides.com, from $145 adults, $135 seniors, $110 children under 16, prices do not include national park passes) offers classic 10-passenger Bombardiers, a fantastic array of tours, and some of the best naturalist guides anywhere. Snow coach tours can be combined with some cross-country skiing in the park. Alpen Guides can also package lodging and meals.

Food

As the southern loop is generally the most heavily traveled section of the park, there are plenty of dining opportunities. In the park restaurants, breakfast and lunch are on a first-come, first-served basis, but reservations are strongly recommended for dinner, particularly if 5pm or 9pm are not your ideal dining hours. In almost all the venues, you will find some good vegetarian options and many items made with sustainable or organic ingredients; these are identified on each menu. If you are planning a day activity away from the center of things, the restaurants or cafeterias offer box lunches for travelers to take with them. Place your order the night before, and it will be ready in the morning. The Yellowstone General Stores at Grant Village, Lake Village, and Old Faithful also have fast-food service, groceries, and snacks.

Inside the Park
The Northern Loop

By far the most distinctive meal available in the park is the ★ **Old West Dinner Cookout** (307/344-7311, www.yellowstonenationalparklodges.com), which departs daily early June through mid-September from the Roosevelt Lodge and is served in Yellowstone's wilderness. The hearty steak-and-potatoes dinner with all the cowboy trimmings can be attended on horseback (1-hour rides from $87 ages 12 and over, $72 children 8-11, 2-hour rides from $94 ages 12 and over, $86 children 8-11) or via covered wagon (from $63 ages 12 and over, $50 children 3-11, free for children under 3).

Breakfast, lunch, and dinner are served daily throughout the season in the **Roosevelt Lodge Dining Room, Canyon Lodge Dining Room, Cafeteria, and Deli,** and the **Mammoth Hotel Dining Room and Terrace Grill** (866/439-7375, www.yellowstonenationalparklodges.com). Each restaurant has its own flair—Roosevelt Lodge tends to be heartier, with options like barbecue beef, bison chili, and Wyoming cheesesteak, while Mammoth is known for elaborate buffets and inventive small plates like goat cheese sliders, mini trout tacos, and Thai curry mussels. Canyon offers a wok station and slow food fast, with ready-made entrées like barbecued ribs, country-fried steak, and rotisserie chicken. Breakfasts include entrées ranging from pancakes and eggs to biscuits and gravy ($6-12). Lunches range $9-16, and dinners are generally $12-36. Generally, breakfast is served 6:30am-10am, lunch 11:30am-2:30pm, and dinner 5:30pm-10pm. Hours vary seasonally by restaurant and are subject to change. Call ahead for reservations or to check hours; menus are available on the website.

The Southern Loop

The **Grant Village Dining Room** (866/439-7375, 6:30am-10am, 11:30am-2:30pm, and 5pm-10pm daily late May-Sept., $17-32) offers a pleasant view of the lake, good service, and a nice variety of American cuisine. In addition to the à la carte menu for breakfast, a buffet is available ($13.95 adults, $7.25 children). Lunch and dinner include dishes such as prime rib sliders, smoked bison bratwurst, or spinach ravioli. Reservations are required for dinner.

The **Lake House** at Grant Village (6:30am-10:30am and 5pm-9:30pm daily high season, shortened hours early/late seasons) sits right on the lake, with great views and a casual ambience. Breakfast ($13.95 adults, $7.25 children) is buffet only, and the dinner menu ($10-25) consists of regional fare like huckleberry chicken, wild game meat loaf, prime rib, and lemon pepper trout.

The ★ **Lake Yellowstone Hotel Dining Room** (307/344-7311 or 866/439-7375, 6:30am-10am, 11:30am-2:30pm, and 5pm-10pm daily mid-May-early Oct., reservations required for dinner, $16-45, breakfast buffet $15.75 adults, $7.25 children) is the most elegant dining room in the park, with a gorgeous view of the lake. The restaurant is committed to creating dishes with fresh, local, organic, and sustainable ingredients. Lunch ($11-15) is a good way to sample some of the gourmet fare without putting too large a dent in your pocketbook. Try the delicious organic lentil soup or blackened wild Alaska salmon wrap. Dinner at the hotel is sure to be a memorable experience with options like Montana elk chops, bison tenderloin, and lamb sliders.

Directly inside the hotel is the **Lake Hotel Deli** (6:30am-9pm daily mid-May-early Sept., shortened hours early/late seasons, $8-11), which serves a nice selection of soups, salads, and sandwiches. The **Lake Lodge Cafeteria** (6:30am-10pm daily early June-late Sept., shortened hours early/late seasons, $7-17) is a casual place for a quick bite. It serves basic breakfast standards, plenty of kids' favorites, and comfort food dishes ranging from spinach pie to fried chicken to apple-glazed pork loin.

Five eateries are located in the Old Faithful complex, but by far the most desirable is the **Old Faithful Inn Dining Room** (307/344-7311, 6:30am-10am, 11:30am-2:30pm, and 4:30pm-10pm daily early June-early Sept., shortened hours in May, Sept., early Oct., $17-30), which offers a buffet for each of the main meals daily (breakfast $13.95 adults and $7.25 children, lunch $16.25 adults and $7.95 children, dinner $30.50 adults and $11.50 children) as well as an à la carte menu. You can dine in the historic inn while enjoying its distinct rustic architecture and Western-style ambience. Lunch is a "Western buffet" with items such as farm-raised pan-fried trout, pulled pork, and wild game sausage. If you don't opt for the dinner buffet (featuring prime rib and trout), you could try pork osso buco, penne with local lamb ragout, wild Alaska sockeye salmon, and New York strip steak. Reservations are required for dinner.

The **Bear Paw Deli** (6am-9pm daily late May-early Sept., shortened hours early/late seasons, $4-9), also inside the inn, is perfect for on-the-go meals. It offers a continental breakfast including bagel sandwiches, salads and deli fare for lunch, as well as serving up several flavors of ice cream. In addition to these two eateries at the inn, there is a cafeteria and bakeshop in the lodge and a dining room and grill in the Old Faithful Snow Lodge.

Outside the Park
Gardiner

Known since 1960 for its "Hateful Hamburgers" and the huge personality of its owner, Helen, this fabulous burger joint was sold to the Wild West Rafting Company and is now known as ★ **Wild West Corral** (U.S. 89 S., across from the Super 8 Motel, 406/848-7627, 11am-10pm daily May-Oct., $7-17). Even without Helen, this is still the kind of place you might easily drive 100 miles (161 km) to for the burgers, shakes, and old-school ambience. The limited seating is mostly outside, and there is often a line of people waiting to order. But none of that will matter when you take your first bite of a bison bacon cheeseburger or a perfectly grilled elk burger. Wild West Corral even managed to improve on Helen's by expanding the menu and cleaning the place up a bit. This is still a little slice of hamburger paradise.

Just over the river toward the park, the **K-Bar Pizza** (202 Main St., 406/848-9995, www.kbarmontana.com, 4pm-9pm Mon.-Thurs., 4pm-10pm Fri., 11am-11pm Sat.-Sun., $18-24) is a classic bar that's been dishing up surprisingly good homemade pizza since 1953. **The Raven Grill** (118 Park St., 406/848-9171, 5pm-10pm daily mid-Apr.-mid-Oct., $10-28) boasts a small but excellent menu long on comfort food and made from scratch. It also serves cocktails, including a mean Montana Huckleberry Moscow Mule. For a good, hearty breakfast, excellent pastries, fresh Mexican food, and burgers, the **Yellowstone Grill** (404 Scott

St., 406/848-9433, 7am-2pm Tues.-Sat., 7am-noon Sun., $7-12) is sure to please. Remember though, this is small-town Montana: Sometimes the place closes when short-staffed. Or when the owners' youngest son has a Legion baseball game. Be glad for that; the important stuff still matters here. You can always have a late lunch.

Cooke City

There are a million ways to work up an appetite in and around Cooke City. Be assured you won't go hungry (or thirsty, for that matter). ★ **Beartooth Café** (14 U.S. 212, 406/838-2475, www.beartoothcafe.com, 11am-9:30pm daily late May-late Sept., $13-27) offers excellent mountain fare—think steak and trout—with just a hint of Asian flair. The front-porch outdoor dining is a treat. Another great spot for a quick bite anytime (except April, May, October, and November when it's closed) is the **Bearclaw Bakery** (309 E. Main, 406/838-2040, 5am-10:30am daily, rolls and coffee served from 5am, hot breakfasts from 6am), which makes from-scratch baked goods, full hearty breakfasts, and light lunch. The bakery also offers a full coffee bar.

The **Prospector Restaurant** (210 U.S. 212, 406/838-2251, www.cookecity.com, 7am-10pm daily, $13-35), inside the Soda Butte Lodge, is open year-round and particularly known for steak and prime rib—not a stretch in these parts. Finally, for those wanting to pick up some supplies, the **Cooke City Store** (101 Main St., 406/838-2234, www.cookecitystore.com, 8am-8pm daily mid-May-Sept., hours may vary slightly) is as much a local museum and community center as it is a place to pick up some bread and a bottle of sunscreen. There's also a fly shop inside, **Trout Rider Fly Shop,** where you can get fishing licenses for Montana, Wyoming, or Yellowstone National Park as well as picking up some flies and other

supplies. It's a wonderful place and worth a visit—plus the nearest grocery store is 90 minutes away.

West Yellowstone

A great spot for a full breakfast, hot lunch, or terrific sack lunches is the long-standing **Ernie's Bakery & Deli** (409 Firehole Ave., 406/646-9467, www.erniesbakery.com, 7am-3pm daily summer, 7am-2pm daily winter, $8-18). **Running Bear Pancake House** (538 Madison Ave., 406/646-7703, www.runningbearph.com, 6:30am-2pm daily, $8-14) offers family-style dining for breakfast and lunch.

For the best soup, salad, and potato bar in town, try the **Timberline Café** (135 Yellowstone Ave., 406/646-9349, www.my.montana.net/timberlinecafe/, 6:30am-4pm and 5pm-10pm daily mid-May-early Oct., breakfast and lunch $6-14, dinner $11-31), an old-school establishment that has been feeding Yellowstone visitors and locals during the summer season since the early 1900s. Don't miss the homemade pie.

A real surprise in this tourist town is the wonderful ★ **Café Madriz** (311 N. Canyon St., 406/646-9245, late May-mid-Sept., 5pm-9pm Mon.-Sat., $11-30), which serves authentic Spanish dishes, from paella and *tortilla española* to hot and cold tapas, and makes the most of fresh, local ingredients. The salads are killer.

Another West Yellowstone institution is **Buckaroo Bill's Ice Cream & BBQ** (24 N. Canyon St., 406/646-7901, 10:30am-10pm Mon.-Sat. May-Oct., $7.75-29), which has excellent bison burgers, steaks, and sandwiches in addition to mouthwatering Montana-made ice cream. The joint is popular, though, and it's not always easy to get a seat; the outside patio is a lively place for a meal.

Canyon Street Grill (22 N. Canyon St., 406/646-7548, 11am-9pm daily May-Oct., 11am-8pm Sun.-Thurs., 11am-9pm Fri.-Sat. summer, reduced hours in off-season, $5-12) is a 1950s-style diner with delicious burgers, fries, and milk shakes. **Pete's Rocky Mountain Pizza and Pasta** (112 Canyon St., 406/646-7820, www.petesrockymountainpizza.com, 11am-10pm summer, seasonal hours vary, $20-27) serves up good pizza and hearty pasta dishes like elk sausage spaghetti and Italian buffalo ravioli. It has gluten-free pizza offerings, too. Delivery is available after 5pm.

If you like Mexican street food, the best place within a day's drive from Yellowstone is, without a doubt, ★ **Taqueria Las Palmitas** (21 N. Canyon St., 406/640-0172, 10am-10pm daily early Apr.-mid-Oct., $5-10), known locally as "The Taco Bus." We're talking soft tacos, beans, and more, piled onto paper plates and served in an old-school bus. It couldn't be less fancy or more satisfying.

For a more gourmet experience, **Serenity Bistro** (38 N. Canyon St., 406/646 7660, www.sydneysbistro.com, 11am-3pm and 5pm-close daily May-Oct., $8-30) is undoubtedly the place. It serves excellent, fresh meals utilizing local ingredients whenever possible. Entrées include the bistro burger, Panang chicken seafood pasta, trout escalope, buffalo tortellini, elk tenderloin, and twice-cooked quail. Pasta lovers won't want to miss the butternut squash. The bistro also offers gourmet salads and sandwiches for lunch and boasts the most extensive wine list in town.

Six miles (9.7 km) outside of town is the **Bar N Ranch** (970 Buttermilk Creek Rd., 406/646-9445, www.bar-n-ranch.com, 7am-10am and 5pm-10pm daily mid-May-mid-Oct., $15-45), a wonderful place for a meal. With beautiful views all around, you can indulge in terrific Western gourmet cuisine including game burgers, bison stir-fry, steaks, and pasta. One favorite is the campfire tacos with pulled pork, jalapeño slaw, and barbecue aioli. Gourmet picnic lunches are available too.

Accommodations

Inside the Park

Reservations for all hotels inside the park should be made through **Xanterra/Yellowstone National Park Lodges** (307/344-7311, www.yellowstonenationalparklodges.com). Nature is the draw here: There are no televisions, radios, or air-conditioning. Internet access can be purchased in the public areas of some hotels in the park.

The Northern Loop

There are three accommodations in the northern loop. The largest is the **Mammoth Hot Springs Hotel and Cabins** (late Apr.-early Oct. and mid-Dec.-early Mar., $109-213 rustic 1- to 2-bedroom cabin without bath, $183 frontier cabin, $177 standard room, $305 hot tub cabin, $587 suite), which has 79 guest rooms and another 116 cabins, four with hot tubs. Mammoth is undergoing a renovation; its cabins are expected to be completed in summer 2019. After the renovation, all 79 rooms will have a private bathroom. Set amid historic Fort Yellowstone, Mammoth provides convenient access to restaurants, gift shops, a gas station, and the visitors center, so guests may forget they're somewhat out in the wild. Despite human and car traffic in Mammoth, wolves have been known to sneak onto the green watered lawns at night to take down an unsuspecting well-grazed elk. You can imagine the surprise when early risers spot a carcass on their way to get a breakfast burrito.

Named for Yellowstone champion Theodore Roosevelt, the ★ **Roosevelt Lodge Cabins** (early June-early Sept.) offer a timeless rustic setting reminiscent of a great old dude ranch in a quiet corner of the park. The Roughrider Cabins (from $102) usually offer double beds and a wood-burning stove. What they lack in amenities they make up for with charming authenticity. Toilets and communal showers are available nearby. The Frontier Cabins (from $170) are slightly larger and include a private bathroom with a shower, toilet, and sink.

Set adjacent to the spectacular Grand Canyon of the Yellowstone, **Canyon Lodge & Cabins** (early June-late Sept.) is the largest single lodging property in the park. The facilities were built in the 1950s and 1960s; they were expanded and renovated significantly in 2016 to bring the total to 590 rooms and cabins. In the lodges, there are standard rooms ($210), premium rooms ($340), superior rooms ($360), superior lodge rooms with patios ($370), and two-bedroom suites ($700). The modest Western Cabins ($204) are basic motel-style units with private full bathrooms.

The Southern Loop

★ **Lake Yellowstone Hotel** (mid-May-early Oct., rooms $515-590, suites $820-980) is both grand and picturesque, perched on the shores of Yellowstone Lake. Originally built in 1891 and completely renovated in 2014 to celebrate its colonial revival influences, the hotel houses the nicest rooms in the park. As is true everywhere in the park, though, the appeal comes from the location and the views. If you are staying in the hotel, request a room with a view of the lake. There is an adjacent building, **The Sandpiper Lodge** ($320), that also offers recently renovated rooms. Individual cabins, called Lake Cottages, are behind the hotel but are part of the Lake Lodge operation. These duplexes were remodeled in 2004 and are simple and modest.

The **Lake Lodge Cabins** (mid-June-late Sept., $246 Western cabin, $158 Frontier cabin, $209 lake cottages) are clean and simple and many underwent renovation in 2016. Located just off the lake, the cabins are clustered around the main lodge, which is an inviting common area for guests to gather. It has a large porch that beckons guests to take a seat in one of the rocking chairs and soak in the view,

as well as two fireplaces, a gift shop, and a cozy lounge. The Western cabins are a bit more spacious, with two beds and a shower-tub in each bathroom. The Pioneer cabins are older and more spartan, with shower-only bathrooms and 1-2 double beds. The Frontier cabins are slated for renovation and will be unavailable in 2019. The setting is tranquil and quiet, and early risers may spot a herd of bison wandering through the property.

The ★ **Old Faithful Inn** (early May-early Oct., $320 standard rooms, $350-370 premium rooms, $390 superior rooms near geyser, $260-400 Old House rooms with bath, $160-320 Old House rooms with shared bath) is the most popular lodging inside the park, and for good reason. The original part of the lodge, known as the Old House, was built in 1904 by acclaimed architect Robert Reamer. Situated close to the Old Faithful geyser, the lodge epitomizes rustic beauty, originality, and strength. It has a large front lobby that houses a massive stone fireplace. The larger rooms are in the wings of the inn, built in the 1910s and 1920s, while the more modest rooms are in the Old House. The inn has a wide assortment of guest rooms and rates, ranging from two-room suites with sitting rooms and fridges to simple rooms without individual baths. This is the most sought-after lodging in the park; make reservations well in advance.

Close to the inn are the **Old Faithful Lodge Cabins** (mid-May-late Sept., $96-159), offering much simpler and rustic lodging. If you are looking for budget-friendly accommodations that put you in the center of park activity, these are a good option. The cabins are small motel-style units that vary in condition. Many of them were renovated in 2016. The lower-priced cabins do not come with baths, but there are communal showers nearby. The cabins are scattered around a main log cabin-style lodge. Built in the 1920s, the main lodge has a large cafeteria, bakery, and fully stocked gift shop, making it popular with park visitors throughout the day.

The **Old Faithful Snow Lodge and Cabins** (late Apr.-mid Oct. and mid-Dec.-late Feb., in summer $301-323 premium lodge rooms, $202 Western cabin, $129 Frontier cabin; and in winter $336-358 premium lodge rooms, $219 Western cabin, $167 Frontier cabin) are among the newest accommodations in the park. The original lodge was torn down and a new structure was built in 1999. Its architecture is intended to complement, though not duplicate, the Old Faithful Inn, and the lodge won a Cody Award for Western Design. It offers comfortable, modern rooms decorated with Western flair. It also has a few motel-style cabins, built in 1989. The Western cabins are a good value for the money; they're large rooms with two queen beds and a full bath. This is one of only two lodges (the other is Mammoth Hot Springs Hotel) open during the winter season in Yellowstone.

Grant Village is about 20 miles (32 km) southeast of Old Faithful on the West Thumb of Yellowstone Lake. Although the accommodations do not have the same rustic feel or character of the other lodges, they do offer a comfortable and modern place to stay away from the crowds. The complex is made up of six small condo-like buildings. Each building has 50 nicely furnished hotel rooms ($270) that come with either two double beds or one queen and full baths. The rooms and exteriors were renovated in 2016.

Outside the Park
Gardiner

Gardiner is built to accommodate the overflow from the park, but in reality, many of the little motels have more charm and much better value, particularly in non-summer months, than those inside the park. For the most part, it's hard to go wrong in Gardiner. There are plenty of small cabins and larger vacation rentals in the area. The folk Victorian ★ **Gardiner Guest House** (112 Main St. E., 406/848-9414, $95-165 summer, $75-115 winter) welcomes both children and pets and offers three modest but comfortable guest rooms and a cabin. Owners Richard and Nance Parks are longtime residents and an extensive source of information on the area. His fly shop and guiding company, **Parks' Fly Shop** (202 2nd St. S., 406/848-7314, www.parksflyshop.com), is one of the oldest businesses in town. **Yellowstone Park Riverfront Cabins** (505 S. Yellowstone, 406/570-4500, www.cabinsontheyellowstone.com, $350/night) offers comfortable cabins in a quiet location above the river. Another option for small, basic, and reasonably priced cottages right in town is **Hillcrest Cottages** (400 Scott St., 406/848-7353 or 800/970-7353, www.hillcrestcottages.com, early May-mid-Oct., $95-187). The cottages come in various sizes that can sleep 1-5 people. The **Flying Pig Adventure Company** (511 Scott St. W., 866/264-8448, www.flyingpigrafting.com) offers a host of higher-end vacation rentals ranging from cozy canvas wall tents on a nearby ranch ($200) to cabins ($175-300) to an enormous private lodge ($599) that can sleep up to 15. Minimum nights apply.

For more standard hotels, there is a decent selection ranging from the riverfront **Absaroka Lodge** (310 Scott St., 406/848-7414, www.yellowstonemotel.com, $85-190), where each room has its own balcony, and the **Comfort Inn** (107 Hellroaring St., 406/848-7536 or 800/424-6423, www.comfortinn.com, $162-325) to the bare-bones but clean and pet-friendly **Super 8** (702 Scott St. W., 406/848-7401, www.wyndhamhotels.com, $71-221).

Cooke City

For a town with a population that is only barely in the double digits, Cooke City has an impressive number of places to hang your hat. Lodging runs the gamut from cabins and vacation rentals to roadside motels, chain hotels, and small resorts, although not all of them are open year-round. Most of the photo galleries on the accommodations' websites are images of moose and bears or snowmobiles buried in powder rather than pictures of beds and baths.

Big Moose Resort (715 U.S. 212, 406/838-2393, www.bigmooseresort.com, $95-150) is 3 miles (4.8 km) east of town and a great place to set up a base camp if you want to explore the region's trails and rivers. Open year-round, the lodge has a collection of seven old and new cabins, all of which are quite comfortable and can accommodate up to four people. There are no phones in the cabins (and no cell service in the area), but free Wi-Fi is provided, and you can schedule a Swedish massage on-site.

The **Cooke City Super 8** (303 E. Main St., 406/838-2070, $125-174) is owned by Bearclaw Bob, who also owns the Bearclaw Bakery and Bearclaw Sales and Service. The rooms are basic and clean, and the service is exceptionally friendly.

In the heart of bustling Cooke City is the **Soda Butte Lodge** (210 E. Main St., 406/838-2251, www.cookecity.com, $110-180), a full-service hotel with 32 guest rooms, a saloon, and a restaurant. The guest rooms are basic, but you didn't come to Cooke City to hang out in your hotel room.

In nearby Silver Gate, ★ **Silver Gate Lodging** (109 U.S. 212, 406/838-2371, www.pineedgecabins.com, $120-300) offers 29 great cabins, plus motel rooms and a big lodge that can accommodate any size group and welcomes pets. The setting is both quiet and communal, with barbecue grills, horseshoe pits, and a playground. And because this is Yellowstone, you can also rent scopes, which will come in plenty handy.

West Yellowstone

In the summer months there are more than 2,000 hotel rooms to be found in West and about 1,300 when the snow covers the ground. Guest ranches, bed-and-breakfasts, and cabin rentals are also available. **Yellowstone Tour & Travel** (800/221-1151, www.yellowstone-travel.com) is a full-service travel agency in West Yellowstone that can book everything from accommodations and tours to complete packages. The **West Yellowstone Chamber of Commerce** (406/646-7701, www.destinationyellowstone.com) also has an excellent website that shows all lodging availability.

Just seven blocks from the west entrance to Yellowstone National Park, the pet-friendly **Pine Shadows Motel & Condos** (229 Hayden St., 406/646-7541 or 800/624-5291, www.pineshadowsmotel.com, $79-250) is open year-round and has a selection of motel rooms and newly built, spacious condos, all of which are clean and comfortable. As is true in much of the town, free Wi-Fi is available. Also open year-round, the **Three Bear Lodge** (217 Yellowstone Ave., 406/646-7353 or 800/646-7353, www.threebearlodge.com, $79-264) offers 44 guest rooms in its recently remodeled pet-friendly motel unit and 26 in the lodge, where no two rooms are alike. All guest rooms have a refrigerator, a microwave, an LCD TV, handmade furniture, and fluffy duvets.

The **Alpine Motel** (120 Madison Ave., 406/646-7544, www.alpinemotel westyellowstone.com, $79-189) is a budget-friendly choice with a variety of units, some including kitchens, just two blocks from the park entrance. The service by owners Brian and Patty is noticeably good. Another good independent property, which is only open mid-May-mid-October, is **Al's Westward Ho Motel** (16 Boundary St., 888/646-7331, www.alswestwardhomotel.net, $129-179), which is just across the street from the park entrance and the Yellowstone Giant Screen Theatre. A couple of blocks farther from the entrance, but a long-standing and reliable choice in town, is the 79-room, pet-friendly **Brandin' Iron Inn** (201

Grizzly and Wolf Discovery Center

If you have your heart set on seeing a grizzly or a wolf in Yellowstone, here's my advice: Get it out of the way before you even go into the park. Seeing a big predator before you enter the park takes the pressure off. The **Grizzly and Wolf Discovery Center** (201 S. Canyon St., 406/646-7001 or 800/257-2570, www.grizzlydiscoveryctr.org, 8:30am-8:30pm daily mid-May-early Sept., 8:30am-7pm daily early Sept.-late Sept. and late Apr.-mid-May, 8:30am-6pm daily late Sept.-late Oct., 8:30am-4pm daily Nov.-late Apr., $13 ages 13 and over, $12.25 seniors 62 and over, $8 children 5-12, free for children under 5, admission valid for two consecutive days) is a nonprofit organization that acts something like an orphanage, giving homes to problem, injured, or abandoned animals that have nowhere else to go.

Although there is something melancholy about watching these incredible beasts confined to any sort of enclosure, particularly on the perimeter of a chunk of wilderness as massive as Yellowstone, there is also something remarkable about seeing them close enough to count their whiskers. Watching a wolf pack interact from a comfy bench behind floor-to-ceiling windows in the warming hut is a worthwhile way to spend an afternoon.

The naturalists on staff are excellent at engaging with visitors of all ages and have plenty to teach everyone. One fantastic opportunity for curious children ages 5-12 is the **Keeper Kids program** ($5), which is offered twice daily during the summer season. For roughly 45 minutes, the kids learn about grizzly eating habits and behavior. They get to then go into the grizzly enclosure while the bears are locked away (obviously) and hide buckets of food for the bears. When the kids exit and the bears come racing out to search for their treats—overturning massive logs and boulders in the process—the kids (and their parents!) are mesmerized. The **Keeper Crew** (free with admission), for kids 13-17, helps the keepers prepare the bears' enrichment for the Keeper Kids program. Space is limited, so enroll at the admissions counter when you arrive (no later than 15 minutes before the program).

The center has gone to great lengths to share the personal story of each animal and why it cannot survive in the wild. They also give the bears all sorts of games and tasks—aiding in the design of bear-proof garbage cans is one example. Because these bears do not hibernate, this is a stop absolutely worth making any time of the year. Ultimately, this is a really nice place to learn a lot about bears, wolves, and raptors before heading into the park to look for them in the wild.

Canyon, 406/646-9411 or 800/217-4613, www.brandiniron.com, $69-299).

There are a number of larger chain hotels in town, including three Best Western options, the nicest of which is probably the **Best Western Weston Inn** (103 Gibbon Ave., 406/646-7373, www.bestwestern.com, $223-369). Other options include **Holiday Inn West Yellowstone** (315 Yellowstone Ave., 406/646-7365 or 800/315-2621, www.ihg.com, $141-468), **Days Inn West Yellowstone** (301 Madison, 406/646-7656, www.daysinn.com, $113-332), **Yellowstone Kelly Inn** (104 S. Canyon, 406/646-4544, www.yellowstonekellyinn.com, $90-350), and, 7.5 miles (12.1 km) from town, **West Yellowstone Super 8** (1545 Targhee Pass, 406/646-9584, www.wyndhamhotels.com, $187-269).

Camping

Inside the Park
The Northern Loop

The only campground in the park's northern loop that can be reserved in advance is the 270-site **Canyon** (307/344-7901 for same-day reservations, 307/344-7311 for advance reservations, late May-early Sept., $30 nightly rate includes two showers/night), which has 15 public restrooms with flush toilets, faucets with cold running water, and pay showers. The other six sites operated by Xanterra, the park's concessionaire—at **Mammoth, Tower Fall, Slough Creek, Pebble Creek, Indian Creek,** and **Norris**—are available on a first-come, first-served basis and cost $15-20. These sites fill up quickly; your best bet is to arrive before 11am. Mammoth is the only campground open all year; all the campgrounds have some RV sites. A great feature on the Yellowstone website (www.nps.gov/yell) shows current availability and what time any given site closed the day before.

In addition to the campgrounds, more than 300 **backcountry campsites** are scattered throughout the park. Overnight permits, which are available at all ranger stations and visitors centers, are only issued in person up to 48 hours in advance; they are required for all the sites. Backcountry campsites can be reserved January 1-October 31 by paying a $25 reservation fee. All requests to reserve sites must be made in person, by fax, or via mail. Pertinent forms and information for backcountry camping in Yellowstone are available online at the National Park Service Backcountry Trip Planner (www.nps.gov/yell).

The Southern Loop

Five of the 12 campsites in the park are in the southern region: **Bridge Bay** (between West Thumb and Lake, late May-early Sept., flush toilets, $25.25); **Fishing Bridge RV Park** (at Fishing Bridge north of Lake Village, early May-late Sept., flush toilets and pay showers, $47.75), the only campground offering water and sewer, for hard-sided vehicles only; **Grant Village** (at Grant Village south of West Thumb, late June-mid-Sept., flush toilets, $30); **Lewis Lake** (at Lewis Lake south of Grant Village, early-June-early Nov., vault toilets, $15); and **Madison** (at Madison Junction between the west entrance and Old Faithful, late Apr.-mid-Oct., flush toilets, $25.25). Advance reservations (307/344-7311 or 866/439-7375) or same-day reservations (307/344-7901) can be made at Bridge Bay, Fishing Bridge RV Park, Grant Village, and Madison.

Outside the Park
Gardiner

The difference between camping outside the park and inside Yellowstone is simply that you need to focus on reservations and availability instead of permits and regulations. There are six campgrounds in Gardiner—four national forest campgrounds and two private ones. The **Yellowstone RV Park & Campground** (121 U.S. 89 S., 406/848-7496, May-Oct., 46 sites including pull-through and tent sites) is ideally situated on the Yellowstone River just 1.3 miles (2.1 km) north of the park entrance.

Those in search of a more rustic experience might enjoy the pack-in, pack-out **Bear Creek Campground** (Forest Rd. 493, 10.5 mi/16.9 km northeast of Gardiner, 406/848-7375, 4 sites with no services, mid-June-late Oct. depending on weather, free) or the **Timber Camp Campground** (Forest Rd. 493, 9.5 mi/15.3 km northeast of Gardiner, 406/848-7375, no services, mid-June-late Oct. depending on weather, free), both of which are small, isolated, and pleasantly rustic.

Cooke City

Three Forest Service campgrounds are in the vicinity of Cooke City. **Soda Butte** (406/848-7375, www.fs.usda.gov,

July-Sept. depending on weather, $9/ vehicle) is 1 mile (1.6 km) east of Cooke City on U.S. 212. It has 27 sites, restrooms, and drinking water, and fishing is available nearby. Please note that due to bear activity, this is a hard-sided campground only, and advance reservations are not accepted. Also strictly a hard-sided campground, **Colter Campground** (406/848-7375, www.fs.usda.gov, July 15-Sept. 7 depending on weather, $8/vehicle) is just 2 miles (3.2 km) east of Cooke City and gives campers access to 18 sites, restrooms, drinking water, and nearby fishing and hiking trails. Reservations are not accepted, so arrive early and have a backup plan in place.

West Yellowstone

With nearly two dozen private and public campgrounds in the vicinity of West, campers have plenty of choices, although most are geared to RV campers. The nearest U.S. Forest Service campground is **Baker's Hole Campground** (U.S. 191, 3 mi/4.8 km northwest of West Yellowstone, 406/823-6961, www.hebgenbasincampgrounds.com, May 15-Sept. 30 depending on weather, $16 for 1 vehicle, $7 for each additional vehicle, plus $6 for electrical sites), with 73 sites (33 with electricity) set on a scenic oxbow of the Madison River. Basic services such as water and trash pickup are provided, there is firewood for sale ($6), and the fishing is excellent.

Right in town, just six blocks from the park's west entrance, is **Wagon Wheel RV Campground & Cabins** (408 Gibbon Ave., 406/646-7872, www.yellowstonervcabin.com, camping May 15-Sept. 30, cabins May 1-Oct. 31, $46-85 full-hookup pull-through sites), offering a forested and quiet setting for RV camping only. The nine cabins ($189-399), reminiscent of the 1930s and '40s architecture found throughout the park, are small but charming. Note that they get booked up quickly and can require three-night stays. At peak season here, there isn't

much elbow room. Free Wi-Fi is available in some public areas.

For a unique experience outside of town, ★ **Yellowstone Under Canvas** (890 Buttermilk Creek Rd., 406/219-0441, www.mtundercanvas.com, Memorial Day-Labor Day) offers "glamping" (glamour-camping) options ($219-634) ranging from modest tipis and safari tents to luxury safari suite tents with king-size beds, private baths with freestanding tubs, and woodstoves. A variety of options are available, from shared bathrooms (the hot-water showers are provided by a generator that runs from 6am to 11pm and is not quiet) to private but separate baths, influencing the price. But all of these tents and tipis are set in a mountain-ringed meadow with a creek running through. And the bedding is nothing short of luxurious. The guests here are largely international, and it can be a treat to listen to campfire or next-tent pillow talk in several different languages. The only downside is that snoring is universally annoying, and with all but the most expensive tents situated so close together, light sleepers are bound to hear plenty of snorers. Still, this is comfortable camping without the work.

Red Lodge

At the edge of the massive Beartooth Plateau, Red Lodge (population 2,237; elevation 5,568 ft/1,697 m) is a mountain town with the Great Plains spread out at its feet. There are a couple of great resorts and some world-class skiing just beyond town, but downtown Red Lodge is a worthwhile destination on its own. Cute shops and wonderful restaurants line Broadway, and the spectacle of nature—the rush of Rock Creek and the drama of the Beartooths—is evident from every part of the street. Even if it's not exactly on the way from Yellowstone to Glacier, the town's Western hospitality combined with its zeal for a good time make Red Lodge a wonderful getaway or a fun launching point to the wildness of the Beartooth Plateau and Yellowstone National Park.

Getting to Red Lodge

From **Cooke City,** Red Lodge is 114 miles (184 km) east on U.S. 212, which takes a minimum of 2.5 hours to drive.

The two major airports closest to Red Lodge are **Billings Logan International Airport** (BIL, 406/657-8495, www. flybillings.com) and **Bozeman Yellowstone International Airport** (BZN, 406/388-8321, www.bozemanairport. com). One of the best options for getting to Red Lodge is by car; both airports have a selection of car-rental companies.

From the Billings airport, **Phidippides Shuttle Service** (307/527-6789, www. codyshuttle.com) transports visitors to Red Lodge.

Sights
Beartooth Scenic Highway and Pass

Considered one of the most beautiful roadways in the country, the **Beartooth Scenic Highway** begins in Red Lodge, climbs and twists its way through 60-million-year-old mountains, and ends 65 miles (105 km) later in Cooke City at the northeast entrance to Yellowstone National Park. The scenic road has numerous switchbacks and steep grades that, once you're driving on it, clearly demonstrate why it is closed during winter. As you ascend, you come upon magnificent vistas of the Beartooth Plateau, Glacier Lake, and the canyons forged by the Clarks Fork River. After about 30 miles (48 km), you reach the mountain summit at 10,947 feet (3,337 m). Here you will encounter the aptly named **Top of the World** rest area, which provides the only services on the route. Keep an eye out for a herd of mountain goats that frequents the area.

If you plan to drive this byway, keep in mind that it is not about getting from A to B—the drive itself is the destination,

and it should be undertaken with plenty of time; it can last up to three hours without stops. You will encounter an array of wildlife, including black bears, bighorn sheep, and mountain goats, as well as a broad display of vibrant wildflowers, depending on the season and moisture levels. Take time to pull over and enjoy the vistas or explore the hiking trails and accessible lakes. With snow falling almost year-round, skiing is popular in the area June to July. Because of the extreme conditions of the mountains, the highway is only open May-October, weather permitting. Contact the **Montana Department of Transportation** (406/444-6200) or the **Red Lodge Visitors Center** (406/446-1718) for opening and closing dates.

Beartooth Plateau

High atop massive mountains is the vast and rugged grandeur of the Beartooth Plateau. It's a nature lover's paradise, with spectacular scenery, unrivaled vistas, abundant wildlife, and a tangle of trails and lakes to get out and enjoy. The Beartooth Scenic Highway makes this remarkable place a Sunday drive destination. But if you have the time, this is a wonderland that begs to be discovered. Take a hike, wet a line—heck, throw on your skis in midsummer; just get out and enjoy this magnificent place.

The plateau is crisscrossed with **trails,** and as long as you are amply prepared, you can't choose a bad one. The **Clay Butte Fire Lookout Tower** is only 1 mile (1.6 km) from the highway and can be accessed by a trail that takes hikers up and above 11,000 feet (3,353 m). The views are incredible, and an interpretive display gives great perspective on the 1988 Yellowstone fires and how they impacted the entire region. **Crazy Creek Falls** is another nice short hike at 1.3 miles (2.1 km) out and back, and the **Clarks Fork Trailhead,** just 3 miles (4.8 km) from Cooke City, offers an abundance of longer trails. Near the summit, an 8-mile (12.9-km) loop around **Beartooth Lake**

Red Lodge

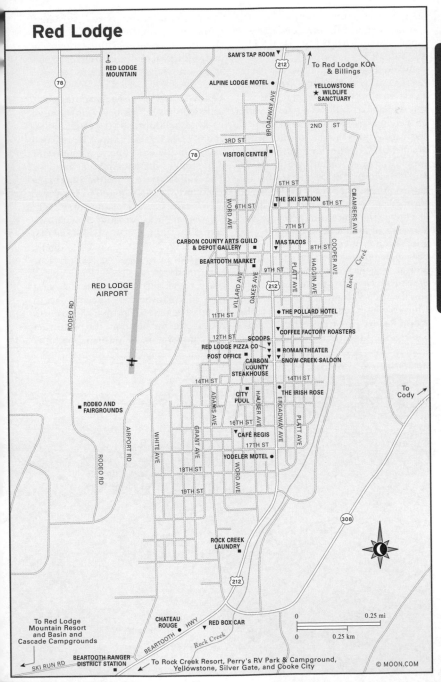

SAM'S TAP ROOM ▼

212

To Red Lodge KOA & Billings

RED LODGE MOUNTAIN

ALPINE LODGE MOTEL ◆

78

YELLOWSTONE
★ WILDLIFE
SANCTUARY

2ND ST

3RD ST

78

VISITOR CENTER ■

BROADWAY AVE

5TH ST

THE SKI STATION ■

CHAMBERS AVE

6TH ST

6TH ST

WORD AVE

7TH ST

CARBON COUNTY ARTS GUILD
& DEPOT GALLERY ■

MAS TACOS ▼

8TH ST

COOPER AVE

HAGGIN AVE

BEARTOOTH MARKET ■

9TH ST

Rock Creek

RED LODGE
AIRPORT

VILLARD AVE

OAKES AVE

PLATT AVE

212

RODEO RD

THE POLLARD HOTEL ●

11TH ST

COFFEE FACTORY ROASTERS ▼

12TH ST

SCOOPS ▼

RED LODGE PIZZA CO ▼

ROMAN THEATER ■

POST OFFICE ■

SNOW CREEK SALOON ▼

CARBON
COUNTY
STEAKHOUSE

14TH ST

ADAMS AVE

CITY
POOL

HAUSER AVE

14TH ST

THE IRISH ROSE ●

AIRPORT RD

RODEO AND
FAIRGROUNDS ■

WHITE AVE

GRANT AVE

16TH ST

BROADWAY AVE

PLATT AVE

To
Cody

CAFÉ REGIS ▼

17TH ST

RODEO RD

YODELER MOTEL ●

18TH ST

WORD AVE

19TH ST

308

ROCK CREEK
LAUNDRY ■

212

To Red Lodge
Mountain Resort
and Basin and
Cascade Campgrounds

CHATEAU
ROUGE ▼

RED BOX CAR ▼

BEARTOOTH HWY

Rock Creek

0   0.25 mi

0   0.25 km

SKI RUN RD

BEARTOOTH RANGER
DISTRICT STATION ■

To Rock Creek Resort, Perry's RV Park & Campground,
Yellowstone, Silver Gate, and Cooke City

© MOON.COM

offers easy terrain and lovely scenery. For trail maps, stop by the **U.S. Forest Service ranger station** (6811 U.S. 212, Red Lodge, 406/446-2103).

Biking the Beartooth Plateau is not for the faint of heart. Never mind the insane elevation climbs and descents, the vast grizzly habitat, and the possibility of a blizzard on virtually any day of the year; the real danger is the automobiles, which are plentiful, often wide, and driven by people who can't help but ogle the mountain vistas instead of the bike traffic. You can eliminate that danger by getting off the road and onto a network of trails.

Though the Beartooth Highway starts and ends in Montana, most of the road goes through Wyoming, including the plateau. In order to **fish** any of the mountain lakes on the Beartooth Plateau, many of which have been stocked with trout, you'll need a Wyoming fishing license, which can be purchased at the **Top of the World Resort** (2823 U.S. 212, 307/587-5368, www.topoftheworldresort.com)

or in Red Lodge or Cooke City. Rental gear ($10/day spincasting setup, $20/day fly rod and reel setup, $10/hour and $40/day paddleboat or canoe) is also available at the Top of the World Resort.

Yellowstone Wildlife Sanctuary

This wildlife refuge is the only one of its kind in Montana. It houses indigenous animals that cannot be released back into the wild due to an injury or unfortunate dependency on humans. The **Yellowstone Wildlife Sanctuary** (615 2nd St. E., 406/446-1133, www.yellowstonewildlifesanctuary.com, 10am-4pm Tues.-Sun. May-Sept., 10am-2pm Tues.-Sun. Oct.-Apr., $30 adults, $15 children 3-12, free seniors, military, and children under 3) cares for some 60 animals that include wolves, black bears, bison, elk, bald eagles, mountain lions, and many more. The center says in its mission that its "primary focus is to educate the public about the protection and conservation of Montana's wildlife

Highway 212, also known as the Beartooth Scenic Highway

and its habitats" by allowing visitors an up-close look at some of the state's most beautiful species. The center's location also affords some spectacular views of the Beartooth Mountains.

Entertainment and Events

Since 1950, the **Festival of Nations** has been a Red Lodge tradition celebrating the wide diversity of ethnic groups that first came to the town during the late-1800s mining boom. The cultural groups honored include both southern and northern Europeans—German, Irish, Finnish, Italian, Norwegian, Scottish, Greek—and a variety of others. The festival takes place in late July or August over 2.5 days, with cultural exhibits, dancing, ethnic food, music, children's activities, and a wide assortment of daytime and nighttime entertainment. People who wear ethnic costumes get admitted free. Contact the **Red Lodge Visitors Center** (406/446-1718) for this year's dates and location.

The **Winter Carnival** (305 Ski Run Rd., 406/446-2610 or 800/444-8977, dates vary each year) takes place at the Red Lodge Mountain Resort and has become a favorite event among locals and visitors alike. Although the carnival selects a different theme each year (in 2019 the theme was "World of Wizardry" in celebration of characters like Merlin, Gandalf, Dumbledore, and Oz), many tried-and-true events make an annual appearance. The Cardboard Classic race tests the skills of its participants as they guide their original crafts—made only from cardboard, duct tape, and glue—in a competitive downhill race. Other popular activities include a scavenger hunt, a snow sculpture contest, a parade of costumes, a jalapeño-eating contest, and a dazzling fireworks show. You may even be crowned King or Queen of Red Lodge Mountain if you can telemark, alpine race, and snowboard yourself to victory.

The **Home of Champions Rodeo and Parade** (406/446-1718, www.redlodgerodeo.com, July 2-4, $15-30, $30 admits 4 on Family Day July 2) takes place each year at the fairgrounds west of Red Lodge just off Highway 78, and the parades run daily in downtown Red Lodge. Rodeo competition in the area dates back to the 1890s, when cowboys used to get together on Sundays to ride broncos at the local stockyards. Formed in 1930, the Red Lodge Rodeo Association has been hosting this annual celebration ever since. The name, Home of Champions, was coined in 1954 after a local cowboy, Bill Linderman, won his third title as World All Around Champion. A different theme is selected for the event every year, and a parade takes place at noon each day; participation is open and there are categories for all age groups. The rodeo is part of the Professional Rodeo Cowboys Association circuit, so you will see many of the nation's top champions compete in a number of different events, including bareback, bull riding, calf roping, and barrel racing.

SODA BUTTE CREEK

Lovers of classical music and fine art are in for a wildly unexpected treat at **Tippet Rise Art Center** (96 S. Grove Creek Rd., Fishtail, www.tippetrise.org, June-Sept.), which brings together nature, art, and music in magnificent ways. Set on an 11,500-acre working ranch, in the shadow of the Beartooths, Tippet Rise brings world-class musicians to the area for intimate performances throughout summer at a variety of indoor and outdoor venues, all of them small and visually spectacular. Tickets for concerts and films are limited to just 100 seats at most—they are available online only for as little as $10, and free for ages 21 and younger—but sell out months in advance. Tickets to the art center are available for free, online, but also in very limited quantities.

Shopping

Shopping in Red Lodge is a leisurely stroll through the historic downtown district. Broadway has still managed to retain the charm and vibrancy of the coal-mining days with a diverse assortment of stores. **Sylvan Peak Mountain Shop** (9 N. Broadway Ave., 406/446-1770, 9am-6pm daily) is a perfect starting point for anyone in need of adventure-related gear. The store carries its own line of clothing as well as familiar brands such as Marmot, Mountain Hardwear, and Osprey. An outlet store on the main floor and the Mountain Shoppe downstairs not only sell equipment but also rent cross-country skis, telemark skis, and snow-shoes. From climbing gear to boating gear, fleeces to bear spray, you will find it—plus the best insider's advice anywhere and a true commitment to protecting the great outdoors—at Sylvan Peak.

Right next door, you'll find the irresistible **Montana Candy Emporium** (7 N. Broadway Ave., 406/446-1119, 9am-9pm daily Memorial Day-Labor Day, 9am-7pm Sun.-Thurs., 9am-9pm Fri.-Sat. Labor Day-Memorial Day). The mouth-watering window displays will draw you in to this world of sweets. It is said to

be the largest candy store in Montana, which is easy to believe while meandering through its selection of more than 800 sugary treats. Located in the former Park Theater, decorated with nostalgic memorabilia, and selling old-fashioned candies, this store will take you back to a simpler time.

Since 1990, **Kibler and Kirch** (101 N. Broadway Ave., 406/446-2226, www.kiblerandkirch.com, 9am-5pm Mon.-Sat.) has been a pillar of the downtown shopping scene in Red Lodge. A home-furnishings store with a nice selection of Western artwork and accessories, the offerings include pottery, glassware, and handcrafted leather. Because many of its products are made in Montana, you may find the perfect gift to take home.

Sports and Recreation
Skiing

Situated in a glacial valley surrounded by the Beartooth Mountains, Red Lodge offers superb downhill and cross-country skiing. **Red Lodge Mountain** (305 Ski Run Rd., 406/446-2610 or 800/444-8977, www.redlodgemountain.com) is just 6 miles (9.7 km) from downtown Red Lodge and boasts slopes free of crowds and with reasonable lift ticket prices ($67-77 adults 19-64, $52-60 seniors 65-69, $22-26 seniors 70 and over, $52-57 juniors 13-18, $28-32 children 6-12, free for children 5 and under) as well as ski runs for beginners to experts. The mountain offers a higher base elevation (7,433 feet/2,266 m) than any other ski hill in the state, a spine-chilling 2,400-foot (731.5-m) vertical drop, 69 runs, and six chairlifts to keep you up to your elbows in the white stuff all day. The diverse terrain is groomed regularly, and the runs' features are frequently upgraded or even changed. Red Lodge offers a full-service lodge, with ski lessons, ski rentals, child care, a restaurant, two bars, and two cafeterias, all on the hill. The resort also has two cross-country trails that offer about 11 miles (17.7 km) of skiing. On top of the outstanding terrain and the jaw-dropping views, one of the things that makes this hill so special is the small-town friendliness of just about everyone here, from the lift ops to the people sharing a chair with you. This feels like what skiing in Montana should be.

Probably the best-known place for cross-country skiing in Red Lodge is the **Red Lodge Nordic Center** (406/446-1771, www.beartoothtrails.org, 8:30am-4:30pm daily in season, $5/day payable at the trailhead), 2 miles (3.2 km) west of downtown off Highway 78. The center is operated by the nonprofit Beartooth Recreational Trails Association (which also maintains several excellent trails for hiking when snow isn't covering the ground) and offers more than 9.3 miles (15 km) of groomed classic and skate trails rated from easy to most difficult. Rentals and lessons can be arranged prior to your arrival via online booking. Other than a porta potty, there are no services at the Nordic Center, so plan ahead.

Golf
To hit the links, head to the 18-hole course at **Red Lodge Resort and Golf Club** (828 Upper Continental Dr., southwest of Red Lodge, 406/446-3344, www.redlodgemountain.com, $39 for 18 holes walking Mon.-Thurs., $50 for 18 holes walking Fri.-Sun., discounts for booking 48 hours in advance, juniors 18 and under, and twilight play after 4pm). On top of the jaw-dropping scenery around this challenging course, your ball will travel farther because of the altitude.

Food
The fanciest place in town these days is the dining room at **The Pollard Hotel** (2 N. Broadway Ave., 406/446-0001, www.thepollard.com, 7am-10am and 5pm-9pm daily, $17-36). Though it offers a nightly vegetarian special, most of the fare is classic Montana meat and potatoes. Think porcini-rubbed beef tenderloin, bison brisket, and beef rib eye. The

Pub at the Pollard (5pm-9pm daily, $7-15) is a much more casual place for a bite. The atmosphere is great, especially when the place hosts live music.

The farm-to-table restaurant **Ox Pasture** (7 Broadway N., 406/446-1212, www.oxpasture.com, 11:30am-10pm Tues.-Sun., $14-32) opened in 2016 to great reviews. The small menu changes frequently to make the most of seasonal produce. From Sicilian specialties like arancini, fritto misto, and eggplant parmesan to grilled sea bass and a variety of handmade pastas, this foodie heaven puts together phenomenal flavors. Another casual restaurant with fresh, inventive food is **Prerogative Kitchen** (104 S. Broadway, 406/445-3232, www.prerogativekitchen.com, 11:30am-8:30pm Fri.-Tues., $5-20), where the menu can change daily and is written on a chalkboard. One of the things that sets this restaurant apart is that it donates a portion of its profits to local nonprofit organizations. Comprising mostly small plates, the menu includes such delights as crispy brussels sprouts, fried mac and cheese, lamb sliders, and the requisite salads, steaks, and fish.

For a casual, inexpensive, old-fashioned drive-in—or better yet, walk-up—experience, head to the **Red Box Car** (1300 S. Broadway Ave., 406/446-2152, 11am-8pm daily early Apr.-Sept., $3.60-13.50). Based in an actual 1906 boxcar from the Rocky Fork Railway, this stand serves some of the best shakes, malts, chili, and burgers you could imagine. Sit outside and enjoy your meal as you take in views of nearby Rock Creek. The Red Box Car may close at any time due to weather, so call ahead or check its Facebook page before visiting.

Set in a cool old Conoco gas station, **Más Taco** (304 N. Broadway Ave., 406/446-3636, 11am-7pm Tues.-Sat., $3-9) is the place for authentic Mexican cuisine in Red Lodge. It has lots of vegetarian options and makes everything from scratch, including the corn tortillas and sour cream. The wet burritos are legendary, and the restaurant is also known for its five versions of *al pastor,* pork roasted with pineapple and paper-thin slices of onion. Sit outside in the summer to enjoy the view, or plant yourself at the counter and watch them cook!

Attached to the Regis Grocery and known for outstanding breakfasts and organic, whole foods, ★ **Café Regis** (501 Word Ave. S., 406/446-1941, www.caferegis.com, 7am-2pm Wed.-Sun., $5-12) is an excellent spot for a hearty, healthy, and very reasonably priced meal. The service is quick and friendly, and every delicious item on the menu—from omelets and breakfast burritos to soup, sandwiches, salads, and mouthwatering daily blue plate specials—is available to go. Grab a ready-to-go picnic lunch or find all the gourmet fixings for whatever adventure you have planned. The Regis Grocery has a huge selection of organic, gluten-free, and other specialty products.

Thirty-five miles (56 km) northeast of town is the tiny hamlet of Fromberg (drive east of Red Lodge on MT-308 to Belfry, then north on MT-72 past Bridger) and the **Little Cowboy Bar & Museum** (105 W. River St., 406/668-9502, noon-2am daily), a rare find. This special place combines a wonderful collection of rodeo and local memorabilia with a good old-fashioned Montana bar. After a fire in December 2013 destroyed much of the memorabilia, the bar was rebuilt and made use of what it could save by hanging it on the walls. Can you imagine a better way to learn about Montana history than with an ice-cold bottle of beer in hand?

Accommodations

In historic downtown Red Lodge, ★ **The Pollard Hotel** (2 N. Broadway Ave., 406/446-0001, www.thepollard.com, $160-300) should not be overlooked. The hotel was the first brick building constructed in Red Lodge and dates to 1893. It has played host to some of the West's most famous legends, including Calamity Jane, Buffalo Bill Cody, and famed orator William Jennings Bryan. Each of the 39 guest rooms and suites are individually decorated, more traditional than modern, and can come with mountain views, jetted tubs, and balconies. All stays include a full breakfast in The Pollard's excellent dining room.

Rock Creek Resort (6380 U.S. 212 S., 800/667-1119, www.rockcreekresort.com, $97-409) is about 5 miles (8 km) south of Red Lodge in a gorgeous canyon at the base of the Beartooth Mountains. The resort has 87 rooms sprawling over a 30-acre site and offers many outdoor activities. The facility has a heated indoor pool, tennis courts, a soccer field, a fully stocked fish pond, and numerous trails for hiking and biking (along with bikes for rent). Accommodations range from hotel rooms and condos to cabins and larger homes; most have impressive views of the mountains.

If you want to stay close to downtown Red Lodge without breaking the bank, try the pet-friendly ★ **Yodeler Motel** (601 S. Broadway Ave., 406/446-1435, www.yodelermotel.com, $105-155). This historic Swiss-themed chalet, owned by delightful former guides Mac and Tulsa Dean, is only three blocks from downtown. Remodeled guest rooms offer nice amenities that include cable TV, free Wi-Fi, jetted tubs, steam showers, and even a wax room to work on your skis. The rooms on the lower level are more budget friendly and do not have balconies like the upper level, but every room is clean, comfortable, and well maintained.

Camping

Thirteen campgrounds along U.S. 212 offer 226 sites between Red Lodge and Cooke City. Because of the elevation and volume of snow, many do not open until late June or July. **Beartooth Lake Campground** (21 sites, $15, July-mid-Sept.) and **Island Lake Campground** (21 sites, $15, July-mid-Sept.) are two excellent choices very near the summit.

Campsites along the Beartooth Highway are managed by the **Custer National Forest** (406/446-2103, www.fs.usda.gov/custergallatin) and range in price from free to $20 per night, depending on the site.

Information and Services

The **Red Lodge Chamber of Commerce** (701 N. Broadway Ave., 406/446-1718 or 888/281-0625, www.redlodgechamber.org, 9am-5pm Mon.-Fri., 10am-4pm Sat.-Sun. summer, winter hours vary) is at the intersection of U.S. 212 and Highway 78. It has a 24-hour brochure room that offers a variety of local information. Inside the center you will find knowledgeable staff and plenty of state publications, visitors guides, and maps.

Access the internet at **Red Lodge Carnegie Library** (3 8th St. W., 406/446-1905, 10am-6pm Tues.-Fri., noon-6pm Sat.). The library has several internet-connected computers available to the public. You can also stop by the **Coffee Factory Roasters** (22 S. Broadway Ave., 406/446-3200, www.coffeefactoryroasters.com, 6:30am-6pm daily), where the Wi-Fi is free.

The **Beartooth Billings Clinic** (2525 N. Broadway Ave., 406/446-2345, 7:30am-6pm walk-in care) offers 24-hour emergency care.

U.S. 212 climbs another 5,000 feet (1,524 m) past Red Lodge. If you want to know the road conditions for the Beartooth Highway, you can stop by the chamber of commerce or check with the state of Montana's **Traveler Road Information** (800/226-7623, TTY 800/335-7592, www.mdt.mt.gov).

Big Sky

In the shadow of Lone Peak, tucked in the winding and rugged beauty of Gallatin Canyon, the resort town of Big Sky (population 2,308; elevation 7,218 ft/2,200 m) actually has three resorts: Big Sky, Moonlight Basin, and the entirely private Yellowstone Club. Although there are not any sights per se, the town and resorts are clearly geographically blessed with mountains for skiing, hiking, climbing, and biking; rivers for fishing and floating; and trails aplenty for horses, hiking, cross-country skiing, and mountain biking. Visitors can take solace in the fact that mountains make up for museums, and the area can be used as a launching point for Yellowstone National Park (51 mi/82 km south) or Bozeman (50 mi/81 km north).

Big Sky has more activities than any visitor could dream of pursuing in a single trip—golf, horseback riding, fishing, skating, skiing, kayaking, wildlife-watching. The town itself, something of an afterthought to the ski hill, has grown tremendously with its own K-12 school (so that kids don't have to be bused 50 winding miles to Bozeman) and the impressive 282-seat Warren Miller Performing Arts Center, which brings a variety of art forms and performers to town. Though the community is growing stronger and more culturally vibrant by the year, Big Sky still feels a bit like a collection of enclaves, resorts, and villages dotting the mountainside. The uniting factor in this area is a zeal for outdoor adventuring.

Getting to Big Sky

From **West Yellowstone,** Big Sky is 51 miles (82 km) north on U.S. 191, a one-hour drive.

From **Gardiner** in winter, it's 120 miles (193 km) north on U.S. 89, west on I-90, then south on U.S. 191, a 2.5-hour drive. In the summer and fall, when park roads are open, it's 105 miles (169 km), on the park loop road to U.S. 191, about a 3.5-hour drive.

The closest airport is **Bozeman Yellowstone International Airport** (BZN, 406/388-8321, www.bozemanairport.com) in Belgrade, about 50 miles (81 km) north.

A variety of shuttle services run from the airport. **Karst Stage** (406/556-3540 or 800/845-2778, www.karststage.com) has a counter next to National Rent-a-Car and provides shuttles ($54 one-way with two-fare minimum, $82 round-trip) to Big Sky. **Shuttle to Big Sky & Taxi** (406/995-4895 or 888/454-5667, www.bigskytaxi.com) offers shuttles from the airport ($82 for two people). Another luxury shuttle service is **Big Sky Shuttle** (406/624-3332, www.bigskyshuttle.net).

Getting Around

Once in Big Sky, take advantage of the free bus service, **Skyline** (406/995-6287, www.skylinebus.com). In addition to covering the Big Sky area, buses also run between Bozeman and Big Sky. Hours vary by season.

Shuttle to Big Sky & Taxi (406/995-4895 or 888/454-5667, www.bigskytaxi.com) offers taxi service around Big Sky.

Dollar Rent-a-Car (1 mi/1.6 km from the airport, Belgrade) will deliver a vehicle to any Big Sky location.

Entertainment and Events

Although it is set up as a winter resort, Big Sky does an excellent job of capitalizing on the relatively short summer with events that draw crowds from near and far. There are few better venues in the state for live music: Concerts are held in a glorious meadow surrounded by rocky peaks at the free **Music in the Mountains** series (changing venues, 406/995-2742, www.bigskyarts.org, June-Sept.). Past headliners in Big Sky have included Willie Nelson, Bonnie Raitt, and the Doobie Brothers. Other annual musical events sponsored by the Arts Council of Big Sky include **Strings Under the Big Sky** (chamber music) and the **Bozeman Symphony Orchestra Pops** concert.

The weekly **Big Sky Farmers Market** (Firepit Park, Big Sky Town Center, 406/480-6579, www.bigskytowncenter.com, 5pm-8pm Wed. June-Sept.) features lots of local vendors in addition to prepared food, a great kids' area, musical entertainment, and personal enrichment that includes yoga and massage.

Sports and Recreation
Skiing

One thing that distinguishes Big Sky from other ski destinations in the Rockies is the plentiful elbow room—there are fewer skiers per skiable acre than in most places. **Big Sky Resort** (snow phone 406/995-5900, reservations 800/548-4486, snow sports school 406/995-5743, www.bigskyresort.com, $95-154 adults; $86-134 children 11-17, college students with ID, and seniors 70 and over; $55-94 children 6-10; free for children 5 and under) calls itself a ski resort without limits. It has 5,800 skiable acres and 4,350 vertical feet (1,326 m), and the area averages more than 400 inches (1,016 cm) of the fluffy stuff annually. The ski season generally lasts from Thanksgiving to mid-April. With virtually nonexistent lift lines (except during holidays), this is an ideal place for ambitious skiers and families.

The resort's **Lone Peak Tram** takes daring skiers 16 feet (4.9 m) shy of the mountain's summit and offers 300 degrees of skiing from the top of Lone Peak. Manicured terrain parks with many groomed features are available for snowboarders. Even with some of the steepest terrain in the country, Big Sky offers plenty of groomers for beginning and intermediate skiers and snowboarders.

In addition to the Mountain Sports School, which offers a wide range of ski and snowboard lessons and programs in winter, Big Sky Resort has the **Basecamp** (406/995-5769), an activity center offering two zip line courses, a high ropes course, a bungee trampoline, a climbing wall, and snowshoeing.

Down the mountain is **Lone Mountain Ranch** (750 Lone Mountain Rd., 406/995-4644 or 800/514-4644, www.lonemountainranch.com, $20 adults, $15 children 13-17 and seniors, free for children 12 and under and adults 70 and over), a cross-country skier's paradise with 85 kilometers of beautifully groomed and forested trails on 5,000 skiable acres with 2,200 vertical feet (671 m). Snowshoeing is another option, as are guided naturalist tours, lessons, and clinics. Rental equipment (skis and snowshoes) and lessons are available, and with such magnificent terrain, this is one of the biggest bargains around. The trails are sublime, and wildlife viewing can be excellent. For winter solitude and exploration, this is a marvelous place to be.

Fishing and Floating

The Gallatin River runs through the canyon beneath Big Sky and offers a plethora of recreational opportunities. U.S. 191 runs parallel to the river for 40 miles (64 km), making fishing access easy. The road is not meant for casual driving—no stopping and looking here—but there are several pullouts that can double as parking lots. Float fishing is prohibited, but the wade fishing is enticing, if somewhat tricky given the number of rapids created as the water tumbles down the canyon over beautiful car-size boulders.

Rainbows, browns, and cutthroats can all be found in these chilly waters, and the fish have to be lean and mean to battle the currents. They tend to be slightly less selective than downriver in Bozeman, where the decline slows and the water flattens out. There are caddis hatches practically all summer, and a killer salmonfly hatch in mid-June-early July. Late in the season, whopping terrestrials are the way to go.

Wild Trout Outfitters (U.S. 191, 0.5 mi/0.8 km south of the turnoff to Big Sky, 406/995-2975 or 800/423-4742, www.wildtroutoutftters.com, half-day Gallatin River wade trip $240 for 1 angler, $280 for 2 anglers, all-day Gallatin River wade trip $350 for 1 angler, $400 for 2 anglers) can offer professionally guided trips—wading or floating—including into Yellowstone National Park. **East Slope Outdoors** (44 Town Center Ave., 406/995-4369 or 888/359-3974, www.eastslopeoutdoors. com, 8am-8pm daily, half-day Gallatin River wade trip $250 for 1 angler, $290 for 2 anglers, all-day Gallatin River wade trip $350 for 1 angler, $400 for 2 anglers) offers equipment, rental gear, and guided fly-fishing trips.

If the tranquility of fishing appeals less than the mayhem of white water, rafting on the Gallatin River is a good option, especially since there are no floating options on rivers inside Yellowstone. **Montana Whitewater** (63960 Gallatin Rd., 800/799-4465, www.montanawhitewater.com, half-day $61 adults, $50 children 6-12, full-day $98 adults, $78 children 6-12) offers a range of trips to suit any adrenaline level, including half-day scenic floats, full-day white-water trips, and paddle-and-saddle overnighters. Plus, from the Gallatin Canyon base camp—which is like a small outdoors-loving city—you can mix and match adventures including rafting, zip-lining, fly-fishing, and horseback riding. The on-site **Blazin' Paddles Café** is a convenient food truck. **Geyser Whitewater** (46651 Gallatin Rd., next to Buck's T-4 on U.S. 191, 406/995-4989, www.raftmontana.com, half-day $68 adults, $58 children 12 and under, full-day $109 adults, $89 children 12 and under, minimum age restrictions vary with water conditions) is another superb local outfitter that specializes in Gallatin River trips. It also offers kayak trips, horseback riding, bike rentals, rock climbing, and zip-lining adventures.

Golf

For those who choose to hoof it around the links instead of a mountain trail, the 18-hole Arnold Palmer-designed **Big Sky Golf Course** (Meadow Village, 406/995-5780, www.bigskyresort.com, $79-159, $49 twilight play after 3pm) is open to nonguests and is well worth playing. There is abundant wildlife often sharing the par-72 course. A driving range, bar and grill, and full pro shop are available.

Food

Something about the high mountain air produces serious appetites, and Big Sky has a substantial selection of eateries for every taste. From the top of the mountain to the bottom, you're never more than a quick jog from your next mouthwatering meal.

The Corral (42895 Gallatin Rd., 5 mi/8 km south of Big Sky, 406/995-4249, www.corralbar.com, 8am-10pm daily, bar until 2am daily, $17-38) offers up an excellent take on the classic Montana menu. From buffalo T-bones to Delmonico steaks, prime rib, and good ol' hamburgers, The Corral's food is consistently good, with plenty of chicken, seafood, and pasta options available. You can't go wrong with the smoked trout appetizer.

The **Gallatin Riverhouse Grill** (45130 Gallatin Rd., 406/995-7427, www.gallatinriverhousegrill.com, 3pm-close daily, $8-26) is known for its excellent smoked barbecue and its views. From their fried pickles, okra, and sweet corn nuggets to beef brisket, baby back ribs, and pulled pork, owners Kyle and Greg don't let anyone leave hungry. As if the sound of the rushing Gallatin weren't enough, this wonderful riverfront venue hosts plenty of live music.

For an elegant meal, **Olive B's Big Sky Bistro** (151 Center Ln., 406/995-3355, www.olivebsbigsky.com, 11am-9pm Mon.-Fri., 4pm-9pm Sat., $25-37) is a great choice. Owned by a couple from the East Coast, the restaurant offers an abundance of good seafood including lobster mac and cheese, ahi, and shrimp and grits. But the spot also serves up the best of the West: Rocky Mountain elk with huckleberry demi-glace, pheasant, and beef tenderloin.

Blue Moon Bakery (3090 Big Pine Dr., 406/995-2305, www.bigskybluemoonbakery.com, 7am-10pm daily, $5-10) is a good bet for everything from breakfast sandwiches and baked goods to salads and gourmet pizza pies. Another good spot for breakfast or lunch is **Bugaboo Café** (47995 Gallatin Rd., Ste. 101, 406/995-3350, 7:30am-2:30pm Wed.-Mon., $8-12), an unassuming little place featuring comfort food with an inventive twist. The menu changes seasonally to take advantage of local products and includes such favorites as blue crab omelets and chicken potpie. The Bugaboo is probably the best value in Big Sky.

★ **Buck's T-4** (46625 Gallatin Rd., 1 mi/1.6 km south of Big Sky, 800/822-4484, www.buckst4.com, 5:30pm-9:30pm daily summer, 6pm-9pm daily winter, $14-40) is fairly unassuming but serves up some of the best cuisine in the region. Known statewide and beyond for wild game—think duck, pheasant, bison, and red deer—Buck's menu reflects Montana culinary traditions with more contemporary, lighter fare. It even packages up duck bacon for diners to take home. Buck's has an extensive and impressive wine list, and its drinks make the most of the local harvest; try a wild huckleberry martini or bacon bourbon old-fashioned. Buck's keeps limited hours in the fall and spring, between ski season and summer.

For a unique meal during the ski season, try the sleigh-ride dinner at ★ **Lone Mountain Ranch** (750 Lone Mountain Rd., 406/995-4644 or 800/514-4644, www.lonemountainranch.com, $145-185 pp), which whisks diners up a snowy trail to a candlelit cabin in the woods for a steak-and-potato dinner. Or try **dinner in a yurt** (via snowcat instead of horse-pulled sleigh) high atop Lone Mountain (406/995-3880, www.bigskyyurt.com, $114 adults, $99 children), which also includes time for sledding. Both experiences offer hearty meals and unparalleled ambience, and both sell out well in advance—so book ahead.

Accommodations

Big Sky was built as a resort, and it caters to visitors and vacationers. There is a wide range of accommodations, from ski-in/ski-out mountainside lodging to rustic roadside motels, inviting guest ranches, luxe resorts, and condo or cabin rentals, that can address your specific needs—staying put or traveling around, skiing or golfing, walking or driving to dinner.

For the best bang for your buck, try the **Corral Motel** (42895 Gallatin Road, 5 mi/8 km south of Big Sky, 406/995-4249 or 888/995-4249, www.corralbar.com, from $100 single, $20 each additional person), which also has a terrific restaurant and bar open year-round. The guest rooms are basic but clean and comfortable, with honeyed pine paneling that evokes the best of Western hospitality. During the winter, a shuttle runs from the motel to Big Sky Resort and Meadow Village.

Closer to Big Sky is **Buck's T-4 Lodge** (46625 Gallatin Rd., 1 mi/1.6 km south of Big Sky, 800/822-4484, www.buckst4.com, $169-319), a very comfortable hotel with newly remodeled rooms, a great bar, and one of the best restaurants in the region. The roadside location leaves something to be desired in ambience and views, but it is convenient.

On top of the mountain is the **Summit at Big Sky** (Mountain Village Center, 800/548-4486, www.bigskyresort.com, studio rooms from $293), a deluxe slope-side facility with the convenience of a hotel and the amenities of a condo. It offers both residences and temporary lodging, all in a comfortable and sophisticated atmosphere. There are indoor and outdoor pools, hot tubs, a sauna and fitness facility, and fireplaces in most

accommodations. Lodging packages can include lift tickets. **Big Sky Resort** (800/548-4486) can arrange a variety of lodging from slope-side rooms and condos to ski-in/ski-out cabins and homes for rent.

Information and Services

The **Big Sky Chamber of Commerce** (55 Lone Mountain Trail, 406/995-3000 or 800/943-4111, www.bigskychamber.com, 8:30am-5:30pm daily summer, 8:30am-5:30pm Mon.-Fri. fall-spring) is an excellent resource for local information.

The **post office** (800/275-8777, 10am-5pm Mon.-Fri., 10am-1pm Sat.) is conveniently located at 55 Meadow Center Drive, Suite 2.

Your best bet for free **internet access** is at the **Big Sky Community Library** (45465 Gallatin Rd., 406/995-4281, 10am-6pm Mon., 4pm-8pm Tues.-Wed., 1pm-5pm Sun.).

The **Mountain Clinic of Big Sky** is in the ski patrol building at Big Sky Resort (100 Beaverhead Trail, 406/995-2797, 9am-5pm Mon.-Fri.). For more serious medical emergencies, **Bozeman Deaconess Hospital** (915 Highland Blvd., 406/585-5000, www.bozemandeaconess.org) has a 24-hour emergency room about an hour's drive from Big Sky.

To wash your clothes and have a few drinks while you wait, **Sit & Spin Laundry Lounge** (115 Aspen Leaf Dr., 1F, 406/600-8416, 11am-2am Wed.-Sun.) is the place. They have great Bloody Marys, fresh-squeezed juices, and house specialty shots that look like Tide pods. They also serve specialty coffees.

Grand Teton National Park

Grand Teton National Park

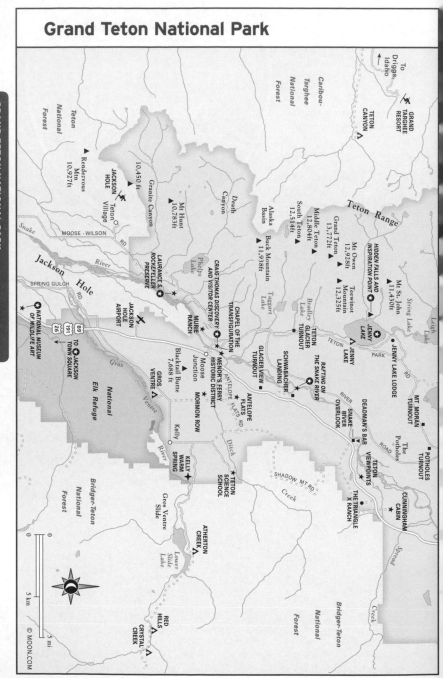

To Driggs, Idaho

GRAND TARGHEE RESORT

TETON CANYON

Caribou-Targhee National Forest

Teton Range

Teton National Forest

Rendervous Mtn 10,927ft

10,450 ft

JACKSON HOLE Village

Teton Village

Granite Canyon

Mt Hunt 10,783ft

Death Canyon

Alaska Basin

Buck Mountain 11,938ft

South Teton 12,514ft

Middle Teton 12,804ft

Grand Teton 13,772ft

Mt Owen 12,928ft

Teewinot Mountain 12,325ft

HIDDEN FALLS AND INSPIRATION POINT

Mt St. John 11,430ft

String Lake

Leigh Lake

Snake River

Jackson Hole

SPRING GULCH RD

MOOSE - WILSON RD

Phelps Lake

LAURANCE S. ROCKEFELLER PRESERVE

CRAIG THOMAS DISCOVERY AND VISITOR CENTER

MURIE RANCH

Taggart Lake

Bradley Lake

TETON GLACIER TURNOUT

JENNY LAKE

JENNY LAKE

JENNY LAKE LODGE

TETON PARK RD

MT MORAN TURNOUT

NATIONAL MUSEUM OF WILDLIFE ART

JACKSON AIRPORT

89
191
26

TO JACKSON TOWN SQUARE

Gros Ventre

CHAPEL OF THE TRANSFIGURATION

MENOR'S FERRY HISTORIC DISTRICT

Moose Junction

GLACIER VIEW TURNOUT

SCHWABACHER LANDING

RAFTING ON THE SNAKE RIVER

SNAKE RIVER OVERLOOK

DEADMAN'S BAR

SNAKE RIVER ROAD

The Potholes

POTHOLES TURNOUT

TETON VIEWPOINTS

GROS VENTRE

Blacktail Butte 7,688 ft

MORMON ROW

Kelly

ANTELOPE FLATS

ANTELOPE FLATS RD

RIVER

National Elk Refuge

Gros Ventre River

KELLY WARM SPRING

Ditch

TETON SCIENCE SCHOOL

SHADOW MT RD

Creek

THE TRIANGLE X RANCH

CUNNINGHAM CABIN

Spread

Bridger-Teton National Forest

Gros Ventre Slide

Lower Slide Lake

ATHERTON CREEK

Slide Lake

RED HILLS

CRYSTAL CREEK

Bridger-Teton National Forest

Creek

0
5 km

0
5 mi

© MOON.COM

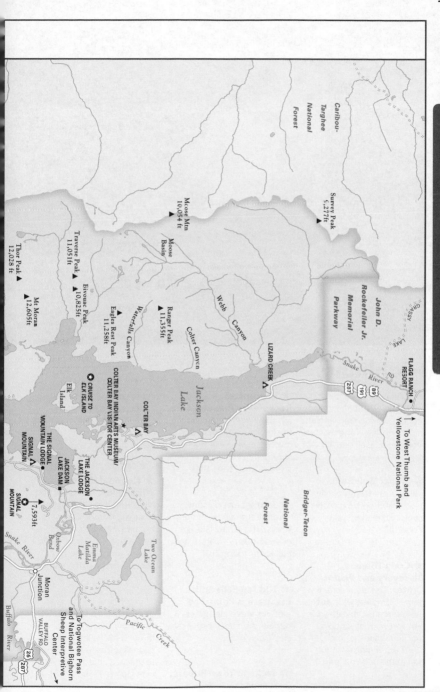

Highlights

★ **Cruise to Elk Island:** Lure yourself out of bed and into this wonderland with an early-morning cruise that features breakfast (page 99).

★ **Signal Mountain:** Follow this exciting 5-mile (8-km) drive with expansive views of the entire valley (page 100).

★ **Craig Thomas Discovery and Visitor Center:** This architectural gem—complete with video rivers running beneath your feet and walls of windows that showcase the Tetons—offers a stunning introduction to the park (page 103).

★ **Laurance S. Rockefeller Preserve:** The longtime summer home of the Rockefeller family, this lovely preserve exemplifies the family's commitment to stewardship (page 104).

★ **Jenny Lake:** Resting like a mirror at the base of the Tetons, this alpine lake is a gem for hikers, boaters, and picnickers (page 105).

★ **Hidden Falls and Inspiration Point:** The glorious views along this popular hike are worth every step (page 105).

★ **Jackson Town Square:** Surrounded by archways constructed entirely from elk antlers, this is the heart of the community for shoppers, art lovers, and diners (page 127).

★ **National Museum of Wildlife Art:** This collection is dedicated to all things wild, spanning George Catlin's bison to incredible works by Georgia O'Keeffe, Charlie Russell, and marvelous contemporary artists (page 129).

★ **Rafting on the Snake River:** The Snake winds through the valley, giving floaters unparalleled access to the area's most stunning views (page 135).

Just south of Yellowstone, Grand Teton National Park is even more dazzling in alpine splendor than its more prominent neighbor. The Tetons soar skyward, 3 in a sea of 12 peaks topping 12,000 feet (3,658 m).

The mountains are young—still growing, in fact—and utterly spectacular, perhaps the most dramatic anywhere in the Lower 48. The park itself contains approximately 310,000 acres (roughly 15 percent the size of Yellowstone), 100 miles of paved road, and, much to the delight of hikers, some 200 miles of trails.

Like Yellowstone, Grand Teton is home to healthy populations of wildlife—this is among the best places in the West to see a moose—but the rugged terrain and limited number of roads afford the animals better places to hide. Still, you always need to be prepared for bear encounters in the park. Beyond the fascinating natural and geological history of the region, Grand Teton offers some interesting human-built attractions—including the historic and elegant Jenny Lake Lodge, the Chapel of the Transfiguration, and the Laurance S. Rockefeller Preserve—that are well worth seeing. At the end of the day, though, Grand Teton is a place for nature lovers and outdoors enthusiasts. The vistas are unparalleled, as are the recreational opportunities.

Getting to Grand Teton National Park

Grand Teton National Park is fairly small in terms of road miles, especially compared to Yellowstone. From the north boundary of the park at the top of Jackson Lake to the south entrance at Moose is 36 miles (58 km) on U.S. 89/191 and the Teton Park Road, about a one-hour drive.

While distances through the park may seem short in actual mileage, your drive time is often extended by lower speed limits, traffic congestion, and animal jams. In addition, most of the park roads are **closed in winter.**

Driving from Yellowstone
70-106 miles (113-171 km); 2-3 hours
From the north entrance of Yellowstone at **Gardiner,** the northern boundary of Grand Teton National Park, just south of the **Flagg Ranch Information Station,** is 100 miles (161 km) south on U.S. 89 and U.S. 191, a three-hour drive that goes through the western side of Yellowstone (this route passes Old Faithful).

If you're coming from Gardiner but driving along the eastern part of Yellowstone (through Tower Junction and Canyon Village), the drive to Flagg Ranch is 106 miles (171 km), which is about a three-hour drive.

From **West Yellowstone,** Flagg Ranch is 70 miles (113 km) west and south on U.S. 191, about a two-hour drive (this route passes Old Faithful).

Driving from Jackson, Wyoming
13 miles (21 km); 30 minutes
From Jackson, Grand Teton's south entrance at **Moose** is 13 miles (21 km) north on U.S. 191/89, about a 30-minute drive.

Driving from Cody, Wyoming
101 miles (163 km); 3 hours
To get from Cody to the Headwaters Lodge & Cabins at Flagg Ranch, it's 122 miles (196 km) west on U.S. 14/16/20, then south on U.S. 89/191. The drive, which begins on the east side of Yellowstone, takes about three hours.

Bus and Shuttle
Mountain States Express (307/733-1719 or 800/652-9510, www.mountainstates

One Day in Grand Teton

Wherever you wake up in Jackson, head straight to breakfast at **Persephone Bakery.** A cappuccino and some quiche Lorraine will get you far in these parts. While you're there, pick up a picnic lunch.

From town, head north into the park to the **Craig Thomas Discovery & Visitor Center.** In addition to the exhibits, check out the schedule of **ranger programs** for the day. You could take a hike, tour the Murie Home, or listen to a talk about bears. Continue on to **Jenny Lake,** where you can find a quiet spot for a picnic and maybe a swim.

After lunch, hit the trailhead for **Hidden Falls and Inspiration Point.** If you aren't eager to climb, you can choose a lovely, flat walk—though still lengthy—to **Leigh Lake.** After your hike, head north again to **Signal Mountain** and drive to the top for a spectacular view. When you come back down, drive northeast to look for moose or other wildlife at the scenic **Oxbow Bend.**

For dinner, make your way to Colter Bay for a **scenic dinner cruise** to **Elk Island.** If there's time, stop into the **Colter Bay Indian Arts Museum.** Bed down at the beautiful **Jackson Lake Lodge.**

express.com), which is operated by **Alltrans** (www.jacksonholealltrans.com), offers a daily **shuttle** (starting at $75) from Salt Lake City, Utah, to Jackson. The ride to Jackson is 5.5 hours.

Greyhound (www.greyhound.com) stops at the Albertsons (105 Buffalo Way) in Jackson.

Air

The only airport in the country within a national park, **Jackson Hole Airport** (JAC, 1250 E. Airport Rd., Jackson, 307/733-7682, www.jacksonholeairport.com) is served by American, Delta, United, and Frontier. The schedules change seasonally but include regular flights from Salt Lake City, Denver, Seattle, Chicago, Minneapolis, Dallas, Houston, Phoenix, San Francisco, and Los Angeles.

Visiting Grand Teton National Park

Planning Your Time

Grand Teton National Park is smaller, and in some ways more manageable, than its northerly neighbor. There are only 100 miles (161 km) of paved road, all of which can be driven easily in less than a day's time. With fewer accommodations than Yellowstone, Grand Teton lends itself to easy day trips from various locations in Wyoming, such as **Jackson Hole** or **Dubois,** 65 miles (105 km) from the east entrance. **Cody** is about a three-hour drive from the park, via Yellowstone, so overnighting there is an option when rooms cannot be found any closer. A destination in its own right, Grand Teton is a paradise for outdoors enthusiasts. Hikers, bikers, boaters, and, in winter, cross-country skiers will have no problem coming up with marvelous weeklong itineraries. Those on a time budget can get an excellent sampling of the park in two days, but even if you are just driving through, there are a few places that should not be missed.

While summer is by far the busiest time in the park, spring and fall can be magnificent with wildflowers, golden aspens, and more active wildlife. **Hiking** and **climbing** in the Tetons is best done in summer and early fall, after the winter snow has melted and before it starts flying again. Still, snow squalls and bad weather can surprise hikers at any time of year, so come prepared. Park rangers offer educational programs throughout

Best Restaurants

★ **Dornans Chuckwagon, Moose:** Eating cowboy cuisine with a view of the Tetons is just plain fun, not to mention the fact that everything tastes better outside (page 122).

★ **The Bunnery, Jackson:** A longtime Jackson favorite for a casual breakfast or lunch, The Bunnery has outstanding bread and pastries, plus hearty and fresh sandwiches, burgers, salads, and more (page 139).

★ **Persephone Bakery, Jackson:** When it comes to buttery French pastries and daily staples, there is no better place than this bakery (page 139).

★ **Hatch Taqueria & Tequilas, Jackson:** Known for its specialty tacos featuring elk, bison, and salmon, this spot is open for breakfast, lunch, and dinner, and has an excellent selection of tequilas (page 140).

★ **Wild Sage, Jackson:** As gourmet as it gets in Jackson, dining at Wild Sage is a culinary adventure (page 141).

the year that are an excellent way to make the most of the time you have. In the fall, for example, drivers can join ranger-led **wildlife caravans** from the Craig Thomas Discovery and Visitor Center that guide visitors to the best places to see wildlife that day. **Ranger-led hikes and eco-talks** are geared to the seasons and offer visitors an insiders' look at the park.

The National Park Service offers an excellent **trip-planning tool online** (www.nps.gov), or you can order a booklet by mail by calling 307/739-3600.

Entrances

Grand Teton National Park has two official entrance stations, but the park can be accessed from the south (Jackson), the east (Dubois), and the north (Yellowstone). Although you will be in Grand Teton National Park starting just 5 miles (8 km) north of Jackson, the southernmost **Moose Entrance Station** is about 20 miles (32 km) north of town. The eastern entrance at **Moran Junction** is 30 miles (48 km) north of Jackson and 55 miles (89 km) west of Dubois, Wyoming, over the Togwotee Pass, which is closed in winter.

From the north, visitors enter Grand Teton National Park from Yellowstone; the $35 admission (for private passenger vehicles) is valid for seven days. Visitors coming in from Yellowstone can stop for information at **Flagg Ranch Information Station** or the **Colter Bay Visitor Center** 18 miles (29 km) south of Yellowstone.

Park Fees and Passes

Single-entry entrance fees are $35 per vehicle, $20 per person for hikers or bicyclists, and $30 per motorcycle for seven days in both Grand Teton National Park and Yellowstone National Park.

With more than 200 miles (320 km) of maintained trails in the park, backpacking and backcountry camping provide a unique way to explore the area. Permits ($35) are required and can be obtained in person on a first-come, first-served basis no more than one day before the start of a trip at the Craig Thomas Visitor Center, Colter Bay Visitor Center, or Jenny Lake Ranger Station. Roughly one-third of **backcountry campsites** in heavily used areas can be reserved in advance online ($45) January 1-May 15 (307/739-3309, www.recreation.gov) and must be picked up in person. After May 15, all permits must be obtained in person. All campers

Best Accommodations

★ **The Triangle X Ranch, Moran to Moose:** The premier guest ranch inside Grand Teton National Park, this fifth-generation family ranch offers warm hospitality and arguably the world's best setting for active vacationers (page 124).

★ **Anvil Motel, Jackson:** Just off Town Square, with comfortable rooms and prices that won't break the bank, this classic spot is a hip, mountain-rustic getaway (page 141).

★ **Rustic Inn Creekside Resort & Spa, Jackson:** Set on 12 lush acres just out of town and next to a nature preserve, this resort offers lodge rooms, cabins, and spa suites with high-end amenities and world-class service (page 141).

★ **Alpine House & Lodge Cottages, Jackson:** A cozy spot for outdoor adventure lovers, this downtown hotel is conveniently located, with superb amenities—from hearty breakfasts to an elegant little spa—to meet guests' every need (page 142).

are required to use bear-proof canisters below 10,000 feet (3,048 m) and at sites without bear boxes. Free canisters are provided when registering for a permit.

Visitors Centers

There are four main visitors centers in the park.

- The impressive **Craig Thomas Discovery and Visitor Center** (307/739-3399, 10am-4pm daily early Mar.-Apr., 8am-5pm daily May-early June and mid-Sept.-Oct., 8am-7pm daily early June-mid-Sept.) is 12 miles (19.3 km) north of Jackson and 0.5 mile (0.8 km) west of Moose Junction. Exhibits include a relief map of the park, an introductory video, and natural history displays.

- The **Jenny Lake Visitor Center** (307/739-3392, 8am-5pm daily mid-May-early June and early Sept.-late Sept., 8am-7pm early June-early Sept.) is 8 miles (12.9 km) north of Moose Junction on Teton Park Road. Visitor services include guided walks and talks, and exhibits focus on park geology.

- Half a mile (0.8 km) west of Colter Bay Junction is the **Colter Bay Visitor**

Center (307/739-3594, 8am-5pm daily mid-May-early June and early Sept.-early Oct., 8am-7pm daily early June-early Sept.).

- Four miles (6.4 km) south of Moose on the Moose-Wilson Road (which is closed to RVs and trailers) is the **Laurance S. Rockefeller Preserve Center** (307/739-3654, 9am-5pm daily early June-late Sept.), which offers 8 miles (12.9 km) of hiking trails, fishing and swimming opportunities in Phelps Lake, and unique sensory exhibits. Opening and closing dates for all visitors centers can change annually and are listed online (www.nps.gov).

Services

Visit the website of the **National Park Service** (www.nps.gov) to help plan your trip to Grand Teton. In the section titled Plan Your Visit, you'll find answers to most of your pressing questions. When you enter the park, you will receive a copy of the park newspaper, *Grand Teton Guide,* which has a lot of useful information about park facilities, hours of operation, and programs and specific activities offered daily or weekly. If you need additional information before you go, you can call the **visitors** information line (307/739-3300, ext. 1). For campground information, call the **Grand Teton Lodge Company** (307/543-2811); for **backcountry** information, contact the permits office (307/739-3309) or book backcountry sites online (www.recreation.gov) in advance.

The main concessionaire in the park is the **Grand Teton Lodge Company** (307/543-2811, www.gtlc.com). Its website can also be a great aid in planning your visit. The company is responsible for the lodging, restaurants, tours, and activities at Jackson Lake Lodge, Jenny Lake Lodge, Colter Bay Village, Headwaters Lodge & Cabins at Flagg Ranch, and campgrounds throughout the park. The restaurants use free-range, naturally raised meat and dairy, organic coffee and produce, and support sustainable farming practices.

For **medical emergencies** within the park, dial 911. **St. John's Medical Center** (625 E. Broadway, Jackson, 307/733-3636) is open year-round, and the **Grand Teton Medical Clinic** (307/543-2514 during business hours or 307/733-8002 after hours, 9am-5pm daily mid-May-mid-Oct.) is located in the Jackson Lake Lodge.

Getting Around

There are no shuttle services in Grand Teton National Park, so visitors will either need to have access to a private vehicle or book a tour.

Private Vehicles

If you are driving through the park, don't forget to keep an eye on your fuel gauge. The only gas station open year-round is at **Dornans** (10 Moose Rd., gas pumps available 24 hours daily if paying with a credit card) in Moose. Other gas stations open May-October are at Signal Mountain, Jackson Lodge, and Colter Bay.

For up-to-date road information and closures in the park, call 307/739-3682, or 307/344-2117 for Yellowstone road reports. For Wyoming road information, contact the **Wyoming Department of Transportation** (888/996-7623, www.wyoroad.info).

Tours

The **Grand Teton Lodge Company** (307/543-2811, www.gtlc.com) offers any number of tours throughout the park, including four-hour tours departing from Jackson Lake Lodge during summer.

A great educational opportunity is provided by the **Teton Science Schools** (307/733-1313, www.tetonscience.org), based in Jackson. The organization is committed to creating a deeper appreciation and understanding of the wilderness and natural ecosystems found in the Greater Yellowstone area. Its experts provide classes and programs to engage every type of learner from small children to adults. The courses focus on everything from ecology and geology to unique plant and animal life. Even if you only plan to be in the park for a day or two, visit the website to see what is being offered. Regular programs can include hikes, campfires, canoe tours, and wildlife-viewing. The school also offers renowned **Wildlife Expeditions** (877/404-6626). These can be half-day, full-day, or multiple-day guided tours with professional wildlife biologists who provide you with an up-close and unique opportunity to experience the natural wonders of the park.

Another tour company that focuses on getting visitors up close and personal with the park's wildlife in comfy 4x4 vehicles is **EcoTour Adventures** (307/690-9533, www.jhecotouradventures.com). Guided half-day tours, often at sunrise or sunset, run roughly four hours and start at $130 for adults and $95 for children 10 and under. Full-day trips last approximately eight hours and can take visitors into Grand Teton and Yellowstone. These tours include lunch at one of the park lodges and start at $225 for adults and $190 for children 10 and under.

Alltrans (307/733-3135 or 800/443-6133, www.jacksonholealltrans.com)

Bear #399 and the Grizzlies of Grand Teton

In July 1975, grizzly bears were listed as "threatened" under the Endangered Species Act. At that time, and for several years afterward, not a single grizzly was known to wander the wilds of Grand Teton National Park. Estimates put the number of grizzlies in Yellowstone around 136 at the time, but in Grand Teton, there wasn't even one.

The animal's listing and, thankfully, passionate involvement by good people have changed that. In early 2016, the number of grizzlies in the Greater Yellowstone Ecosystem—which includes Yellowstone and Grand Teton National Parks and their surrounds—hovered somewhere around the 700 mark. And at the end of 2015, Grand Teton National Park was home to some 60 of these totemic animals.

Because it's true that we protect what we love, and love what we know, perhaps no bear has done as much for grizzly protection as #399. First captured and collared in 2001 when she was five years old, #399 has become the most famous grizzly in the world. She has had more than 15 cubs and grandcubs and been watched along roadsides by thousands upon thousands of park visitors over the years. "Along with her cubs, she made you want to protect her," said acclaimed photographer Tom Mangelsen, who, with writer Todd Wilkinson, put out a marvelous book on #399, *Grizzlies of Pilgrim Creek* (www.mangelsen.com).

Because she is so visible, Bear #399 has shown us the challenges bears face to simply survive. According to Wilkinson, nearly 75 percent of her descendants have died as a result of human encounters—struck by cars, killed illegally by big-game hunters, euthanized for preying on cattle or for coming too close to human development. She has lost other cubs to starvation or encounters with dominant males. But it's the day-to-day glimpses of #399, often with her cubs, that endear her to people the world over and give people a vision of something worth fighting for.

Even with postcard bears like #399 and citizen advocates, the fight to protect bears is far from won. After the success of their recovery over the last 40 years, in the early part of 2016, the U.S. Fish and Wildlife Service proposed that grizzly bears be removed from the federal List of Endangered and Threatened Wildlife, which strips away various protective measures and eventually opens grizzlies to hunting. In 2017, 56 grizzlies died from poachers, conflicts with hunters and ranchers, and car collisions. Even amid all these threats, in the fall of 2018, plans for a sport hunt that could kill as many as 22 grizzlies, 12 of them females, were nearly enacted before a federal judge overturned the ruling and extended protections for grizzlies. The decision is being appealed. As the status of grizzly bears is questioned, their value in our wild world should not be.

While scientists call the grizzly an "umbrella" or "indicator" species—meaning that when the grizzlies thrive, so too do the other plants and animals that inhabit their world—naturalist and writer Doug Peacock, who has dedicated his life to making the world a safer place for grizzlies, goes further in asserting the importance of their survival. "Really, we are as much endangered as the grizzly bears. The fate of humans and grizzlies is a single, collective one," he said.

Twenty-two years old in 2018, when she emerged from hibernation with year-old twin cubs, Bear #399 will not be around much longer. But let us hope—and fight—to make sure grizzly bears still are.

offers **full-day tours** (Tues., Thurs., and Sun. late May-late Sept., starting at $245 for adults) of Grand Teton National Park out of Jackson Hole.

Sights

Flagg Ranch and Colter Bay

Just south of the Yellowstone border, Flagg Ranch was at one time a U.S. Cavalry outpost. Converted to a guest ranch in 1910 and now known as Headwaters Lodge & Cabins at Flagg Ranch, it is ideally situated for visitors looking to explore both Yellowstone and Grand Teton National Parks from one location. In addition to full resort lodging and services, Flagg Ranch offers activities and services—a gas station, a grocery store, a deli and coffee shop—for those just passing through.

One of the busiest spots in the park, with a marina, lodging, a campground, a visitors center, and a museum on the shores of Jackson Lake, Colter Bay is a practical, if not exactly quiescent, place to stay, and it is a worthwhile region to explore.

Colter Bay Indian Arts Museum

The unassuming **Colter Bay Indian Arts Museum** (307/739-3594, 8am-7pm daily early June-Labor Day, 8am-5pm daily Labor Day-early Oct., free) is tacked onto the visitors center almost as an afterthought. But the relatively unknown gem includes important Native American artifacts that belonged to tribes across the country. The David T. Vernon collection—which comprises more than 1,000 objects including dolls, shields, pipes, weapons, and photographs—was donated by the Rockefeller family with the provision that it be displayed permanently in Grand Teton National Park. In 2012, almost the entire collection was sent to a conservation facility; it is slowly being returned to the park, at both the Colter Bay and Craig Thomas Visitor Centers. It

is a remarkable collection that could just as easily be on display at the Smithsonian were it not for the wishes of an extremely generous family. Meanwhile, Native American artisans practice their crafts in the museum intermittently through the summer, and a number of prominent lecturers and daily educational events are scheduled on-site.

★ Cruise to Elk Island

Because nothing builds an appetite like time spent on an alpine lake, there are wonderful breakfast, lunch, and dinner cruises (307/543-2811, www.gtlc. com) departing from the marina that whisk guests across Jackson Lake to Elk Island, in the shadow of Mount Moran. Each cruise takes approximately three hours. The **breakfast cruise** ($50 adults, $25 children 3-11), offered daily except Thursday (which can change from year to year), serves hearty fare with eggs and trout, pancakes, pastries, fresh fruit, and the all-important cowboy coffee. Typically, it departs at 7:15am from June to August and at 8am late August to early September. The **lunch cruise** ($50 adults, $25 children 3-11) includes a sack lunch and plenty of time to explore the island. It departs Monday, Wednesday, Friday, and Saturday at 12:15pm. The **dinner cruise** (5:15pm Fri.-Wed. June-Sept. 5, $72 adults, $42 children 6-11) includes such delectable mountain fare as steak and trout, baked beans, corn on the cob, a salad bar, roasted potatoes, and mouth-watering fruit cobbler. Scenic **lake cruises** (10:15am, 1:15pm, and 3:15pm daily, $36 adults, $18 children 3-11) last about 90 minutes and are geared to different aspects of the park (with one cruise designed especially for kids). An extra tour departs at 6:15pm on Thursdays.

Jackson Lake Lodge and Signal Mountain

Its breathtaking setting, coupled with excellent amenities and access to hiking and sightseeing in the park's northeastern

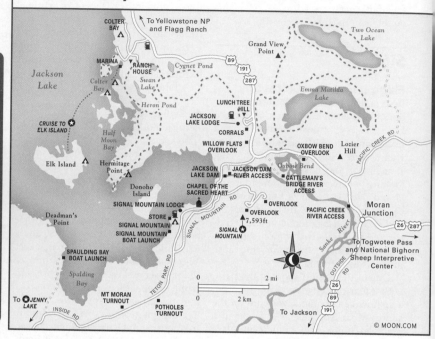

Colter Bay

corner, make Jackson Lake Lodge a vacation destination all its own. Though the lodge is not adjacent to Jackson Lake in the way that the Colter Bay Village is, the views over the lake to the Tetons are magnificent. Nearby, the rustic Signal Mountain Lodge is situated immediately on the water, offering unlimited opportunities for enjoying Jackson Lake and its proximity to hiking and adventuring.

Oxbow Bend

Just southeast of Jackson Lake Lodge on the main road is Oxbow Bend, a picturesque area created when the Snake River carved a more southerly route. One of the most photographed sites in the park, the slow-moving water perfectly reflects towering Mount Moran. The serenity of the area attracts an abundance of wildlife, including moose, beaver, and otters along with a vast number of birds. White

pelicans can occasionally be spotted passing through, as can sandhill cranes, majestic trumpeter swans, nesting great blue herons, and bald eagles. Avid boaters like to paddle the area in their canoes and kayaks. Don't forget your binoculars and your camera.

★ Signal Mountain

One mile (1.6 km) south of Signal Mountain Lodge is the turnoff to Signal Mountain Road and one of the greatest viewpoints in Grand Teton National Park. The winding 5-mile (8-km) road is completely **unsuitable for RVs and trailers.** Along the way, there are ample spots for wildlife-viewing—look for moose in the pond on the right as you start up the road, and the pond lilies blooming in June. Two small parking lots are near the summit. The first offers the best view of the Tetons; sunsets are sensational. From the second, a short walk takes you down to an overlook with a view of Oxbow Bend. Visitors in August might even have a chance to pick some succulent huckleberries as the berries ripen in the late-summer sun.

The story of Signal Mountain's name is a rather tragic one. Around the turn of the 20th century, a local rancher named Roy Hamilton got lost when he was out hunting. Rescuers agreed to light a fire on the mountain as soon as anyone found Hamilton. After nine days, a fire was lit atop the mountain, signaling the end of rescue efforts. Tragically, Hamilton's body was found in the Snake River, and some speculated his business partner had suggested he cross the river in a particularly dangerous spot.

Moran to Moose

The stretch of road between Moran Junction and the southernmost entrance to the park at Moose is scenic and full of interesting sights, both natural and artificial. From the historic crossing at **Menors Ferry** to the architecturally inspired **Craig Thomas Discovery and Visitor Center** to the wildlife-rich **Antelope Flats,** this part of the park is heavily traveled for good reason.

Cunningham Cabin

A relic of hardscrabble ranching days before the turn of the 20th century—and the site of the murder of two alleged horse thieves—**Cunningham Cabin** is 6 miles (9.7 km) south of Moran Junction. The cabin reflects the common building materials and style of 1890, the year it was built. Known as a "dogtrot," it consists of two small structures connected by a breezeway and topped with a dirt roof.

Pierce Cunningham built a modest home for his family on Flat Creek in 1888. A neighbor introduced Cunningham to two strangers, George Spenser and Mike

Top to bottom: Jackson Lake; Oxbow Bend; view from the summit of Signal Mountain.

Moran to Moose

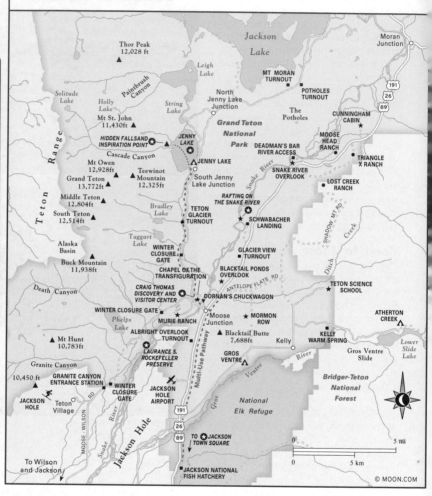

Burnett, who were seeking hay for their horses. Cunningham sold them 15 tons of hay and arranged for them to winter in his cabin near Spread Creek. The rumor among the locals was that the men were in fact horse thieves.

In April 1893, Spenser and Burnett were the target of a posse of vigilantes from Montana. Sixteen men on horseback rode up to the little cabin on Spread Creek under cover of darkness and waited

in silence for dawn. Spenser and Burnett's dog barked in the early-morning hours, perhaps warning the men of the ambush that awaited them. Spenser dressed, armed himself, and walked out the front door. When the posse called for him to hold his hands up, Spenser fired his revolver in the direction of the speaker and was immediately shot. He propped himself up on one elbow and continued to fire until he collapsed. Burnett came out next, armed with a revolver and a rifle. The men shot at him, but Burnett managed to shoot the hat off one of the posse members and "crease his scalp" with the bullet. Burnett was shot and killed moments later. The two men were buried in unmarked graves a few hundred yards southeast of the cabin on the south side of a draw. Some of their bones were eventually excavated by badgers.

Mormon Row and Antelope Flats

Interesting both for its wildlife and its human history, the area around **Mormon Row** is instantly recognizable from some of the region's most popular postcards, featuring a weathered barn leaning into the jagged mountains behind it. Listed in the National Register of Historic Places, Mormon Row is a collection of six fairly dilapidated homesteads that can be explored on a self-guided tour (brochures are available near the pink house). The area was settled around the turn of the 20th century by a handful of Mormon families who built homes, a church, a school, and a swimming hole. The settlement was abandoned and left to the elements when the Rockefellers bought up much of the land and transferred it to the National Park Service. In the 1990s the historical and cultural value of the site was recognized; the area was added to the National Register of Historic Places in 1997, and steps were taken to preserve the structures.

The **Antelope Flats** area—excellent for walking or biking on a flat, unpaved road—offers prime habitat for pronghorn, bison, moose, coyotes, ground squirrels, northern harriers, kestrels, and sage grouse. In the winter, the first mile (1.6 km) of Antelope Flats Road is plowed to a small parking area, giving visitors easy snowshoe or cross-country ski access to Moulton Ranch, one of the homesteads on Mormon Row. On the NPS website, visitors can access **audio tours** (www.nps.gov/grte/learn/photosmultimedia/audio-descriptions.

htm) of Mormon Row and other historical spots and places of interest.

★ Craig Thomas Discovery and Visitor Center

Twelve miles (19.3 km) north of Jackson in Moose, the **Craig Thomas Discovery and Visitor Center** (307/739-3399, 10am-4pm daily early Mar.-Apr., 8am-5pm daily May-early June and mid-Sept.-Oct., 8am-7pm daily early June-mid-Sept.) is, among other things, an architectural masterpiece, mimicking the nearby natural masterpiece of the Teton Range. The $21.6 million structure has more than 22,000 square feet (2,044 sq m) and is being used as a model for other national parks—in that more than half the funds used to build the center were donated by private individuals. The state-of-the-art facility, including video rivers that flow beneath your feet, places emphasis on the connection between humans and the natural world. Fantastic interpretive displays include a large relief model of the park that uses technology to show glacier movement and animal migration; there is also a photographic tribute to mountaineering in the region. Many of the excellent ranger-led hikes and tours depart from the Craig Thomas Discovery and Visitor Center.

Menors Ferry Historic District

In 1894, William D. Menor came to Jackson Hole and built a homestead along the Snake River. He built a ferryboat on cables to carry settlers and hopeful miners across the river, which was otherwise impassable during spring runoff. Entire wagon teams crossed on the ferry, paying $0.50 per trip, while a horse and rider paid $0.25. In 1918, Menor sold the ferry operation to Maud Noble, who doubled the fares ($1 for automobiles with local plates, $2 for out-of-staters) in the hope of attracting more tourists to the region. When a bridge was built in 1927, the ferry became obsolete, and in 1929 (the same year the park was created) Noble

sold her land to the Snake River Land Company. She had earlier donated a parcel for the construction of the Chapel of the Transfiguration.

Today, a replica of the ferryboat and cables has been built on-site, and visitors can meander down the 0.5-mile (0.8-km) self-guided **Menors Ferry Trail** past Menor's cabin, which doubled as a country store. On the NPS website, there are **audio tours** (www.nps.gov/grte/learn/photosmultimedia/audio-descriptions.htm) of Menors Ferry, Mormon Row, and the Murie Ranch, along with other historical spots and places of interest.

Chapel of the Transfiguration
Built in 1925 to serve the ranchers and dudes in the Teton Valley, the **Chapel of the Transfiguration** (307/733-2603, services 8am and 10am Sun. Memorial Day-Sept.) is a humble log cabin structure with the most spectacular mountain view framed in the window behind the altar. An Episcopal church, operated by St. John's in Jackson, it was built on land donated by Maud Noble and is a favorite spot for summer weddings. A candlelit Christmas night service and sunrise Easter service are particularly wonderful ways to experience this historic place of worship.

★ Laurance S. Rockefeller Preserve
Four miles (6.4 km) south of Moose on the Moose-Wilson Road, the former JY Ranch and longtime summer home of the Rockefeller family, known as the **Laurance S. Rockefeller Preserve** (307/739-3654, 9am-5pm daily late May-late Sept., center closed late Sept.-late May, trails open year-round), offers 8 miles (12.9 km) of trails through forest, wetlands, and meadows on reclaimed property along Phelps Lake and Lake Creek. The 1,106-acre preserve was donated to the Park Service in 2007 by the

Top to bottom: canoe for rent at Jenny Lake; Antelope Flats; old barn at Mormon Row.

Rockefeller family with the mission of giving people access to the natural world that Laurance Rockefeller found so inspiring and sustaining.

The Laurance S. Rockefeller Preserve Center is the first platinum-level LEED-certified building constructed in a national park and was designed to give visitors a sensory experience of the natural elements found on the preserve. A poem by beloved writer Terry Tempest Williams features prominently, and visitors can learn about the preserve and Rockefeller's beliefs about land stewardship in a comfortable and environmentally sustainable building. Several ranger programs, including sunrise hikes and children's programs, are available from the center daily throughout summer. The preserve is accessible by car from May to October.

Murie Ranch

The onetime STS Ranch and former residence of wilderness champions Olaus and Mardy Murie, the **Murie Ranch** (1 Murie Ranch Rd., Moose, 307/732-7752, www.tetonscience.org/murie-center/home, 9am-5pm Mon.-Fri. mid-Mar.-mid-Oct.) is dedicated to connecting people and wilderness. It is where the Wilderness Act was authored in the 1950s and early 1960s. The ranch itself is a National Historic Landmark and the site of ongoing conservation seminars and educational workshops. On-site accommodations are available to participants, and the entire facility can be rented for conservation education programs. An excellent library and bookstore is on-site, and rangers host naturalist programs throughout the summer. Free tours of the Murie home are given from 2:30pm to 3:30pm daily in summer.

Jenny Lake and Vicinity

Carved some 12,000 years ago by the same glaciers that dug out Cascade Canyon, Jenny Lake is perhaps the most picturesque and popular spot in the park.

The hiking—to places like Inspiration Point and the even more beautiful Leigh Lake—is sublime, and the water activities—scenic cruising, canoeing, kayaking, swimming, and fishing—are plentiful. The park's fanciest and most expensive lodging and dining can be found at the historic Jenny Lake Lodge.

In much the same way that Old Faithful embodies the Yellowstone experience for many visitors, so too does Jenny Lake conjure all that is wonderful about Grand Teton. A scenic drive from North Jenny Lake to South Jenny Lake skirts the water and affords breathtaking views of the Grand Teton, Teewinot, and Mount Owen. Those who are more interested in solitude would be well advised to get off the main drag here, away from the crowds and into the wilderness.

★ Jenny Lake

In 1872 an English-born mountain man, known widely as "Beaver Dick" Leigh for his enormous front teeth and his penchant for the animal, guided Ferdinand Hayden around the Tetons. Hayden named the alpine lake for Dick's wife, Jenny, a member of the Shoshone tribe. In the fall of 1876, pregnant Jenny took care of an ailing Native American woman, not knowing the woman had smallpox. Jenny and all four of her children became ill. Her baby was born just before Christmas and, along with Jenny and the other four children, died within a week. Beaver Dick buried his family in Jackson Hole.

Despite the tragic story of its namesake, Jenny Lake is indeed one of the most beautiful and visited spots in the park. From cruising across the lake to hiking along its shores, there are an endless number of ways to enjoy this idyllic spot.

★ Hidden Falls and Inspiration Point

One of the area's most popular hikes is to the spectacular **Hidden Falls.** From Jenny Lake's south shore, the hike follows

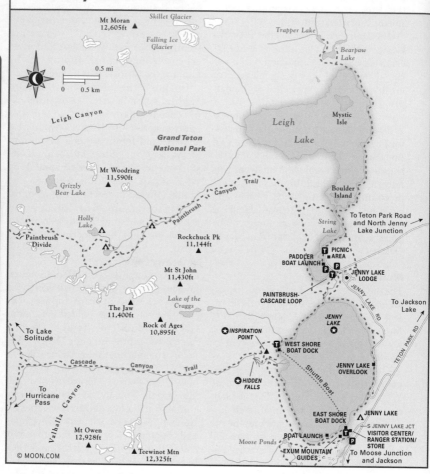

Jenny Lake Area

a moderate 2.5-mile (4-km) trail (one way) with 550 feet (168 m) of elevation gain to the cascade. Visitors who want to put fewer miles on their feet can take the **Jenny Lake Shuttle** (307/734-9227, www.jennylakeboating.com, 10am-4pm mid-May-early June, 7am-7pm early June-early Sept., round-trip $15 adults, $12 seniors, $8 children 2-11, one-way $9 adults, $6 children), which runs every 10-15 minutes throughout the day, to shorten the hike to 1 mile (1.6 km) with

150 feet (45.7 m) of elevation gain. The breathtaking overlook at **Inspiration Point** is visited via a 5.8-mile (9.3-km) round-trip hike with 700 feet (213.4 m) of elevation gain from the trailhead, or a 2.2-mile (3.5-km) round-trip with 420 feet (128 m) of elevation gain from the boat shuttle.

Leigh Lake
Named for mountain man "Beaver Dick" Leigh, Leigh Lake is much quieter and

perhaps even more beautiful than the more southerly Jenny Lake. The lake offers unrivaled views of Mount Moran, Mount Woodring, and Rockchuck Peak, and it is dotted with sandy beaches ideal for picnics. The 5.4-mile (8.7-km) round-trip (out-and-back) trail is flat and weaves in and out of the forest with a constant water view. The Leigh Lake Trailhead is at the northwest corner of the String Lake Picnic Area. The trail can be hiked as early as May or June, depending on snowmelt, and is typically passable well into September. Although popular, Leigh Lake does not attract the crowds that Jenny Lake does.

Adventure and Recreation

Hiking
Flagg Ranch and Colter Bay
Colter Bay Lakeshore Trail
Distance: 2-mile (3.2-km) loop
Duration: 1.5 hours
Elevation change: 100 feet (30 m)
Effort: easy
Trailhead: Colter Bay Visitor Center

For a short walk with minimum hills and maximum scenery, the Colter Bay Lakeshore Trail provides a double loop that follows the shoreline of the small promontory with multiple inlets. Begin on the paved trail that rims the north shore of the **marina** to tour a breakwater spit. After walking the spit, head west on the trail toward a tiny **isthmus** of rocks that connects the two parts of the peninsula. Once across the isthmus, go either way to circle the **1.1-mile loop.** Side trails reach beaches that yield views across Jackson Lake to the Teton Mountains. Upon returning to the causeway, follow your original tracks back to the visitors center, or take the other **spur trail** northeast toward the swimming beach and then return to the visitors center on a trail paralleling the road.

Heron Pond and Swan Lake
Distance: 2.6 miles (4.2 km) round-trip
Duration: 1.5 hours
Elevation change: 200 feet (61 m)
Effort: easy
Trailhead: Swan, Heron, and Hermitage Point Trailhead at Colter Bay Village

A series of ponds named for birds flanks the hillside east of Colter Bay Village. They have significant growths of yellow pond lilies, leaving little visible water, but make for prime habitat for a variety of wildlife: sandhill cranes, trumpeter swans, osprey, muskrats, river otters, and great blue herons. You'll pass multiple junctions, all well signed on this forest-and-meadow trail. A map from the visitors center can help in navigating the junctions. Be ready for mosquitoes. Hikers can also access this loop from Jackson Lake Lodge, which will add 10 miles round-trip.

The trail starts on an **old service road** that curves around the south edge of Colter Bay. After leaving the bay, climb over a loosely forested hill to **Heron Pond,** where the trail follows the northeastern shore to several ultra-scenic viewpoints of Mount Moran and Rockchuck Peak in the Teton Mountains. At the southeast corner of the pond, turn left at the trail junction to reach **Swan Lake.** After following the shore northward, the trail returns to a junction where going straight will curve around **Jackson Lake Overlook** back to the trailhead.

Hermitage Point
Distance: 9.7 miles (15.6 km) round-trip
Duration: 5 hours
Elevation change: 690 feet (210 m)
Effort: moderate
Trailhead: Hermitage Point Trailhead at Colter Bay Village

The hike out to Hermitage Point can take in Jackson Lake Overlook, Heron Pond, and Swan Lake. Hermitage Point sits on the end of a long forest-and-meadow peninsula. The rocky beach at the point offers a scenic place for lunch on Jackson

Finding a Guide

Setting off into the wilds of Grand Teton National Park can be slightly intimidating, making guided tours a good option. The Park Service maintains a list of licensed, permitted, and park-approved guides.

For any type of technical **rock climbing,** a guide is as necessary as a helmet and rope. **Exum Mountain Guides** (307/733-2297, www.exumguides.com) has been offering instruction and guided mountain climbing since 1931, making it the oldest guide service in North America and certainly one of the most prestigious. Exum offers numerous programs, from easy day climbing for families with kids to guided expeditions up the 13,770-foot (4,197-m) Grand Teton. Detailed information, including climbing routes and trail conditions, can be found at www.tetonclimbing.blogspot.com.

The Hole Hiking Experience (307/690-4453, www.holehike.com) offers a range of **guided hikes** and **snowshoe or ski tours** in and around the park for all interests and ability levels, from sunrise or sunset discovery tours to all-day wildlife-watching hikes. Kids will love the family day hikes with fun survival-like activities that include eating "lemon drop" ants and using butterfly nets. Winter cross-country ski and snowshoe tours are guided by naturalists and show off the best winter has to offer.

There are several options for guided **horseback riding** trips, May-September, from a number of lodges in the park, including Colter Bay Village, Flagg Ranch, and Jackson Lake Lodge. The **Grand Teton Lodge Company** (307/543-2811, www.gtlc.com) can arrange everything from a horseback ride ($45-90 1-3 hours) to breakfast wagon rides ($45) and dinner rides ($79-84 adults, $59-64 children 8-13) to pony rides ($5). All riders in the park must be at least eight years old and under 225 pounds (102 kg).

With so many varied bodies of water, there are a number of **fishing** outfitters that can guide any type of trip you can dream up. A good place to start is the **Grand Teton Lodge Company** (307/543-3100, www.gtlc.com), which can arrange trips from any of the accommodations inside the park. Fishing trips on the Snake River or Jackson Lake can also be arranged through the lakefront **Signal Mountain Lodge** (307/543-2831, www.signalmountainlodge.com) or **Grand Teton Fly Fishing** (307/690-0910, www.grandtetonflyfishing.com).

Rafting is popular in Grand Teton National Park, and there are 11 licensed outfitters to guide visitors down the Snake River. As with all activities, **Grand Teton Lodge Company** (307/543-3100, www.gtlc.com) can make arrangements for the park's most popular 10-mile (16.1-km) scenic float. Other outfitters include **Barker-Ewing** (307/733-1800 or 800/365-1800, www.barkerewing.com) and **Solitude Float Trips** (307/733-2871, www.grand-teton-scenic-floats.com).

Throughout the year, Park Service rangers offer excellent **naturalist-guided tours.** Late December-March, depending on conditions, daily guided **snowshoe hikes** depart from the **Craig Thomas Discovery and Visitor Center** (307/739-3399, reservations required, $5 donation suggested). During the summer months, the range of offerings is vast—from 30-minute map chats and campfire programs to three-hour hikes, evening astronomy programs, and tipi demos. For more information on ranger programs, pick up the park newspaper at any of the entrance stations, call 307/739-3300, or check out the visitors centers in Moose, Jenny Lake, Colter Bay, and the Laurance S. Rockefeller Preserve.

Lake with views of several islands, Mount Moran, and the Teton Mountains. But be prepared for winds on this treeless point, mosquitoes in early summer, and shadeless heat in midsummer. With plenty of wetlands on this trail, you'll see tracks: moose, bears, and deer. While the main trail junctions are well signed, plenty of unmarked spur trails head off to viewpoints and explorations. Pick up a map at the visitors center to aid with navigation.

Grand View Trails

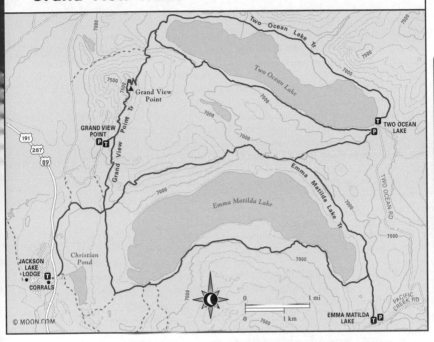

For the quickest route to the point, start on the **old service road** at the trailhead. At every junction, **turn right** to reach Hermitage Point via the west side of the peninsula. The route will take you past **Jackson Lake Overlook** and **Heron Pond.** The trail goes through a lodgepole forest broken by sagebrush and wildflower meadows with lupine, paintbrush, and harebells until it emerges at **Hermitage Point.** From the point, continue up the east side of the peninsula. When you reach a broad meadow, the view eastward spans Willow Flats, Jackson Lake Lodge a few miles away, the Absaroka Mountains, and the Teton Wilderness. At the next trail junction, **go left** to return to your previous trail and back to the trailhead via Heron Pond or Swan Lake.

Jackson Lake Lodge and Signal Mountain
Grand View Point

Distance: 2.2-8.8 miles (3.5-14.2 km) round-trip

Duration: 3-5 hours

Elevation change: 550-800 feet (168-244 m)

Effort: moderate

Trailhead: Grand View Point

Directions: Drive 0.9 mile north of Jackson Lake Lodge on U.S. 89/191/287. Take the unmarked, rough, narrow dirt road east, veering right at 0.1 mile and climbing 0.7 mile farther to the trailhead.

Multiple trailheads lead to Grand View Point, an aptly named 7,286-foot summit with huge panoramic views of Jackson Lake and the Tetons. From the signed Grand View summit, you overlook Two Ocean and Emma Matilda Lakes. West of the summit, a large rocky bluff takes in the jagged peaks of Mount Moran and the Cathedral group of Grand Teton, Mount Owen, and Teewinot Mountain.

The shortest route, a **2.2-mile** out-and-back with only 550 feet of climbing, goes from the **Grand View Point** parking area to the viewpoint. From the trailhead, hike up a steep 0.2-mile connector trail to reach the **Grand View Point Trail.** The trail ascends steeply through meadows and forest.

From **Jackson Lake Lodge,** the trail is **6.1 miles** round-trip with 790 feet elevation gain. From the trailhead near the corrals, cross under the highway and gently ascend across sagebrush meadows. At **Christian Pond** (mostly grown in with greenery), take the left junction toward Grand View Point. En route to the point, you'll pass several trail junctions. At the **four-way junction,** turn left and continue straight, climbing into the forest and meadows of pink sticky geranium. Most of the elevation gain packs into the last mile.

The longest route at **8.8 miles** and 800 feet elevation gain goes from **Two Ocean Lake Trailhead.** Because Grand View Point sits above the head of the lake, hikers can loop around the lake, adding in an ascent of Grand View Point. From the trailhead, circle the north side of **Two Ocean Trail** through meadows and forest to the junction at the head of the lake. Turn right for 0.3 mile to another junction, where ascending straight up the ridge leads to Grand View summit and then the overlook. Return to the head-of-the-lake trail junction and turn right to circle back around the forested south side of Two Ocean Lake.

Two Ocean Lake

Distance: 6.4 miles (10.3 km) round-trip
Duration: 3 hours
Elevation change: 395 feet (120 m)
Effort: easy
Trailhead: Two Ocean Lake Trailhead
Directions: From Highway 89/191/287 one mile north of Jackson Lake Junction, take the paved Pacific Creek Road 2 miles to a junction with Two Ocean Road. Turn left and drive 2.4 miles on dirt road to the trailhead at Two Ocean Lake.

The view from Inspiration Point is worth every step of the hike.

A mostly flat trail loops around Two Ocean Lake, a trough gouged from the Pacific Creek glacial lobe. Two Ocean Plateau, which straddles the Continental Divide, sheds water to the Pacific and Atlantic Oceans, hence the name. However, the misnamed Two Ocean Lake only drains to the Pacific. The trail travels through forests and meadows, with more open meadows on the north shore and denser forest on the south shore. In June, yellow arrowleaf balsamroot dominates the meadows, while in fall, golden aspens light up the hillside. Distant views of the Tetons line the horizon. The lake is home to trumpeter swans, waterfowl, and moose. Bears move in for food sources: cow parsnip in early summer and patches of huckleberries and thimbleberries in midsummer.

From the trailhead, start on the **north-shore trail** for the bigger views first. The meadow-lined trail goes 3.4 miles with a short climb and descent to a **junction** at the head of the lake. From the junction, a steep trail grunts up to **Grand View Point.** If you tack on the point up and back, it will add 2.2 miles to your total. To continue around the lake from the junction, turn left to return 3 miles along the forested south side to the trailhead.

Many hikers opt to combine Two Ocean Lake with **Emma Matilda Lake** and **Grand View Point.** The distance ranges 9.3-13.2 miles depending on the routes chosen around the lakes.

Emma Matilda Lake

Distance: 9.9-10.7 miles (15.9-17.2 km) round-trip
Duration: 5-6 hours
Elevation change: 1,050 feet (320 m)
Effort: moderate
Trailhead: Emma Matilda Trailhead on Pacific Creek Road or Two Ocean Lake Trailhead at Two Ocean Lake
Directions: From Highway 89/191/287 one mile north of Jackson Lake Junction, take the paved Pacific Creek Road 1.5 miles to the Emma Matilda Trailhead for the shorter loop. For the longer loop, drive 0.5 mile farther to Two Ocean Road. Turn left and drive 2.4 miles on dirt road to the trailhead at Two Ocean Lake.

Two different trailheads access Emma Matilda Lake. From the **Emma Matilda Trailhead** on Pacific Creek Road, hike **0.6 mile** to the lake. From **Two Ocean Lake Trailhead,** hike **1 mile** to the lake. Once there, the trail loops **8.7 miles** around Emma Matilda Lake. Circling the lake will take you through two lightning fire zones from burns in 1994 and 1998 where new growth is changing the flora.

On the north shore of the lake, the trail climbs about 400 feet up a ridge that yields views of the lake backed by the Teton Mountains. A loose Douglas fir forest covers the ridge, and you can see Jackson Lake Lodge in the distance. Near the trail junction that goes to Jackson Lake Lodge, a **spur trail** cuts to **Lookout Rock** for views of the lake. From the junction, bear left to circle the south shore of the lake, where the trail travels through a dense forest of spruce and fir.

From Jackson Lake Lodge, trails link into the Emma Matilda Loop. The total distance of the loop is **10.7 miles,** but

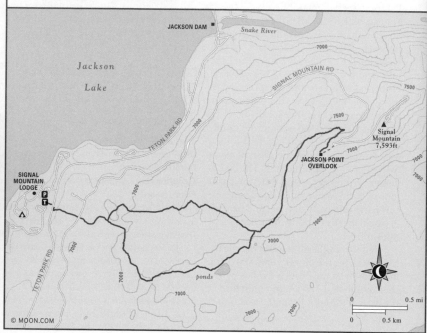

Signal Mountain

elevation gain is about 750 feet. As another alternative, many hikers opt to combine Two Ocean Lake with Emma Matilda Lake and Grand View Point. From the Two Ocean Lake Trailhead, the distance ranges 9.3-13.2 miles depending on the routes chosen around the lakes.

Signal Mountain

Distance: 13.4 miles (21.6 km) round-trip
Duration: 6.5 hours
Elevation change: 920 feet (280 m)
Effort: moderately strenuous
Trailhead: At Signal Mountain Lodge, park in the main lot and walk uphill opposite the employee housing to the trailhead.

Although you can drive to viewpoints on Signal Mountain, a trail also climbs to Jackson Point Overlook near the summit. Because of the mountain's island-like perch in the middle of Jackson Hole, it offers tremendous views of Jackson Lake, Jackson Hole, and the Teton Mountains despite its diminutive size in comparison to surrounding peaks. In its first mile, the trail crosses **Teton Park Road** and **Signal Mountain Road.** Once past those, you'll feel more in the wilderness.

At the **signed junction,** opt for ascending via the right fork to the ponds. This portion loops through meadows, wetlands, ponds, aspens, and conifers, a good mix of habitat for wildlife. At a second junction, the climb to the summit begins. The final ascent to **Jackson Point Overlook** is steep, gaining 600 feet in one mile. Intermittent Douglas fir and aspen offer bits of shade on a hot day, and the sagebrush meadows yield bursts of wildflowers in early summer including cinquefoil and pink sticky geranium. At Jackson Point Overlook, the view is huge. Lower forested ridges below are glacial moraines from 15,000 years ago, with

Taggart and Bradley Lakes

glacial kettles or potholes to the southeast. These features often get lost below the sweeping panorama of the Teton Mountains, Jackson Lake, Jackson Hole, and the Snake River.

Moran to Moose
Taggart and Bradley Lakes

Distance: 3-5.9 miles (4.8-9.5 km) round-trip
Duration: 2-4 hours
Elevation change: 400-900 feet (122-274 m)
Effort: easy to moderate
Trailhead: Taggart Lake Trailhead off Teton Park Road between Jenny Lake and Moose

Two lower-elevation lakes cower around 7,000 feet at the base of Avalanche and Garnet Canyons. For a shorter three-mile hike, go to Taggart Lake and back. It's scenic, but the longer 5.9-mile loop adds on Bradley Lake, where you can stare straight up at Grand Teton. When the lake is glassy, the Grand reflects like

a mirror. Get an early start in order to claim a parking spot at this popular trailhead. Anglers fish both lakes, and on hot days, both lakes make good swimming holes.

From the trailhead, the trail curves north to cross a tumbling stream before ascending through conifers and meadows growing on glacial moraines to a **signed junction** at 1.1 miles. If you are planning to hike both lakes, you will loop back to this junction. To reach **Taggart,** turn left to hike 0.5 mile to the lake. Explore the small peninsula to the south for a place to enjoy the water and views.

To continue the loop to **Bradley Lake,** circle north around the shore of Taggart Lake to climb two switchbacks that crest a forested glacial moraine. After dropping to a **signed junction,** turn left to visit Bradley Lake. Beaches flank the east shore while the north side contains a footbridge crossing the outlet. After the lake, retrace your steps back to the last junction and take the fork heading left to climb over the moraine again and complete the loop to the first junction to return to the trailhead.

Phelps Lake

Distance: 1.8-9.9 miles (2.9-15.9 km) round-trip
Duration: 2-5 hours
Elevation change: 350-975 feet (107-297 m)
Effort: easy to moderate
Trailhead: Laurance S. Rockefeller Preserve Center or Death Canyon Trailhead on Moose-Wilson Road north of Granite Canyon Entrance
Directions: To reach Death Canyon Trailhead from the signed turnoff, drive one mile on pavement followed by one mile of rugged rock, mud, and dirt road (high-clearance vehicles only). Park at the end of the pavement or at a pullout on the dirt road (add one mile to walk the dirt road).

A maze of trails surrounds the low-elevation Phelps Lake in the Laurance S. Rockefeller Preserve, a special area where hiking the trails is more about the experience than reaching destinations. Visiting the preserve's center adds to the hiking experience. Trails circle the lake, which sits at 6,645 feet at the bottom of Open and Death Canyons. From various viewpoints around the lake, hikers are rewarded with stunning views of the Teton Mountains. The lake provides a year-round destination, although you'll need skis or snowshoes in winter.

Most hikers opt to park at the **Laurance S. Rockefeller Preserve Center.** Arrive before 9am to claim a parking spot in the small 50-car lot that is designed to limit crowds and create a climate of solitude. If it's full, you'll need to hike via the Death Canyon Trailhead. From the center, you can design your own route through the maze of trails. Junctions are well signed to help in selecting routes. The shortest and easiest route to Phelps Lake is the **Lake Creek-Woodland Trail Loop** (3.1 miles). The loop tours forests and meadows on both sides of a creek, offering opportunities to watch moose. At the lake,

enjoy contemplation from several different constructed rock-slab overlooks. The **Aspen Ridge-Boulder Ridge Loop** (5.8 miles) climbs through large talus fields and aspens that shimmer gold in fall to reach Phelps Lake. The longest hike, the **Phelps Lake Loop** (6.6 miles), climbs via Lake Creek to reach the lake and then loops around the lake for a changing perspective on the Teton Mountains.

From **Death Canyon Trailhead,** climb 400 feet in 0.9 mile through Douglas firs and aspens to **Phelps Lake Overlook,** which takes in the lake plus the Gros Ventre Mountains. You can appreciate the view from here, or drop to the lake. To descend to the lake, drop westward down switchbacks to a trail junction, and turn left. At the lake, a 4.5-mile trail loops around the shoreline. The return to the overlook requires climbing 575 feet in elevation. The lake loop tallies 9.9 miles with 975 feet elevation gain.

Death Canyon, Static Peak Divide, and Fox Creek Pass

Distance: 16.3-18.4 miles (26.2-29.6 km) round-trip
Duration: 9-12 hours
Elevation change: 2,800-5,250 feet (853-1,600 m)
Effort: very strenuous
Trailhead: Death Canyon Trailhead on Moose-Wilson Road
Directions: To reach Death Canyon Trailhead from the signed turnoff, drive one mile on pavement followed by one mile of rugged rock, mud, and dirt road (high-clearance vehicles only). Park at the end of the pavement or at a pullout on the dirt road (add one mile to walk the dirt road).

Death Canyon is a place to go to get away from hordes of people. This trail's destinations require lengthy hikes with major elevation gain. Rewards are huge, with views of glaciated canyons, alpine wonderlands, and vertical rock walls. The two main destinations are Static Peak Divide with 5,250 feet of elevation gain, and Fox Creek Pass on the Teton Crest with 18.4 miles of hiking round-trip. Both have knee-pounding returns. Many hikers opt for backpacking for these trails, although

Phelps Lake and Death Canyon

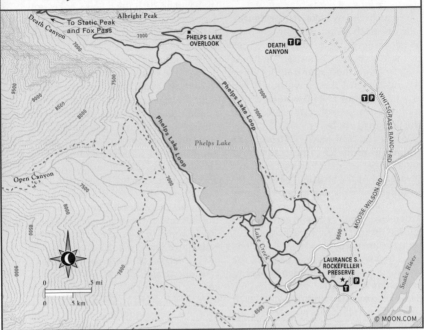

ADVENTURE AND RECREATION

strong hikers can do them in a day. You may need ice axes for steep snowfields that linger well into August in the upper elevations.

The trail traverses 2.2 miles along the base of **Albright Peak** to squeeze through the boulder-strewn canyon carved by a glacier 15,000 years ago. Flanked by immense rock walls, the trail steepens through avalanche swaths, talus fields, and coniferous forests to reach a **patrol cabin,** listed in the National Register of Historic Places, at 7.9 miles.

From the junction at the patrol cabin, take the north fork up the ultra-steep trail that climbs 4.1 miles up the rocky scree and cliff ridge to the 10,790-foot **Static Peak Divide.** Views up-valley take in Fox Pass and Death Canyon Shelf. Another 300 feet in elevation follows a climber's trail to the summit for views of Buck Mountain and Grand Teton. For the

9,570 foot **Fox Creek Pass,** take the south fork to follow the less steep trail through meadows and sparse trees 5.5 miles along Death Canyon Creek. This fork eventually reaches the **Teton Crest** and the pass, with miles of immense meadows below Spearhead Mountain.

Jenny Lake and Vicinity
Jenny Lake Loop
Distance: 7.1 miles (11.4 km) round-trip
Duration: 3.5 hours
Elevation change: 456 feet (139 m)
Effort: moderate
Trailhead: String Lake Trailhead or Jenny Lake Village. Plan to arrive early to claim a parking spot at the popular trailheads.

This trail loops completely around Jenny Lake; part of the path is paved near the visitors center, but most of the trail is dirt. Unless you hike in early morning or late evening, expect to meet crowds in midsummer. All trail junctions are well signed; unsigned spur trails cut to the lakeshore for views or fishing.

From the **Jenny Lake Visitor Center,** take the north trail heading to Big Lake Overlook. From there, turn right to circle the lake counterclockwise. You'll pass Rock Beach, a short **spur trail** (for those staying at Jenny Lake Campground), and eventually **Jenny Lake Overlook** as the trail cuts 3 miles between the lake and North Jenny Lake Drive.

When the trail reaches **String Lake Trailhead,** head 0.3 mile west, crossing a bridge over the String Lake outlet stream. At the junction, head left for 1.7 miles above the north shore of Jenny Lake through the remains of the 1999 Alder Fire. You'll pass large boulders (glacial erratics) before reaching multiple trail junctions. Continue straight as trails break off to **Cascade Canyon,** the boat dock (two trails), **Hidden Falls,** and **Inspiration Point.** After crossing Cascade Creek on a **wooden bridge,** you'll reach another junction. Continue straight for 1.5 miles south along the shore of Jenny Lake, passing two junctions with the upper traverse followed by two junctions for **Moose Pond Loop;** stay left at all junctions. Pass the boat launch to reach the **bridge** crossing the Jenny Lake outlet at the tour boat dock.

Hidden Falls and Inspiration Point
Distance: 2.4-7.2 miles (3.9-11.6 km) round-trip
Duration: 1.5-4 hours
Elevation change: 1,250 feet (381 m)
Effort: moderately strenuous
Trailhead: Jenny Lake Visitor Center

This hike combines Hidden Falls, a 200-foot tumbler in Cascade Canyon, and Inspiration Point, a rocky knoll at 7,257 feet squeezed between Mount Teewinot and Mount St. John. Given the point's perch, the scope of views from the summit lives up to its name. You'll look straight down on the blue waters of Jenny Lake, up to the peaks on both sides, and across Jackson Hole to the Gros Ventre

Mountains. Hordes of hikers clog this trail, except in early morning or late in the day. The $18 million Jenny Lake project upgraded the eroded trails in 2015-2017 with 5,000 linear feet of stonework. The boat shuttle (fee) reduces this hike to a 2.4-mile loop from the west boat dock.

From the **visitors center,** head west toward the **boat dock** and cross the **bridge** at the outlet of Jenny Lake at Cottonwood Creek. Continue 0.9 mile west along the south shore of Jenny Lake, passing the boat launch and two junctions for **Moose Pond Loop.** At the second Moose Pond Loop junction, take either the upper or lower trails to reach Hidden Falls Trail; the lower trail travels 1.5 miles along the scenic lakeshore. Before reaching the Chasm Bridge over Cascade Creek, you'll come to a junction for **Hidden Falls.** Turn left to ascend the south side of Cascade Creek. At the next junction, continue straight to reach the spur that goes to Hidden Falls Overlook. Hikers wanting to skip Inspiration Point can drop back one junction to loop across Cascade Creek on the middle bridge and descend the creek's north side to the **Chasm Bridge** over a frothy spillway and the return trail.

To continue to Inspiration Point from the overlook, cross the two upper **bridges** below the falls for more views, then climb four south-facing switchbacks to **Inspiration Point.** (The slope can get hot in midsummer; mornings are best for hiking to the point.) At Inspiration Point, plenty of other trails cut off to various viewpoints and places for lunch. From the point, retrace your steps back to the visitors center or loop west to connect with the **Cascade Canyon Horse Trail** and descend the north side of the canyon toward Jenny Lake. After reaching the **Jenny Lake Trail,** turn south, passing two boat dock junctions and crossing the lower bridge over Cascade Creek to reach the junction for the lakeshore trail back to the visitors center. Retrace your earlier steps.

String and Leigh Lakes

Distance: 3.7 miles (6 km) round-trip
Duration: 2 hours
Elevation change: 325 feet (99 m)
Effort: easy
Trailhead: String Lake Trailhead from North Jenny Lake

This trail circles String Lake and takes in the southern tip of Leigh Lake; it's a less-crowded loop than Jenny Lake. Hike counterclockwise to get the big views down the western side of the loop.

Start from the **String Lake Trailhead** and hike 1.4 miles north along the forested eastern shore of String Lake. Stop frequently along the shallow sand-bottomed lake to look for moose and waterfowl. To the north, Mount Moran rises into view while Teewinot Mountain pokes above the trees southward. At the south end of Leigh Lake, a trail junction splits right and continues up the east side of Leigh Lake to Bearpaw Lake. Stay straight instead to follow a **short spur** to the edge of the deeper **Leigh Lake** for the views.

Return to the junction and head west to cross the **bridge** at the rocky outlet of Leigh Lake. Enjoy the view of Boulder Island from the bridge, then continue westward as the trail climbs 0.7 mile through a lodgepole forest to a second **junction.** Turn left to break out of the woods and onto the open slopes of **Rockchuck Peak** and Mount St. John with views of Teewinot Mountain. The trail gradually descends 1.6 miles to the foot of String Lake where it meets the **Jenny Lake Trail.** Turn left and cross the **bridge** at the outlet of String Lake to return to the String Lake Trailhead.

Hikers can add on to this trail with a round-trip walk to Leigh Lake (1.8 miles) or by going past Leigh Lake to Bearpaw Lake (8 miles round-trip).

Biking

Some of the best biking in the park is on the paved **multiuse path** that heads north from Jackson and parallels U.S. 89/191 to Antelope Flats Road, where secondary paved roads meander through sagebrush flats. From Moose Junction, the path follows the Teton Park Road to **South Jenny Lake.** A 7-mile (11.3-km) scenic loop starts at South Jenny Lake, follows the Teton Park Road for 3 miles (4.9 km), and then turns left at North Jenny Lake Junction and left again on the one-way return to South Jenny Lake.

North of Colter Bay, near the **Flagg Ranch,** is **Grassy Lake Road,** a 52-mile (84-km) dirt road—great for mountain biking—that follows an ancient Indian thoroughfare all the way to Ashton, Idaho. Along the way are hiking trails, streams, ponds, and splendid scenery.

A nice area for bicyclists is in the vicinity of **Two Ocean Road,** southeast of **Jackson Lake Lodge** and northeast of **Signal Mountain Lodge.** The road itself is just 3 miles (4.8 km) long, but the scenery is sublime for a short, sweet ride. **River Road** is 15 miles (24 km) of gravel running along the west side of the Snake River between Signal Mountain and Cottonwood Creek. Do remember that this is bear country; every precaution—including bear spray—should be taken.

There are plenty of biking opportunities on the paved and unpaved portions of **Antelope Flats Road,** which runs all the way to Kelly, just over 4 miles (6.4 km) away; the **Shadow Mountain Road;** and the **Moose-Wilson Road** linking Moose and the Laurance S. Rockefeller Preserve.

Bike racks are available at Taggart Lake Trailhead and in Moose. Bicycles can be rented from **Dornans** (12170 Dornan Rd., Moose, 307/733-2415, www.dornans.com, 9am-6am daily). In addition to a range of adult bikes ($16-25/hour, $38-55/half day, $44-65/day or 24 hours), Dornan's rents kids' bikes, Trail-a-Bikes, bike racks, and Burley carriers for toddlers.

Boating and Fishing

With so much beautiful water in the park, boating is a fantastic way to explore.

Rafting on the **Snake River,** canoeing or kayaking on any number of lakes, or cruising across **Jackson Lake**—there are options for adrenaline junkies and die-hard landlubbers alike.

On the shores of Jackson Lake, by far the largest body of water in the park, **Colter Bay** and the **Colter Bay Village Marina** (307/543-2811, ext. 1097, or 307/543-2811, www.gtlc.com) are excellent launching points for a variety of boating expeditions. From the marina, you can arrange cruises, canoe or kayak excursions, motorboat rentals, and guided fishing trips.

The best-known trout stream in the region is the Snake River, which winds more than 60 miles (97 km) on lazy flats and then blasts through the Snake River Canyon, which offers more white-knuckle rafting than graceful casting. The Upper Snake, much of which is in Grand Teton National Park, is characterized by braided channels with cutbanks and logjams, and the water holds native cutthroats. Drift boating is popular as a way to maximize the water covered (and scenery enjoyed), but there are ample opportunities to get out and wade-fish. Guided trips on both the Snake River and Jackson Lake can be arranged through **Grand Teton Lodge Company** (307/543-3100 and ask for the marina, www.gtlc.com), from $112 per hour for 1-2 adults with a two-hour minimum and $23/hour per additional person; day trips start at $600 per day for 1-2 anglers and $125 each additional person. The price includes use of rods, reels, and waders, as well as transportation and a streamside lunch. From **Signal Mountain Lodge** (307/543-2831, www.signalmountainlodge.com), anglers can go out with experienced guides (late May-mid-Sept.) in pursuit of Jackson Lake's cutthroat, brown, and lake trout for $130 per hour for 1-2 people (two-hour minimum) and $35/hour per additional person; half-day trips are $370 for 1-2 people and $109 per additional person. Half-day and multiple-day

fishing trips on Jackson Lake can also be arranged through **Grand Teton Fly Fishing** (307/690-0910 or 307/690-4347, www.grandtetonflyfishing.com, all-day floats from $625, half-day floats from $550 for two people). Fishing is also permitted in Jenny, String, Leigh, Bradley, and Taggart Lakes.

With all the blue-ribbon water in the region, Jackson has no shortage of fly-fishing guides or fly shops. Among the best is a small outfit, **Teton Fly Fishing** (544 Clark St., 307/413-1215, www. tetonflyfishing.com), run by Nate Bennett, who loves teaching his clients about the art of fishing as much as he loves hooking a fish. He books only one trip daily so that the pace can be less breakneck and far more enjoyable. Bennett gets his clients on a variety of types of water and, like a good fish whisperer, somehow gets the fish to bite. An artist by training, Bennett ties all his own flies and loves to share. His trips ($495 half day, $535 full day for up to 2 anglers) on the Snake, Salt, and Green Rivers include all equipment, flies, transportation, streamside lunch, and full access to his unlimited knowledge and expertise.

A Wyoming **fishing license** is required for all fishing in the park and can be purchased at **Snake River Angler at Dornan's** (12170 Dornan Rd., 307/733-3699, www.snakeriverangler.com), **Signal Mountain Marina** (307/543-2831, www. signalmountainlodge.com), or **Colter Bay Marina** (307/543-3100, www.gtlc.com). Pick up a fishing brochure from any of the visitors centers to learn about park regulations.

Scenic 10-mile (16.1-km) floats down the Snake River can be arranged through **Signal Mountain Lodge** (307/543-2831, www.signalmountainlodge.com, $80 adults, $50 children 6-11), **Grand Teton Lodge Company** (307/543-3100, www. gtlc.com, $78 adults, $50 children 6-11), or **Solitude Float Trips** (307/733-2871, www.grand-teton-scenic-floats.com,

$80 adults, $60 children 5-15, $900 for a private boat for up to 12 guests). Most floats on the Snake River inside the park last about two hours. Both GTLC and Solitude offer a wonderful sunrise float, perfect for spotting wildlife. GTLC also offers four-hour luncheon floats May through Labor Day (Mon.-Sat., $89 adults, $59 children 6-11) and dinner floats (4:30pm Tues.-Thurs. and Sat. May-early Sept., $95 adults, $65 children 6-11) with fun riverside cookouts.

Scenic one-hour **cruises** (noon and 2pm daily mid-May-early June and early Sept.-late Sept.; 11am, 2pm, and 5pm daily early June-early Sept., $19 adults, $17 seniors 62 and over, $11 children 2-11), **boat shuttles** to Cascade Canyon hiking trails (round-trip $15 adults, $8 children, depart every 10-15 minutes), and canoe or kayak **rentals** ($20/hour, $75/day) can be arranged through **Jenny Lake Boating** (307/734-9227, www.jennylakeboating.com).

Human-powered boats such as kayaks and canoes are permitted on Emma Matilda Lake and Two Ocean Lake, east of Jackson Lake Lodge. Jackson Lake is open to motorboats, human-powered boats, sailboats, waterskiing, and windsurfers. **Permits** are required for motorized boats ($40) and nonmotorized crafts ($10), including SUPs, and can be purchased at the visitors centers in Moose, Jenny Lake (cash only), or Colter Bay. A variety of boats can be rented through **Signal Mountain Lodge** (307/543-2831, www.signalmountainlodge.com), including deck cruisers ($145/hour, $725/day for up to 10 people), pontoon boats ($110/hour, $535/day for up to 10 people), runabouts ($71/hour, $349/day for up to 5 people), fishing boats ($42/hour, $185/day for up to 5 people), canoes ($25/hour, $99/day for up to 3 people), and sea kayaks ($21/hour, $89/day single, or $26/hour, $110/day for 2 people). The **Grand Teton Lodge Company** (307/543-3100, www.gtlc.com) can also arrange various boat rentals throughout the park.

Horseback Riding

The **Grand Teton Lodge Company** (307/543-2811, www.gtlc.com) can arrange one-hour ($48) or two-hour ($75) horseback tours that depart from Jackson Lake Lodge and can include trips to Emma Matilda Lake and an overlook of Oxbow Bend. All riders must be at least eight years old and under 225 pounds (102 kg).

Winter Sports

In the winter, when snow blankets the park, most park roads are closed to vehicles. The 14-mile (22.5-km) unplowed section of **Teton Park Road,** from the Taggart Lake Trailhead parking area to Signal Mountain Lodge, is groomed and open to **cross-country skiing** and **snowshoeing.** Dogs are permitted on leash. Accessible trailheads from the groomed section of the road include **Jenny Lake Trail** (8 mi/12.9 km round-trip, 200 feet elevation gain, easy) and the **Taggart Lake-Beaver Creek Loop** (4 mi/6.4 km round-trip, 500 feet elevation gain, moderate-difficult).

Some popular destinations for cross-country skiing and snowshoeing expeditions include the **Phelps Lake Overlook** (5.2 mi/8.4 km round-trip, 730 feet elevation gain, moderate), **Phelps Lake** (4 mi/6.4 km round-trip, 300 feet elevation gain, moderate), and the **Moose-Wilson Road** (5.8 mi/9.3 km round-trip, 500 feet elevation gain, easy). All three trailheads can be accessed from parking areas on the Moose-Wilson Road, including the Granite Canyon Trailhead (from Teton Village) and the gate at the Death Canyon road (coming from Moose).

In Jackson Hole, cross-country skis and snowshoes can be purchased or rented from **Skinny Skis** (65 W. Deloney Ave., 307/733-6094 or 888/733-7205, www.skinnyskis.com, general touring package $20/full day, skate-skiing package $25/full day) or **Teton Mountaineering** (170 N. Cache St., 307/733-3595, www.tetonmtn.com).

None of the park trails are marked or flagged, so planning and caution are important. Skiers and snowshoers should always carry water, high-energy snacks, and additional weather-appropriate clothing. For those who want to cover ground with a ranger, **guided snowshoe hikes** (307/739-3399, Tues., Thurs., and Sat. late Dec.-mid-Mar.) are offered three times a week from late December through mid-March. Call for more details or to make reservations.

Food

Flagg Ranch and Colter Bay

The main lodge at Headwaters Lodge & Cabins at Flagg Ranch is the center of all activity at the ranch. It has a gas station, a general store, and **Sheffields Restaurant & Bar** (800/443-2311, www. gtlc.com, 6:30am-10am, 11:30am-2pm, and 5:30pm-9:30pm daily June-late Sept., $20-31), which serves a solid range of local cuisine—including bison and elk meat loaf and Wyoming prime rib—in a family-friendly setting.

The **Café Court Pizzeria** (11am-10pm daily late May-early Sept., $8-24) in Colter Bay Village serves up specialty salads, toasted subs, and pizza, both by the slice and whole pies. Also at Colter Bay is the **Ranch House Restaurant** (6:30am-10:30am, 11:30am-1:30pm, and 5:30pm-10pm daily late May-late Sept.). The restaurant offers family-style meals with an emphasis on barbecue. The breakfast buffet ($10-16 adults, $7-9 children) can include eggs, French toast, hot specials, and organic oatmeal, or if you want to order à la carte ($7-15), you can easily fill up on the New York steak and eggs, pan-fried oatmeal, or the breakfast burrito. Lunch ($11-17) consists of a good selection of salads, burgers, and sandwiches, while dinner ($18-25) offers hearty

Top to bottom: String Lake; trail in the Jenny Lake area; Jenny Lake Lodge.

steaks, chops, and seafood dishes. The bar is open 11:30am-10:30pm daily and has a small food menu as well.

Jackson Lake Lodge and Signal Mountain

There are a lot of options for dining at the **Jackson Lake Lodge** (307/543-3100, www. gtlc.com). The **Mural Room** (307/543-3463, 7am-9:30am, 11am-2:30pm, and 5:30pm-9pm daily mid-May-early Oct., $22-46) has unmatched ambience with its windowed wall looking out onto the lake, Mount Moran, and the Teton Range along with the colorful murals by famed artist Carl Routers depicting Western life. The food is upscale and innovative—also known as Rocky Mountain cuisine—and when coupled with the view, it makes this one of the most pleasurable dining experiences in the park. Breakfast includes classic eggs Benedict and huckleberry French toast. Lunch is a mix of sandwiches and salads as well as regional cuisine including Idaho rainbow trout and beef bourguignon. Dinner is a hearty affair with delectable main entrée items including grilled elk loin, Idaho ruby red trout, and wild mushroom saffron risotto. A delightful end to the meal is the flourless dark chocolate cake or the huckleberry pound cake. Kids menus are available. Dinner reservations are recommended.

Also in the lodge is the much more casual and less pricey **Pioneer Grill** (6am-10pm daily mid-May-early Oct., $10-26), a true-to-style 1950s diner; supposedly it has the largest soda fountain counter still in use. A fun place for a meal, the counter snakes 200 feet (61 m) through the room and encourages guests to interact with other diners. The Pioneer Grill offers American cuisine with a slight gourmet twist (try the poutine) and has a takeout service if you decide you'd rather watch the sunset while munching on your burger. Its famous desserts keep customers returning, and you should not leave without ordering a huckleberry shake.

The **Blue Heron Lounge** (307/543-2811, 11am-midnight daily mid-May-early Oct., food served until sunset, $11-26) is another casual dining experience in Jackson Lake Lodge. It has a bar menu with a good selection of appetizers and creative sandwiches and offers draft beer from local breweries. Enjoy your meal on the deck with a huckleberry mojito and a beautiful view of the mountains.

If you are at the pool or with your kids at the playground, you may want to fill up on the terrific Mexican food at the outdoor **Poolside Cantina** (food service 11am-4pm, beverage service 11am-8pm daily early June-late Aug. depending on weather, $6-12), which also serves salads, plus burgers and hot dogs for the kids.

There are three options for dining at the **Signal Mountain Lodge** (307/543-2831, www.signalmountainlodge.com). **The Trapper Grill** (7am-10pm daily early May-early Oct., $11-18) has a large menu for all three meals of the day. It mostly sticks to American fare with some Tex-Mex thrown in. The nachos are a favorite. The breakfast menu is vast, with an egg menu, an omelet menu, and griddle options. The lunch and dinner menu is filled with specialty sandwiches, salads, and burgers, but the restaurant prides itself on its homemade desserts. You may want to share an entrée so that you'll have room for the Wyoming Whiskey chocolate pecan pie. **The Peaks Restaurant** (5:30pm-10pm daily early May-early Oct., $18-41) serves delicious dinners and is committed to offering an environmentally sustainable menu. Dine on Snake River Farms Kurabota pork shank, bison meatball, or grilled Colorado white bass. **Leek's Pizzeria** (11am-10pm daily late May-early Sept., $10-25) is at the marina on Jackson Lake. It serves specialty pizzas and calzones, sandwiches, salads, and microbrews in a fantastic outdoor setting. For a drink, snack, and a glimpse of television, you may want to stop at **Deadman's Bar** (noon-midnight daily), which serves the largest plate of fully loaded nachos you've ever seen. They pair perfectly with a blackberry margarita and a Wyoming sunset.

Moran to Moose

You'll find most of your food options in this area at Dornans ranch. ★ **Dornans Chuckwagon** (Dornans, Moose, 307/733-2415, ext. 203, 7am-11am, noon-3pm, and 5pm-9pm daily mid-June-Labor Day, weather dependent) serves up hearty "cowboy cuisine" during the summer. Dornan's uses beef from its own butcher shop and cooks in Dutch ovens heated over wood fires. Breakfast ($7-10) offers great sourdough pancakes, and dinner ($25-29 adults, $13-15 children 5-11) is an all-you-can-eat affair with prices based on your choice of barbecued beef or chicken, pork ribs, or trout. Lunch ($8-16) is served as well. The restaurant is used for private events on weekend evenings. And Monday night is the hootenanny starting at 6pm, an evening of acoustic delight. There's often live music Tuesday-Saturday between 5:30pm and 8:30pm. It's a good idea to call ahead for evening reservations and check that it's not privately booked for the evening.

Dornans Pizza and Pasta Company (Dornans, Moose, 307/733-2415, ext. 204, 11:30am-9pm daily, $9-17) offers a large variety of salads, hot sandwiches, gourmet pizzas, rich pasta dishes, and calzones. If you are looking to pick up food for your hike, stop at **Dornans Trading Post & Deli** (Dornans, Moose, 307/733-2415, ext. 201, 8am-8pm daily) for everything from freeze-dried meals and cold drinks to gourmet groceries and any camping equipment you might need. The deli is open May-September; it's a good option for a quick meal or a sweet treat. If you have the time, don't miss a visit to **Dornans Wine Shop** (Dornans, Moose, 307/733-2415, ext. 202, 10am-9pm daily summer, reduced hours off-season). It is a find for wine connoisseurs and novices alike, with an award-winning selection

of around 1,600 wines and 150 types of cheese. *Food & Wine* magazine named it one of the 50 most amazing wine experiences in the country, and *Wine Spectator* has bestowed its Wine Award on the shop for 28 consecutive years and counting.

Built in 1906 and operated for years as Beaver Tooth Charlie Neil's trading post, **Buffalo Valley Café** (Heart Six Ranch, 16945 Buffalo Valley Rd., Moran, 307/543-2062, www.heartsix.com, 7am-7:30pm daily, $8-16) is open daily for breakfast, lunch, and dinner, and serves delicious burgers, sandwiches, and cowboy fare.

Hatchet Grill & Whetstone (19980 U.S. 287, Moran, 307/543-2413, www.hatchetresort.com, 7am-11am, 11:30am-2pm, and 5pm-10pm daily May-mid-Oct., $15-40) is a local resort that serves meals to hungry travelers. The menu is hearty mountain cuisine—burgers, steak, trout, pasta and more—served in a classic log building.

Jenny Lake and Vicinity

The **Jenny Lake Lodge Dining Room** (307/543-3352, www.gtlc.com, 7:30am-10am, 11:30am-1:30pm, and 6pm-9pm daily June-early Oct.) offers a fine-dining experience in an original log cabin. Reservations are required for all three meals and should be booked well in advance. Men are required to wear dinner jackets. The food is incredibly creative and incorporates local flavors. Crab cake Benedict and a prime rib cowboy skillet appear on the breakfast menu ($12-18), and lunch ($15-20) consists mostly of upscale sandwiches and salads. The main event at the restaurant is the prix fixe five-course dinner ($94, not including gratuity or alcohol). There are options for each course that rotate every night. Depending on the day, you may be dining on Lockhart beef tartare, Heluka pork tenderloin, Alaskan Pacific halibut, or duck leg confit—no matter what's on the menu, it is sure to be a memorable meal (and an expensive one).

Accommodations

Flagg Ranch and Colter Bay

The **Headwaters Lodge & Cabins at Flagg Ranch** (307/543-2861 or 307/543-3100, www.gtlc.com, June-Sept.) is touted as the oldest continuously operating resort in upper Jackson Hole. It is ideally situated to take advantage of both Yellowstone and Grand Teton National Parks. The accommodations options include deluxe or premium log cabins ($301-320); camper cabins (from $77), which are four-walled structures with permanent roofs and cots; and RV sites (from $74). Log cabins have two queen or one king bed, coffee makers, private baths, and patios furnished with rocking chairs. The camper cabins (built in 2012), RV sites, and campsites all include access to 24-hour hot shower and laundry facilities. Note there is no cell service or Wi-Fi in the area.

Colter Bay Village (307/543-3100, www.gtlc.com, late May-early Oct.) on the northern shore of Jackson Lake offers some of the park's most affordable lodging. The village has rustic cabins ($179-265), an RV site, and a tent village. The original homestead cabins, purchased by the Rockefellers and moved to the area, have been refurbished but still offer a glimpse into the past. Each cabin displays a description of its own history. While most of the one-room cabins sleep 2, one can sleep up to 6 people, and the two-room cabin can sleep up to 10 with rollaways. Prices vary depending on the number of occupants in the room and the arrangement of double, twin, and rollaway beds. Pull-through RV sites are available for $72. The tent cabins ($74) consist of two log walls, two canvas walls and a canvas roof, a single lightbulb, and a wood-burning potbellied stove. Each log wall has two pull-down bunks with thin mattresses; additional cots can be rented. Guests are encouraged to bring their own bedding, but a limited number of sleeping bags can be rented from the cabin office. Each tent cabin has a picnic and grilling area, and showers are located in the launderette with a fee for use.

Jackson Lake Lodge and Signal Mountain

The **Jackson Lake Lodge** (307/543-3100, www.gtlc.com, mid-May-early Oct., $330-449 cottages, $330-439 lodge rooms) is one of the largest resorts in the park and commands an unparalleled view of Jackson Lake and the Teton Range from the lobby's panoramic 60-foot-high (18.3-m) windows. There are 385 guest rooms in the main lodge and surrounding cottages, and the grounds also house a playground and swimming pool. The cottages are in clusters and come in a range of styles. The classic cottage guest rooms have one king bed and sleep a maximum of three. The cottage guest rooms with a view of the Tetons can sleep up to five people and have a mini fridge and a patio or balcony. The mountain-view suite has a spectacular view of Willow Flats and the majestic Tetons; it comes with a king bed and a comfortable sitting area. The lodge guest rooms are on the third floor and also come in three price ranges. Unlike the cottages, these guest rooms do not accommodate rollaways.

The **Signal Mountain Lodge** (307/543-2831, www.signalmountainlodge.com, early May-mid-Oct.) is an independently owned resort on the banks of Jackson Lake with a gorgeous view of the Tetons. It has a variety of options for lodging, ranging from rustic log cabins (1-room cabin $217-242, 2-room $247-277) to motel-style rooms ($261-367) to one- or two-room bungalows ($261-407) on the beach. The two-room lakefront retreats ($367-407) are ideal for families; they overlook the lake with fantastic views of the mountains and have kitchenettes. Many of the rooms in the lodge were remodeled in 2015, and all of them are carpeted and comfortably furnished. There is one three-bedroom cabin aptly named Home Away from Home ($492); if you are lucky enough to get it, you'll have a bedroom, dining area, living room with a gas fireplace, kitchen, and small laundry room all to yourself; the only drawback is that there is no view.

Moran to Moose

★ **The Triangle X Ranch** (2 Triangle X Ranch Rd., 307/733-2183, www. trianglex.com, late May-mid-Oct. and Dec. 26-mid-Mar., $1,958-2,713 pp/week summer when paid with credit card, discounts for paying in cash, $150 pp/night winter) has been in operation since 1926. Twenty-six miles (42 km) north of Jackson and 32 miles (52 km) south of Yellowstone, it is the only authorized guest ranch concessionaire in the entire national park system and sits right inside Grand Teton National Park. Not surprisingly, the setting is gorgeous, and you can see the entire Teton Range from this secluded getaway.

The lodge, which is the center of activity and meals, is the original main house used by two generations of the Turner family. The 20 log cabins are also originals that once housed families in different parts of Jackson Hole. The cabins come with 1-3 bedrooms; all have modern amenities and are decorated with cozy Western charm.

The ranch is also the only concession in the park that is open during winter. During the peak season (early-June-late Aug.), the minimum stay is one week (Sun.-Sun.). During the spring and fall seasons, the ranch requires a minimum four-night stay but offers reduced rates, and during the winter season, visitors can book per night. All meals, served family-style in the main lodge, are included in the price, as are the endless horseback rides, cookouts, square dancing, and special programs for children. Winter activities include cross-country skiing, snowshoeing, and snowmobiling. Regardless of the season, there are always great opportunities for wildlife-viewing.

Dornans Spur Ranch Cabins (12170 Dornan Rd., Moose, 307/733-2522, www. dornans.com, year-round) sits idyllically on the Snake River in the middle of a wildflower meadow, affording alpine views in all directions. This is a small, family-owned business that provides quality service with personal touches, and the location affords easy access to fly-fishing and floating adventures. There are eight one-bedroom cabins ($235-275 summer, $150-170 fall-spring) and four two-bedroom duplexes ($375 summer, $175-225 fall-spring) on the premises. The cabins were built in the early 1990s and are bright, airy, and furnished with lodgepole pine furniture. They each have queen beds, kitchens, living-dining areas, and covered porches with a barbecue grill nearby. The 10-acre property has a grocery and camping store, two restaurants, and an award-winning wine shop. Visitors can rent mountain bikes, canoes, and kayaks during the summer and cross-country skis and snowshoes in the winter to make the most of the surrounding area.

The **Hatchet Resort** (19980 U.S. 287, Moran, 307/543-2413, www. hatchetresort.com, May-mid-Oct., $89-499) is a historic gem, built in the mid-1950s and beautifully renovated in 2014. Set at the edge of the forest, with meadows and views of Mount Moran, these simple and comfortable rooms and cabins give great access to both Grand Teton and Yellowstone.

To rent your own modern log cabin for a night or a week, visit **Luton's Teton Cabins** (24000 N. Gun Barrel Flats Rd., Moran, 307/543-2489, www.tetoncabins. com, $257-507/night or $1,708-3,374/week), which offers a variety of log cabin accommodations, plus easy access to activities like horseback riding, float trips, fishing, and covered wagon cookouts.

A wonderful all-inclusive dude ranch in the area is **Heart Six Ranch** (16985

Buffalo Valley Rd., Moran, 307/543-2477, www.heartsix.com, $99-399/night, $1,043-2,793/week), which offers cozy accommodations and year-round adventures, including horseback riding all summer, hunting in the fall, and snowmobiling in winter and spring. You can also book myriad Grand Teton and Yellowstone adventures through the ranch. Glamping is an option, too. Heart Six allows you to book by the night or the week.

Jenny Lake and Vicinity

A former dude ranch for sophisticated Easterners, **Jenny Lake Lodge** (307/543-3100, www.gtlc.com, mid-May-early Oct., cabins $530-1,000/night for 2 people) is the finest lodging in the park. The cabins have authentic log walls, renovated baths, and touches such as handmade bed quilts that add to the charm of each room. Situated among the three lakes, the lodge is comfortably secluded but offers beautiful vistas in all directions. The rooms are pricey, but guests get a lot for their dime. A gourmet breakfast, five-course dinner, horseback riding, and access to bicycles are all included in the rates. Each week, different activities are available and include options such as live raptor displays on the front patio, stargazing, interpretive programs, live music, and garden games like bocce ball and croquet. If you are looking for a romantic getaway, consider booking one of the suites, which come with wood-burning stoves.

A much more affordable, and truly rustic, option is the **Grand Teton Climbers Ranch** (307/733-7271, www.americanalpineclub.org, June-Sept. 10, $17.28 AAC members, $27 nonmembers), owned by the American Alpine Club and located just 3 miles (4.8 km) south of Jenny Lake. The ranch has small log cabins that serve as dormitories for 4-8 people. Guests must bring their own sleeping bags and pads, towels, cooking equipment, and food. Cooking and dishwashing facilities, toilets, and showers

with hot water are available. No camping is allowed. There is also a general store on the grounds where you can stock up on groceries as well as hiking and camping supplies. The ranch often offers a work week in early June during which volunteers can stay at the ranch for free.

Camping

Flagg Ranch and Colter Bay

The **Colter Bay Campground** (800/628-9988, late May-late Sept., $31/vehicle, $12 pp for hikers or bicyclists) has 330 sites. Some campsites and RV sites are discounted if you have a lifetime version of the National Parks Senior Pass. Electric RV sites are $53/night.

Located 30 miles (48 km) north of Moose between Flagg Ranch and Colter Bay Village, the **Lizard Creek Campground** (307/543-2831, mid-June-early Sept., $30) has 60 individual sites with no hookups. It rarely fills.

Jackson Lake Lodge and Signal Mountain

The **Signal Mountain Campground** (800/672-6012, mid-May-mid-Oct., $32/vehicle standard site, $54 electric site) is nestled among spruce and fir trees with views of the mountains, lakes, and hillside. It is also wildly popular and often fills up between 8am and 10am on a first-come, first-served basis. There are 86 smallish sites, each with a picnic table and fire ring, and RVs up to 30 feet (9.1 m) in length are permitted. Restrooms with cold running water are available but no showers.

Moran to Moose

Gros Ventre (307/543-2811 or 307/543-3100, www.gtlc.com, early May-early Oct., tent and dry RV sites $29, electric sites $53) is the closest park campground to Jackson and among the largest campgrounds in the park; it's situated at the park's southeast end, 11.5 miles (18.5 km) southeast of Moose. The 318 first-come, first-served individual sites and 5 large group sites usually fill between noon and 5pm mid-June through mid-August, and rarely fill outside that time frame. Each individual site has a fire pit and picnic table and can accommodate two tents, two vehicles, and up to six people. The campground isn't far from the river, and there are sites to be had in the cottonwoods and open sage. Nearby bathrooms include flush toilets, but no shower facilities are available. A grocery store and service station are within 2 miles (3.2 km) of the campground. Some campsites and RV sites are discounted if you have the lifetime version of the National Parks Senior Pass.

Located 6 miles (9.7 km) east of the Moran Junction gate, **Fireside Buffalo Valley RV Park** (U.S. 26/287, 307/733-1980, www.yellowstonerv.com, year-round, tent sites $29-39, RV sites $79) offers tent sites, RV sites, camping cabins, condos, suites, and pet-friendly fireside cabins. Most sites offer a view of the Tetons. Activities like float trips and snowmobile tours can be arranged. There's also a restaurant and convenience store on the property, plus clean restrooms and hot showers.

Jenny Lake and Vicinity

The **Jenny Lake Campground** (307/543-3100 or 307/543-2811, early May-Sept., $29/vehicle, $12 hikers and bicyclists) is the smallest in the park and is available on a first-come, first-served basis only; it is usually full by 8am. It has 49 sites that can each accommodate one vehicle, two tents, and up to six campers. Ten additional sites are set aside for hikers or bicyclists. There are no large group sites, nor are trailers, campers, or generators allowed in the area. Because of its size and popularity, the maximum stay is 7 days (at the other campgrounds it is 14 days). Flush toilets are available but no shower facilities. Payment is by cash or check only; credit cards are not accepted.

Jackson Hole

Visitors love Jackson (population 10,529; elevation 5,672 ft/1,729 m) because it encompasses the best of the West in a charming town with a spectacular setting. Western indeed, Jackson boasts a classic boardwalk around town, saloons with swinging doors and saddles for barstools, and architecture built on elk antlers. At the same time, Jackson is clearly mountain chic, with a number of high-end boutiques and art galleries, a phenomenal performing arts center, gourmet dining, and ritzy accommodations.

The valley itself, known as Jackson Hole because it is entirely surrounded by mountains, is 48 miles (77 km) long and up to 8 miles (12.9 km) wide in places. With the Tetons as the most significant landmark, Jackson Hole gives rise to the headwaters of the Snake River, fed by numerous mountain streams. Because of its remarkable setting, Jackson Hole is a natural playground with offerings for just about anyone. In winter, outdoors enthusiasts can ski downhill at two well-known ski areas, Snow King and Jackson Hole Mountain Resort, or go the cross-country route just about anywhere, including nearby Grand Teton National Park. For those less interested in working up a sweat, a sleigh ride in the National Elk Refuge is a memorable experience. When the snow melts, there is no end to the amount of adventurous options this valley offers, with fly-fishing and wildlife-watching among the less exhausting. From hiking and mountain biking to rafting and rock climbing, Jacksonians do it all.

Planning Your Time

Jackson Hole boasts easy (but pricey) air access. It could easily occupy visitors for **2-3 days,** and is an excellent launching pad for day trips into Yellowstone and

Grand Teton National Parks. The dude ranches outside Jackson offer tremendous opportunities to experience the state's vast open spaces close to the hustle and bustle of town. For many people, this is the ideal way to spend a week enjoying the best of Wyoming's offerings.

Getting to Jackson Hole

The major routes into Jackson Hole—including U.S. 89/191/287 from Yellowstone and Grand Teton National Parks, U.S. 26/287 from the east, Highway 22 from the west over Teton Pass, and U.S. 189/191/89 from the south—can all experience **weather closures** in the winter, particularly over Teton Pass. There is no car traffic in the southern portion of Yellowstone during the winter. For Wyoming road reports, call 800/WYO-ROAD (800/996-7623, www.wyoroad. info).

Keep in mind that while distances through the national parks may be shorter in actual mileage, your drive time is often extended by lower speed limits, traffic congestion, and animal jams. In addition, most of the park roads are **closed in winter,** and it won't be possible to drive directly between Bozeman and Jackson or between Cody and Jackson. Driving around the parks increases distances and drive times significantly.

Driving from Yellowstone
130-150 miles (209-242 km); 2.5-4 hours
To get from the north entrance of Yellowstone at **Gardiner** to Jackson, it's 150 miles (242 km) south on U.S. 89/191, a route that takes you through both national parks. This drive takes about four hours.

From **West Yellowstone** to Jackson is 165 miles (265 km) west and south on U.S. 191, a four-hour drive that takes you through both parks. To avoid driving through the parks, you can take U.S. 20 from West Yellowstone to Ashton, then ID-32 to ID-33 East for a 130-mile (209-km), 2.5-hour drive to Jackson.

Air
Jackson Hole Airport (JAC, 1250 E. Airport Rd., Jackson, 307/733-7682, www.jacksonholeairport.com) is served by American, Delta, United, and Frontier. The schedules change seasonally but include regular flights from Salt Lake City, Denver, Seattle, Chicago, Minneapolis, Dallas, Houston, Phoenix, San Francisco, and Los Angeles.

Getting Around

The airport has on-site car rentals from **Alamo, National, Hertz,** and **Enterprise. Avis/Budget, Dollar,** and **Thrifty** are available off-site.

In town, **The Driver Provider** (800/700-2687, http://driverprovider.com) and **Alltrans** (307/733-3135 or 800/443-6133, www.jacksonholealltrans.com) provide various ski shuttles and tour options. Shuttles can also be arranged through **Jackson Hole Shuttle** (307/200-1400, www.jhshuttle.com).

Somewhat amazingly for this part of the country, Jackson has 32 taxi companies serving the area, including **Broncs Taxi** (307/413-9863, www.jackson-hole-taxi.com), **Snake River Taxi** (307/413-9009, www.snakerivertaxi.com), and **Teton Mountain Taxi** (307/699-7969, www.jacksonholecab.com). Transportation to Jackson from the airport runs roughly $40 for 1-2 people. A taxi to Teton Village averages $70. A complete list of taxi services can be found under the transportation heading on the airport website.

Sights
★ Town Square

Jackson's **Town Square** is uniquely distinguished by four dramatic archways constructed in 1932 entirely from naturally shed and sun-bleached elk antlers. It is the focal point of town and a good meeting spot, with shady trees and the occasional musician. In the summer, late May-early September, Town Square is the site of the free **Jackson Hole Shootout,** a

Jackson

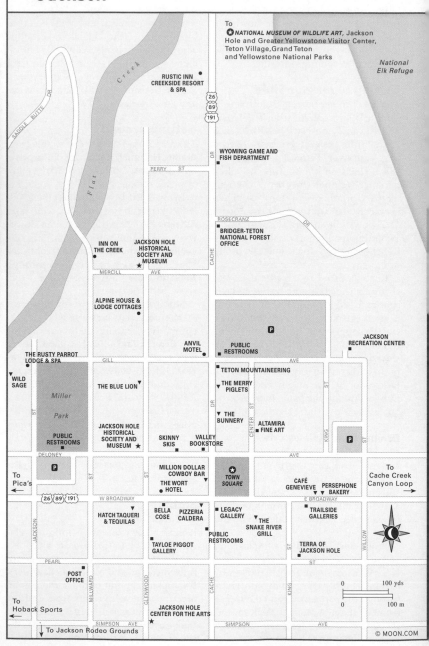

To ★ NATIONAL MUSEUM OF WILDLIFE ART, Jackson Hole and Greater Yellowstone Visitor Center, Teton Village, Grand Teton and Yellowstone National Parks

National Elk Refuge

Creek

Flat

SADDLE BUTTE DR

RUSTIC INN CREEKSIDE RESORT & SPA

26 89 191

DR

PERRY ST

WYOMING GAME AND FISH DEPARTMENT

ROSECRANZ

DR

CACHE

BRIDGER-TETON NATIONAL FOREST OFFICE

INN ON THE CREEK

JACKSON HOLE HISTORICAL SOCIETY AND MUSEUM ★

MERCILL

AVE

ALPINE HOUSE & LODGE COTTAGES

P

JACKSON RECREATION CENTER

THE RUSTY PARROT LODGE & SPA

ANVIL MOTEL

PUBLIC RESTROOMS

AVE

WILD SAGE

Miller Park

GILL

THE BLUE LION

TETON MOUNTAINEERING

ST

THE MERRY PIGLETS

KING ST

P

PUBLIC RESTROOMS

JACKSON HOLE HISTORICAL SOCIETY AND MUSEUM ★

DR

THE BUNNERY

CENTER ST

ALTAMIRA FINE ART

SKINNY SKIS

VALLEY BOOKSTORE

DELONEY

AVE

P

To Pica's ←

26 89 191

ST

MILLION DOLLAR COWBOY BAR

THE WORT HOTEL

TOWN SQUARE

CAFÉ GENEVIEVE

PERSEPHONE BAKERY

To Cache Creek Canyon Loop →

W BROADWAY

E BROADWAY

JACKSON ST

HATCH TAQUERI & TEQUILAS

BELLA COSE

PIZZERIA CALDERA

LEGACY GALLERY

THE SNAKE RIVER GRILL

TRAILSIDE GALLERIES

WILLOW

TAYLOE PIGGOT GALLERY

PUBLIC RESTROOMS

TERRA OF JACKSON HOLE

PEARL

ST

POST OFFICE

CACHE

KING ST

0   100 yds

To Hoback Sports ←

MILLWARD

GLENWOOD

JACKSON HOLE CENTER FOR THE ARTS ★

0   100 m

SIMPSON AVE

↓ To Jackson Rodeo Grounds

SIMPSON

AVE

© MOON.COM

spirited reenactment of frontier justice, which plays for crowds Monday through Saturday around 6pm-6:30pm. In winter, the arches are illuminated by strings of twinkling lights, creating a magical setting.

Within easy walking distance of the square are more than 70 eateries—from mouthwatering pizza joints with ski-bum prices to the very tony—and a number of fine art galleries and shops that sell everything from high-end furs to T-shirts and knickknacks. There are also plentiful espresso and ice-cream shops for those in need of instant energy.

Jackson Hole Historical Society and Museum

Just down Cache Street from Town Square, the **Jackson Hole Historical Society and Museum** (225 N. Cache St., 307/733-2414, www.jacksonholehistory. org, 10am-5pm Tues.-Sat., $6 adults, $4 seniors over 60 and students, free for children 6 and under) is actually two museums within easy walking distance of one another. One is dedicated to the history of homesteading and dude ranches in the area, and the other to Indians of the Greater Yellowstone (the latter is open only in summer). The collections include historical photos of the region, Indian artifacts, fur trade-era tools, and firearms. Admission is good for both museums. The society also operates the hands-on Mercill Archaeology Center, which is open on a program basis only. In summer, the historical society offers free Jackson **walking tours** (10:30am Tues.-Fri., Memorial Day-last full week in Sept.). Tours depart from the center of Town Square. For a historical perspective on the town and valley, this is the best place to begin.

★ National Museum of Wildlife Art

Just 3 miles (4.8 km) north of Town Square overlooking the National Elk Refuge, the **National Museum of Wildlife Art** (2820 Rungius Rd., 307/733-5771,

www.wildlifeart.org, 9am-5pm daily May-Oct., 9am-5pm Tues.-Sat., 11am-5pm Sun. Nov.-Apr., $15 adults, $13 seniors, $6 for one child 5-18, $2 each additional child, free for children under 5) is an absolute find. In existence in various forms since 1984, the museum's 14 galleries represent the lifetime study and collection of wildlife art by Bill and Joffa Kerr. More than 5,000 objects reside in the permanent collection, primarily paintings and sculptures by artists that range from early Native American artists to masters both past and present, including Pablo Picasso, Carl Rungius, John James Audubon, Robert Bateman, and Kent Ullberg. A 0.8-mile (1.3-km) sculpture trail, which is free and open to the public, was added in 2013. The trail combines marvelous art with the stunning landscape around Jackson, and often plays host to live music, theater, yoga, and other programs. Audio guides to the museum are included with paid admission, and coupons for discounts on admission are offered on the museum's website.

The museum itself is a work of art: Inspired by the ruins of a Scottish castle, the red Arizona sandstone building emerges from the hillside like a natural outcropping of rock and often reminds visitors of Ancestral Puebloan ruins.

National Elk Refuge

During the winter months, more than 5,000 elk—often as many as 7,000—descend from their mountain habitat to the nearly 25,000-acre **National Elk Refuge** (532 N. Cache St., 307/733-9212, www. fws.gov/refuge/national_elk_refuge/) in Jackson Hole. The large number of elk make the refuge a popular wintertime attraction (in the summer, birds and other wildlife populate the range). Forty-seven different mammal species and nearly 175 species of birds have been observed on the refuge. Horse-drawn sleigh rides through the refuge are offered mid-December-first Saturday in April. The elk are accustomed to the vehicles, allowing

The Elk Conundrum

Established in 1912, the National Elk Refuge was the first Wyoming state-run feeding ground for elk. In the 1930s and 1940s, more feeding grounds were created to help the animals survive the harsh winters, and in part to keep them from entering areas reserved for cattle grazing. The thriving herd in Jackson ultimately was used to replenish other herds of elk and aid the reintroduction of elk throughout the country. However, as a result of the large number of elk concentrated in these feeding grounds, the animals are much more susceptible to contagious diseases including brucellosis and, more recently, chronic wasting disease. Wyoming lost its federal brucellosis-free status in 2004 when cattle acquired the disease after coming into contact with elk from the refuge.

In 2005 the U.S. Department of Agriculture's Animal Plant Health Inspection Service reported that there was a 50-80 percent rate of brucellosis infection among elk on feedlots, and though that number has dropped to 30 percent in more recent reports, it is still substantially higher than the 1-3 percent infection rate in wild free-ranging elk. Before the National Elk Refuge was created, the elk from southern Yellowstone would migrate and spread past the area of the refuge into southwestern Wyoming. As the winter came to a close, they moved back to their summer habitat. Today it's believed that the 11,000 elk in the Jackson herd migrate to and from the refuge at the risk of spreading both brucellosis and chronic wasting disease. As of 2018, the National Elk Refuge is one of 22 feeding grounds for elk in the western part of the state. A study published in 2016 showed that four of the five strains of brucellosis are found on Wyoming feeding grounds, a discovery that pinned the blame for the spread of brucellosis outside Yellowstone on the elk, as opposed to the bison that have long been treated as the culprits.

The question now is, what can be done? The argument has been made that the elk should return to their historic migration routes and original winter ranges rather than being concentrated in the feedlots. Today, however, many of those routes and ranges have been developed for housing, ranches, or other businesses. Furthermore, the idea of elk and cattle competing for food on the open range is worrisome to many Wyoming ranchers. So, although the scientific consensus is that it would be best for the elk to return to their natural migration patterns, the challenge is finding places in the wild that can sustain them throughout the year.

visitors to travel easily through the herds. Reservations (307/733-0277 or 800/772-5386) are strongly suggested. Tickets can be purchased from the **Jackson Hole and Greater Yellowstone Visitor Center** (532 N. Cache St., 307/733-3316, $25 adults, $15 children 5-12, free for children under 5, $450/private sleigh), and a free shuttle will take visitors 3 miles (4.8 km) north of Jackson to the departure point. Tours run 10am-4pm daily and last about an hour. Dress warmly as the wind can be quite biting during the tour.

Jackson Hole and Greater Yellowstone Visitor Center

A terrific place to start any type of exploration of the area, including the National Elk Refuge, which operates out of the same building, the **Jackson Hole and Greater Yellowstone Visitor Center** (532 N. Cache St., 307/733-3316, www.fws.gov, 8am-7pm daily Memorial Day-Sept., 9am-5pm daily Oct.-Memorial Day) is a phenomenal resource with seven agencies represented, including the local chamber of commerce, the National Park Service, and the Bridger-Teton National Forest. Visitors can obtain annual park passes and hunting and fishing licenses as well as get trip-planning assistance, directions, and maps aplenty. The wildlife exhibits inside are matched by sweeping wildlife observation decks outside that overlook the National Elk Refuge. The real treasure here, though, is the staff, all of whom are friendly, knowledgeable, and more than willing to roll up their sleeves for whatever help you need. Short interpretive talks are offered throughout the season, and naturalists are often on hand at the upper viewing deck with spotting scopes, binoculars, and field guides.

Teton Village

Twelve miles (19.3 km) northwest of Jackson is **Teton Village,** an Alps-like enclave nestled around the state's largest and most popular ski hill. The area pulses with energy and activity as soon as the snow flies, and although it quiets down in the shoulder seasons, it is an enormously popular destination in summer as well. Even so, these days it's quite a bit quieter than the center of Jackson. In addition to the abundant lodging, shopping, and dining options, the area is a hub for outdoor activities such as hot-air ballooning, paragliding, horseback riding, and, of course, myriad mountain-oriented sports. Plenty of concerts and special events are also held year-round.

National Bighorn Sheep Interpretive Center

Set in Dubois, 85 miles (137 km) east of Jackson on U.S. 287/26, the **National Bighorn Sheep Interpretive Center** (10 Bighorn Ln., 307/455-3429 or 888/209-2795, www.bighorn.org, 9am-6pm daily late May-early Sept., 10am-4pm Mon.-Sat. early Sept.-mid-Dec. and Apr.-late May, 10am-4pm Tues.-Sat. late Dec.-late Mar., $6 adults, $3 children 8-17, free for children under 8) is dedicated to educating the public about these majestic creatures and their habitats. Visitors are welcomed by a stunning bronze of a ram and led inside to several hands-on

Top to bottom: an archway made of antlers at Jackson's Town Square; Jackson Hole Historical Society and Museum; aerial tram at Jackson Hole Mountain Resort.

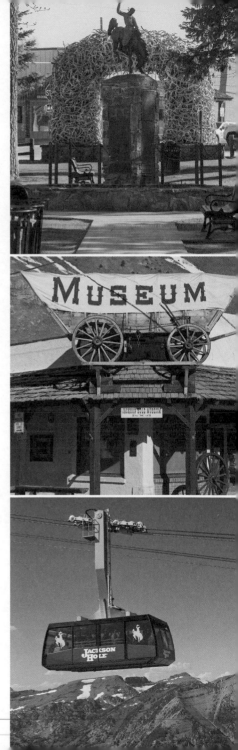

exhibits that will delight little ones and fascinate animal lovers. There are 16 mounts of wild sheep from around the world and a great little gift shop with everything from T-shirts to children's toys and wares by local artists. November-March, the center offers tours to the winter range of the **Whiskey Mountain Habitat Area,** providing an excellent opportunity to see the bighorn sheep in their natural, windswept environment. Reservations for the 3- to 5-hour tours ($100 pp, min. 2 people) should be made at least 48 hours in advance by calling the center.

Entertainment and Events
The Arts
Among the most impressive facilities in the state is the **Jackson Hole Center for the Arts** (265 S. Cache St., 307/734-8956 or 307/733-4900, www. jhcenterforthearts.org), a truly inspired art campus in the heart of downtown that offers educational programs and facilities along with professional theater, dance, and music as well as a remarkable space for major community events. Rickie Lee Jones, Lyle Lovett, and John Hiatt have all made recent appearances. Check out the schedule online—there is always something happening. Of particular note at the Center for the Arts is the **Off Square Theatre Company** (240 S. Glenwood St., 307/733-3021, www. offsquare.org), which produces excellent and wildly diverse shows ranging from family-favorite American musicals (*Beauty and the Beast*) to dramatic masterpieces (*Macbeth*) to side-splitting improv by Laff Staff. Regardless of the offerings, a night at the theater in Jackson is a night well spent.

Art Galleries
The art scene in Jackson is both rarefied and approachable, and an increasingly important part of both the community and the local economy. There are more than 30 galleries in town. Among the favorites are **Trailside Galleries** (130 E. Broadway, 307/733-3186, www. trailsidegalleries.com, 10am-5:30pm Mon.-Sat., noon-5pm Sun. June-Oct., 10am-5:30pm Mon.-Sat. Nov.-May) and **Legacy Gallery** (75 N. Cache St., 307/733-2353, www.legacygallery.com, 10am-5pm Mon.-Sat.), both with classic examples of Western art in its traditional and contemporary forms. **Altamira Fine Art** (172 Center St., 307/739-4700, www. altamiraart.com, 10am-5pm daily or by appointment) has a more loftlike urban feel and represents groundbreaking contemporary artists, including Rocky Hawkins, Duke Beardsley, Ed Mell, Mary Roberson, and John Nieto. The **Tayloe Piggot Gallery** (62 S. Glenwood St., 307/733-0555, www.jhmusegallery. com, 10am-6pm Mon.-Wed., 10am-8pm Thurs.-Sat., 11am-5pm Sun.) is cutting-edge cool with both emerging and mid-career artists in a variety of media. For more information on all the galleries in Jackson, visit the **Jackson Hole Gallery Association** (www. jacksonholegalleryassociation.com).

Festivals and Events
Weekly events in Jackson during the summer season (Memorial Day-Labor Day) include the **Jackson Rodeo** (447 Snow King Ave., 307/733-7927, www. jhrodeo.com, 8pm Wed. and Sat. June, 8pm Wed., Fri., and Sat. July-Labor Day, $20-35), a fun family event with bull riding, team roping, barrel racing, bareback broncs, and plenty of other action. Food and refreshments are sold at the chuck wagon.

For one of Jackson's favorite regular events, check out the **Town Square Shootout** (6pm Mon.-Sat.) on the Town Square. It's free, loud, and a lot of fun for visitors.

An annual event built around the well-known Boy Scout Elk Antler Auction, where the boys sell the shed antlers they collect from the National Elk Refuge, **Elk Fest** (307/733-5935 or 300/733-3316, www.elkfest.org) takes place the weekend before Memorial Day and includes plenty of food, community concerts, children's activities, and many opportunities to learn about elk.

Happening each year over Memorial Day weekend all around town is Jackson's long-running **Old West Days** (307/733-3316, www.jacksonholechamber.com), which features a horse-drawn parade, a rodeo, a mountain man rendezvous, and a host of other events that celebrate Jackson's rough-and-tumble origins.

Happening in late July-early August, the nearly weeklong **Teton County Fair** (Teton County Fairgrounds at 305 West Snow King Ave., 307/733-5289, www.tetoncountyfair.com) includes family-friendly events like pig wrestling ($5-15), a rodeo ($15-25), a demolition derby ($15-30), concerts, a carnival, and plenty of agricultural and animal exhibits.

The equivalent of Cody's Rendezvous Royale, Jackson's **Fall Arts Festival** (307/733-3316, www.jacksonholechamber.com) is a 10-day event in mid-September that unites the community and attracts a crowd of art lovers with a phenomenal range of art-related events, including the prestigious **Jackson Hole Art Auction** (www.jacksonholeartauction.com) and **Western Design Conference** (www.westerndesignconference.com), gallery walks, open-air art fairs, and historical ranch tours.

The **Grand Teton Music Festival** (McCollister Dr., Teton Village, 307/733-1128, www.gtmf.org, $15-85, free for students) takes place annually during July-August. It is held in the all-wood Walk Festival Hall, which recently underwent a $4.85 million renovation to improve the intimate setting and provide top-notch acoustics. Known as one of the top classical music festivals in the country, it showcases an impressive list of musicians and singers. Running annually since 1962, past performers include Sarah Chang, Itzhak Perlman, the New York Philharmonic, and the Mormon Tabernacle Choir. In addition to the summer festival, the organization hosts concerts during the winter. Family concerts are free, as is student admission, and open rehearsals (Friday mornings at 10am) can be attended for as little as $15.

One of the most renowned bluegrass festivals in the country takes place on the western slopes of the Tetons in Targhee during mid-August. Held at the Grand Targhee Resort (800/827-4433), the **Grand Targhee Bluegrass Festival** (3300 Ski Hill Rd., 307/353-2300, www.grandtarghee.com, 3-day pass from $239, day passes also available starting at $85, camping $40-110) draws some of the best bluegrass musicians in the country, including Brother Mule, Danny Barnes, and Sarah Jarosz, along with a large number of fans. In addition to performances all day long, there is also plenty of food, arts, and crafts available.

Also taking place at Grand Targhee Resort, in mid-July, the decade-old **Targhee Fest** (www.grandtarghee.com, 3-day pass from $239, day passes also available from $85, camping $40-110) is a lively three-day music festival with an eclectic mix of artists such as Los Lobos and John Hiatt.

The **Jackson Hole Film Festival** (307/200-3286, www.jhfestival.org) is a biennial event dedicated to nature conservation, held in late September-early October. The six-day festival attracts leaders in science, conservation, and media as numerous films are screened and related social events and activities are organized throughout the week. The festival is held at the Jackson Lake Lodge, except for the final event, a screening of selected finalists at the Center for the Arts in downtown Jackson. The festival is slated to run in 2019, 2021, and 2023.

Winter Fest (307/733-3316, www.jacksonholechamber.com) gives residents and visitors alike one more reason to celebrate the snow. Happening over two weeks in February, the celebration includes events like snow sculpting, skiing, ice-skating, and wine-tasting.

Another winter event everyone looks forward to is the **Pedigree Stage Stop Dog Race** (307/734-1163, www. wyomingstagestop.org). It takes place from the last weekend in January through the first week of February. Begun in 1996, it is the largest U.S. dogsled race outside Alaska. The race begins in Jackson and runs 500 miles (805 km) to Park City, Utah. It is unusual in that the participants stop for the night in towns along the way, including Lander, Pinedale, Big Piney-Marbleton, Alpine, Kemmerer, Lyman, Evanston, and Uinta County. Each town along the route celebrates with different festivities as crowds greet and cheer on the racers.

Shopping

For those with time and money, shopping can practically be an athletic pursuit in Jackson, particularly in the streets and alleyways around **Town Square.** In the early 1990s, Jackson was populated with a number of outlet stores, but today most of those have been pushed out by more sophisticated boutiques. There are lots of fascinating little shops to pop into, from gorgeous high-end art galleries to the few remaining tacky but fun T-shirt and tchotchke shops.

A wonderful independent bookstore, **Valley Bookstore** (125 N. Cache St., 307/733-4533, www.valleybookstore. com, 9am-9pm daily June-Aug., 9am-7pm Mon.-Sat., 10am-6pm Sun. Sept.-May) has been providing local readers with fabulous books and stellar recommendations since the 1970s. The owners grew up in Jackson and have a superb local and regional section. **Jackson Hole Book Trader** (970 W. Broadway, 307/734-6001, www.jhbooktrader.com, 10am-6pm Mon.-Sat.) is another fantastic find for new, used, and rare books. There's a fireplace and cozy chairs, helpful staff, and an adorable dog to be petted. What more could you want from a bookstore?

rafting the Snake River in Jackson Hole

For top-of-the-line women's and children's clothes in a spacious, almost Zen-like setting, visit **Terra of Jackson Hole** (105 E. Broadway, 307/734-0067, www.terrajh.com, 11am-6pm Mon.-Sat., noon-5pm Sun.), which would not be out of place in Manhattan or San Francisco. Another glorious place filled with beautiful things is **Bella Cose** (48 E. Broadway, 307/733-2640, www.bellacose.com, 10am-6pm Mon.-Sat., noon-5pm Sun.), which offers elegant home decor as well as kitchen and dining items; it clearly caters to the second-home crowd. For a chance to actually play with some cool toys, visit the **Jackson Hole Toy Store** (165 Center St., 307/734-2663, www.jacksonholetoystore.com, 10am-8pm daily in high season, 10am-6pm daily in off-season). There's a wireless Wild West shooting gallery ($5) and the owner can tell you anything about any of the creative toys they stock from all over the world.

One of the most exquisite design studios anywhere, **WRJ Design** (30 S. King St., 307/200-4881, www.wrjdesign.com, 10am-6pm Mon.-Fri., weekends by appointment) has a Jackson showroom filled with furnishings, unique objects, fine art, and curated lines from around the world. Owned by renowned designers Klaus Baer and Rush Jenkins, WRJ's style is elegant, earthy, and contemporary.

A great resource for fishing are the friendly folks at **JD High Country Outfitters** (50 E. Broadway, 307/733-3270, www.jdhcoutfitters.com, 9am-8pm daily summer, reduced hours in winter). The staff are experts on waters all over the region. The shop has a great selection of flies, equipment, and clothing. They even teach casting lessons for novices, as well as offer guiding services on the Snake River ($475/half day, $575/full day).

Sports and Recreation
★ Rafting on the Snake River
One of the greatest attractions for summertime visitors to Jackson is rafting the Snake River. There are close to two dozen rafting companies to choose from in the area, and most are open mid-May-September. Below are a few options for those who are interested in experiencing the river, whether it be a tranquil day float through Grand Teton National Park or white-water adventure a little farther south in the canyon. Most adult fares average $80-90 for an 8-mile (12.9-km) trip. Increasingly popular are combination trips, which include a scenic float or white-water raft trip with other activities ranging from wildlife tours to horseback rides to gourmet Dutch oven meals.

Barker-Ewing (800/448-4202, www.barker-ewing.com, $82-88 adults, $65-88 children) is a family-operated business that has been running trips for more than 50 years.

Dave Hansen Whitewater (800/732-6295, www.davehansenwhitewater.com, $82-88 adults, $65-88 children) has been in the business since the late 1960s. Dave actually named two of the largest waves on the river, the Lunch Box and the Big Kahuna. Another option with a variety of trips down the Snake River is **Mad River Boat Trips** (800/458-7328, www.mad-river.com, $79-99 adults, $59-94 children).

For experienced floaters who want to tackle the Snake unguided, **Rent-a-Raft** (U.S. 89, Hoback Jct., 13 mi/20.9 km south of Jackson, 307/733-2728, www.rentaraft.net) offers 11-foot ($65), 12.5-foot ($90), 13-foot ($105), and 14-foot rafts ($125) as well as sit-on-top kayaks, one- and two-person ducks ($40), and shuttle service from its headquarters.

Hiking

Snow King Mountain

Distance: 3.6 miles (5.8 km) round-trip
Duration: 3-4 hours
Elevation change: 1,500 feet (457 m)
Effort: strenuous
Trailhead: at the corner of Snow King Avenue and Cache Street

Hiking up Snow King Mountain in Bridger-Teton National Forest is something locals do for exercise, but it's also a worthy climb for scenery. The 360-degree view from the summit takes in the Tetons, National Elk Refuge, Gros Ventre Mountains, Sleeping Indian, and the town of Jackson. Prepare for a grunt and carry water: The route climbs 1,571 vertical feet. To avoid the knee-pounding descent, take the chairlift down from **Snow King Mountain** (100 E. Snow King Ave., 307/734-3194 or 307/734-9442, http://snowkingmountain.com, 9am-6pm daily late May-early Sept., $5).

From the base area, find the **Snow King Summit Trail** above the ticket office at the chairlift. The path is a combination of trail and service roads. Climb three switchbacks, passing the Sink or Swim Trail, to a signed junction with a mountain road. Turn west and traverse the slope to the end of a switchback, where the steep work begins. Climb up three more switchbacks on the dirt road. The route crests out on the ridge, where

a dirt road reaches the summit and the top of the chairlift. Alternate trails also go to the summit.

Cirque Trail

Distance: 1.8 miles (2.9 km) one-way
Duration: 1.5 hours
Elevation change: 1,323 feet (403 m)
Effort: moderate down, strenuous up
Trailhead: summit of Rendezvous Mountain at Jackson Hole Mountain Resort

The Cirque Trail connects the top of the Aerial Tram with Bridger Gondola. Most hikers take the tram up and hike down to the gondola before riding back down to Teton Village, but reversing the route works, too, if you want more challenge. From below Corbet's Cabin, follow the trail in a steep descent of a ridge. Stop en route to look down the dizzying Corbet's Couloir. After short switchbacks descend a boulder spine with rough block steps, the trail swings north into the cirque below the couloir. It drops through steep wildflower meadows and under dramatic cliffs to the top of the gondola. Views sweep across Jackson Hole on the entire route. To add more scenery, extend the hike from the junction above the gondola onto **Casper Ridge** (1.75 mi rt, 1.5 hours).

Rock Springs Loop

Distance: 4.3 miles (6.9 km) round-trip
Duration: 2.5 hours
Elevation change: 1,000 feet (305 m)
Effort: moderately strenuous
Trailhead: summit of Rendezvous Mountain at Jackson Hole Mountain Resort

From the top of the tram on Rendezvous Mountain, hike a combination of service roads and trails to take in views of Jackson Hole, the Gros Ventre Mountains, and the Tetons. Begin by taking the **Top of the World Loop** (a service road) along the ridge southward. Those looking for a short jaunt (0.5 mile round-trip) can just walk the loop back to the summit. En route, you'll pass spur trails going to **Green River Overlook,**

Rock Springs Overlook, and **Cody Bowl Overlook.**

From the lower end of the loop, continue downhill following the signed route across Rendezvous Bowl into wildflower meadows alternating with forest patches. Listen at talus slopes for the high-pitched "eep" from pikas. After passing wet seeps of Rock Springs, the route climbs back to the summit via a service road.

Guided Hikes

For excellent guided hiking in the Tetons and around the valley, contact **The Hole Hiking Experience** (307/690-4453 or 866/733-4453, www.holehike.com, half day from $250 for up to 2 hikers, $95 pp for 3 or more, full day $485 for up to 2 hikers, $195 pp for 3 or more), which offers a wide variety of trips from half-day naturalist-guided trips geared to families to strenuous all-day hikes and even yoga-hiking combinations.

Mountain Biking

For guided mountain bike trips for the whole family (including kids on Trail-a-Bikes and in trailers) or more extreme riders, contact **Teton Mountain Bike Tours** (545 N. Cache St., 307/733-0712, www.tetonmtbike.com) for half-day (from $75 pp), full-day (from $115-165 pp plus $10 box lunch), multiday, and specialty trip offerings. They also rent bikes.

Hoback Sports (520 W. Broadway Ave., 307/733-5335, www.hobacksports.com, 9am-7pm daily) has all kinds of rental bikes for adults and kids, from road bikes ($59-79 for 3 hours, $69-89 full day) and hybrids ($39 for 3 hours, $49 full day) to full-suspension mountain bikes ($69-79 for 3 hours, $79-89 full day), and can point bikers in the direction of any kind of ride they seek. They also offer a handy trail guide on their website.

Horseback Riding

Another popular way to experience the great outdoors in Jackson is on horseback. Several options, including hourly rentals, half-day trail rides, or overnight pack trips, are available from the many local outfitters in and around town. For half-day trail rides, expect to pay around $120-150 per person.

Located 35 miles (56 km) south of Jackson, **Jackson Hole Outfitters** (307/699-3541, www.jacksonholetrailrides.com, early June-early Sept.) starts its trail rides in the secluded Greys River camp and follows trails through the Bridger-Teton National Forest. It offers half-day rides ($120), full-day rides ($175), 5.5-hour extreme rides ($210), and overnight stays ($95) in comfortable canvas tents and real beds.

Spring Creek Ranch (1600 N. East Butte Rd., 307/733-8833 or 800/443-6139, www.springcreekranch.com, mid-May-mid-Oct.) offers one-hour rides ($49), two-hour rides ($69), and half-day rides ($159) along the East Gros Ventre Butte. It also offers wagon rides to a chuck wagon dinner ($75 adults, $45 children 12 and under) Sunday, Tuesday, and Thursday nights at 6pm. Age restrictions vary for the different rides.

Mill Iron Ranch (307/733-6390 or 888/808-6390, www.millironranch.net), 10.5 miles south of Jackson on U.S. 89/191, offers two-hour ($80), four-hour ($140), or full-day trips ($220-280) that can be combined with breakfast, lunch, fishing, or a steak dinner for an additional charge.

Golf

Golf is becoming increasingly popular in Jackson Hole (maybe because the ball seems to fly so much farther at altitude), and there are a couple of world-class public courses. The **Jackson Hole Golf & Tennis Club** (5000 Spring Gulch Rd., 307/733-3111, www.jhgtc.com, $70-190 with twilight discounts after 2pm) offers an award-winning 18-hole course designed by Bob Baldock and renovated twice by Robert Trent Jones II, most recently in 2004. Local conservation hero Laurance Rockefeller once owned the course, which says a lot about its natural beauty. The 18-hole course at **Teton Pines Country Club** (3450 Clubhouse Dr., 307/733-1005 or 800/238-2223, www.tetonpines.com, $130-175 for 18 holes, $85 for 9 holes) in Teton Village was designed by Arnold Palmer and has been highly ranked by *Condé Nast Traveler, Audubon International,* and *Golf Digest,* among others.

Skiing and Mountain Sports

Jackson's reputation among the West's premier ski towns is not hard to explain. There are three developed downhill ski resorts, the closet one being right in town.

For avid Nordic skiers, the blanket of snow transforms many favorite local hiking trails into first-rate **cross-country skiing** trails. There's terrain for everyone. Hit the groomers at local golf courses, including **Teton Pines** (3450 N. Clubhouse Dr., 307/733-1733 or 800/238-2223, www.tetonpines.com, 9am-4pm mid-Dec.-mid-Mar., $17 adults, $12 seniors, $10 children 6-12, rentals from $25), or hoof into the backcountry in Grand Teton National Park.

The **Jackson Hole Nordic Center** (3395 Village Dr., 307/739-2629, www.jhnordic.com) at Teton Village offers 11 miles (17.7 km) of groomed trails for classic and skate skiers. Rentals are available on-site. In town, alpine, cross-country, skate, or snowshoeing gear can be purchased or rented from **Skinny Skis** (65 W. Deloney Ave., 307/733-6094 or 888/733-7205, www.skinnyskis.com, from $20) or **Teton Mountaineering** (170 N. Cache St., 307/733-3595, www.tetonmtn.com).

Snow King Mountain

Jackson is a ski town in the most literal sense. **Snow King Mountain** (400 E. Snow King Ave., 307/201-5464, www.snowkingmountain.com, full-day $55 adults, $45 juniors 6-14 and seniors, free for children 5 and under; half-day $45 adults, $30 juniors and seniors; night

skiing 4pm-7pm $30 adults, $25 juniors and seniors) soars skyward just six blocks from Town Square. The mountain was developed for skiing in 1939, making it the first in the Jackson area and one of the first in the country.

The area boasts 1,571 feet (479 m) of vertical drop over 400 acres with two double chairlifts, one triple lift, a surface tow, and the ever-popular **Snow Tubing Park** ($20 first hour, $10 each additional hour). The area is open for day and night skiing. Discounts are available for lodging guests.

Nonskiers can pay to ride the **lift** ($20 adults, $15 seniors and kids 12 and under) just to enjoy the breathtaking views of town and the valley from the summit. In the summer, the trails and lifts are open for hiking, mountain biking, and paragliding, plus a cowboy roller coaster, an alpine slide, and a ropes course.

Jackson Hole Mountain Resort

In nearby Teton Village, the ski area at **Jackson Hole Mountain Resort** (307/733-2292 or 888/DEEP-SNOW, www.jacksonhole.com, $104-158 adults, free for children 5 and under) is in fact two mountains. Apres Vous and Rendezvous together offer skiers 2,500 skiable acres, a vertical drop of 4,139 feet (1,262 m), and open access to more than 3,000 acres of backcountry terrain. There are 129 trails, of which a whopping 50 percent are geared to experts, 40 percent are for intermediate skiers, and 10 percent are for beginners. The ski hill averages 459 inches (1,166 cm) of snow annually, and in 2018, it topped 500 inches (1,270 cm)! In Jackson, this is the mountain to ski and be seen. Prices rise as the season progresses, especially around the holidays. Discounts are available online.

The resort's **aerial tram** (9am-5pm daily late May-mid-June, 9am-6pm daily mid-June-early Sept., single ride from $34 adults, $27 seniors, $18 juniors 6-14, $89 family with up to four children, free for children under 6), known as Big Red or the Red Heli, takes hikers, bikers, paragliders, backcountry skiers, and lookie-loos up to the summit of Rendezvous Peak (4,139 ft/1,262 m) in nine minutes. At the top, a fabulous little waffle hut, **Corbet's Cabin** (307/739-2688, 9am-4:30pm daily in season), makes you wish you had hiked the whole way.

Grand Targhee Resort

Although you need to go through Idaho to get there, **Grand Targhee Resort** (3300 Ski Hill Rd., 307/353-2300, www.grandtarghee.com, full day $90-95 adults, $65-70 seniors, $37-42 juniors 6-12, free for children under 6) in Alta, Wyoming, is a destination in itself. The skiing is out of this world, with huge dumps of powder and expansive terrain. The resort also offers Nordic skiing, tubing, guided snowcat tours, sleigh-ride dinners, snowmobile tours, and ice climbing. In summer, the mountain stays awake for hiking, mountain biking, horseback riding, and a couple of renowned musical events, including **Targhee Fest** and the **Grand Targhee Bluegrass Festival.**

Food

For every opportunity this region provides to exert energy by skiing, hiking, biking, or other pursuits, Jackson offers many more ways to replenish your supply. The number of outstanding restaurants in this town puts just about every other town in Wyoming—and many Western states—to shame.

As a rule, every day in Jackson should start with a trip to ★ **The Bunnery** (130 N. Cache Dr., 307/733-5474, www.bunnery.com, 7am-3pm daily, $10-17). The food is entirely made from scratch and utterly scrumptious. The baked goods—including its trademark OSM (oats, sunflower, millet) bread and homemade granola—are beyond compare, and the enormous and diverse menu offers plenty of healthy options as well as a few decadent ones. The "Get Your Buns in Here" bumper stickers are also good for a laugh. Be prepared to wait, however: The Bunnery is beloved by visitors and locals alike.

Just as the best days in Jackson should start at The Bunnery, so too should they finish at the **Million Dollar Cowboy Bar** (25 N. Cache Dr., 307/733-2207, www.milliondollarcowboybar.com, 11am-2am daily summer, noon-2am daily winter, Fri.-Sat. 9pm-1:30am off-season, bar food $9-17), right on Town Square. The bar has been a centerpiece of Jackson since 1937 when the first liquor license was issued in the state. The saddle barstools should absolutely be sat upon and visitors are encouraged to check out the impressive collection of Western memorabilia adorning the bar. There is live music regularly, and patrons who don't want to go too far can enjoy a hearty meal next door in the **Million Dollar Cowboy Steakhouse** (307/733-4790, www.jhcowboysteakhouse.com, 5:30pm-10pm daily, $24-29), featuring specialties like beer and bone marrow fondue, short rib nachos, grilled halibut, and any kind of steak you can imagine. Reservations are recommended. During the "Hidden Hour" from 8pm to 9pm daily, take half off the Den Menu ($13-17), well cocktails, and wines by the glass.

Inspired by New York's popular food hall Eataly, but every bit Jackson Hole, **Bin 22** (200 W. Broadway, 307/739-9463, www.bin22jackson.com, wine bar 11am-10pm Mon.-Sat., 3pm-10pm Sun., retail shop 10am-10pm daily, $9-16) is a great spot for a light bite or to pick up a bottle of wine to go. It has all sorts of salamis and cheeses, plus appetizers and tapas-style plates.

Newer on the Jackson scene, and often with a line out front, ★ **Persephone Bakery** (145 E. Broadway, 307/200-6708, www.persephonebakery.com, 7am-3pm daily, pastry case and beverages 7am-6pm Mon.-Sat. and 7am-5pm Sun. summer, call for winter hours, $9-14) is an artisanal bakery and café known for French-style rustic, elegant breads and pastries, and excellent salads and sandwiches for lunch. Don't miss the quiche Lorraine. It also offers afternoon high tea service (reservations required) and a nice wine list and cocktail menu. How's that for a Jackson Hole bakery?

Set in a 1910 log cabin, one of the oldest residential structures in town, **Café Geneviève** (135 E. Broadway, 307/732-1910, www.genevievejh.com, 8am-9pm daily, $24-38) serves inspired home cooking with dishes like red curry baby back ribs, smoked turkey leg, and steak frites. It serves a killer breakfast until 3pm with specialties like grits and eggs, sweet and spicy candied bacon (known as "pig candy"), corned beef hash, and fried chicken and waffles. Fido will appreciate the pet-friendly deck. There's also a daily happy hour (3pm-5:30pm) and a nice wine list.

A fresh and lively arrival on Jackson's culinary scene is ★ **Hatch Taqueria & Tequilas** (120 W. Broadway, 307/203-2780, www.hatchjh.com, 8am-10pm daily, $18-23), which offers the freshest take on 10 varieties of tacos, plus specialties like elk quesadilla, braised bison enchiladas, chili-spiced yellowfin tuna, and delicious standbys like burgers and eggs Benedict. It has phenomenal margaritas and other cocktails, as well as a significant menu of tequilas. Another terrific Mexican restaurant right in town is **The Merry Piglets** (160 N. Cache St., 307/733-2966, www.merrypiglets.com, 11:30am-9pm daily, $10-26), which serves classic taco, burrito, chimichanga, and enchilada plates with fresh salsas, sauces, and tortilla chips, all made in-house daily. The fish is wild-caught, the meat is pasture-raised, and no partially hydrogenated oils are used. The portions are big, and the flavors are very satisfying.

Known for its rack of lamb, but accomplished at everything on the menu, **The Blue Lion** (160 N. Millward St., 307/733-3912, www.bluelionrestaurant.com, 5:30pm-9pm daily, $23-44) has been a staple of the Jackson food scene for more than two decades, with menu items ranging from elk and buffalo tenderloin and Idaho trout to rack of lamb and hazelnut-crusted chicken. There's also a children's menu. Reservations are recommended.

For burger lovers, the best spot in town is **MacPhail's Burgers** (399 W. Broadway, 307/733-8744, www.macphailsburgers. com, 4pm-9pm Tues.-Sat., $14-32), a classic burger joint—but not cheap! MacPhail's uses premium Angus beef from local ranches that is ground fresh daily. They also serve bison burgers, cheesesteaks, chicken sandwiches, and steak meals, plus salads and smaller meals. As is true at any good burger joint, the milk shakes are great—but so too are the local brews.

Every ski town worth its salt needs a good hometown pizza joint. **Pizzeria Caldera** (20 W. Broadway, 307/201-1472, www.pizzeriacaldera.com, 11am-9:30pm daily, $10-17) serves up thin-crust Napoletana-style pizza baked over stone-hearth fires. Options range from classic Italian margherita to pure Jackson Hole, like the Bisonte, with bison sausage and fresh sage. There is also a great beer and wine list, plus yummy salads, pastas, and tapas.

Although it is every inch a Four Seasons, this is still Wyoming, and there is a casualness that puts visitors at ease here. The hotel has some exquisite restaurants, **Westbank Grill** (serving breakfast, lunch, and dinner) among them, but a great little spot is the **Ascent Lounge** (7680 Granite Loop Rd., Teton Village, 307/732-5000, www.fourseasons.com/jacksonhole, 3pm-11pm daily, $13-29), which feels like an oversize living room and serves casual but still elegant light fare with pan-Asian flair, including Thai chicken lettuce cups, tuna poke bowl, and salmon-hamachi avocado roll. It's smaller than the resort's other restaurants, with seating for 38. As it's quite popular with the locals, the overflow spills out onto the gorgeous mountainside patio that is heated in winter.

In Teton Village, a longtime favorite is the **Mangy Moose Restaurant and Saloon** (3295 Village Dr., 307/733-4913, www.mangymoose.com, 8am-9pm daily, saloon 11:30am-late daily summer and ski season, $17-40). The menu is packed with upscale pub fare including a bison burger with truffle fries, prime rib, baby back ribs, and grilled rainbow trout.

Right on the Town Square is one of Jackson's most celebrated eating establishments, the **Snake River Grill** (84 E. Broadway, 307/733-0557, www.snakerivergrill.com, 5:30pm-9:30pm daily summer, from 6pm daily winter, $21-66). A visual feast in addition to being a gastronomical delight, the Snake River Grill has largely defined Jackson Hole cuisine with offerings like crispy pork shank, cast iron-roasted elk chop, and Wagyu boneless beef rib eye. The menu is diverse, constantly changing, and completely mouthwatering. It's worth noting that although children are welcome in the restaurant, no high chairs or children's menus are available.

An elegant option for an unforgettable meal is at the Rusty Parrot Lodge & Spa's ★ **Wild Sage** (175 N. Jackson St., 307/733-2000, www.rustyparrot.com, 5:30pm-9:30pm daily, $29-41). With only eight tables, the service is as notable as the food. From dry-aged duck to bison short ribs, Wild Sage has made quite a name for itself in the intermountain West culinary scene. Reservations are strongly recommended.

Accommodations

While there are plenty of places to hang your hat in Jackson, during the prime seasons those places will not come cheap. In summer, there really is no such thing as a good deal. Just off Town Square, the ★ **Anvil Motel** (215 N. Cache St., 800/234-4507, www.anvilmotel.com, $94-375), might be as close as you can get. The rooms are mountain-rustic with thoughtful details and custom furnishings, and some have air-conditioning.

Almost as close to Town Square but quite a bit higher on the luxury scale is **The Wort Hotel** (50 N. Glenwood St., 800/322-2727, www.worthotel.com, $158-799), built in 1941 and a landmark in town, complete with the legendary Silver Dollar Bar & Grill, which has more than 2,000 inlaid silver dollars as time capsule-type decorations. The rooms are plush, and the location is great. Just down the street, the **Rusty Parrot Lodge & Spa** (175 N. Jackson St., 307/733-2000 or 888/739-1749, www.rustyparrot.com, $230-515) is like a little oasis at the edge of town. From the on-site spa to the world-class dining at Wild Sage Restaurant, every little detail is well considered. The 31 rooms and suites are luxurious; some even have fireplaces and jetted tubs.

Just four blocks from Town Square, ★ **Rustic Inn Creekside Resort & Spa** (475 N. Cache St., 800/323-9279 or 307/733-2357, www.rusticinnatjh.com, double queen rooms $149-809) is an oasis of calm set on 12 beautifully landscaped acres of. The creek-side cabins are farther from the road and quieter, but the whole property is lovely. The log cabins are cozy and elegantly appointed. The spa is excellent, as are the on-site dining options.

Although independent hotels and inns tend to reflect more of Jackson's charm, there are plenty of nice chain hotels, some of which can offer good deals, particularly in the off-season. Among them are **Hampton Inn** (350 U.S. 89 S., 307/733-0033, www.hamptoninn3.hilton.com, $149-458); **Jackson Hole Super 8** (750 U.S. 89 S., 307/733-6833, www.jacksonholesuper8.com, $79-284), which is steps away from the free bus service in town; and **Motel 6** (600 U.S. 89 S., 307/733-1620, www.motel6.com, $82-209).

A comfortable bed-and-breakfast with easy access to both town and country is **Inn on the Creek** (295 N. Millward, 307/739-1565, www.innonthecreek.com, $149-359), which offers balconies, fireplaces, king beds, and private Jacuzzis in some of its rooms. Another very peaceful place to stay with a babbling creek to help lull you to sleep is the **Wildflower Lodge at Jackson Hole** (3725 Shooting Star Ln., Wilson, 307/733-4710, www.jhwildflowerlodge.com, 2 nights from $598), which boasts cozy handcrafted log beds, fluffy comforters, and delicious food. There's even a kids' bunk room with eight beds for families traveling together.

A cozy, welcoming property within walking distance of everything downtown, ★ **Alpine House Lodge & Cottages** (285 N. Glenwood St., 307/739-1570, www.alpinehouse.com, $190-705) is geared toward people who want to make the most of their time in the mountains. Alpine House boasts free cruiser bikes, a little spa, a self-service bar, and a common fridge for restaurant leftovers and hiking snacks. The 22 lodge rooms are small and super comfortable, and the service is beyond friendly. (There are also five rustic cottages.) Breakfasts are substantial and delicious, and the common spaces are always inviting with good books, interesting people, and yummy treats around every corner. There is a two-night minimum stay for the cottages in summer.

For unparalleled luxury in the heart of this mountain village, Jackson has plenty of options. **Amangani** (1535 NE Butte Rd., 307/734-7333, www.amanresorts.com, from $800-2,450) is perched on the edge of a butte with stunning views of meadows and mountains from every window. In addition to deluxe suites and first-class service, Amangani rents spectacular homes.

In Teton Village at the base of the ski hill, the five-star **Four Seasons Resort** (7680 Granite Loop Rd., 307/732-5000, www.fourseasons.com, from $315-3,500) offers ski-in/ski-out access with exquisite amenities including outstanding dining, a spa, and flawless service.

Away from the bustle of town, perched on a ridge overlooking the entire valley, is the **Spring Creek Ranch** (1800 Spirit Dance Rd., 307/733-8833 or 800/443-6139, www.springcreekranch.com, from $200 spring and fall, $320 early summer, $400 summer, $200 winter), which boasts a variety of accommodations, including hotel rooms, cabins, condos, and exclusive mountain villas. The property is entirely self-contained with two restaurants on-site, a spa, and a slew of activities. The views from here beat just about everything else in the region, and the quiet gives Spring Creek Ranch tremendous appeal.

At Teton Village, **Hotel Terra** (3335 W. Village Dr., 307/201-6065 or 800/318-8707, www.hotelterrajacksonhole.com, $188-1,200) is a hip choice, at once luxurious and sustainable. The ecofriendly rooms have clean lines, retro-funky appointments, and lots of gadgets for techies, including iPod docking stations, flat-screen high-definition TVs, and Bose surround sound. The 132 guest rooms and suites range in size and style from studios to one- to three-bedroom suites. There are two restaurants on-site, a lively bar, a rooftop swimming pool and hot tub, a day spa, and a fitness center.

Guest Ranches

For many visitors, the best way to enjoy Jackson Hole is to while away the days at a scenery-soaked dude ranch somewhere in the valley; after all, it was the dude ranches that jump-started Jackson's economy in the 1920s and 1930s. A multitude of wonderful choices are available, ranging from the historic and rustic, like the **Flat Creek Ranch** (15 bumpy mi/24 km from Jackson in isolated splendor, 307/733-0603 or 866/522-3344, www.flatcreekranch.com, all-inclusive, 3-night stays in summer from $3,150 for 2 people, 3-night stays in spring or fall $2,400 for 2 people, 7-night stays in summer $7,350 for 2 people), to the extravagant, like **Lost Creek Ranch & Spa** (17820 Old Ranch Rd., Moose, 30 minutes north of Jackson, 307/733-3435, www.

lostcreek.com, cabins from $5,500/week per cabin for 1-2 people), to the family-oriented, like the **Heart Six Guest Ranch** (Moran, 35 mi/56 km north of Jackson, 307/543-2477, www.heartsix.com, 1- to 3-bedroom cabins $199-299 nightly). There are options for every preference: proximity to town, emphasis on riding, this century or last, weekend or week-long stays, and more.

For a comprehensive listing of the dude ranches in the vicinity of Jackson Hole, contact the **Dude Ranchers' Association** (866/399-2339 or 307/587-2339, www.duderanch.org).

Camping

Camping is by far the most economical way to stay in and around Jackson, and there are 14 campgrounds within a 15-mile (24-km) radius of downtown. Among the closest to town is the **Curtis Canyon Campground** (Flat Creek Rd., 8 mi/12.9 km northeast of Jackson, 307/739-5400, www.fs.usda.gov/btnf, mid-May-early Sept., $15), which offers phenomenal views of the Tetons, immediate access to the National Elk Refuge, and terrific mountain hiking trails.

For more information on specific public campgrounds, contact the **Bridger-Teton National Forest** (340 N. Cache Dr., Jackson, 307/739-5500, www.fs.usda.gov).

For RV parks in Jackson, try the large and conveniently located **Virginian Lodge** (750 W. Broadway, 307/733-2792 or 800/262-4999, May 1-Oct. 15, www.virginianlodge.com), which has both motel rooms ($159-259 summer, $64-175 winter) and 103 RV sites (full hookups $110) in addition to all the amenities you could want, including laundry, a pool, a hot tub, a salon, a restaurant, and a saloon.

Information and Services

The most comprehensive spot to get information on the area is the **Jackson Hole and Greater Yellowstone Visitor Center** (532 N. Cache St., 307/733-3316, www.fws.gov, 8am-7pm daily Memorial Day-Sept. 30, 9am-5pm daily Oct. 1-Memorial Day), which houses representatives from the Jackson Hole Chamber of Commerce (307/733-3316), the National Park Service, the Bridger-Teton National Forest, and four other agencies all under the same sod roof.

Rocky Mountain Front

Rocky Mountain Front

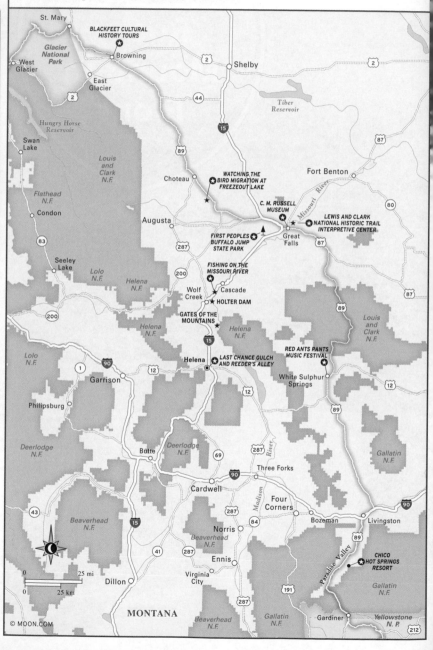

© MOON.COM

Highlights

★ **Chico Hot Springs Resort:** Chico has all the trappings of a resort—hiking, riding, pool, day spa, and sumptuous cuisine—with none of the attitude (page 156).

★ **Last Chance Gulch and Reeder's Alley:** One of the few pedestrian malls in Montana is both the historic and modern heart of Helena (page 160).

★ **Red Ants Pants Music Festival:** Voted Montana's best event of the year in 2018, this family-friendly weekend-long festival in late July offers pastoral beauty, fantastic music, and a real sense of community (page 166).

★ **C. M. Russell Museum:** The most beloved and impressive art museum in the state is an extraordinary tribute to the life and work of the consummate Western artist (page 170).

★ **Lewis and Clark National Historic Trail Interpretive Center:** This compelling museum enables visitors to learn about the extraordinary challenges faced by Lewis and Clark and to appreciate how what they found parallels what exists today (page 171).

★ **First Peoples Buffalo Jump State Park:** One of only three protected buffalo jumps in the state, this mile-long cliff is considered the largest buffalo jump in North America, if not the world (page 171).

★ **Fishing on the Missouri River:** America's longest river attracts anglers from all over the world. The tailwater stretch between Holter Dam and Cascade serves up thousands of trout per mile (page 175).

★ **Watching the Bird Migration at Freezeout Lake:** Around mid- to late March, hundreds of thousands of birds of more than 200 species use this lake as a staging point on their flight back north (page 180).

★ **Blackfeet Cultural History Tours:** Let Blackfeet culture and history come alive on this fascinating guided tour (page 183).

One of the things that makes driving from Yellowstone to Glacier so memorable is that the landscapes and towns along the way are beautiful and interesting in their own right. There's no rush to get from one park to the next. Savor the journey by taking time to explore the back roads, and you'll have a much fuller experience.

There are a number of ways to travel between Yellowstone and Glacier, and not one of them is ugly. But there is something special about cruising along the Rocky Mountain Front, stopping in tiny towns that dot the map, moving back and forth between the mountains and the plains. Traveling between the high, heavily forested Yellowstone plateau and the jagged peaks of Glacier, this wide-open stretch of Montana feels like breathing room. Time moves slowly as you watch the sun drift across the sky and eventually sink behind the spine of the continent. It's also a taste of real Montana—in small communities like Choteau, White Sulphur Springs, and Browning. There are excellent tours, fascinating museums, and some of the best small-town rodeos in the West.

There are bigger towns along the route, too—small cities, even, such as Bozeman, Helena, and Great Falls—where you can find great meals, wonderful art museums, and a most unexpected tiki bar. Don't rush. Plan to spend your time outside, whether at mom-and-pop ski hills along the Rocky Mountain Front, or hiking some of the great trails that are outside every town. There's world-class fishing on the Yellowstone and Missouri Rivers, and plenty of unique and beautiful state parks along the way. Between parks, the point is to go slow. Take it in. Fill the day. Or, better yet, make it two.

Planning Your Time

Just above the northern entrance of Yellowstone is the aptly named **Paradise Valley.** The mountains surrounding the valley are spectacular and beg to be hiked. **Chico Hot Springs Resort** is the place to stay; it boasts some of the best dining in the state, plus a long list of activities.

Just north of Chico is the artsy town of **Livingston,** a small but vibrant community. You could happily spend a morning or afternoon browsing the **shops** and **galleries** downtown, and sampling from its excellent restaurants. The town explodes with enthusiasm and visitors over the **Fourth of July,** and if you can secure a parking spot for the parade and a ticket to the rodeo, dealing with the crowds will be well worth the effort.

The state's capital, **Helena,** is a bustling city that has transitioned into modernity while preserving its past. Recreational opportunities just outside the city are plentiful.

There is as much to do in **Great Falls** as time will allow. Spend a day in the city to see some of the excellent **museums** and nearby natural attractions, including **First Peoples Buffalo Jump State Park.** Known for its consistent wind, this city is ideally located on the **Missouri River** between the Rocky Mountains and Montana's Big Open. Any number of outdoor adventures can be dreamed up and launched from Great Falls.

West of Great Falls, the Rocky Mountains soar skyward, with towns such as **Augusta, Choteau,** and the reservation town of **Browning** in their shadows. **Dude ranches** are available for those who have enough time to spend outside the parks, but at the very least this is a magnificent corner to drive through en route to Glacier National Park. Dinosaur aficionados will want to allow enough time to visit some of the plentiful **paleontological sites,** including **Egg Mountain** and the **Old Trail Museum** in Choteau.

The Rocky Mountain Front in Two Days

With the Rocky Mountain Front behind you, the plains seem to stretch out forever.

Day 1

Whether you wake up in Yellowstone or Grand Teton, make your way north to **Livingston,** where you can stroll downtown and peek into the shops and galleries that line Main Street.

From here, you have a choice to make: Do you want to continue to Glacier on smaller, single-lane roads or larger highways? The difference between choosing the **back roads through White Sulphur Springs** (225 mi/360 km) or the **highways through Helena** (260 mi/420 km) is only about 20 minutes of driving time, with the longer highway route taking slightly more time. Either way, you'll end up in Great Falls for the night, which will set you up for a full day before entering Glacier.

OPTION A: BACK ROADS

Head north on U.S. 89 to the cowboy town of **White Sulphur Springs.** Grab lunch at **Bar 47** and take a soak in the **hot springs** that give the town its name. Continue north, stopping at **Sluice Boxes State Park** to stretch your legs.

Continue to tiny Belt, Montana, where you can sip an excellent microbrew at **Harvest Moon Brewing Company.** From there, drive to **Great Falls,** where you can grab dinner at **Mighty Mo Brewing Company** and see a mermaid show at the **Sip-N-Dip Lounge** before you settle in for the night at the **O'Haire Motor Inn.**

OPTION B: HIGHWAYS

Drive west on I-90 through Bozeman to U.S. 287, which will take you to **Helena.** Stroll around **Last Chance Gulch** and enjoy lunch on the deck at **Karmadillos Southwestern Café** and something sweet at **The Parrot Confectionery.** If you like contemporary art, swing by the always-free **Holter Art Museum** to see outstanding local and regional art.

From Helena, head north past **Gates of the Mountains** and along the **Missouri River** into **Great Falls.**

Day 2

No matter how you get there, make the most of your time in Great Falls with a trip to either the **C. M. Russell Museum** or the **Lewis & Clark National Historic Trail Interpretive Center.** Have a bite to eat at **Bert & Ernie's Tavern & Grill** and then head northwest on U.S. 89 to **Browning.**

In Browning, you can take a fascinating **Blackfeet Cultural History Tour** before you settle in for the night with an outstanding home-cooked meal, stories around the campfire, and a bedroll in a traditional tipi at **Lodge Pole Gallery and Tipi Village.** You'll wake up with the sun, ready to head into Glacier National Park.

Best Restaurants

★ **Chico Hot Springs Resort, Paradise Valley:** Known for exquisite food—often fresh from the on-site garden—and a romantic setting that's popular with Hollywood types, dinner at this resort will be a highlight of your trip (page 154).

★ **Pine Creek Lodge & Café, Paradise Valley:** This is comfort food through and through—burgers, smothered chicken, tacos, and panang coconut curry—all served in a cozy cabin (page 154).

★ **Karmadillos Southwestern Café, Helena:** The best way to enjoy Karmadillos is on the deck, soaking in the view and tucking into a plate of slow-cooked pork or beef with fresh-made sauces and salsas (page 163).

★ **Benny's Bistro, Helena:** A small, farm-to-table restaurant in the heart of downtown Helena, Benny's serves a delicious meal you can feel good about, even if you didn't hike all day (page 164).

★ **Bar 47, White Sulphur Springs:** Serving an eclectic menu with awesome burgers, salads, and tacos, this upscale bar reflects the new West in an Old West town (page 166).

★ **Rose Room, Pendroy:** Spend an evening here for the tiny-town experience and to feel like the restaurant is open just for you—which it may be (page 182).

Livingston and Paradise Valley

Rough-and-tumble Livingston (population 7,401; elevation 4,501 ft/1,372 m) has always been a crossroads of cultures. A railroad town, it was long the launching point for expeditions—both professional and leisurely—into Yellowstone National Park. Paradise Valley, the stunning agricultural and recreational corridor linking Livingston to the north entrance of Yellowstone National Park, was the stomping ground of the Crow, a prized region for fur trappers, and the end point of the great cattle drive from Texas. The town was surrounded by mines, which drew a unique crowd, and today it probably has more literary figures and artists per capita than any other community in the state.

At one point in the early 1880s, there were 40 businesses in town, 30 of which were saloons. Such legendary characters as Calamity Jane and Madame Bulldog were residents. Evidence of those wild days is still visible in various establishments—for example, as bullet holes through the ceiling. The town still has a healthy number of bars, but in a nod to foodies, there are now an equal number of excellent restaurants.

Livingston's transformation into a haven for legendary artists, writers, and actors probably started in the 1960s. Iconic film director Sam Peckinpah took up residence in the town's Murray Hotel, and writers Tom McGuane, Doug Peacock, Tim Cahill, and Richard Brautigan all called Livingston home—and some still do. Actors including Peter Fonda, Jeff Bridges, Michael Keaton, and Dennis Quaid have ranches outside town.

Indeed, Livingston has a rich blended culture that is evident in everything from its sophisticated galleries and gourmet restaurants to its bawdy bars, rollicking rodeo, and fly-fishing paradise.

Best Accommodations

★ **Chico Hot Springs Resort, Paradise Valley:** This resort offers a range of accommodations, from cozy lodge rooms to cabins and more. It also has the best swimming anywhere and an exquisite restaurant (page 156).

★ **O'Haire Motor Inn, Great Falls:** It's the tiki bar and the mermaid shows that make this motel a great place to stop for the night (page 178).

★ **Bunkhouse Inn, Augusta:** In the center of a great little town at the edge of the Rockies, the charming Bunkhouse Inn welcomes guests with comfortable rooms and reasonable prices (page 182).

★ **Lodge Pole Gallery and Tipi Village, Browning:** If sleeping under a blanket of stars sounds like your kind of night, this is the place for you. Bed down in a tipi and dream about Blackfeet history and culture (page 185).

Getting to Livingston
Driving from Jackson, Wyoming
190-240 miles (305-385 km); 5-6.5 hours
From **Jackson Hole,** Livingston is 190 miles (305 km) away, traveling up the east side of Yellowstone National Park—past Lake, Canyon, and Tower Junction—a little over a six-hour drive. Getting to Livingston from Jackson Hole via the west side of Yellowstone—past Old Faithful and Norris Geyser Basin—is 200 miles (320 km), a roughly 6.5-hour drive. When park roads are closed, the only route is via U.S. 20 and U.S. 191 north outside the western boundary of Yellowstone, a 240-mile (385-km), five-hour drive.

Driving from Yellowstone
55 miles (89 km); 1 hour
From the north entrance of Yellowstone at **Gardiner,** Livingston is 55 miles (89 km) north on U.S. 89, a one-hour drive.

Sights
The town's **Depot Center** (200 W. Park St., 406/222-2300, www.livingstonmuseums.org, 10am-5pm Mon.-Sat., 1pm-5pm Sun. Memorial Day-Labor Day, donation) is a majestic building anchoring Livingston to its railroad heritage. In addition to being something of a community center where the town gathers for concerts

and special events, the depot houses a worthwhile museum featuring history, art, and culture of the region. Electric-train buffs should ask for a tour of the basement, where the region's train fanatics have built a wonderland.

On the other side of the tracks, the **Yellowstone Gateway Museum** (118 W. Chinook St., 406/222-4184, www.yellowstonegatewaymuseum.org, 10am-5pm daily Memorial Day-Sept., 10am-5pm Thurs.-Sat. Oct.-Memorial Day, $5 adults, $4 seniors 55 and over, free for children 18 and under), housed in a historic schoolhouse, holds the county's archives and presents some excellent local exhibits on railroad history, pioneer life, Native American cultures, and military history.

Entertainment and Events
The Arts
One of the area's best-kept secrets is **Music Ranch Montana** (4664 Old Yellowstone Trail N., 9 mi/14.5 km south of Livingston, 406/222-2255, www.musicranchmontana.net), a unique music venue for indoor/outdoor concerts in summer. Founded by a well-known entrepreneur and his wife in 1995, Music Ranch has a large barn with both indoor and outdoor seating, including terraces built into the hillside. Talk about an

amphitheater with a view! The ticket prices for the concerts, largely country and folk musicians, are reasonable, and a dance floor right next to the stage keeps the energy up for each concert. Family-owned and operated in the best possible way, attending a concert at Music Ranch feels like a festive family reunion.

Art Galleries

Livingston is a railroad town, but to its core it is also an artists' town. There are over a dozen galleries and many more artists, both brilliant amateurs and sophisticated professionals.

Livingston Art Museum (106 N. Main St., 406/222-6510, www.livingstonartmuseum.org, 11am-5pm Tues.-Fri., noon-5pm Sat., extended summer hours) is the town's oldest gallery. The well-respected gallery focuses on contemporary art with constantly changing exhibitions, and it even promotes school-age child artists through some inspired installations.

Local character and talented artist Parks Reece captures the beauty of the region with a delightful and often mischievous sense of humor. The **Parks Reece Gallery** (119 S. Main St., Ste. A3, 406/222-5724, www.parksreece.com, 9am-5pm Tues.-Fri., 11am-4pm Sat.) should not be missed.

Festivals and Events

Since 1924, the annual **Livingston Roundup Rodeo** (406/222-3199, www.livingstonroundup.com) has enticed cowboys from across the country with its fat purse on the Fourth of July holiday. As crowds overtake the town's fairgrounds with rabid rodeo fever, regular events include barrel racing, bareback team roping, tie-down roping, saddle bronc, steer wrestling, and bull riding. The three-day event—held July 2-4—kicks off with a hometown parade and ends each evening with fireworks. This is without a doubt when Livingston shines brightest. General admission and reserved seating

---

Livingston is a railroad town, an art mecca, and an angler's idea of paradise.

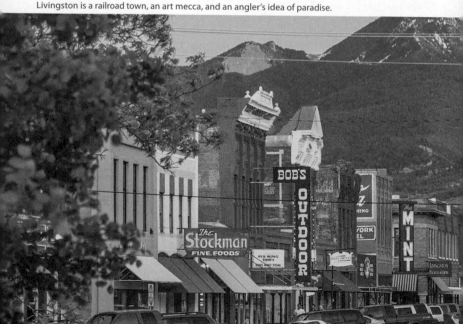

rodeo tickets are available online or by calling; note that both sell out well before July.

In a town as food-savvy as Livingston, it's no surprise that there are a handful of great events at which to sample the local offerings. The wonderful, community-centered **Livingston Farmers Market** (at the band shell in Sacajawea Park, River Dr., 406/222-0730, 4:30pm-7:30pm Wed. early June-mid-Sept.) offers up the region's fresh local bounty in a friendly and festive environment. Live music is performed until 9pm. Sponsored by the Western Sustainability Exchange (www.northrock.org), the event supports a Young Entrepreneur Leadership Program that teaches kids about the intricacies of business and the value of giving back to the community, and a Senior Farmers Market Nutrition Program provides local low-income seniors with $50 vouchers for locally grown veggies, herbs, fruit, and honey at the market.

If you want a fantastic overview of the art scene, and consequently the entire community, hit the town **art walks,** held the fourth Friday of every month late June-September; there is also a single holiday art walk each year in November-December. The town comes out in force to celebrate the arts.

Shopping

Downtown Livingston is a wonderful place to shop, with stores all within walking distance of one another offering a convenient escape from the town's ever-present wind along with an eclectic assortment of wares, from art and clothes to books and equipment. Most shops are closed on Sunday.

Sax & Fryer (109 W. Callender St., 406/222-1421, 9am-5pm Mon.-Fri.) is an anchor for the town and a direct link to its origins. Founded in 1883, the year after Livingston was incorporated, and still run by the Fryer family, the store offers a meaty selection of books from regional and local authors as well as magazines, cards, gifts, and office supplies. An excellent section is devoted to children's books.

B-Hive Artisan Cooperative (113 W. Park St., 406/222-5996, 10am-5pm Mon.-Sat.) is a hip little boutique that is artist-owned and staffed. The collection blends various media—jewelry, yard art, ceramics, hand-blown glass, handbags, and bronze sculpture—and is perfect for those who don't necessarily want their gifts detailed with rusty nails or old barbed-wire.

The Obsidian Collection (108 N. Second St., 406/222-2022, www.theobsidiancollection.com, 10am-6pm Mon.-Sat.) offers an appealing selection of gifts, children's items, jewelry, cards, stationery, soaps, and lotions. Customers are loyal, often driving significant distances to see the latest and greatest collections.

Sports and Recreation
Fishing and Floating

If art defines Livingston, fishing feeds it. The Yellowstone River curves around the town and always makes its presence known. Paradise Valley lives up to its name in countless ways, fishing among them. **Nelson's, Armstrong's, and De Puy's Spring Creeks** are just minutes from town and offer some of the best and most consistent fishing in the state. Winter is an especially good time to fish the spring creeks because the springs flow constantly at a consistent temperature, the crowds are gone, and the rod fees go down significantly. Matson Rogers's **Angler's West Flyfishing** (206 Railroad Ln., off U.S. 89 S., Emigrant, 406/333-4401, www.montanaflyfishers.com) is a great resource, with both a fly shop and complete guiding service for the Yellowstone River and waters around the state. In Livingston, **Dan Bailey's Fly Shop** (209 W. Park St., 406/222-1673, www.dan-bailey.com, 8am-6pm Mon.-Sat., 8am-noon Sun. summer, 8am-6pm Mon.-Sat. winter) is as venerable a fly shop as ever there was, anywhere. In addition to a living history lesson—the shop was established in 1938—the staff at Dan Bailey's can offer superbly qualified advice along with renowned gear and world-famous flies.

To cover a lot of water in this country, with or without a rod, floating on a raft or drift boat can be a great option. While just about any outfitter can arrange to float and fish, **Flying Pig Adventure Company** (888/792-9193, www.flyingpigrafting.com, half day $43 adults, $33 children 12 and under, full day $90 adults, $69 children) and **Montana Whitewater** (603 Scott St., Gardiner, 800/799-4465, www.montanawhitewater.com, half day $43 adults, $32 children 12 and under, full day $82 adults, $62 children) both offer scenic and white-water floats on the Yellowstone River. In addition to its standard menu of day trips,

Flying Pig also offers half-day, all-day, and three-day "Paddle and Saddle" trips.

Hiking

With mountains towering in every direction—the Absarokas and the Gallatins south of town, the Bridgers to the west, and the Crazies to the northeast—and a stiff wind usually blowing, heading out for a hike is never a bad idea in Livingston. Six miles (9.7 km) south of town on the east side of River Road in Paradise Valley, **Pine Creek** is a stunning and popular spot with camping (spots fill up early) and hiking options for every ability level. A nice leisurely amble is the 2-mile (3.2-km) out-and-back trail to **Pine Creek Falls.** Hard-core hikers could hike the steep but mostly shaded 10 miles (16.1 km) to **Pine Creek Lake. Suce Creek, Deep Creek,** and **Mill Creek** all have first-rate trails and stunning scenery, but be aware of bears in the region.

For gear or just good ideas, talk to Dale at **Timber Trails** (309 W. Park St., 406/222-9550, noon-6pm Tues., 9am-6pm Wed.-Mon.), on the main thoroughfare into downtown Livingston. His wonderful little gem of a store also rents mountain bikes.

Food

If the pools bring people to ★ **Chico Hot Springs Resort** (163 Chico Rd., off U.S. 89 S., 23 mi/37 km south of Livingston, Pray, 406/333-4933, www.chicohotsprings.com, $28-50), the food is what transforms them into regulars. From the first taste of baked brie en croûte with Montana huckleberry coulis, through the house-smoked rainbow trout and the gorgonzola filet mignon to the legendary flaming orange, Chico has gone a long way in defining Montana cuisine with fresh local ingredients in simple, hearty, and outstanding dishes. The Chico cookbook, available at the resort, should be in every kitchen.

Closer to town but still set in the grandeur of Paradise Valley, the ★ **Pine**

Cranky Yankee Jim's Road

James George, who earned the moniker Yankee Jim as well as a reputation for being more than a little cantankerous, came to Montana Territory as a young prospector in 1863. When gold eluded him, Jim began to hunt professionally, for meat for the Crow Indian Agency. In 1873, Jim took possession of the road from Bottler's Ranch in Paradise Valley, near present-day Emigrant, to Mammoth by squatting in the canyon along the Yellowstone when the road builders stopped construction. Jim set up a toll booth in the narrowest section of the canyon, today called Yankee Jim Canyon, and charged exorbitant fees to all travelers passing through. At the time, it was the only way for travelers to get from Livingston to Gardiner, Montana, and the brand-new Yellowstone National Park. By all accounts, Yankee Jim made a lot of money but few friends in those days.

In 1883, the Northern Pacific Railway appropriated his roadbed, much to Yankee Jim's chagrin. He negotiated the construction of another road through the canyon (parts of which are still visible along the west side of U.S. 89 South) and used his location above the train tracks reportedly to spit on, curse at, and occasionally fire rifle shots at passing trains. His tirades were supposedly fueled by copious amounts of whiskey.

By 1893, with his road in disrepair and his alcohol intake steadily on the rise, Yankee Jim agreed to surrender his road for a lump sum of $1,000. Local lore inserts Teddy Roosevelt, a frequent visitor to Yellowstone National Park, as the person who convinced Yankee Jim to give up his road and his antics (or else). In 1924, Yankee Jim died penniless in Fresno, California. There are many who believe that his fortune, amassed by all those years of price-gouging in the canyon that bears his name, is buried in the hills between Emigrant and Gardiner.

Creek Lodge & Café (2496 E. River Rd., 10 mi/16.1 km south of Livingston, 406/222-3628, www.pinecreeklodgemontana.com, 4pm-9pm Mon.-Wed., 11am-9pm Thurs.-Fri., 10am-9pm Sun., $9-24) is a longtime favorite and an off-the-beaten-path gem. The menu changes frequently but boasts such fare as pasta with elk sausage and rainbow trout tacos you won't soon forget. Live music and outdoor barbecues take place in summer, and readings by local authors are held in winter. The place was nearly burned down in a big 2012 forest fire, but this little enclave continues to be a wonderful part of the community. Call for reservations.

Not gourmet by any stretch of the imagination, **Mark's In & Out Drive-In** (801 W. Park St., Livingston, 406/222-7744, 11am-10pm daily late spring-early fall, $2-5) just might be the town favorite. There is no seating at this seasonal walk-up or drive-up joint right out of the 1950s, but the burgers, fries, and shakes are so good that you won't mind. There's a park with benches across the street, so you'll be just fine.

Housed in the venerable Murray Hotel, **2nd Street Bistro** (123 N. 2nd St., Livingston, 406/222-9463, www.secondstreetbistro.com, 5pm-close Wed.-Sun., $16-38) serves simple but inspired cuisine—both small and large plates—with French flair and Western attitude. The Mediterranean fish stew is a local favorite, as are the upscale pizzas. All of the meat served is raised locally, as is much of the produce. On Friday and Saturday nights, Montana prime rib is served all night.

Immediately adjacent to the Murray Hotel is **Gil's Goods** (207 W. Park St., Livingston, 406/222-9463, www.gilsgoods.com, 7am-10pm daily, $10-17), a local favorite. Set in a defunct curio shop, the restaurant features an enormous wood-fired oven and such delicious staples as chicken-fried steak, Angus beef burgers, towering sandwiches, salads, and, of course, wood-fired pizzas. The pastries and coffee make a perfect end to any meal.

An excellent regional chain is the **Rib & Chop House** (305 E. Park St., Livingston, 406/222-9200, www.ribandchophouse. com, 11am-9:30pm Mon.-Thurs., 11am-10pm Fri.-Sat., 4pm-9:30pm Sun., $15-45), which serves top-notch steak, seafood, and, obviously, ribs. It's a popular spot (in all of its six Montana and Wyoming locations, plus Pennsylvania and Utah), so reservations are strongly recommended.

Every Western town worth its salt should have a **Stockman** (118 N. Main St., Livingston, 406/222-8455, 11am-2pm and 5pm-9pm Mon.-Thurs., 11am-2pm and 5pm-10pm Fri.-Sat., $9-29). It is an old-school bar with the essence of a supper club. The steaks, prime rib, and burgers are second to none; this is the real Montana.

Accommodations

It's true that Livingston has quite a collection of funky roadside motels that have seen better days, but there are some treasures around town and down the valley. Right in town, the **Murray Hotel** (201 W. Park St., Livingston, 406/222-1350, www. murrayhotel.com, from $229, pets welcome for $25) is a Montana standard. It hasn't been glamorously overhauled, but the authenticity works well, and the place is rich with history, including the story of Will Rogers and Walter Hill trying to bring a saddle horse to the 3rd floor in a 1905 hand-cranked elevator. Guest rooms are well appointed, with elegant details.

Nestled between town and Paradise Valley is the **Blue Winged Olive Angler's Rest** (5157 U.S. 89 S., 3 mi/4.8 km south of Livingston, 406/222-8646, Apr.-Oct., $110 s, $150 d, 3-night minimum), a cute vacation rental geared to anglers (you can hang your waders on the deck to dry). The owners also have a fully outfitted year-round vacation rental cabin ($1,250/

week), which can sleep up to four, along Mill Creek, not far from the Yellowstone River. Either place offers a quiet, comfortable respite for hard-core anglers.

For travelers who long to stay in one place and experience life as a dude, **Mountain Sky Guest Ranch** (480 National Forest Development Rd. 132, Emigrant, 406/333-4911, www.mountainsky.com, all rates weekly Sun.-Sun., $4,430-5,860 adults, $3,790-4,790 children 7-12, $2,950-3,510 children 6 and under) sets the gold standard for summertime family ranch vacations. Set on 10,000 acres of mountains and forests, Mountain Sky offers impeccable service, gourmet dining, charming log cabins, and fantastic activity possibilities, including golf on a Johnny Miller course, a high-energy kids' program, endless alpine trails for horseback riding and hiking, swimming, and even a spa. With such superlative options for balancing family time and adult relaxation, it's small surprise that 87 percent of the guests return year after year, and that entire summers are often booked more than a year in advance.

★ Chico Hot Springs Resort

Built around a natural hot spring that was discovered in the late 1800s, the ★ **Chico Hot Springs Resort** (163 Chico Rd., 23 mi/37 km south of Livingston, Pray, 406/333-4933, www.chicohotsprings. com) has become a Montana icon, as much for its sensational food and raucous saloon as for its heavenly year-round outdoor pools. The resort got its start when Bill and Percie Knowles offered weary miners a clean bed, a hot bath, and fresh strawberries with every meal. The resort has stayed true to its humble origins by offering simple, no-frills guest rooms with shared baths in the main lodge starting at $73-110. Modern accommodations are available in Warren's Wing (from $155), the Lower Lodge (from $155), and in elegant cabins ($245) or pet-friendly rustic cabins ($125-135). Cottages, houses, and chalets (from $260-525) can accommodate larger parties.

For travelers in search of more than a memorable meal and a luxurious soak, Chico offers a number of activities, all of which take advantage of its spectacular location just north of Yellowstone National Park in Paradise Valley. From horseback riding and dogsledding to hiking and cross-country skiing, Chico affords every visitor ample opportunity to earn their dinner.

Information and Services
The **Livingston Chamber of Commerce** (303 E. Park St., Livingston, 406/222-0850, www.livingston-chamber.com, 9am-5pm Mon.-Fri., 9am-1pm Sat.-Sun. Memorial Day-Labor Day, 9am-5pm Mon.-Fri. Labor Day-Memorial Day) is housed in the former crew quarters of the Burlington Northern Railroad. It offers a wide assortment of information about summer and winter activities. Stop by to meet the friendly people and pick up information on restaurants, accommodations, fishing, dude ranches, and more. A computer is available for visitors to check their email or browse the internet.

The **Livingston-Park County Public Library** (228 W. Callender St., Livingston, 406/222-0862, www.livingstonparkcountylibrary.blogspot.com, noon-8pm Mon.-Tues., 10am-8pm Wed.-Thurs., 10am-6pm Fri., 10am-5pm Sat.) offers cozy spaces to work or browse through your guidebook. It has a terrific collection of fly-fishing material and even offers a genealogy service for visitors in the summer. It also has **free internet access.** Computers are available for up to an hour at a time. Internet access can also be found at the internet café **Chadz** (104 N. Main St., Livingston, 406/222-2247, 6:30am-2:30pm daily).

The **main post office** (406/222-0912, 8:30am-5pm Mon.-Fri., 10:30am-12:30pm Sat.) is at 105 North 2nd Street in Livingston.

Livingston HealthCare (320 Alpenglow Ln., Livingston, 406/222-3541) has a 24-hour emergency room. For nonemergency medical care, visit **Urgent Care** (104 Centennial Dr., Livingston, 406/222-0030, 8am-7pm Mon.-Fri., 8am-4pm Sat.-Sun.).

Wash clothes at **Off the Cuff** (322 E. Park St., Livingston, 406/222-7428, 24 hours daily). It has coin-operated washers and dryers, laundry drop-off service, dry cleaning, and free Wi-Fi.

⊕ Detour: Helena

Montana's capital, Helena (population 31,169; elevation 4,090 ft/1,247 m) is an elegant city, the demure little sister to Butte. The city has done a particularly good job of preserving its history by maintaining architecture. The State Capitol Building, for example, is Greek Renaissance style, and the myriad mansions around town are largely Victorian. With its soaring spires and remarkable stained glass, the St. Helena Cathedral would look at home in Europe. There are also humble miners' cabins and historic businesses lining the streets in Last Chance Gulch, the site of the city's origins.

But Helena is not living in the past. The city is growing rapidly, and with that growth comes culture. Helena is becoming recognized as the arts capital of the state, with an edgy, contemporary fine arts scene in addition to extensive performing arts. Located as it is in a wide-open valley surrounded by mountains, lakes, and rivers, Helena also offers endless opportunities to get out of the city and into the wilderness.

Getting to Helena
Driving from Livingston
125 miles (201 km); 2 hours
From **Livingston,** Helena is a 125-mile (201-km), two-hour drive west on I-90 and north on U.S. 287.

Helena

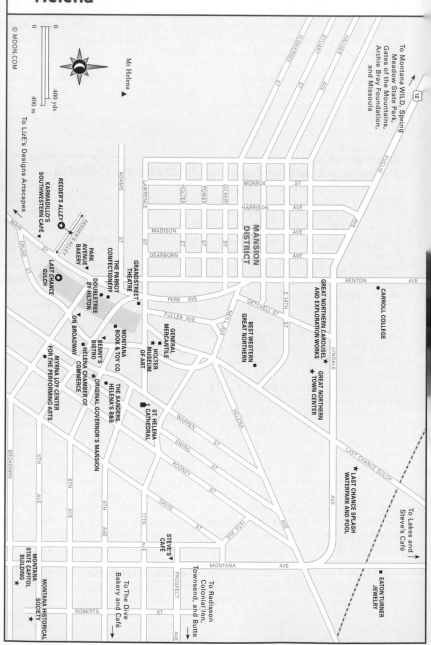

© MOON.COM

0 400 yds
0 400 m

Mt Helena ▲

To Montana WILD, Spring
Meadow State Park,
Gates of the Mountains,
Archie Bray Foundation,
and Missoula

12

To LizE's Designs Artscapes

REEDER'S ALLEY
KARMADILLO'S
SOUTHWESTERN CAFÉ

PARK
AVENUE
BAKERY

THE PARROT
CONFECTIONERY

GRANDSTREET
THEATRE

LAST CHANCE
GULCH

DOUBLETREE
BY HILTON

ON BROADWAY

MONTANA
BOOK & TOY CO.

BENNY'S
BISTRO

HELENA CHAMBER OF
COMMERCE

ORIGINAL GOVERNOR'S MANSION

GENERAL
MERCANTILE

HOLTER
MUSEUM
OF ART

THE SANDERS,
HELENA'S B&B

ST. HELENA
CATHEDRAL

MYRNA LOY CENTER
FOR THE PERFORMING ARTS

MONTANA
STATE CAPITOL
BUILDING

MONTANA HISTORICAL
SOCIETY

STEVE'S
CAFÉ

To The Dive
Bakery and Café

To Radisson
Colonial Inn,
Townsend, and Butte

EATON TURNER
JEWELRY

To Lakes and
Steve's Café

LAST CHANCE SPLASH
WATERPARK AND POOL

GREAT NORTHERN CAROUSEL
AND EXPLORATION WORKS

GREAT NORTHERN
TOWN CENTER

BEST WESTERN
GREAT NORTHERN

CARROLL COLLEGE

MANSION
DISTRICT

MONROE   ST
HARRISON   AVE

LAWRENCE   ST
HOLTER ST
POWER ST
GILBERT ST

MADISON   AVE

DEARBORN   AVE

ADAMS ST

PARK   AVE

FULLER AVE

GETCHELL ST

E 14TH ST

NEILL AVE

LYNDALE

BENTON   AVE

HELENA ST

WARREN   AVE

EWING   ST

ROONEY   ST

DAVIS   ST

LAST CHANCE GULCH

MAIN ST
CRUISE ST

BROADWAY

6TH   AVE

8TH   AVE

9TH   AVE

11TH   AVE

13TH AVE

PROSPECT   AVE

MONTANA   AVE

ROBERTS   ST

EUCLID

FLORENCE ST
STUART AVE
HAUSER AVE

Driving from White Sulphur Springs
75 miles (121 km); 1.5 hours
From **White Sulphur Springs** to Helena, it's 75 miles (121 km) west on U.S. 12 and north on U.S. 287, a 1.5-hour drive.

Driving from Great Falls
90 miles (145 km); 1.5 hours
To get to Helena from **Great Falls,** it's a 90-mile (145-km) drive southwest via I-15, which will take about 1.5 hours.

Air
The **Helena Regional Airport** (HLN, 2850 Skyway Dr., 406/442-2821, www.helenaairport.com) is just 2.5 miles (4 km) from the city center and is served by Delta/SkyWest, Alaska/Horizon, and United. The car-rental agencies at the airport are **Alamo, Avis, Budget, Hertz,** and **National.**

Shuttles to the airport are provided by hotels in town. The courtesy phone to contact them is located in the baggage claim area. There is also a courtesy phone to call **Capitol Taxi** (406/449-5525). **Helena Towncar** (406/437-8585, www.helenatowncar.com) is another option for getting to your hotel.

Bus
Greyhound (www.greyhound.com) has a station at the **Capital Transit Center** (1415 N. Montana Ave.) in Helena. It runs several bus routes to and from nearby cities, including Bozeman, Billings, and Butte.

Getting Around
Capital Transit (406/447-8080, www.ridethecapitalt.org, $0.85 single ride, $2.60 all-day pass) operates fixed-route **bus service** (7am-6pm Mon.-Fri.), with nine loops around the city.

Capitol Taxi (406/449-5525) and **Helena Towncar** (406/437-8585, www.

Top to bottom: section of the Yellowstone River in Gardiner; Helena cityscape at night; Montana State Capitol building.

helenatowncar.com) provide service throughout the city.

Sights
Last Chance Tour Train

One of the best ways to get an overview of the city and some historical perspective is by hopping on one of the **Last Chance Tours** (tours depart from Montana Historical Society, 225 N. Roberts, on the corner of E. 6th Ave., 406/442-1023, www.lctours.com, Mon.-Sat. June-Sept. 15, $10 ages 13-59, $9 seniors 60 and over, $8 children 4-12, free for children under 4). The wheeled trains and trolley cruise around town with commentary on places like Reeder's Alley, the Old Fire Tower, Last Chance Gulch, and the city's tree-lined Mansion District. Tours depart at 11am and 3pm June 1-14 and September 1-15; 11am, 1pm, and 3pm June 15-30; and 11am, 1pm, 3pm, and 5:30pm July-August. Plan to arrive 15 minutes before departure time for any tour.

Montana State Capitol

Its weathered copper dome visible for miles around, the **Montana State Capitol** (225 N. Roberts St., 406/444-2694 or 406/444-4789, www.visit-the-capitol. mt.gov, 7am-6pm Mon.-Sat., 11am-5pm Sun.) unites Montana's past and present in a very ornate and interesting way. The building itself is something of a Greek Renaissance masterpiece. Started in 1898, the main portion of the building was completed in 1902, and the wings were unveiled 10 years later. The building is filled with dramatic art by some of Montana's most recognizable legends, among them Charles M. Russell and Edgar Paxson.

Self-guided tours are possible 9am-5pm daily. **Guided tours** (free) are offered on the hour 10am-2pm Monday-Saturday in summer, and on the hour 10am-2pm Saturday only mid-September-mid-May. When the legislature is in session, in odd-numbered years, tours are offered 9am-2pm Monday-Saturday January-April.

The capitol is always closed on state holidays and on Sunday when the legislature is in session.

Montana Historical Society

With a phenomenal collection spanning 12,000 years of history, the **Montana Historical Society** (225 N. Roberts St., 406/444-2964, www. montanahistoricalsociety.org, 9am-5pm Mon.-Wed. and Fri.-Sat., 9am-8pm Thurs., $5 adults, $1 children, $12 family, free admission the second Sat. of every month) is the best historical resource in the state. There is an impressive art gallery, photo archives, a Native American collection, and decorative arts—more than 50,000 artifacts in all. A wonderful long-term exhibit explores what Montana must have been like at the time of Lewis and Clark. There are also several special exhibits and traveling exhibits. The institution was founded in 1865, making it among the oldest of its kind in the western United States.

Original Governor's Mansion

Built in 1888 by a wealthy businessman, this Queen Anne-style mansion was owned by a number of important Helena residents before it was acquired by the state of Montana in 1913 as the **Original Governor's Mansion** (304 N. Ewing St., 406/444-4789, www. montanahistoricalsociety.org, guided tours hourly noon-3pm Tues.-Sat. summer, noon-3pm Sat. only mid-Sept.-mid-May, $4 adults, $1 children, $10 family, combination tickets for museum and tour $8 adults, $1.50 children, $19 family). Since 1959, the mansion has been owned, meticulously restored, and maintained by the Montana Historical Society.

★ Last Chance Gulch and Reeder's Alley

Rarely in the West have important gold or other mineral discovery sites gone on to become the center of big modern cities. Helena is an exception. Four prospectors (known as "the four Georgians") discovered gold in a small tributary of Ten Mile Creek. A mining camp quickly grew up around them, and the discovery site became the camp's main drag. Businesses sprouted up around the creek and never left.

Nearly 150 years after that first discovery, **Last Chance Gulch** (between W. 6th Ave. and Pioneer Park) is still at the heart of the city. But rather than a dusty collection of saloons and brothels, the area has been transformed into a marvelous pedestrian mall that includes dozens of great eateries, a few museums and galleries, wonderful shopping, and one of the most popular candy shops in the state. The area is even home to the **Last Chance Splash Waterpark and Pool** (1203 N. Last Chance Gulch, 406/447-1559, www.lastchancesplash.com, 12:15pm-7pm Mon.-Fri., 1pm-5pm Sat.-Sun., lap swim 9:30am-7pm Mon.-Fri., 1pm-5pm Sat.-Sun. mid-June-mid-Aug, $4.50 adults, $3.50 children 4-12 and seniors, free for children under 3), a welcome stop on a hot day, only about 1 mile (1.6 km) from the mall. If your time in Helena is limited, Last Chance Gulch should be your first stop.

Nearby, **Reeder's Alley** (between S. Park Ave. and S. Benton Ave., across from Pioneer Park, www.reedersalley.com) is a unique little corner of downtown that reflects its humbler origins. The area has remained authentic visually, while some of the small miners' shacks, tenements, stables, and other buildings have been transformed into upscale shops and eateries. The buildings have been designated a historic district in the National Register of Historic Places and are maintained by the Montana Heritage Commission (406/843-5247, www.montanaheritagecommission.mt.gov). Both Reeder's Alley and Last Chance Gulch are worth spending an afternoon or evening, enjoying a meal and some shopping.

Montana WILD

On the west side of Helena, near Spring Meadow Lake State Park, **Montana WILD** (2668 Broadwater Ave., 406/444-9944, http://fwp.mt.gov/education/montanawild, 8:30am-5pm Mon.-Fri.) is the state's flagship education and conservation center, dedicated to all things wild. The 7,000-square-foot refurbished historic building sits on five acres and includes a wildlife rehabilitation center. Naturally a favorite destination with local schoolchildren, it's a great place to get an overview of the wildlife that lives in every corner of the state.

Great Northern Carousel and Exploration Works

The must-see corner of town for kids includes the **Great Northern Carousel** (989 Carousel Way, 406/457-5353, www.gncarousel.com, 11am-8pm Mon.-Fri., 11am-9pm Sat., 11am-7pm Sun., $1.50), a modern, hand-built, Montana lovers' carousel with 37 animals including a grizzly bear, bobcats, bison, and trout, as well as the hands-on **Exploration Works** (995 Carousel Way, 406/457-1800, www.explorationworks.org, 10am-5pm Mon.-Sat., noon-5pm Sun. June-Aug., check website or call ahead for winter hours, $9 adults, $6.50 seniors and students with ID, $5.50 children 2-18, free for children under 2). The museum is an interactive science center with frequently changing exhibits on topics such as space exploration, waterworks, and amazing airways. After you've exhausted your brain in the museum, head next door to the carousel for a leisurely ride and a fantastic ice-cream cone. It's kid paradise.

Gates of the Mountains

Just north of Helena, on the way to Great Falls, is one of the loveliest canyons in Montana. Named Gates of the Mountains by Lewis and Clark in 1805 because of the 1,200-foot (366-m) limestone cliffs that tower on either side of the Missouri River, it has become a favorite recreation area for Helena residents.

There are many ways to enjoy this scenic area on your own, but for those interested in tours, **Gates of the Mountains Boat Tours** (3131 Gates of the Mountains Rd., 20 mi/32 km north of Helena at I-15 exit 209, 406/458-5241, www.gatesofthemountains.com, 8am-8pm daily) has 120-minute cruises ($16 adults 18-59, $14 seniors 60 and over, $10 children 4-17, free for children under 4, dinner cruise $44) from the marina; schedules change daily, so call or go online for details. Abundant wildlife inhabit the area, including bighorn sheep, mountain goats, and more than 120 bird species. You can bring a picnic lunch and get off the boat at Meriwether Picnic Area, returning later on another one. It is also possible to hike from here to **Mann Gulch,** where 13 firefighters were killed by a fast-moving wildfire in 1949.

Entertainment and Events
The Arts
In a town that is becoming known for its art, the **Holter Museum of Art** (12 E. Lawrence St., 406/442-6400, www.holtermuseum.org, 10am-5:30pm Tues.-Sat., noon-4pm Sun., free) is a fascinating place to spend some time. The building was constructed in 1914 and expanded in 1999 to add 6,000 square feet of gallery space. The museum's contemporary collection includes art in a variety of media displayed in more than 25 exhibitions annually, creating a unique voice in the Northwest art scene. The museum makes art education a priority and has managed to keep admission free.

Another cutting-edge artists' workshop and gallery is the **Archie Bray Foundation** (2915 Country Club Ave., 406/443-3502, www.archiebray.org, 10am-5pm Mon.-Sat. year-round, 1pm-5pm Sun. June-Aug., free), an international hotbed of ceramic art in what was once a brick factory. Hundreds of well-known artists have come to work and

exhibit here. Classes and workshops are available for people of all ages and abilities, and some of the studio spaces are open to visitors. The grounds are open daily, year-round, during daylight hours.

There are two marvelous theaters in town that host both musical and dramatic events. The **Myrna Loy Center for the Performing Arts** (15 N. Ewing St., 406/443-0287, www.myrnaloycenter.com) presents contemporary media and performing arts from its glorious theater in the castle-like old county jail. The **Grandstreet Theatre** (325 N. Park Ave., 406/442-4270, www.grandstreettheatre.com) presents classic plays and musicals in a beautifully restored Unitarian church.

Festivals and Events
For a full listing of daily events in Helena, visit www.helenamt.com or www.helenaevents.com.

Every Wednesday throughout summer, a different block of Helena comes to life for **Alive at 5** (406/447-1535, www.downtownhelena.com, 5pm-9pm June-Aug.), a fun and family-oriented event that combines live music, food, and drink for a fantastic summer evening. Happening the first Friday of every month is **First Friday** (406/447-1535, www.downtownhelena.com, 5pm-9pm), which invites visitors to explore downtown shops, galleries, and restaurants.

Once each summer, the Helena Symphony joins Carroll College in presenting **Symphony Under the Stars** (406/442-1860, www.helenasymphony.org, 8:30pm, free) on the hillside at Carroll College. Concerts feature classical, opera, or Broadway-oriented music, and all of them end with a spectacular fireworks display.

In late July-early August, Helena puts on the annual **Last Chance Stampede and Fair** (98 W. Custer Ave., 406/457-8516, www.lewisandclarkcountyfairgrounds.com) at the fairgrounds. In addition to big country-music concerts, the fair includes a rodeo, a carnival, food, and a variety of entertainment.

Shopping

Eaton Turner Jewelry (1735 N. Montana Ave., 406/442-1940, www. eatonturnerjewelry.com, 10am-5:30pm Mon.-Fri.) is the oldest jeweler in the state and has been family owned and operated since 1885. History aside, this is a special store that offers a great selection of jewelry, including local stones like Montana and Yogo sapphires.

A wonderful independent bookstore, **Montana Book & Toy Co.** (331 N. Last Chance Gulch, 406/443-0260 or 877/844-0577, www.mtbookco.com, 9:30am-6pm Mon.-Fri., 9:30am-5pm Sat.) offers a diverse collection of books for all readers, as well as children's toys.

The **General Mercantile** (413 N. Last Chance Gulch, 406/442-6078, www. generalmerc.com, 8am-5:30pm Mon.-Fri., 9am-5pm Sat., 11am-4pm Sun.) is like a step back in time. The Merc serves every variety of coffee and tea, including espresso from vintage machines, and there are all sorts of cozy nooks to sip a latte while perusing a book. The store has gifts and cards galore, but it's the atmosphere in the Merc that makes it so welcoming.

Another unique destination in Helena is **LizE Designs Artscapes** (330 Fuller Ave., 406/459-4081, 10am-5:30pm Wed.-Fri., 10am-4pm Sat.), which sells fine and funky art as well as one-of-a-kind gifts, many of which are crafted from found objects. In addition to her own mixed-media work, Liz showcases various guest artists who work in raku pottery, photography, painting, and jewelry, among other media.

For a real taste of Montana, look no further than **The Parrot Confectionery** (42 N. Last Chance Gulch, 406/442-1470, www.parrotchocolate.com, 9am-6pm Mon.-Sat.), a Montana standard when it comes to candy shops and diners. The shop makes 130 different varieties of candy, and its reputation for hand-dipped chocolates has won customers worldwide. Try a cherry phosphate from the original soda fountain, and sit at the bar for a bowl of the secret-recipe chili. A local favorite since 1922, The Parrot should not be missed.

Food

For a quick bite between sights, and breakfast all day, try **Steve's Café** (1225 E. Custer, 406/444-5010, and 630 N. Montana Ave., 406/449-6666, both locations 6:30am-2:30pm daily, $5-15) for wonderful huckleberry pancakes, breakfast burritos, steak and eggs, burgers, sandwiches, and the like. Another good spot for a quick bite is **The Dive Bakery & Café** (1609 11th Ave., 406/442-2802, www.thedivebakery.com, 6am-4pm Mon.-Fri., $3-9), which is known for its from-scratch pastries, bread, and soup, plus delicious crepes and salads.

For the best artisan bread in town (or maybe the state) try **Park Avenue Bakery** (44 S. Park Ave., 406/449-8424, www. parkavenuebakery.net, 7am-6pm Mon.-Fri., 7am-5pm Sat., 8am-2pm Sun., $4-8), where you can fill up on gorgeous European-style breads, pastries, pizza, quiche, calzone, homemade soups, salads, and dessert.

Atop a hill overlooking Last Chance Gulch and the Helena Valley, ★ **Karmadillos Southwestern Café** (139 Reeder's Alley, 406/442-2595, 11am-9pm Tues.-Sat.) is a perfect spot to sit outside and enjoy a summer afternoon or evening. The food is sensational, all slow-cooked and served with salsas and crèmes prepared fresh daily. Lunch ($7-14) options include nachos, homemade chicken tortilla soup, tacos, enchiladas, and even a savory barbecue-beef sandwich. Dinner ($8-16) offers some of the same items as well as tamales, chiles rellenos, and combo plates. Karmadillos also has a number of vegetarian items and a children's menu. Even if the food weren't so good, you would come just for the incredible view and the spacious outdoor seating. Check their Facebook page for the code word of the day to receive free chips and salsa.

For fine dining in Helena, **On Broadway** (106 Broadway, 406/443-1929, www.onbroadwayinhelena.com, 5:30pm-close Mon.-Sat., $18-43) is the elegant favorite, with mouthwatering pasta dishes, steaks, and seafood, and live jazz on Thursday evenings. For great Italian food, **Lucca's** (56 N. Last Chance Gulch, 406/457-8311, www.luccasitalian.com, 5pm-close Wed.-Sun., $22-34) is a gustatory delight.

Another nice spot just off Last Chance Gulch is ★ **Benny's Bistro** (108 E. 6th St., 406/443-0105, www.bennysbistro.com, 11am-3pm Mon.-Tues., 11am-3pm and 5:30pm-9pm Wed.-Sat., lunch $9-14, dinner $21-31). Set in a renovated historic building, Benny's does a phenomenal job of catering to the "locavore" movement by using as many fresh, locally grown ingredients as possible. Its list of Montana suppliers is vast. You can taste the best of the state in dishes like Mediterranean lamb burger with Montana lamb and local greens, pork and beans with candied bacon made with ginger-rubbed Montana pork loin and a Flathead cherry reduction, plus jerk chicken with chicken from the Hutterite colony. This is Montana cuisine at its best.

Accommodations

While Helena is long on hotels (perhaps for all the legislators who come to govern for four months every other year), most fall into the category of nice upscale chain hotels or nice upscale bed-and-breakfasts.

Still, there are plenty of quality rooms all around town. The **Best Western Great Northern** (835 Great Northern Blvd., 800/829-4947, $153-304) is shiny and new, with decor intended to conjure the Great Northern Railway days. It has all the amenities you could want in a city hotel, and small pets (under 25

pounds/11.3 kg) are welcome for $15 per night per animal for up to two animals. The hotel is ideally located in the **Great Northern Town Center** within walking distance of an eight-screen movie theater, shopping, a children's museum, and a carousel.

Closer to the highway is the **Radisson Colonial Hotel** (2301 Colonial Dr., 406/443-2100, www.radisson.com, $135-244), a large, full-service, very comfortable hotel.

Additional chain hotels and motels that line the major thoroughfares here include the pet-friendly **Baymont Inn & Suites** (750 Fee St., 406/443-1000, www.baymontinns.com, $89-129), the **Comfort Suites** (3180 N. Washington St., 406/495-0505, www.comfortsuiteshelena.com, $99-150), **Days Inn** (2001 Prospect Ave., 406/442-3280, www.wyndhamhotels.com, $76-120), **Holiday Inn Express & Suites** (3170 N. Sanders St., 406/442-7500, www.ihg.com, $134-178), and **Super 8** (2200 11th Ave., 406/443-2450, www.wyndhamhotels.com, $62-80). Situated right downtown in the heart of Last Chance Gulch is the pet-friendly **Doubletree by Hilton Helena Downtown** (22 N. Last Chance Gulch, 406/443-2200, www.doubletree3.hilton.com, $124-213).

For a more historic option near downtown and the state capitol, **The Sanders, Helena's Bed and Breakfast** (328 N. Ewing St., 406/442-3309, www.sandersbb.com, $145-165) offers seven guest rooms in its beautifully appointed 1875 Queen Anne mansion. Many of the furnishings are original to the home, and the owners are gracious and welcoming.

Information and Services

A good source of visitor information is the **Helena Chamber of Commerce** (225 Cruse Ave., 406/442-4120 or 800/743-5362, www.helenachamber.com, 8am-5pm Mon.-Fri.). The **Helena Tourism Alliance** (406/449-1270, www.helenamt.com) is located at 105 Reeder's Alley; hours are determined daily, so call ahead.

A terrific website for planning a trip to Helena is www.helenamt.com. The site allows you to plug in your dates of travel and shows you all the available hotels and their average nightly rates.

The **main post office** (406/443-3304, 8am-6pm Mon.-Fri., 9am-noon Sat.) is at 2300 North Harris Street, and the **Lewis and Clark Library** (406/447-1690, www.lewisandclarklibrary.org, 10am-9pm Mon.-Thurs., 10am-6pm Fri., 10am-5pm Sat., 1pm-5pm Sun.) is at 120 South Last Chance Gulch.

St. Peter's Hospital (2475 Broadway, 406/442-2480, www.stpetes.org) has a 24-hour emergency room. The hospital also runs the **St. Peter's Urgent Care Clinic** (2475 Broadway, 406/447-2488, www.stpetes.org, 9am-8pm daily) and **North Clinic** (3330 Ptarmigan Ln., 406/495-7901, www.stpetes.org, 7am-6pm daily).

The **Clean and Coin Laundromat** (1411 11th Ave., 406/442-9395, 6am-8:50pm daily) has a Ms. Pac-Man machine to entice you while your duds dry.

White Sulphur Springs

Named for the white deposits found around the hot sulfur springs here, White Sulphur Springs (population 908; elevation 5,043 ft/1,537 m) was a gathering spot for various Native Americans tribes for years before James Brewer stumbled on the area in 1886 and developed the hot springs into a resort. The town boomed, first as the "Saratoga of the West," then with lead and silver mines, and then as a cattle town and commercial center for this vast agricultural area. There is nothing booming about White Sulphur Springs these days, but it does have its own charm. In the midst of the prairies, it is close to excellent floating on the Smith River and skiing at Showdown Ski Area, and there are wonderful relics from its glory days: A castle sits atop the hill in town, and the hot springs still gurgle with purportedly healing waters. And every summer the Red Ants Pants Music Festival brings great musicians (country, folk, bluegrass) to a dreamed-up stage in the middle of a cow pasture in the middle of nowhere.

Getting to White Sulphur Springs

From **Livingston,** White Sulphur Springs is 70 miles (113 km) north on U.S. 89, a 75-minute drive.

From **Great Falls,** it's 100 miles (161 km) south on U.S. 89, a one-hour and 45-minute drive. From **Helena,** White Sulphur Springs is 75 miles (121 km) east via U.S. 12, an 80-minute drive.

Sights
Castle Museum
Built in 1892 by merchant Bryon Roger Sherman, **The Castle** is a remarkable Victorian mansion that now houses the **Meagher County Museum** (310 2nd Ave. NE, 406/547-2324, 10am-5pm daily Memorial Day-Labor Day, 10am-5pm Wed.-Sun. Labor Day-Oct., last guided tour of the day at 4pm, $5 adults, $3 seniors and children 4-12, free for children under 4). It was constructed with hand-cut granite blocks hauled by oxen from the Castle Mountains, 12 miles (19.3 km) away. It is appointed with period furniture and original fixtures—Italian marble sinks as well as crystal and brass light fixtures. Sherman supplied electricity to the entire town, making White Sulphur Springs one of the first towns in the state to have electricity.

Spa Hot Springs
These are the waters that give the town its name, and a soak in one of the three pools at **Spa Hot Springs** (202 W. Main St., 406/547-3366, www.spahotsprings.com, 6am-11pm daily) is good for the soul any time of year. Outside, two pools are kept at 98°F (26.7°C) and 103°F (39.4°C). Inside, the pool is 105°F (40.6°C). All are drained and cleaned nightly so that no chemicals have to be added to the natural

hot water. There is a motel attached to the pools, and overnight guests swim for free. Nonguests can use the pools for a fee ($7 adults, $6 seniors and children 13-17, $5 children 6-12, $3 children 3-5, $2 children under 3). Towels and swimsuits can be rented by the brave for $1 each. The springs are open year-round.

Entertainment and Events
★ Red Ants Pants Music Festival
Voted the Best Event of the Year for the State of Montana in 2018, the **Red Ants Pants Music Festival** (Jackson Ln., 3 mi/4.8 km northeast of White Sulphur Springs, 406/209-8135, www.redantspantsmusicfestival.com, $60 day pass, $160 3-day pass, $25 camping pass, free for kids 12 and under, early bird discounts available) is held in late July. It's a family-friendly, three-day weekend of music, food, and camping for those who don't mind the dust. Past headliners have included Dwight Yoakam, Shooter Jennings, Lucinda Williams, Lyle Lovett, and the Wailing Jennies. There's a kids' tent, a beer garden, hayrides, great food vendors, and room to dance. It can be hot and windy with very little shade (bring your own!), but this is a wholesome place to listen to great music. Tickets go on sale with early bird specials in April. The festival was founded in 2011 by Sarah Calhoun, the genius behind the Red Ants Pants brand of workwear for women. Along with her staff and army of volunteers, she is transforming the region by bringing youth and vibrancy and music. In town, stop into **Red Ants Pants** (206 E. Main St., 406/547-3781, www.redantspants.com, 10am-5pm Mon.-Sat.), which sells T-shirts, gifts, and awesome work gear, including pants that don't wear out and are made for women's bodies.

Sports and Recreation
Showdown Montana Ski Area
Showdown Montana Ski Area (2850 U.S. 89, 406/236-5522 or 800/433-0022, www.showdownmontana.com, $47 adults, $37 seniors and ages 11-17, $25 children 6-10, free for children 5 and under) is one of Montana's oldest ski hills, in operation since 1936. In the middle of the not-so-little Little Belts, Showdown sees an average of 245 inches (622 cm) of powder annually. There are four lifts and 34 trails on 620 skiable acres at this family-friendly ski hill, with 40 percent of the runs geared to intermediates and 30 percent each aimed at beginners and experts. Mountain biking is also offered when the snow melts, with the primary season running mid-June-October. Showdown is on U.S. 89, about 30 miles (48 km) north of White Sulphur Springs, on the way to Great Falls.

Food
Dori's Café (112 E. Main St., 406/547-2280, 6am-2pm Mon.-Fri., 6am-1pm Sat., 6am-11am Sun., hours can vary, $5-12) is just what you'd hope to find in a small, middle-of-nowhere Montana town: a friendly place with good, hearty food and the ambience of a wildlife museum.

For dinner and a glimpse of the local nightlife, head to the **Stockman's Bar and Barnwood Steakhouse** (2nd Ave. NE, 406/547-9985, 5pm-10pm daily, bar opens 11am daily, $7-25) for a steak or juicy burger.

For a gourmet experience and a glimpse of the New West, try ★ **Bar 47** (24 E. Main St., 406/547-6330, 11am-2am daily, $10-29), which serves excellent and inspired comfort food including poutine, sea salt caramel fries, cheese curds, pulled pork sliders, phenomenal burgers, street tacos, and steaks. There's also a kids' menu and awesome desserts. Try the grown-up milk shakes too!

Accommodations
To enjoy White Sulphur Springs in the way the earliest settlers intended, make a point to visit the **Spa Hot Springs Motel** (202 W. Main St., 406/547-3366, www.spahotsprings.com, $99-139). The guest

rooms are basic and clean, though some have been recently updated and have pillow-top mattresses, leather recliners, and flat-screen TVs; some pet-friendly rooms are available for a $10 fee. But it's the three hot springs pools that make this place special. There are two outdoor pools and one indoor, all of which are drained and cleaned nightly so that no chemicals have to be added to the natural hot water. Swimming and towels are included for hotel guests. Nonguests can use the pools for a fee ($7 adults, $6 seniors, $6 children 13-17, $5 children 6-12, $3 children 3-5, $2 children under 3). The springs are open 6am-11pm daily year-round.

For nonswimmers, the nearby **All Seasons Inn & Suites** (U.S. 89 S., at the south end of town, 406/547-8888 or 877/314-0241, www.allseasonsinnandsuites.net, $89-160) is a smoke-free modern hotel with a hot tub, free Wi-Fi, and continental breakfast. Dogs are welcome for a $25 fee.

Information

For information about White Sulphur Springs, contact the **Meagher County Chamber of Commerce** (406/547-2250, www.meagherchamber.org). Hours here vary daily and seasonally, so please call before you visit.

Great Falls

At the meeting place of the mountains and the plains, Great Falls (population 58,638; elevation 3,674 ft/1,120 m) has more romantic origins than its modern-day grittiness may suggest. A few days ahead of William Clark, Meriwether Lewis stumbled on the region in June 1805, calling the falls themselves "the grandest sight I ever beheld." Seventy-five years later, Fort Benton merchant Paris Gibson sought the same views that had captivated Lewis and later recollected,

I had never seen a spot as attractive as this... I had looked upon this scene for a few moments only when I said to myself, here I would found a city.

Just three years later, in 1883, the city of Great Falls was named and platted.

With the falls long since dammed to create power—Great Falls is known as the "Electric City" for all its dams and power plants—the city has worked to capitalize on the beauty of the Missouri River with a scenic roadway (River Drive), trails, parks, and picnic areas along the waterway. The Lewis and Clark National Historic Trail Interpretive Center sits atop a bluff and affords visitors an unspoiled view of what the area might have looked like 200 years ago. Another kind of beauty celebrated by this city is art: There are a couple of excellent—and surprising—art museums to visit.

But Great Falls is still a rough-and-tumble Montana town. There is cowboy culture, military culture, and serious wind, all of which give the state's third-largest city a little bit of an edge. Its location between the mountains and plains and amid rivers is ideal for lovers of the outdoors, and Great Falls is an excellent launching point for adventures in any direction.

Getting to Great Falls

From **White Sulphur Springs,** Great Falls is 100 miles (161 km) north on U.S. 89, about an hour and 45-minute drive.

From **Choteau,** Great Falls is 50 miles (81 km) southeast along U.S. 89, a little less than an hour's drive. From **Helena,** it's 90 miles (145 km) north on I-15, a 90-minute drive.

The **Great Falls International Airport** (GTF, 2800 Terminal Dr., 406/727-3404, www.flygtf.com) is southwest of the city. It is served by Alaska Airlines, Allegiant, Delta, and United. The airport's on-site car-rental companies are **Alamo, Avis, Enterprise, Hertz,** and **National. Budget**

Great Falls

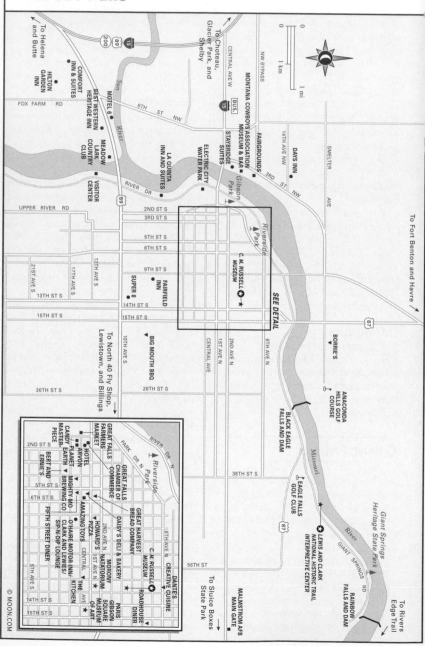

To Helena
and Butte

To Choteau,
Glacier Park, and Shelby

200
89
15

HILTON
GARDEN
INN
COMFORT
INN & SUITES
BEST WESTERN
HERITAGE INN
MOTEL 6
MEADOW
LARK
COUNTRY
CLUB
VISITOR
CENTER

FOX FARM RD

Sun River

CENTRAL AVE W
NW BYPASS

6TH ST NW

MONTANA COWBOY'S
ASSOCIATION
MUSEUM & BAR

FAIRGROUNDS

BUS.
15

STAYBRIDGE
SUITES

ELECTRIC CITY
WATER PARK

LA QUINTA
INN AND SUITES

RIVER DR

89

UPPER RIVER RD

14TH AVE NW

DAYS INN

3RD ST NW

SMELTER AVE

To Fort Benton and Havre

2ND ST S
3RD ST S

5TH ST S
6TH ST S

9TH ST S

SUPER 8
FAIRFIELD
INN

13TH AVE S
17TH AVE S

21ST AVE S

13TH ST S

14TH ST S
15TH ST S

Gibson Park

Riverside Park

C. M. RUSSELL
MUSEUM

SEE DETAIL

To North 40 Fly Shop,
Lewistown, and Billings

10TH AVE S
BIG MOUTH BBQ

26TH ST S
26TH ST S

CENTRAL AVE

1ST AVE N
2ND AVE N

8TH AVE N

BORRIE'S

87

ANACONDA
HILLS GOLF
COURSE

BLACK EAGLE
FALLS AND DAM

Missouri River

38TH ST S

EAGLE FALLS
GOLF CLUB

87

18TH AVE N

56TH ST

To Sluice Boxes
State Park

LEWIS AND CLARK
NATIONAL HISTORIC TRAIL
INTERPRETIVE CENTER

MALMSTROM AFB
MAIN GATE

GIANT SPRINGS RD

Giant Springs
Heritage State Park

RAINBOW
FALLS AND DAM

To Rivers
Edge Trail

0   1 mi
0   1 km

Detail:

2ND ST S
5TH ST S
6TH ST S

FIFTH STREET DINER

5TH AVE S

14TH ST S
15TH ST S

CANDY
MASTER
PIECE
BERT AND
ERNIE'S

PLANET
EARTH
ARVON
HOTEL

MIGHTY MO
BREWING CO

AMAZING TOYS
O'HARE MOTOR INN/
CLARK AND LEWIES/
SIP-N-DIP LOUNGE

GREAT FALLS
FARMERS
MARKET
GREAT FALLS
CHAMBER OF
COMMERCE

HOWARD'S
PIZZA

DAISY'S DELI &
BAKERY
GREAT HARVEST
BREAD COMPANY

2ND AVE N
1ST AVE N
CENTRAL

MORONY
NATATORIUM

C. M. RUSSELL
MUSEUM

PARIS
GIBSON
SQUARE
MUSEUM
OF ART

THE AVE.

DANTE'S
CREATIVE CUISINE

ROADHOUSE
DINER

RIVER DR N

PARK DR N

Riverside Park

© MOON.COM

Nancy Russell: The Force Behind the Artist

Charles M. Russell's name is synonymous with great Western art and Montana. He is not only the pride and joy of Great Falls but a hero to the entire state. Although today Charlie Russell's art is heralded around the world, there is little debate that the world may not have known him had it not been for his savvy and determined wife, Nancy.

Born Nancy Bates Cooper in 1878, she was 14 years younger than Charlie and worked as a housemaid for one of his friends when they met. Their pairing seemed an unlikely match, and when news of the engagement spread, it seemed clear that Charlie was marrying beneath himself. What soon became apparent was that not only could Nancy hold her own in any social circle, she would be the single greatest asset to her husband's career.

Nancy Russell had fended for herself from the age of 16, when her mother had died. She was a strong woman capable of achieving whatever she set her mind to; some would argue that's how she nabbed Charlie. In his book *More Rawhide,* Charlie wrote, "It's the women that make the men in this world." There is no doubt that he was a talented artist, but his wife's belief in his work and her drive to see him properly recognized are what made him a success. As his business-minded partner, Nancy ultimately organized the shows that gained him worldwide attention.

Nancy quickly earned the moniker "Nancy the Robber" because of the high prices she would ask (and receive) for Charlie's work. Charlie once told a newspaper that the worst fight the couple ever had was when she had asked for $75 for a painting that he thought would sell for $5. Initially setting up a home in the town of Cascade, the couple moved to Great Falls to aid Charlie's burgeoning career. On their arrival, the mayor's wife commissioned a painting, and Nancy asked her husband if she could deliver it. He warned her that the painting was to be sold for $25, and she should not ask for a penny more or the painting would not sell. Nancy met the mayor's wife, delivered the painting, and with a lump in her throat asked for $35. The mayor's wife replied, "I'll get my checkbook."

Ultimately, it was evident that Charlie was proud of his wife and relieved to have her handle the financial part of his business. In 1919, when asked by a reporter if marriage hinders an artist's expression, Charlie replied, "I still love and long for the Old West, and everything that goes with it. But I would sacrifice it all for Mrs. Russell."

also offers car-rental services off-site with shuttles to and from the airport.

The Great Falls **bus terminal** (326 1st Ave. S., 406/453-5261) accommodates service from **Salt Lake Express** (www.saltlakeexpress.com), **Greyhound** (www.greyhound.com), and **Jefferson Lines** (www.jeffersonlines.com).

Getting Around

Diamond Cab (406/453-3241) serves the Great Falls area and will pick you up from the airport (look for the direct phone in the terminal) or shuttle you around town. **Blacked Out 406 Taxi** (406/781-5218) is another option for airport transfers, regular taxi service, or crazy-fancy limousine SUVs, buses, and the like.

Sights
Blackfeet Tours

A remarkable way see and better understand the city—and the landscapes that encircle it—is by booking a **Blackfeet Tour** (406/450-8420, www.blackfeettours.com), led by local Blackfeet guides. You'll hear interpretive stories of Native culture and history and the ways they shape and influence sites in and around Great Falls. You can choose from a menu of half-day tours ($85 pp for 2-10 people) and full-day tours ($120 pp for 2-10 people), with options that visit the C. M. Russell Museum, First Peoples Buffalo Jump, St. Peter's Mission, Giant Springs State Park, and Fort Benton. They provide comfortable air-conditioned buses, plus lunch. It's a unique and important perspective that you won't likely get any other way.

Great Falls Historic Trolley

If you only have a few hours and want to see as much of the city as possible, the **Great Falls Historic Trolley** (406/868-2913, www.gftrolley.com, June-Sept., late Nov.-Dec. for holiday lights tours) takes you to the most important natural and human-built places. The company was sold in the spring of 2018. The new owner has updated the trolley and revamped the tour options, including ghost tours, brothel tours, and art tours.

★ C. M. Russell Museum

One of the best and most intimate Western art museums in the country, the **C. M. Russell Museum** (400 13th St. N., 406/727-8787, www.cmrussell.org, 10am-5pm Tues.-Sun. mid-May-Oct., 10am-5pm Wed.-Sat. Nov.-mid-May, $9 adults, $7 seniors and veterans, $4 students, free for children 5 and under) has amassed the world's largest collection of Charlie Russell art and personal objects, including his illustrated letters. His home (11am-4pm Tues.-Sun. mid-May-Oct.) has been meticulously maintained on the museum grounds and is open to visitors. In addition to a significant number of important works by Western masters, the museum takes an interesting approach to art through its permanent bison exhibit. The iconic western ungulate had significance to Russell himself, and the importance of the animal and its near extinction is traced through more than 1,000 exquisite Native American artifacts. Don't leave Great Falls without spending a few hours at the C. M. Russell.

Paris Gibson Square Museum of Art

At the eastern end of downtown Great Falls, the **Paris Gibson Square Museum of Art** (1400 1st Ave. N., 406/727-8255, www.the-square.org, 10am-5pm Mon.

The falls in Great Falls are part of the landscape.

and Wed.-Fri., 10am-9pm Tues., noon-5pm Sat., free) is known as "The Square" and occupies an entire city block. Built in 1896, the impressive structure served the community as Central High School and later as Paris Gibson Junior High until it closed in 1975. Renovated, renamed after the city's founder, and reopened in 1977, this National Historic Landmark houses an impressive permanent collection of contemporary art as well as important traveling exhibitions. In addition to classes, lectures, tours, and performances, the museum has a café and gift shop. Don't miss a stroll through the sculpture garden on the beautifully landscaped grounds.

★ Lewis and Clark National Historic Trail Interpretive Center

Beautifully built into a bluff overlooking the Missouri River, the **Lewis and Clark National Historic Trail Interpretive Center** (4201 Giant Springs Rd., 406/727-8733, www.fs.usda.gov, 9am-6pm daily

Memorial Day-Sept., 9am-5pm Tues.-Sat., noon-5pm Sun. Oct.-Memorial Day, $8 adults, free for children under 15 and federal pass holders) provides visitors with a hands-on interpretation of the intrepid explorers' cross-country journey. With a two-story diorama of the portage at the Missouri River's five great falls, impressive videos by Ken Burns and others, and ranger-led programs, the center does an excellent job of portraying the importance of Native Americans to the journey alongside its comprehensive natural history exhibit. The center offers a wealth of worthwhile special events that include concerts, lectures, and reenactments (check the website for upcoming events). There is also a nice outdoor component to the center with a network of self-guided trails, one of which leads you to the nearby Giant Springs Heritage State Park.

Giant Springs Heritage State Park

Among the largest freshwater springs in the country, Giant Springs was discovered by Lewis and Clark in 1805. The spring, now in **Giant Springs Heritage State Park** (4600 Giant Springs Rd., 406/454-5840 or 406/727-1212, www.stateparks.mt.gov, 8am-sunset daily, $6/vehicle or $4/pedestrian or biker for nonresidents), produces 156 million gallons (590.5 million liters) of crystal-clear water each day. The water stays at a constant 54°F (12.2°C) all year, making it an ideal spot for fishing. There is a fish hatchery on-site, a **visitors center** (8am-5pm daily), a picnic area, and several trails that wind through the lush area. For trivia buffs, the 201-foot-long Roe River, the second shortest in the world, flows from the springs.

★ First Peoples Buffalo Jump State Park

Considered to be among the largest buffalo jumps in North America, and in use more than 1,000 years before Lewis and Clark explored the area,

The History of Buffalo Jumps

Used by Native Americans for more than 5,000 years, buffalo jumps are rocky cliff formations that entire herds of bison were driven over, causing mortal injury to the animals and providing the hunters with ample meat, fur, and bones to make into weapons, tools, and decorative objects. Throughout Montana, the jumps have become significant archaeological sites, with discoveries of bones and tools guiding scientists to a better understanding of the various cultures of the people who hunted in this way.

What is surmised about the process is that the hunters first would spot herds of bison within a reasonable distance of the jump. Using rock cairns, they would carefully construct an ever-narrowing pathway from the base of the jump, up the gradual slope to the cliff's edge. Several warriors would dress in animal hides and intersperse themselves undetected among the herd. At a specific moment, the warriors would throw off their hides and stand up to startle the bison into a stampede, hopefully in the direction of the jump. As the bison headed toward the jump, other hunters would line the way, waving a variety of things to frighten the animals and prevent them from leaving the trail. By the time the animals reached the precipice, they were moving so fast that they were unable to stop at the cliff's edge even when they saw it. Hundreds of bison could go over the jump in one event, providing a substantial harvest for the hunters.

All of the animals were processed on-site, a painstaking process since every piece of the animal was used for meat, clothing, shelter, tools, and even toys. Archaeologists have uncovered significant prehistoric camps at the bases of many jumps. In some places, bison bones continue to be found more than 15 feet (4.6 m) beneath the surface.

Buffalo jumps were used by a great variety of Native American tribes until the 19th century, when the Spanish brought horses to North America and the Indians began hunting on horseback.

First Peoples Buffalo Jump State Park (342 Ulm-Vaughn Rd., Ulm, 406/866-2217 or 406/454-5840, www.stateparks. mt.gov, 8am-6pm daily Apr.-Sept., 10am-4pm Wed.-Sat., noon-4pm Sun. Oct.-Mar., $6/vehicle nonresidents) is exceptional in that it offers an extensive on-site education center that houses buffalo culture exhibits, a storytelling circle, a gallery, and an outdoor pow-wow area. The site itself is impressive, with a mile-long sandstone cliff from which the bison were chased to their deaths, but more than anything, this is the best place in the state to learn about buffalo jumps. Watch your step on or off the trails for both rattlesnakes and prickly pear cacti. An adjacent prairie dog town is home to protected black-tailed prairie dogs and worth the short detour. Check the website for upcoming events like the guided **Rock Art Hike** ($4 pp), a strenuous hiking tour that takes visitors to prehistoric petroglyphs and pictographs by Native Americans as well as carvings in stone made by early European settlers.

The park is 10 miles (16.1 km) south of Great Falls off I-15 at Ulm; follow signs for the state park 3.5 miles (5.6 km) northwest on a county road.

Sluice Boxes State Park

A rugged state park combining natural beauty, old mines, and a railroad, plus historic cabins and a limestone canyon, **Sluice Boxes State Park** (38 Evans Riceville Rd., Belt, 406/454-5840, www. stateparks.mt.gov, $6 nonresidents) is about a 35-mile (56-km), 45-minute drive southeast of Great Falls. Hikers can amble along the creek, admiring the soaring cliffs of Belt Creek Canyon, and peek into the old prospector cabins.

Entertainment and Events
Nightlife

An authentic and unforgettable tiki bar in the heart of cowboy country, the **Sip-N-Dip Lounge** (17 17th St. S., 406/454-2141 or 800/332-9819, www.ohairemotorinn.com, 11:30am-midnight Sun.-Mon., 11:30am-2am Tues.-Sat.) is housed in the O'Haire Motor Inn. You can sip exotic cocktails as you gaze at the window into the pool behind the bar, watch exhibitionist guests, or, most evenings depending on the season, see mermaid- and (occasionally) merman-costumed performers (6pm-9pm Mon., 6pm-10:30pm Tues., 6pm-midnight Wed.-Sat., 9:30am-2:30pm every second Sunday for mermaid brunch). Daryl Hannah, the quintessential mermaid, has even taken a dip here. You can also catch Piano-Pat Spoonheim singing covers of Elvis, Neil Diamond, and other legendary crooners (starting around 9:30pm Wed.-Fri.)— she has been a mainstay at the lounge for close to 50 years. Once voted the best bar on the planet by *GQ* magazine and recognized as one of the world's best bars by *Condé Nast Traveler,* this kitschy, cool watering hole should not be missed.

Another one-in-a-million bar in Great Falls is the **Montana Cowboys Association Museum & Bar** (311 3rd St. NW, 406/453-0651, www.cowboysbarmca.com, 8am-2am daily). Whether this is a bar in a museum or a museum in a bar is open to debate, but either way there is no shortage of cool old stuff to look at while you sip something frosty. An authentic log cabin built in 1941, it boasts two fireplaces and hundreds of artifacts from the Old West, including a sizable gun collection, Charlie Russell's well-worn boots, a rare photo of Jeremiah "Liver-Eating" Johnson, and a handsome collection of saddles. An evening spent bellied up to the bar is bound to be unforgettable. Bring some friends; the bar closes earlier when the number of guests drops below five.

The Arts

The **Great Falls Symphony** (venues vary, 406/453-4102, www.gfsymphony.org) is a dynamic organization that has been in existence for more than half a century, offering marvelous year-round entertainment in the form of classical symphonic masterpieces and contemporary compositions, chamber music, a youth orchestra, a symphonic choir, and ballet. For an evening of refined culture in the heart of cowboy country, the symphony is a rare treat. Larger performances are held at the **Mansfield Theater** (2 Park Dr. S.) in the lovely 1930s Great Falls Civic Center.

Festivals and Events
Western Art Week

With major art-related events held across Great Falls over a long weekend closest to Charlie Russell's birthday (Mar. 19), **Western Art Week** puts Great Falls on the map of top destinations for serious Western art collectors. In addition to three major auctions—which include **The Russell: The Sale to Benefit the C. M. Russell Museum** (400 13th St. N., 406/727-8787, www.cmrussell.org), **Out West Art Show** (1700 Fox Farm Rd., 406/899-2958, www.outwestartshow.com), and **March in Montana** (1411 10th Ave. S., 307/635-0019, www.marchinmontana.com)—the weekend offers an impressive collection of fine art by living and deceased masters, as well as cowboy and Indian collectibles. Considered *the* social event of the year for lovers of Western art, the celebration takes over several hotels, where artists and art dealers set up mini galleries and provide a rare opportunity for collectors to mingle with the artists they collect. Lectures, tours, artist demonstrations, parties, and a quick-draw event are scheduled throughout the week.

Lewis and Clark Festival

For 25 years, Great Falls has been celebrating the Corps of Discovery's 1806 monthlong stay in the city. The **Lewis and Clark Festival** (event venues vary, many held at Gibson Park on the River's Edge Trail, 406/791-7732, www.lewisandclarkfoundation.org) takes place each year, usually in mid-June. For a full weekend, history comes alive in various locations around the city. Highlighting events from Lewis and Clark's experience in Great Falls, the festival is as much about education as it is about fun. There are children's activities such as a discovery camp and storytelling, float trips, tours of Lewis and Clark sites, and presentations by Native American groups. Actors help re-create daily life from this period with dramatic readings and plays, and there is a traditional arts and crafts show, concerts, food, nature outings, and exhibits.

Montana State Fair

The **Montana State Fair** (Montana ExpoPark, 400 3rd St. NW, 406/727-8900, www.goexpopark.com, general admission $8 adults, $5 youth 6-17) takes place in Great Falls around the end of July and into August. It is one of Montana's largest parties and a true celebration of the state's unique history and culture. It includes a five-day rodeo (the largest in the state), horse racing, carnival rides, and big-name entertainment at the Montana ExpoPark. There are more than 250 vendor booths selling arts, crafts, clothes, music, and plenty of food as well as local, national, and international exhibits.

Great Falls Farmers Market

During summer, wander over to the **Great Falls Farmers Market** (Civic Center Park, 2 Park Dr. S., www.farmersmarketgf.com, 7:45am-noon Sat. June-Sept., 4:30pm-6:30pm Wed. mid-July-Sept.), which was started in 1982 by some of the local Hutterite colonists. Claiming to be the

Giant Springs Heritage State Park

largest farmers market in the state, more than 150 vendors gather to sell their goods, and you'll find the best home-grown fruits and vegetables, delicious jams, tasty baked goods, and handmade gifts and crafts. Pony rides are available for the little ones, and musicians wander among the stalls to keep you entertained.

Shopping

Great Falls has a number of unique specialty stores that line either side of Central Avenue downtown. You can start at the beginning of Central Avenue at Park Drive and stroll down the avenue. If you have a sweet tooth, don't miss **Candy Masterpiece** (120 Central Ave., 406/727-5955, www.candymasterpiece. com, 9:30am-5:30pm Mon.-Fri., 9:30am-5pm Sat.). Friendly staff are extremely generous with samples, and you'll find a delicious array of sweets, from childhood favorites straight off the candy rack to mouthwatering handmade chocolates. There are 30 different types of fudge

available: Try the Heavenly Goo (chocolate with marshmallow and caramel) or, for the more adventurous, jalapeño fudge. Leaving Montana without a bag of huckleberry saltwater taffy is a mistake.

Next door to the candy store is the fun and funky **Planet Earth** (116 Central Ave., 406/761-7000, 10am-5:30pm Mon.-Thurs. and Sat., 10am-7pm Fri.), a shop full of eclectic gifts. Browse the assortment of cards, accessories, and jewelry. It also has a fragrance bar where you can create your own scent from essential oils and add it to specific bath or skin-care products.

Every town should have a great toy store, and Great Falls certainly does. The aptly named **Amazing Toys** (515 Central Ave., 406/727-5557, www.amazingtoys. net, 9:30am-5:30pm Mon.-Thurs., 9:30am-6pm Fri., 9:30am-5pm Sat.) has an abundance of games, puzzles, and other toys and has been a local favorite since 1987.

Sports and Recreation
★ Fishing on the Missouri River

With no shortage of world-class waters in the region, including the Missouri and Sun Rivers, there are endless opportunities to wet a line in and around Great Falls. Among the fish that can be found in local waters are northern pike, walleye, perch, catfish, large- and small-mouth bass, plus, of course, the venerable trout. For **trout fishing** on the Missouri, the 30-mile (48-km) stretch of river running from **Holter Dam to Cascade** is the most productive (and the most heavily fished!) for both rainbows and browns. Average size for rainbows is 14-18 inches (36-46 cm), and browns are generally a bit bigger. Blue-winged olive hatches start in late April and often last through June, and then hit again in the fall. The river's biggest hatch, the pale morning dun, can happen anytime from June well into August and gives skilled anglers a thrilling chance to catch very big fish on very small flies. Fish in these parts see a lot of flies and thus are wary of clumsy anglers.

North 40 Outfitters (which used to be Big R) is one of the West's best all-around ranch supply stores, selling everything from baby chicks and barbed wire to snakeskin cowboy boots. It also has a well-respected fly-fishing shop staffed by passionate local anglers: **North 40 Fly Shop** (4400 10th Ave. S., 406/761-7441, www.north40flyshop.com, 7am-7pm Mon.-Sat., 9am-5pm Sun.) is an excellent place to start for advice on local waters and current hatches.

For a guided trip on any number of local waters, try **Fin Fetchers Outfitters** (406/240-3715, www.finfetchers.com, from $425 half day, $525 full day for up to 2 people). Owner Brian Neilson was born in Bozeman and raised in Great Falls, and he knows as much as you could ever hope to learn about the sport. Another well-respected guide is Dirk Johnsrud of **Johnsrud Outfitters** (406/253-8408, www.johnsrudoutfitters.com, from $375 half-day, $495 full-day), who can take anglers to a variety of rivers and lakes in the region.

River's Edge Trail

The **River's Edge Trail** is the envy of nearly every town in Montana. With 60 miles (97 km) of trail, some 20 miles (32 km) of which are paved for wheelchair access, the River's Edge Trail accommodates single-track and double-track riders on 19 miles (31 km) of dirt, as well as walkers on graveled paths. Started in the 1990s, the trail winds along both sides of the Missouri River, past five waterfalls including Black Eagle Falls, Rainbow Falls, Crooked Falls, and the renowned Great Falls of the Missouri below Ryan Dam. The art-lined trail also provides access to numerous parks, reservoirs, and other attractions, including the **Lewis and Clark National Historic Trail Interpretive Center** (4201 Giant Springs Rd., 406/727-8733, www.fs.usda.gov). There are 11 parking areas for easy access, and a trail map can be downloaded online (www.thetrail.org) or picked up at the **visitor information center** (15 Overlook Dr.).

Swimming

The **Electric City Water Park** (100 River Dr. S., 406/771-1265, www.greatfallsmt. net, noon-6pm daily, Wed. family nights until 8pm, early June-late Aug., $5-12 adults, $3-10 children 2-17, free for children under 2) is a favorite with kids and includes surfing features, giant slides, a lazy river, and a toddler-friendly waterplay structure. The facility boasts the largest heated outdoor swimming pool in the state, **Mitchell Pool,** and concessions are available on-site. Two other outdoor neighborhood pools in Great Falls with small splash parks are **Jaycee Pool** (4th St. and 26th Ave. NE, www.greatfallsmt. net, $3.50 adults, $2.50 children 3-17, free for children under 3) and **Water Tower Pool** (34th St. and 7th Ave. S., www. greatfallsmt.net, $3.50 adults, $2.50 children 3-17, free for children under 3). Both are open daily (1pm-5:45pm late June-mid-August) depending on weather.

When the weather is not conducive to outdoor swimming, **Morony Natatorium** (111 12th St. N., 406/452-3733, www. greatfallsmt.net, $3.50 adults, $2.50 children 3-17, free for children under 3) is a good option for open swimming and classes. The pool is kept at 83-86°F (28.3-30°C). Life vests are provided free of charge at all municipal pools in Great Falls, but swimmers need to provide their own towels. Hours vary for lap swim, classes, and open swim, so call ahead or check online for the day's schedule.

Golf

Golfers not afraid of a stiff breeze can find a few places to play in Great Falls. There are three 18-hole public courses: **Eagle Falls Golf Club** (1025 25th St. N., 406/761-1078, www.greatfallsmt.net, $19 for 9 holes or $32 for 18 holes Mon.-Fri., $20 for 9 holes or $35 for 18 holes Sat.-Sun.), **Anaconda Hills Golf Course** (2315 E. Smelter Ave., Black Eagle,

406/761-8459, www.greatfallsmt.net, $16 for 9 holes or $26 for 18 holes Mon.-Fri., $18 for 9 holes or $30 for 18 holes Sat.-Sun.), and **Hickory Swing Golf Course** (1100 American Ave., 406/452-9400, www.hickoryswinggolf.com, $14 for 9 holes or $24 for 18 holes). **Meadow Lark Country Club** (300 Country Club Blvd., 406/454-3553, www.meadowlarkclub.com) is a lovely old private club at the confluence of the Missouri and Sun Rivers that allows reciprocal fees ($80) for members of other private clubs.

Food

In a historic building downtown, **Bert & Ernie's Tavern and Grill** (300 1st Ave. S., 406/453-0601, www.bertandernies.com, 11am-8pm Mon.-Wed., 11am-9pm Thurs., 11am-10pm Fri.-Sat., $10-24) is something of a Great Falls institution. The food is simple and hearty with a variety of homemade soups, big salads, sandwiches, and burgers.

Another iconic restaurant in Great Falls is **Borrie's** (1800 Smelter Ave., 406/761-0300, www.borriesrestaurant.com, 5pm-9:30pm Mon.-Thurs., 4:30pm-10pm Fri., 4pm-10pm Sat., 4pm-9pm Sun., $10-40), an old-school supper club with excellent steaks, seafood specials (including Australian lobster), and legendary homemade pasta sauce and ravioli. The atmosphere leaves something to be desired, but this is a classic Montana dining experience with great specials several nights a week.

Though it has changed names and owners many times over the decades, the **Roadhouse Diner** (613 15th St. N., 406/788-8839, www.roadhousegf.com, 11am-8pm Wed.-Sat., last seating at 7:30pm, 9am-2pm Sun., $9-16) is the real deal when it comes to burgers and fries. It has inventive and strangely delicious, options like the Bacon Mac-N-Cheeseburger and PB&J Burger—which pairs bacon, cheddar, peanut butter, and grape jelly—but the basics here are plenty good. Try the breakfast burrito and the

hand-cut fries. A true mom-and-pop outfit, the Roadhouse gets as many of its ingredients as possible locally and makes most everything from scratch.

One of Great Falls's most well-known restaurants is a local pizza joint, **Howard's Pizza** (713 1st Ave. N., 406/453-1212, www.howardspizzamt.com, 4pm-midnight daily, $12-21), started in 1959. Much beloved for its signature thin crust, famous sauce, and homemade ranch dressing, four locations citywide are now available for dining in, takeout, or delivery.

Another Montana success story, **Great Harvest Bread Company** (515 1st Ave. N., 406/452-6941, www.greatharvestgreatfalls.com, 6am-5:30pm Mon.-Fri., 6am-4pm Sat.) is a national chain that started in Great Falls in 1976. Its motto starts, "Be loose and have fun," and the food follows suit with inventive offerings ranging from cranberry crunch bread with flaxseeds and oat bran to white chocolate cherry bread and the savory buttery basil oregano bread. The menu revolves around fresh-baked bread and is filled with delicious hot and cold sandwiches. And the cinnamon rolls, muffins, and brownies will leave you begging for mercy.

For a step back in time, **Fifth Street Diner** (500 Central Ave., 406/727-1962, 8:30am-2:30pm Tues.-Sun., $4-11) is located in a refurbished Woolworth's and centered on the original F. W. Woolworth stainless steel lunch counter. The menu offers standard comfort food ranging from steak and eggs to burgers and meat loaf. The fries, called "smiles," are mashed potatoes shaped into smiley faces. The shakes and malts should not be missed—even for breakfast!

Newer on the scene, and an excellent addition to Great Falls, is **Mighty Mo Brewing Company** (412 Central Ave., 406/952-0342, www.mightymobrewing.com, 11am-8pm daily, $6-19). Housed in a beautifully refurbished historic building, this microbrewery serves fine beer with perfectly paired food—wings, pizza, nachos, breadsticks, pretzels, and the like.

Big Mouth BBQ (1720 10th Ave. S., 406/727-7095, www.greatfallsbbq.com, 11am-8pm Mon.-Thurs., 11am-9pm Fri.-Sat., $9-15) is not for the faint of heart. The $20 Big John Challenge entices diners to eat three chicken-fried steaks with gravy sandwiched between two grilled cheese sandwiches served with 1 pound (0.5 kg) of fries topped with chili and cheese. Those who can finish in 30 minutes or less get the whole shebang (and some serious heartburn) for free. Less maniacal eaters can enjoy Texas-style pit-smoked meats, po'boys, fried pork tenderloin, ribs, and all the fixings. There's another location (215 3rd St. NW, 406/952-0872) west of the river.

A stark contrast to Big Mouth BBQ, **Dante's Creative Cuisine** (1325 8th Ave. N., 406/453-9599, 11am-9pm Mon.-Thurs., 11am-10pm Fri.-Sat., $16-25) is within a beautiful, old brick ironworks building. It's white linens all the way with Italian and Southwestern fare, seafood, and steak. The Thursday night lobster tail is a local favorite at this decidedly upscale establishment.

A weekday takeout restaurant with traditional family-style restaurant grub is **The Kitchen** (1225 Central Ave., 406/727-5820, 11am-6:30pm Mon.-Fri., $5-11), which offers two homemade soups daily, plus classic dinners like baked ham, meat loaf, cabbage rolls, and shepherd's pie. In the summer, picnic benches out front provide a place for on-site eating.

About a half-hour's drive southeast of Great Falls on U.S. 89 is the tiny town of Belt, and the wonderful **Harvest Moon Brewing Company** (7 5th St. S., Belt, 406/277-3188, www.harvestmoonbrew. com, 10am-4pm Mon.-Fri., 11am-8pm Sat.-Sun.), which uses untreated water from the Madison aquifer and barley that is grown and malted a few miles away for its outstanding selection of beers.

Accommodations

If you are looking for a memorable motel stay in downtown Great Falls, look no further than the ★ **O'Haire Motor Inn** (17 7th St. S., 406/454-2141 or 800/332-9819, $90-150), with 68 guest rooms, an indoor pool, indoor parking, and free Wi-Fi. Its full-service restaurant, **Clark and Lewie's** (6am-10pm Mon.-Thurs., 6am-midnight Fri.-Sat., 6am-9pm Sun., $13-25), offers up hearty meals and even room service. The biggest draw at the inn is its authentic and unforgettable tiki bar, the Sip-N-Dip Lounge.

The upscale **Hotel Arvon** (118 1st Ave. S., 406/952-1101, www.hotelarvon.com, $129-189) is a 33-room boutique hotel with a coffee shop, wine bar, restaurant, and pub in the city's oldest commercial building.

Another option just south of downtown is the **La Quinta Inn & Suites** (600 River Dr. S., 406/761-2600 or 800/531-5900, www.laquintagreatfalls.com, $114-229), built in 2000 on the banks of the Missouri River. Ask for a room with a view of the river. The hotel is styled as a Western lodge, with a fireplace in the lobby, as well as an indoor pool and a fitness center. The guest rooms are large and comfortable with amenities such as high-speed internet, microwaves, and fridges, and continental breakfast is included.

Along the River's Edge Trail, the spacious **Staybridge Suites** (201 3rd St. NW, 406/761-4903 or 877/238-8889, www. staybridgesuites.com/greatfallsmt, $145-300) is a pet-friendly, all-suite hotel offering fully equipped kitchens, free Wi-Fi, a 24-hour business center, and an indoor pool.

Among the chain hotel offerings in town, the **Best Western Heritage Inn** (1700 Fox Farm Rd., 406/761-1900, www.bestwestern.com, $109-149) offers 231 rooms plus an indoor swimming pool, fitness center, restaurant, casino, and sports bar. Other comfortable chain hotels in Great Falls include **Comfort**

Inn & Suites (1801 Market Place Dr., 406/455-1000, www.choicehotels.com, from $120), the pet-friendly Days Inn (101 14th Ave. NW, 406/727-6565, www.daysinngreatfalls.com, $106-133), the Fairfield Inn (1000 9th Ave. S., 406/454-3000, www.marriott.com/fairfieldinn, $114-145), and the Hilton Garden Inn (2520 14th St. SW, 406/452-1000, http://greatfalls.hgi.com, $134-404), which is located next to several restaurants, a shopping mall, and a 10-screen movie theater. More budget-friendly options include Motel 6 (2 Treasure State Dr., 406/453-1602, www.motel6.com, from $67-78) and Super 8 (1214 13th St. S., 406/727-7600, www.greatfallssuper8.com, $56-78).

Information and Services

Most services are conveniently located in a walkable downtown area. The Great Falls Chamber of Commerce (100 1st Ave. N., 406/761-4434, www.greatfallschamber.org, 8am-5pm Mon.-Fri.) and the Visitor Information Center (15 Overlook Dr., 406/771-0885, www.greatfallsmt.net, 10am-4pm Mon.-Fri., 10am-2pm Sat.-Sun. Oct.-Apr., 9am-6pm Mon.-Fri., 10am-4pm Sat.-Sun. May-Sept.), under the huge U.S. flag in Overlook Park, both have city brochures, books, Made in Montana goods for sale, and friendly, knowledgeable volunteers.

The main post office (215 1st Ave. N., 406/771-2160, 8:30am-5:30pm Mon.-Fri., 10am-1pm Sat.) is at 1st Avenue and 2nd Street.

The public library (301 2nd Ave. N., 406/453-0349, www.greatfallslibrary.org, 10am-8pm Tues.-Thurs., 10am-6pm Fri.-Sat.) is just two blocks from the post office and offers computers and free internet access.

Falls Cleaners & Laundry Center (614 9th St. S., 406/453-9361, 8am-9pm daily) offers same-day laundry service, dry-cleaning service, and coin-op machines to do it yourself.

Benefis Health Systems (1101 26th St. S., 406/455-5000, www.benefis.org) is a first-class hospital with a 24-hour emergency room as well as a walk-in clinic (1401 25th St. S., 406/731-8300, 7am-8pm Mon.-Fri., 9am-6:30pm Sat.-Sun.) for immediate medical care.

Choteau and Augusta

Established with a post office under the name Old Agency in 1875, Choteau (population 1,686; elevation 3,819 ft/1,164 m) is one of the region's oldest active towns. The name was changed in 1882 to honor Pierre Chouteau, president of the American Fur Company and responsible for bringing the first steamboat up the Missouri River. This ranching town at the edge of the Rockies is a dinosaur lover's dream, with paleontological museums and sites galore. In addition to its obvious attractions, Choteau is simply a charming Montana town—small, friendly, and ideally situated for visitors.

Just under 30 miles (48 km) southwest of Choteau is the wonderful little town of Augusta (population 315; elevation 4,068 ft/1,240 m). The town—with classic Western storefronts and warm hospitality—hosts the state's oldest and biggest one-day rodeo, known as the "Wildest One Day Show on Earth," the last Sunday in June. It also has an outstanding general store, a beautiful art gallery and coffee shop, a great little hotel, and plenty of places to get a good burger. What else do you need on a road trip?

Getting to Choteau and Augusta

Choteau is 50 miles (81 km) northwest of Great Falls along U.S. 89, a little less than an hour's drive. Augusta is 25 miles (40 km) southwest of Choteau on U.S. 287, a 25-minute drive.

From Browning, Choteau is 70 miles (113 km) south on U.S. 89, a drive of about one hour and 15 minutes.

Sights

The remains of the most famous inhabitants of **Egg Mountain** (U.S. 287, between mileposts 57 and 58) were discovered in 1977 by Marion Brandvold and studied extensively by dinosaur guru Jack Horner. The discovery has yielded the largest collection of dinosaur eggs, embryos, and baby skeletons in the Western Hemisphere. The findings entirely changed our notion of how dinosaurs raised their young. The baby remains were found alongside an enormous number of adult remains, which scientists determined was a monumental herd of maiasaura (good mother reptile) along with a lesser number of troodons killed in a catastrophic event such as a volcanic eruption or a hurricane. Egg Mountain is one of 16 sites in Montana deemed "geological wonders" by a team of historians, geologists, and paleontologists. An interpretive sign on U.S. 287 provides information about the site. There is also a small parking area, and visitors are welcome to wander the site, which is more a hill than a mountain. Naturalist guides occasionally offer narrated tours of the area; for more information contact the Museum of the Rockies in Bozeman (406/994-2251).

At the north end of Choteau, the **Old Trail Museum** (823 N. Main St., Choteau, 406/466-5332, www.oldtrailmuseum. com, 9am-5pm daily Memorial Day-Labor Day, $2, children under 3 are free) celebrates both the natural and cultural history of the Rocky Mountain Front. In the Dinosaurs of the Two Medicine paleontology gallery, there are dinosaur bones and fossils aplenty, along with a good maiasaura exhibit. The museum also has a number of other interesting local history exhibits, including Native American artifacts collected by A. B. Guthrie Jr. and details of Choteau's last hanging. Right next door to the museum is the **Old Trail Ice Cream Parlor** (406/466-2257, 1pm-9pm daily Memorial Day-Labor Day), which dishes up Montana-made Wilcoxen's ice cream. Don't leave town without a cone!

★ Freezeout Lake

Between Choteau and Fairfield, off U.S. 89, is **Freezeout Lake** (406/467-2646, www.fwp.mt.gov, mid-Mar.-autumn), a birder's paradise and for many Montanans the best place to gauge the imminent arrival of an ever-elusive spring. The scenic lake is a staging area for hundreds of thousands of snow geese and thousands of tundra swans on their way north. The snow geese typically arrive at Freezeout in early March. As with most wildlife, dawn and dusk offer the best viewing opportunities. A variety of other birds pass through the area, including raptors and upland game birds in winter, waterfowl in spring and fall, and shorebirds in summer. The interior roads have ample parking and pullouts, and are open to vehicles mid-March to the beginning of waterfowl season. The lake is plenty scenic any time of year, but

what makes this a must-see is the massive migration in March.

Entertainment and Events

Held annually the last Sunday in June, the **Augusta American Legion Rodeo and Parade** (American Legion Rodeo Grounds, Augusta, 406/562-3477, www.augustamontana.com) is the biggest and oldest one-day rodeo in the state. For more than 80 years, this small town has put on an amazing show with a parade, a Professional Rodeo Cowboys Association-sanctioned rodeo complete with bull riding, and a huge party atmosphere.

Shopping

Don't leave Choteau without a stop at **Choteau Trading Post** (106 N. Main Ave., Choteau, 406/466-5354 or 406/229-0279, 9am-5:30pm Mon.-Sat.), which offers Western wares, boots galore, work clothes, jewelry, and gifts. Another place to take a step back in time is **Days Gone By Antiques** (38 N. Main Ave., Augusta, 406/466-3435, 9am-5pm Tues.-Sat. winter, 9am-6pm daily spring-summer), which specializes in vintage furniture, but also has an abundance of glassware, dishes, linens, jewelry, old photos, and more. They also claim the largest collection of tobacco tins in the state.

One of the best gift shops in the state is **Latigo and Lace** (122 Main St., Augusta, 406/562-3665, 10am-5pm Wed.-Sun. Mar., 10am-6pm Tues.-Sun. Apr., 10am-6:30pm daily May Dec.), which has books, clothing, an espresso bar, and fantastic local art including ceramics, photography, paintings, jewelry, rugs, baskets, and beadwork. Just up the street, **Allen's Manix Store** (10 Main St., Augusta, 406/562-3333, 7:30am-7:30pm daily Jan.-May and Sept.-Dec., 7am-8pm daily June-Aug.) is a classic country store with everything from groceries and meats to hunting and fishing licenses, sporting goods, and gifts. The staff are friendly and helpful, and just listening to

snow geese taking flight from Freezeout Lake

the chatter as you wait in line to check out makes you feel like you know this place a little bit.

Sports and Recreation

Teton Pass Ski Resort (18 mi/29 km west of Choteau, 406/466-2209, www. tetonpassresort.com, $39 adults full day or $36 half day, $36 seniors, $33 youth 7-17, $15 beginner lift, free for kids 6 and under) is a small ski area—two lifts and 36 trails geared largely to experts—with an enormous amount of snow (the area averages 20 feet/6.1 m of snow annually) and some pretty fierce terrain.

Food

Choteau has some good options for regional cuisine. The **Log Cabin Cafe** (102 Main Ave. N., Choteau, 406/466-2888, 11am-9pm Tues.-Fri., 8am-9pm Sat.-Sun., $5-11) is precisely what you would expect from its name: a cozy spot with hearty servings of good old-fashioned comfort food. The burgers are great, but so too are the salads, soups, and breakfast dishes. Don't miss the desserts!

For a quick, fresh lunch or snack, **9th and Main Gourmet** (825 Main Ave. N., Choteau, 406/466-3880, 11am-5pm Thurs.-Sun. summer, 7am-2pm Thurs.-Fri., 6am-3pm Sat.-Sun. winter) offers soups, sandwiches, lettuce wraps, smoothies, and a mouthwatering assortment of fresh-baked goodies. From the maple sticks and blueberry scones to the ham-and-cheese breakfast rolls and deli sandwiches, **Bylers Bakery** (425 Main Ave. S., Choteau, 406/466-9900, 6am-2pm Wed.-Sat., $2-8) is a great little coffee shop and café open for breakfast and lunch.

In Augusta, the **Buckhorn Bar** (120 Main St., Augusta, 406/562-3344, 7am-2am daily, $9-23) is a great place for burger and a beer and to soak in the scene, particularly during bird-hunting season.

★ **Rose Room** (Main St., Pendroy, 406/469-2205, hours vary, call for

reservations, $12-40) calls itself "downtown Pendroy's finest dining," and is consistently ranked "number 1 of 1 restaurants in Pendroy"—but that's not the point. You won't forget an evening at the Rose Room. It's an old bank building in the middle of nowhere—a redbrick structure with a lighted sign out front that creaks in the wind, and a room in back that serves food. You'll need to call the owner, Dorene, a few days in advance if you want a meal. You can say what time you'd like, but after 44 years in business, she may have other ideas. There is carpet on the floor *and* on the ceiling, and one wall is mirrored with gold swirls on it. The wallpaper might be velvet. There is seafood on the menu—and it's good! (There are also steaks and burgers.) Start with fry bread served with butter and honey. Finish with an ice cream sundae, whether you want it or not. This is what it used to be like to go to a fine restaurant. The server is a musher, meaning she runs sled dogs. She'll tell you all about it if you ask. Dorene might pop out of the kitchen to say hello, too. You may have the place to yourself. There's a pool table in the bar. And drinks are pretty cheap. The point is, you should eat here. There is no place like the Rose Room. The Rose Room is about 25 miles (40 km) north of Choteau via U.S. 89, on the way to Browning.

Accommodations

Sadly, most of the small, mom-and-pop motels in Choteau have gone the way of the dinosaur. The best hotel in town today is the relatively new **Stage Stop Inn** (1005 Main Ave. N., Choteau, 406/446-5900, www.stagestopinn.com, $114-150), which is spacious, comfortable, and clean but without any of the charm of days gone by.

In Augusta, the ★ **Bunkhouse Inn** (124 Main St., Augusta, 406/562-3387, www. yourgatewaytoadvenuture.com, $60-79) is small, charming and old-fashioned in ambience, but very welcoming and spotlessly clean. It was built as a boardinghouse in 1912, and beautifully restored by new owners in 2017. The rooms are small; some have their own sink and vanity, but all share three bathrooms at the end of the hall. Gas fireplaces keep all the rooms toasty and rocking chairs on the front porch beckon. There are no TVs or phones, but there is high-speed internet. This is a place where you will feel at home.

The **Deep Canyon Guest Ranch** (2055 Teton Canyon Rd., 406/466-2044, www.deepcanyonguestranch.com, from $2,190 weekly pp double occupancy, $1,380 children under 12) is a charming old guest ranch 28 miles (45 km) west of Choteau, set in the heart of Teton Canyon with easy access to the Bob Marshall Wilderness Complex. Some of the buildings date back to the 1920s, but others were constructed in the 1980s. Available daily activities include horseback riding, fishing, and hiking.

Another favorite family-friendly guest ranch west of Augusta is the **Triple J Wilderness Ranch** (80 Mortimer Rd., 406/562-3653, www.triplejranch.com, $2,300 weekly pp double occupancy all-inclusive, $2,100 children 13-17, $2,000 children 6-12), tucked in the magnificent Sun River Canyon above Gibson Lake. In addition to all-inclusive vacations catering to riders, hikers, and anglers, the Triple J offers fantastic kids' programs and awesome pack trips in the Bob Marshall Wilderness Complex. Early June-late September, the ranch offers six-day stays with discounts for children and teens. Shorter stays may be available in June and September.

Information

The **Choteau Chamber of Commerce** (703 Main Ave. N., 406/466-5316 or 800/823-3866, www.choteaumontana.us, 10am-4pm Mon.-Fri.) has hours that can vary from season to season; call ahead to make sure it is open. The **Augusta Chamber of Commerce** (www.augustamontana.com)

has a great website with information on the area, but no physical presence.

Browning

Agency headquarters for the Blackfeet Indian Reservation, home to Montana's largest tribe, Browning (population 1,031; elevation 4,377 ft/1,334 m) has retained much of the culture of the Blackfeet people. The setting is spectacular, at the eastern edge of Glacier National Park, but the town doesn't offer anything in the way of striking architecture or high-end hotels. What it does offer, though, is an exceptional opportunity to learn about and experience Blackfeet culture. In addition to the important Museum of the Plains Indian, there are a number of annual events open to visitors as well as tours given by well-versed local guides. There is even a place where guests can camp in tipis, feast on gourmet regional cuisine, and enjoy a thoughtfully curated Blackfeet experience.

Getting to Browning

From **Choteau,** Browning is 70 miles (113 km) north on U.S. 89, a little over a one-hour drive. From Glacier National Park's eastern entrance at **St. Mary,** Browning is 30 miles (48 km) south on U.S. 89, a 45-minute drive.

Sights
★ Blackfeet Cultural History Tours
Led by Blackfeet tribe member, historian, and well-known artist Darryl Norman, **Blackfeet Cultural History Tours** (U.S. 89, 2.5 mi/4 km west of Browning, www.blackfeetculturecamp.com, tipicamp@3rivers.net, half-day tours for 1-4 people from $100, full-day tours for 1-4 people $160) offers a remarkable opportunity to explore the reservation and its history. Norman operates as a step-on guide, joining guests in their own vehicles and taking them to various buffalo jumps, tipi rings, medicine lodges, and

historic sites. You can also arrange to ride horses on ancient Blackfeet paths or hike and fish on streams tumbling out of Glacier National Park. All of the experiences add up to a deeper understanding of Blackfeet history and culture, and its great significance to the region.

Museum of the Plains Indian

Just west of Browning at the junction of U.S. 2 and U.S. 89 is the **Museum of the Plains Indian** (19 Museum Loop, 406/338-2230, www.doi.gov/iacb/museum-plains-indian-location, 9am-4:45pm Tues.-Sat. June-Sept., 10am-4:30pm daily Oct.-May, $5 adults, $4 seniors 65 and over, $1 children 6-16 June-Sept., free Oct.-May). The museum exhibits the arts and crafts of the Northern Plains Indians. The permanent collection highlights the diversity of tribal arts and displays artifacts from everyday life, including clothing, weapons, toys, and household implements. Two galleries are dedicated to showcasing contemporary Native American artists. During summer, painted tipis are assembled on the grounds.

Entertainment and Events

Held annually the second week in July over four days, the **North American Indian Days** (406/338-7521 or 406/338-7103, www.blackfeetnation.com) is an excellent powwow giving insight into the Blackfeet culture and traditions. Events include contest dancing, games, sporting events, drum contests, and plenty of food. Another traditional powwow happening annually on the reservation is the **Heart Butte Society Celebration,** held over four days the second week of August in Heart Butte, 26 miles (42 km) south of Browning.

Food

The best local food, including buffalo, deer, and elk, is served in traditional style for guests only at the **Lodge Pole Gallery and Tipi Village** (U.S. 89, 2 mi/3.2 km west of Browning, www.blackfeetculturecamp.

com, tipicamp@3rivers.net, $19.50-30). If sleeping in a hand-painted tipi weren't cool enough, eating native cuisine is more than worth the trip. Memorial Day-Labor Day, the Aspenwood Resort also offers dining to the public in its **Outlaw Kitchen** (102 SW Boundary St., U.S. 89, 9.5 mi/15.3 km west of Browning, 406/338-3370, 8am-11am and 1pm-close daily, $4-20). The Outlaw Kitchen offers standard fare ranging from fluffy pancakes to sandwiches, salads, burgers, pizza, and barbecue.

Right in town, across from the Museum of the Plains Indian, the **Junction Café** (Starr School Rd., 406/338-2386, 8am-2pm Mon.-Fri., $3-17) is locally owned and serves up hearty breakfasts of corned beef hash, breakfast burritos, and biscuits and gravy, as well as hamburgers and steaks. Try the fry bread! With usually only one server and a local clientele, the restaurant is very friendly. Don't be surprised if a neighboring diner offers to refill your coffee cup.

Another very friendly local restaurant serving everything from burgers to Indian tacos is **Nation's Burger Station** (205 Central Ave., 406/338-2422, www.nationsburgerstation.com, 10:30am-9:30pm Mon.-Fri., 10:30am-10:30pm Sat.-Sun. May-mid-Aug., 10:30am-8:30pm Mon.-Sat. mid-Aug.-Apr., $6-12). In addition to the aforementioned, Nation's Burger Station serves salads and wraps, plus an impressive menu of frozen treats including root beer floats, slushies, and snow cones. On a hot day, this is the place.

Accommodations

Browning itself doesn't offer a lot in the way of accommodations; the best bets are toward Glacier National Park. Just under 10 miles (16.1 km) west of Browning is the **Aspenwood Resort** (U.S. 89, 406/338-3009, mid-May-early Oct., suites from $95-150), ideally located close to Glacier National Park between Browning and St. Mary. There are three suites in the rustic lodge in addition to RV sites ($40), a campground ($25), and a restaurant.

The ★ **Lodge Pole Gallery and Tipi Village** (U.S. 89, 2 mi/3.2 km west of Browning, www.blackfeetculturecamp.com, tipicamp@3rivers.net, tipis $70 pp, plus $16 for each additional person, $10 children under 12, $12 to rent sleeping bag and mattress) is a rare and special place. Part art gallery and part tipi camp, the Lodge Pole offers an extraordinary, unique experience and a true taste of Blackfeet culture with Native American art, Spanish mustangs, and various cultural events.

Information
The **Blackfeet Country Chamber of Commerce** (380 1st Ave. SW, 406/338-4015 or 406/338-7521, www. blackfeetnation.com, 8am-4:30pm Mon.-Fri.) is open year-round and has an active Facebook presence.

Getting to Glacier National Park
The drive from Browning to Glacier's east entrance at St. Mary is short, but scenic. Just 30 miles (48 km) west on Starr School Road and north on U.S. 89, the drive takes just over half an hour. Even as you drive the open country and rolling hills, the relief of Glacier's jagged peaks is always in view, reminding you that you're pointed someplace beautiful, someplace wild. At this point, you'll want to get into the park, and the spectacular blue-green of St. Mary Lake is a wonderful place to do just that.

Glacier
National
Park

Glacier National Park

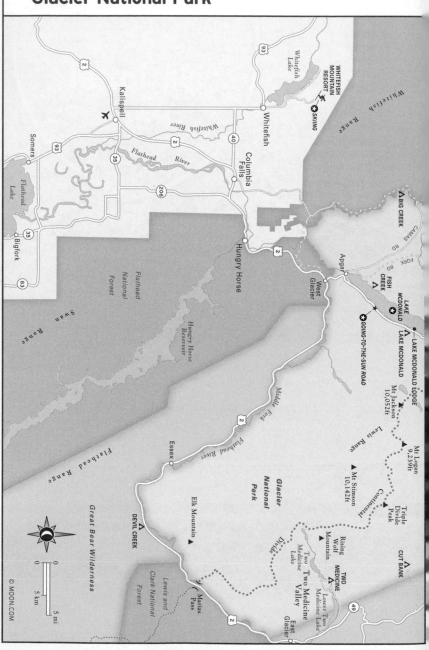

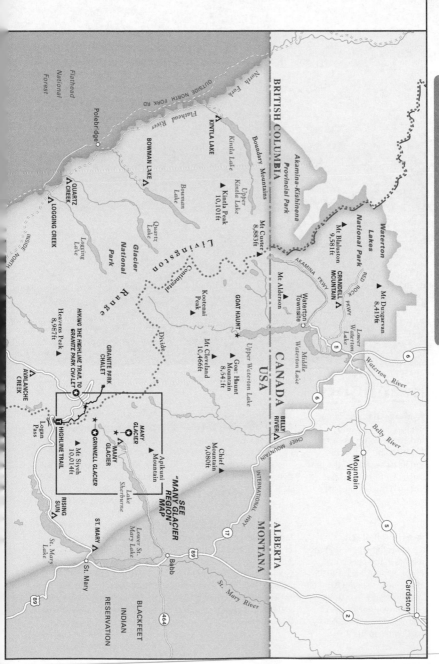

Flathead National Forest

BRITISH COLUMBIA

North Fork

OUTSIDE NORTH FORK RD

Flathead River

Polebridge

Boundary Mountains

KINTLA LAKE

BOWMAN LAKE

Kintla Lake

Upper Kintla Lake

▲ Kintla Peak 10,101ft

QUARTZ CREEK

LOGGING CREEK

INSIDE NORTH

Logging Lake

Bowman Lake

Quartz Lake

Glacier National Park

Li v i n g s t o n

Mt Custer 8,883ft

Akamina-Kishinena Provincial Park

Mt Alderson

Waterton Lakes National Park

▲ Mt Blakiston 9,581ft

CRANDELL MOUNTAIN

AKAMINA PKWY

RED ROCK PKWY

▲ Mt Dungarvan 8,419ft

Continental

Kootenai Peak ▲

R a n g e

Divide

GOAT HAUNT

★

Mt Cleveland 10,466ft ▲

Upper Waterton Lake

Waterton Townsite

Middle Waterton Lake

Lower Waterton Lake

CANADA

USA

5

6

Waterton River

6

Heavens Peak 8,987ft ▲

HIKING THE HIGHLINE TRAIL TO GRANITE PARK CHALET

GRANITE PARK CHALET

AVALANCHE CREEK

Logan Pass

HIGHLINE TRAIL

★

▲ Goat Mountain 8,541ft

MANY GLACIER

★

GRINNELL GLACIER

MANY GLACIER

Apikuni Mountain

▲ Mt Siyeh 10,014ft

Lake Sherburne

Chief Mountain 9,080ft ▲

BELLY RIVER

CHIEF MOUNTAIN

INTERNATIONAL HWY

Belly River

Mountain View

"MANY GLACIER REGION" MAP SEE

RISING SUN

ST. MARY

St. Mary Lake

MONTANA

ALBERTA

5

Lower St. Mary Lake

Babb

89

17

St. Mary

BLACKFEET INDIAN RESERVATION

St. Mary River

89

464

2

Cardston

Highlights

★ **Many Glacier:** Prime hiking, canoeing, and horseback-riding country, this stunning area in the northeast section of the park is popular but often less crowded than other parts (page 201).

★ **Grinnell Glacier:** Scientists anticipate that the glaciers in the park could disappear entirely by 2030, which means seeing Grinnell Glacier may be a once-in-a-lifetime opportunity. The ranger-led hike is especially worthwhile (page 201).

★ **Going-to-the-Sun Road:** Stretching just over 50 miles (81 km), this phenomenal feat of engineering gives viewers an extraordinary overview of Glacier (page 202).

★ **Lake McDonald:** The largest lake in the park and arguably one of the most beautiful, glacially carved Lake McDonald is easy to access. Pack a picnic for the rocky beach or cruise the waters on a boat tour (page 202).

★ **Hiking the Highline Trail to Granite Park Chalet:** Among the best-loved trails in the park is the Highline, which climbs to the historic Granite Park Chalet and then drops back to Going-to-the-Sun Road. The views are staggering but the hike is not for the faint of heart (page 209).

★ **Skiing at Whitefish Mountain Resort:** This phenomenal ski area has a view over Whitefish Lake, the most haunting trees anywhere, and perhaps the best après-ski scene in the state (page 227).

Known as the "Crown of the Continent," Glacier National Park is one of the largest intact ecosystems in the Lower 48, an amalgam of stunning landscapes that, for many visitors, defines the entire state of Montana.

The beauty of Glacier is rugged, raw, and dynamic. The mountains thrust skyward, and the gravity-defying roads are ribbons that snake toward the summits. The legendary Going-to-the-Sun Road is one of the West's most impressive engineering feats and one of the best scenic drives in the country. There are still 25 "active" glaciers (at least 25 acres in area) to be found within the park, along with countless waterfalls and hundreds of crystalline lakes. In summer the landscape is heavy with huckleberries and dotted with fuzzy, white bear grass. While wildlife-viewing from the road can be challenging in this mountainous terrain, the animals—grizzly and black bears, mountain goats, bighorn sheep, wolves, and more—are here in abundance. With 1,583 square miles of alpine majesty, the scenery, if not the altitude, will leave you breathless.

Glacier National Park is a haven for nature lovers, and visitors can enjoy the natural beauty in a number of ways—hiking, bicycling, boating, and cross-country skiing, to name a few. There are 745.6 miles (1,210 km) of trails throughout the park and a smattering of historic lodges and chalets for cozy accommodations. Yet despite its extensive offerings, Glacier still provides visitors a rare and precious sense of solitude. The crowds disperse as soon as your feet hit the trail, and there are miles of shoreline where the only other picnickers are four-legged. More than just the Crown of the Continent, Glacier is like no place on earth.

Getting to Glacier National Park

Driving from Yellowstone
St. Mary: 375-380 miles (605-610 km); 6-6.5 hours

The fastest route between the north entrance of Yellowstone at **Gardiner** and Glacier's east entrance at St. Mary is 380 miles (610 km) via U.S. 89 through Livingston and Great Falls, about a 6.5-hour drive.

Just a few miles and minutes shorter, the northward route via U.S. 287 and U.S. 89 is 375 miles (605 km) and will take just over six hours, traveling along the Rocky Mountain Front through Bozeman, Helena, and Choteau.

West Glacier: 390-420 miles (630-675 km); 7-7.5 hours

From Gardiner to West Glacier, via I-90 West and U.S. 93 North, the drive is roughly 420 miles (675 km) and will take approximately 7.5 hours without stops. This drive takes you through Bozeman, Missoula, and Kalispell.

The route from West Yellowstone north through the Seeley-Swan Valley on MT-83 is 390 miles (630 km) and will take roughly seven hours.

Driving from Great Falls
155 miles (250 km); 2.5 hours

From Great Falls, the east entrance of Glacier National Park at St. Mary is 155 miles (250 km) north on I-15 and U.S. 89, just over a 2.5-hour drive.

Driving from Kalispell and Missoula
35-140 miles (56-225 km); 1-2.5 hours

From Kalispell, the west entrance of Glacier National Park is 35 miles (56 km) northeast on U.S. 2, just under an hour's drive.

From Missoula, the shortest route to

Two Days in Glacier National Park

Day 1

Enter Glacier on the west side after fueling up with an early breakfast and a killer piece of pie at **Loula's Café** in Whitefish.

Stop at **Lake McDonald** to soak in the glorious views and even take a morning dip. Indulge in a huckleberry elk burger in the **Russell's Fireside Dining Room** at the historic **Lake McDonald Lodge.**

After a leisurely lunch, enjoy the scenery as you climb the **Going-to-the-Sun Road** and stop at the Logan Pass Visitor Center, behind which you'll find the **Hidden Lake Overlook** trailhead. Often covered with snow until late June or even July and frequented by both mountain goats and bighorn sheep, the trail climbs through wildflower meadows and beneath rocky peaks to the shores of Hidden Lake. Anglers can cast a line before heading back up the trail to the visitors center.

With tired legs, make your way down the east side of the Going-to-the-Sun Road and through St. Mary and Babb before heading back into the park for a cozy room and delicious meal at the **Many Glacier Hotel.**

Day 2

Plan to spend the day adventuring around **Many Glacier,** where canoeing, kayaking, and hiking are all options. You could combine a scenic cruise across both **Swiftcurrent Lake** and **Lake Josephine** with a short hike up to the famed Many Glacier, or hike the longer version with a ranger departing from the Many Glacier dock. Be sure to bring a lunch, plenty of water, foul-weather gear, and bear spray.

From here you'll head back out of the park and fill up on roasted Mexican chicken or chili burgers or nachos at the fun **Two Sisters Café** in Babb, before traveling on to your next stop.

the park is 140 miles (225 km) north on U.S. 93 and MT-35 to West Glacier and will take a little over 2.5 hours. Longer routes through the Seeley-Swan Valley via MT-83 (165 miles, 265 km) or along the west side of Flathead Lake via MT-200 and MT-28 (175 miles, 280 km) will take roughly three hours.

Driving from Calgary
180 miles (290 km); 3 hours
From Calgary, Alberta, the east entrance of Glacier National Park at St. Mary is 180 miles (290 km) south on AB-2, and takes roughly three hours without time allotted for crossing the border at Carway.

Air
The closest airport to Glacier is 30 miles (48 km) away in Kalispell. The **Glacier Park International Airport** (FCA, www. iflyglacier.com) is served by Delta, Alaska Airlines, United, and Allegiant.

At the airport **Avis, Budget, Hertz,** and **National/Alamo** have car-rental counters, and **Dollar, Thrifty,** and **Enterprise** have car-rental lots off-site but near the airport. **Glacier Taxi** (406/250-3603) and **Wild Horse Limousine** (406/756-2290 or 800/841-2391, www.wildhorselimo. com) offer taxi and limo services, respectively.

Great Falls International Airport (GTF) is 130-165 miles (209-265 km) southeast of the park entrances at St. Mary, Two Medicine, and Many Glacier.

Missoula International Airport (MSO) is roughly 138 miles (222 km) south of the park entrance at West Glacier.

Calgary International Airport (YYC) is approximately 187 miles (301 km) north of the entrance at St. Mary and should take just over three hours to reach by car. Among the car-rental companies at the airport are **Avis, Budget, Hertz, Dollar, Thrifty, Enterprise, National,** and **Alamo.**

Best Restaurants

★ **Park Café & Grocery, St. Mary:** An institution since 1952, this spot is known for breakfasts that'll stick to your ribs, hearty burgers and sandwiches, and excellent homemade pies (page 219).

★ **Two Sisters Café, Babb:** On a fairly lonesome highway, this unexpected restaurant boasts delicious handmade meals—from bison steaks to huckleberry pie—and a festive atmosphere (page 219).

★ **The Belton Grill Dining Room, West Glacier:** Set in a beautifully appointed 1910 railroad chalet, this upscale place serves innovative and gourmet cuisine including Montana Wagyu beef, lamb linguini, and wild salmon (page 219).

★ **Loula's Café, Whitefish:** Serving three meals a day, Loula's offers family-friendly comfort food—like chicken potpie and country-fried steak—using fresh local ingredients. But the pie is the thing here (page 229).

Train

Amtrak runs the **Empire Builder** from Chicago to Seattle, with daily stops in both directions in East Glacier (summer only), Essex, and West Glacier.

Visiting Glacier National Park

Planning Your Time

Depending on the amount of time you have to spend in Montana, Glacier National Park could easily absorb all of it, but often it is a spectacular route to get from one side of the Continental Divide to the other, in which case some sights take priority.

The 50-mile (81-km) **Going-to-the-Sun Road** is one of the most scenic drives you will ever take and the best way to get an overview of the park if your time is limited. The alpine vistas provide a marvelous sense of the geography, and the park's history comes alive for those who stop to notice the architecture of the road itself. The drive will likely take at least two hours, not accounting for construction, traffic, or weather-related delays, but if time permits even just an extra hour, there are plenty of turnouts

and hiking opportunities along the way. **Hidden Lake Overlook** is a wonderful 3-mile (4.8-km) round-trip hike from the **Logan Pass Visitor Center** that provides opportunities to view seasonal wildflowers and wildlife. Any time in Glacier's backcountry will be time well spent, but visitors should be prepared for changes in the weather (dress in layers and bring water) and wildlife encounters.

With more than a day, visitors can see some of the park's idyllic corners. **Many Glacier** is a launching spot for day hikes to numerous alpine lakes and glaciers. **Lake McDonald,** the park's largest, is a favorite place to spend the day. The southern section of the park, accessed from U.S. 2, is especially popular in winter with cross-country skiers who make tracks from the **Izaak Walton Inn** in Essex.

Planning is critical in Glacier, as accommodations within and immediately surrounding the park fill up months in advance. The 1,004 campsites throughout the park, on the other hand, are filled primarily on a first-come, first-served basis (with a few notable exceptions: Fish Creek and St. Mary can be reserved in advance, as can half the group sites at Apgar and some of the campsites at Many Glacier). Still, last-minute travelers

Best Accommodations

★ **Glacier Park Lodge, East Glacier Area:** Opened in 1913, the Glacier Park Lodge is still the grand dame of Glacier's historic hotels. Built just outside the park, the hotel offers a variety of accommodations with excellent ambience (page 220).

★ **Granite Park Chalet, East Glacier Area:** You have to hike to get here, and unless you consider alpine views and grizzly bear sightings amenities, it's not glamourous, but a night at Granite Park is unforgettable (page 221).

★ **Many Glacier Hotel, Many Glacier:** Set on the idyllic shores of Swiftcurrent Lake, this Swiss-style chalet puts guests in the heart of the Many Glacier region with old-world accommodations and loads of activities (page 222).

★ **Belton Chalet, West Glacier:** Small and rustic, the Belton Chalet was magnificently restored in 1999 and offers charming rooms and cottages with one of the best restaurants in the area (page 223).

are not necessarily out of luck. For park brochures, which can be immensely helpful in planning your trip, visit www.nps.gov/glac. For those who are willing to stay outside of the park and launch day trips, the gateway towns of Whitefish and Kalispell have many more choices for accommodations.

Although pets are allowed in drive-in campgrounds, picnic areas, and on roads open to car traffic, they are required to be on a leash no longer than 6 feet (1.8 m) at all times. They are not permitted on any trails within the park, and park officials strongly discourage the presence of pets in Glacier. Because of this policy, it is nearly impossible to find pet-friendly accommodations in the area.

Entrances

The two main entrances to Glacier National Park are at either end of Going-to-the-Sun Road. **West Glacier,** on the west side of the park, can be accessed from U.S. 2, and **St. Mary,** on the park's east side, can be accessed from U.S. 89.

Entrance stations on the west side are at **Camas Creek** and the **Polebridge Ranger Station** off Outside North Fork Road, and on the east side at **Two Medicine** off Highway 49, **Many Glacier**

off U.S. 89, and at **Waterton Lakes National Park** accessible from Alberta Provincial Highways 5 and 6. Entrance fees must be paid even when entrance stations are closed.

Park Fees and Passes

Entrance to **Glacier National Park** (406/888-7800, www.nps.gov/glac) costs $35 per vehicle for seven days May 1 through October 31, $30 for motorcycles, and $20 for hikers and bikers. From November 1 through April 30, the rate is reduced to $25 per vehicle, $20 for motorcycles, and $15 for hikers and bikers.

An annual park pass for Glacier costs $70. An annual America the Beautiful Pass is $80 and will gain you entrance into any and all national parks for one year.

Visitors Centers

At the park entrance, visitors are given a copy of *Vacation Planner,* which provides important general information about the park. Once inside the park, visitors centers and ranger stations are the best sources of information. Hours of operation vary, but during the summer the centers and stations are open every day.

The **Visitor Information Headquarters**

Planning a Last-Minute Trip to Glacier

Rooms in Glacier's historic lodges and chalets can already be full up to a year ahead, but spontaneous travelers are not necessarily out of luck. Last-minute cancellations and room openings are possible and well worth a couple of phone calls. **Glacier Park Collection** (844/868-7474, www.glacierparkcollection.com) is the booking service for the Grouse Mountain Lodge, Glacier Park Lodge, St. Mary Village, Apgar Village Lodge & Cabins, Motel Lake McDonald, West Glacier RV Park & Cabins, and Prince of Wales Hotel. Call and ask specifically for cancellations. You may have better luck if you are open to whatever they have to offer, but you just may get the property you were hoping for. Being flexible with your dates helps.

view from Granite Park Chalet

Glacier National Park Lodges (855/733-4522, www.glaciernationalparklodges.com) is the booking service for Cedar Creek Lodge, Many Glacier Hotel, Swiftcurrent Motor Inn & Cabins, Rising Sun Motor Inn & Cabins, Lake McDonald Lodge, and Village Inn at Apgar. In this case, too, a phone call to ask about cancellations can lead to a windfall.

For visitors willing to hike in to their accommodations, **Granite Park Chalet** (888/345-2649, www.graniteparkchalet.com, from $108 pp, $80 additional person in same room, optional linen and bedding service $20 pp) is a fantastic option and well worth a call to see if they have last-minute openings.

For true spontaneity, pitch a tent in one of Glacier's 1,000-plus campsites in 13 campgrounds, at least some of which are open May-mid-October. With the exception of St. Mary, Fish Creek, half the campsites at Many Glacier, and half the group sites at Apgar, all campgrounds are available on a first-come, first-served basis, with nightly fees of $10-23. An excellent page on the National Park Service website (www.nps.gov/glac) shows updated availability at campsites across the park, and even gives the time of day each campground was filled the day before. Apgar is the largest campground, with 194 sites, followed by Fish Creek (178 sites), St. Mary (146 sites), and Many Glacier (110 sites). For advance reservations no more than six months ahead of time at Fish Creek or St. Mary, contact the **National Park Reservation System** (877/444-6777, www.recreation.gov).

In the spirit of spontaneity, almost anything you need for your recreational purposes can be rented from **Glacier Outfitters** (196 Apgar Loop, 406/219-7466, www.goglacieroutfitters.com), from bear spray to camping gear.

Building (64 Grinnell Dr., 8am-4:30pm Mon.-Fri., excluding holidays, year-round) is just inside the West Glacier park entrance before the actual entrance station; turn right after passing the "Glacier National Park" sign. Staff can issue a variety of passes and permits as well as answer most questions.

The park's visitors centers all have knowledgeable staff, guidebooks and maps, and basic amenities. In West Glacier, visit the **Apgar Visitor Center** (9am-4:30pm daily mid-May-mid-Oct., only open Sat.-Sun. winter) in the central part of Apgar Village. It is two doors down from the **Backcountry Permit**

Bear Safety

Glacier has significant concentrations of both grizzly and black bears, both of which can be threatening in any encounter. The keys to safe travel in the backcountry are acting to prevent bear encounters and knowing what to do in the event you do meet a bear. The following are simple guidelines for responsible behavior in bear country:

♦ **Don't surprise bears.** Make noise, even on well-traveled trails, to allow bears the opportunity to get away from you. Bells can be effective, as can singing, hand-clapping, and loud talking. Never assume that a bear has better senses than you and will see, hear, or smell you coming.

♦ **Don't approach bears.** Be aware of their feeding opportunities and behavior so that you can avoid potential feeding locations and times of day. Avoid hiking through berry patches, cow parsnip thickets, or fields of glacier lilies. Never approach a carcass, which could be under the surveillance of a bear. Try not to hike before sunrise or at dusk, both active times for bears. Always keep children close.

♦ **Minimize the possibility that a bear would be attracted to your belongings or campsite.** Abide by all the park regulations about hanging your food and garbage away from your sleeping area. Don't carry odiferous food, and never bring anything potentially edible, including medicines and toothpaste, into your tent. Take special care with used feminine hygiene products by sealing them in several zip-top bags with baking soda to absorb the odor.

♦ **Be prepared for an encounter.** Carry pepper spray that is not out of date and know how to use it. Familiarize yourself with the behaviors most likely to ensure your safety in a bear encounter.

If you do surprise a bear, keep your wits about you. While there is no easy and universal answer about how to react—bears are as individual and unpredictable as humans—the following are accepted behaviors outlined on Glacier's website:

♦ **Talk quietly and calmly.** If you have surprised a bear, don't attempt to threaten it; if possible, try to detour around it.

♦ **Never run.** Don't turn your back; instead, back away slowly, unless it agitates the bear. Running could trigger its predatory instincts.

♦ **Use peripheral vision.** Bears may perceive direct eye contact as aggressive behavior on your part.

♦ **Drop something (not food) to distract the bear and keep your pack on for protection in case of an attack.** If you have bear spray, grab it and be prepared to use it in the event of an attack.

♦ **Protect yourself if the bear attacks.** Protect your chest and abdomen by falling to the ground on your stomach or assuming the fetal position. Cover the back of your neck with your hands, and if the bear tries to roll you over, attempt to stay on your stomach. If the attack is defensive, the bear will leave once it has determined you are not a threat. If the attack is prolonged, *fight back!*

Center (406/888-7800, open daily late May-mid-Sept., or by appointment when closed for the season), which also provides trip planning. The **St. Mary Visitor Center** (8am-5pm daily late May-mid-Sept.) inside the eastern park entrance, is the park's largest visitors center and offers backcountry permit services.

The **Two Medicine Ranger Station** and **Many Glacier Ranger Station** (both 7am-5pm daily late May-mid-Sept., backcountry permits available), close to the campgrounds, provide visitor information and permits.

Services

If you have questions before arriving in Glacier, check out the Plan Your Visit section on the **Glacier National Park website** (www.nps.gov/glac) or call the **Park Headquarters** (406/888-7800, 8am-4:30pm daily).

Lodging in Glacier is available through three separate providers. **Glacier National Park Lodges** (855/733-4522 or 303/265-7010 from outside the U.S., www.glaciernationalparklodges.com) operates the Cedar Creek Lodge, Village Inn at Apgar, Lake McDonald Lodge, Rising Sun Motor Inn & Cabins, Swiftcurrent Motor Inn & Cabins, and Many Glacier Hotel. **Glacier Park Collection** (844/868-7474, www.glacierparkcollection.com) operates Grouse Mountain Lodge, Glacier Park Lodge, St. Mary Village, Prince of Wales Hotel, Apgar Village Lodge & Cabins, West Glacier RV Park & Cabins, and Motel Lake McDonald. Both the **Belton Chalet** (406/888-5000, 888/345-2649, http://beltonchalet.com) and **Granite Park Chalet** (888/345-2649, www.graniteparkchalet.com) can be booked directly. You can book accommodations as well as a variety of tours and park transportation online or by phone.

If you arrive and discover you are missing some important piece of recreational equipment—or more important, bear spray—almost anything you need can be rented from **Glacier Outfitters**

(196 Apgar Loop, 406/219-7466, www.goglacieroutfitters.com). From camping gear and backpacks to a variety of bicycles, paddleboards, kayaks, canoes, fishing rods, GoPro cameras, and, yep, bear spray, this is the place to make sure you have what you need in the way of toys and gear.

Getting Around
Private Vehicles

Vehicles and vehicle combinations longer than 21 feet (6.4 m), including bumpers, and wider than 8 feet (2.4 m), including mirrors, are not permitted on Going-to-the-Sun Road between Avalanche Campground and the Rising Sun Parking Area. Vehicles and vehicle combinations taller than 10 feet (3 m) may have difficulty navigating Going-to-the-Sun Road westbound from Logan Pass to the Loop because of rock overhangs. Stock trucks and trailers can access Packers Roost on the west side and Siyeh Bend on the east side.

Shuttles

Glacier's **free shuttle system** (406/892-2525, 7:30am-7pm daily July-September 23) picks up and drops off at 16 different stops, including Apgar Visitor Center, Avalanche Creek, Logan Pass, St. Mary Visitor Center, and a number of trailheads. West-side shuttles depart every 15-30 minutes and east-side shuttles depart every 40 minutes. The shuttle is an excellent option for hiking from the Logan Pass Visitor Center, which often has a full parking lot otherwise, or for doing trails that start at one trailhead and end at another. Be warned that at peak season, even seats on the shuttle can be scarce and hikers can wait hours for a ride. To travel the entire Going-to-the-Sun Road from the Apgar Visitor Center to the St. Mary Visitor Center and back, or vice versa, takes approximately seven hours on the shuttle. The last service to Logan Pass with time to visit and return departs Apgar Visitor Center at 4:15pm

Hands-On Learning

Founded in 1983, the **Glacier Institute** (406/755-1211, www.glacierinstitute.org) is a private nonprofit organization that offers hands-on educational experiences using Glacier National Park and Flathead National Forest as its classrooms. Its mission is to provide "an objective and science-based understanding of the area's ecology and its interaction with people." The Glacier Institute fulfills its mission by providing field-based experiences in and around the park for all ages and levels of fitness.

The Glacier Institute offers 3- to 5-day youth camps ($125-350), which have a variety of focuses. Whether it is the first overnight camp experience for children away from their parents, an introduction to the basic concepts of ecology, or a focus on art and nature, the institute offers experienced guides and experts to foster each child's learning. It also has a variety of outdoor education courses open to young and old. You can enroll for a daylong course (from $65) with expert instructors on topics such as, for instance, wolves of the North Fork Valley, for a unique learning experience.

To peruse the institute's extensive and fascinating offerings, visit its website; if you see a course that interests you but is not being offered when you plan to be in Glacier, the Glacier Institute creates custom programs and can plan a half-day to several-day course just for your group (1-6 people, $425) based on the courses or expert instructors that you select.

and St. Mary Visitor Center at 6:31pm. Check daily schedules for early-morning express service from Apgar Visitor Center to Logan Pass.

Tours

Scenic, interpretive **Red Bus Tours** (855/733-4522 or 303/265-7010 from outside the U.S., www.glaciernationalparklodges.com, from $36 adults, $18 children) are another way to see the park. These snazzy vintage buses, known locally as "Jammers," were originally built by the White Motor Company 1936-1939. The vehicles, which have been overhauled for safety purposes, are 25 feet (7.6 m) long, seat 17 passengers, and have the added bonus of roll-back canvas tops, ideal for sunny summer days. Numerous tours of varying lengths are available, and informative guides entertain with facts and stories about Glacier. It's an excellent way to leave the driving to someone else.

Slightly less flashy but quite comfortable are the air-conditioned and large-windowed coaches of **Sun Tours** (406/226-9220 or 800/786-9220, www.glaciersuntours.com, June-Sept. 1, $60-100 adults, $30-50 children 5-12, free for children under 5). Tours last four, six, or eight hours, and what makes them unique is that they are guided from a Blackfeet perspective. Plants and roots used for Blackfeet medicine are pointed out, for example, as are the natural features that relate to the Blackfeet Nation. The coaches can accommodate 25 passengers and depart daily from East Glacier, Browning, St. Mary, and West Glacier. Sun Tours also offers a hiker shuttle service and private custom tours.

Sights

East Glacier Area

Located on the Blackfeet Indian Reservation at the southeast corner of the park, East Glacier (population 363; elevation 4,799 ft/1,463 m) has long been a primary entrance into Glacier National Park. Early visitors from the east often arrived by rail at East Glacier and spent the night in the grand Glacier Park Lodge before heading into the wilds of the park.

Today the town of East Glacier bustles year-round and is a hub of activity during the summer months as visitors stream in and out of the park. There are numerous accommodations, including the still-majestic Adirondack-style Glacier Park Lodge, several good restaurants, local outfitters, and a smattering of shops. There is also a tremendous amount of wilderness to be explored both inside the park and in immediate proximity to East Glacier. The stunning Two Medicine Valley is just a few miles away, and hiking, skiing, and even snowmobiling trails are within steps of the main drag.

Two Medicine Valley

Geographically, Two Medicine Valley is not at the heart of Glacier, but this remote southeastern corner is staggeringly beautiful and seemingly less known among the mass of summer visitors. The rocky peaks and glacially carved valleys meet in clear alpine lakes, and the area offers plenty of activity. There are boat tours that intersect with hiking trails, numerous waterfalls to ogle, fishing, and a lovely campground.

St. Mary to Many Glacier

This place feels like it's at the edge of two worlds: mountains to the west, vast plains to the east. St. Mary is a small village nestled between St. Mary Lake and Lower St.

Top to bottom: Grinnell Glacier; hikers in Two Medicine Valley; Lake McDonald.

Many Glacier Region

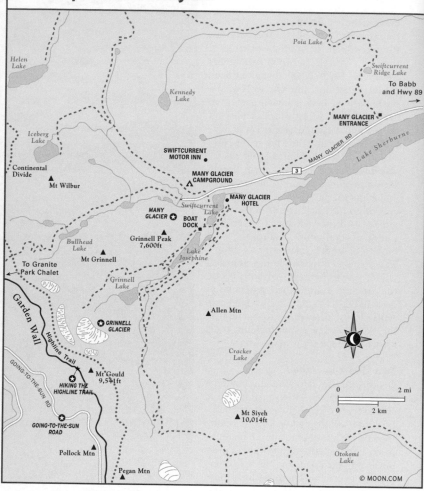

Poia Lake

Helen Lake

Swiftcurrent Ridge Lake

To Babb and Hwy 89

Kennedy Lake

MANY GLACIER ENTRANCE

Iceberg Lake

MANY GLACIER RD

Lake Sherburne

SWIFTCURRENT MOTOR INN

Continental Divide

Mt Wilbur

MANY GLACIER CAMPGROUND

3

MANY GLACIER HOTEL

MANY GLACIER

Swiftcurrent Lake

BOAT DOCK

Bullhead Lake

Grinnell Peak 7,600ft

Mt Grinnell

Lake Josephine

To Granite Park Chalet

Grinnell Lake

Garden Wall

Highline Trail

Allen Mtn

GRINNELL GLACIER

GOING-TO-THE-SUN RD

Cracker Lake

Mt Gould 9,541ft

HIKING THE HIGHLINE TRAIL

GOING-TO-THE-SUN ROAD

0   2 mi

0   2 km

Mt Siyeh 10,014ft

Pollock Mtn

Pegan Mtn

Otokomi Lake

© MOON.COM

Mary Lake that marks another entrance to the park and the start of Going-to-the-Sun Road. With all the splendor of the jagged peaks and the wide-open vistas created by sparse stands of aspen and sweeping prairie, the recreational opportunities are abundant and the scenery spectacular.

Farther north, Many Glacier is the ideal base camp for avid and active outdoors lovers, with extensive opportunities

for hiking, canoeing, and horseback riding. The popular boat tours and Red Bus Tours are also accessible from Many Glacier. Grinnell Glacier is a dwindling but still phenomenal work of nature, and daily ranger-led hikes take visitors up to its toe. The Many Glacier Hotel is a historic 1915 Great Northern Railway Swiss chalet-style lodge that welcomes guests with a rambling veranda and cozy guest rooms.

St. Mary Lake

One of the most photographed lakes in the park for its absurdly beautiful mountain backdrop, St. Mary Lake is among the best places in Glacier to watch the sun rise. The lake and its many hiking trails are accessible from Going-to-the-Sun Road. The **Sun Point Nature Trail** is 1.4 miles (2.3 km) round-trip, and the trailhead is 9.5 miles (15.3 km) west of the St. Mary Visitor Center. It is worth the short walk for views of Baring Falls and the lake itself. An even quicker stop is **Sunrift Gorge,** 0.6 mile (1 km) west of Sun Point, an incredible cascade slicing between two rock walls; it's just 200 feet (61 m) from the parking area. Baring Falls is another 0.3-mile (0.5-km) walk down the trail.

★ Many Glacier

The Many Glacier region is a palpable reminder of why Glacier has long been known as the Switzerland of America. Marked by grand accommodations and a landscape that was visibly scoured and carved by glaciers, from the U-shaped valleys and milky-blue glacial lakes to the rocky moraines and the last remaining glaciers themselves, this region is among the most dramatic and startlingly beautiful in the park.

This is not a place to be enjoyed from inside a car, although those on a tight schedule would still benefit from making the journey just to walk around the hotel and drink in the stunning surroundings. Many Glacier is best suited for active travelers: The hiking and boating are exceptional, and it is one of the rare places in the Lower 48 where a day hike can lead you to an actual glacier. Come to Many Glacier to see the splendid scenery, but if possible, stay a few days to truly enjoy it.

★ Grinnell Glacier

Named for conservationist and explorer George Bird Grinnell, Grinnell Glacier lies in the heart of Many Glacier and is a symbol both of the park's wilderness and of the dramatic climatic changes that are occurring. Because the glacier is accessible within a day's hike, its startling shrinkage—from 710 acres in 1850 to 152 acres in 2005—has been captured on film. Still, as long as it exists, this glacier is well worth visiting.

The options for seeing the glacier up close and personal are to hoof it from the **Many Glacier Hotel** (5.5 mi/8.9 km one-way with a 1,600-ft/488-m elevation gain) or to take a boat across Lake Josephine with **Glacier Park Boat Company** (406/257-2426, www.glacierparkboats.com, $27.50 adults, $13.75 children 4-12, free for children under 4) and hike the remainder of the trail from the head of Lake Josephine (3.8 mi/6.1 km one-way with a 1,600-ft/488-m elevation gain). There is also an excellent ranger-guided hike to the glacier that makes use of the boat, leaving the Many Glacier dock daily at 8:30am starting in mid-July (weather and conditions permitting). The 8.5-mile (13.7-km) round-trip outing lasts almost nine hours. The trail twists and climbs above impossibly blue alpine lakes and within sight of the aptly named Salamander Glacier. In the early season, hikers will get wet with runoff from the overhanging waterfalls along the trail; come prepared! Though the trail is one of the oldest and most popular hikes in the park, and thus heavily trafficked, wildlife is plentiful in the area too, and grizzly bears are commonly spotted on or near the trail. The trail often does not open until late July and is seldom clear of snow until well into August.

Upper Waterton Lake and Goat Haunt

You'll need your passport to see one of the natural highlights of Canada's Waterton Lakes National Park, but you may feel like you've traveled even farther afield—the fjord-like valley is reminiscent of Norway, especially when it is shrouded in fog and mist. Upper Waterton Lake runs north-south, straddling the border.

Boats run between the Canadian town of Waterton (headquarters for the park) and **Goat Haunt** at the lake's southern end, accessible only by hiking or by boat.

On the Canadian side, **Crypt Lake Trail** (10.8 mi/17.4 km round-trip) is an ambitious hike that includes a natural tunnel through a rock wall, stomach-dropping heights, waterfalls galore, and a dazzling hidden cirque. There are a handful of hikes, ranging from mellow to death-defying, from the Goat Haunt ranger station, and several ranger-led hikes daily in summer. A few favorites are **Rainbow Falls** (2 mi/3.2 km round-trip, no elevation gain), **Kootenai Lakes** (5 mi/8 km round-trip, 200-ft/61-m elevation gain), **Lake Janet** (6.6 mi/10.6 km round-trip, 750-ft/229-m elevation gain), and **Lake Francis** (12.4 mi/20 km round-trip, 1,050-ft/320-m elevation gain). For those willing to huff and puff, but only briefly, **Goat Haunt Overlook** (2 mi/3.2 km round-trip, 800-ft/244-m elevation gain) offers a phenomenal view of the valley. The isolation and lack of roads tends to keep visitor numbers down around Upper Waterton Lake, but the mosquitoes are abundant; come prepared.

There is a limited port of entry at Goat Haunt that's open 11:15am-5pm daily. Travel between Waterton Lakes National Park, Canada, and the Goat Haunt Ranger Station on the U.S. side will require an official government-issued photo identification card for U.S. or Canadian citizens or permanent residents; all others must carry a valid passport. Persons seeking to travel beyond the Goat Haunt Ranger Station into the United States must present documents that are WHTI compliant.

★ Going-to-the-Sun Road

Completed in 1932, the famed Going-to-the-Sun Road is a marvel of modern engineering. Spanning 50 miles (81 km) from West Glacier to St. Mary, the road snakes up and around mountains that include its namesake, Going-to-the-Sun Mountain,

giving viewers some of the most dramatic vistas in the country. The road, which crosses the Continental Divide, required more than two decades of planning and construction. It climbs more than 3,000 feet (914 m) with only a single switch-back, known as The Loop. Going-to-the-Sun is an architectural accomplishment as well: All of the bridges, retaining walls, and guardrails are built of native materials, so the road itself blends seamlessly into its majestic alpine setting.

In addition to being an experience all on its own, Going-to-the-Sun is also the primary access road to the park and the only way to get to some of Glacier's best-known highlights: the visitors center at Logan Pass, the Highline Trail, Lake McDonald, and an array of hiking trails. For visitors who are not keen on driving the road themselves, there are a few excellent options, including free shuttles, vintage-vehicle tours, and Blackfeet-themed tours, to see the road as a sightseer.

★ Lake McDonald

The largest lake in the park at 9.4 miles (15.1 km) long and 464 feet (141 m) deep, Lake McDonald was gouged out by a glacier that was likely 2,200 feet (671 m) thick. Surrounded by jagged peaks on three sides, it is bordered by the Lewis Range to the east, which creates a rain block and makes the Lake McDonald Valley one of the mildest and lushest environments in the region. Not unlike the Pacific Northwest, the Lake McDonald Valley boasts dense forests of towering western red cedars and hemlocks.

Although the lake and surrounding forests are exquisitely serene, the area is a hub of activity in the summer months for human visitors and the bear population alike. Modeled after a Swiss chalet and opened in 1914, the grand and slightly worse-for-wear **Lake McDonald Lodge** sprawls along the northeast shore and provides relatively expensive lodging with unmatched views. The dining

Ranger Programs

Some of the best resources on Glacier National Park are the Park Service rangers—encyclopedias in hiking boots. Their stations are conveniently located at major sights throughout the park, and the rangers host a number of outdoor educational events geared to the whole family. The ranger programs in Glacier begin in late spring and run throughout the summer, with most activities offered at St. Mary, Apgar, Logan Pass, Many Glacier, Goat Haunt, and Two Medicine. Rangers lead several guided hikes each day that allow visitors to learn about the park's geology, history, wildlife, flora, fauna, and more. The St. Mary Visitor Center, Fish Creek Amphitheater, Lake McDonald Lodge, and Many Glacier Hotel host slide lectures as part of the ranger program. Full-day hikes, boat tours, and Junior Ranger programs also are available.

One of the most noteworthy park programs is "Native America Speaks," where members from the Blackfeet, Salish, Kootenai, and Pend d'Oreille tribes provide campfire talks about their life, culture, and influence in Glacier. The speakers range from artists and musicians to historians who intersperse their talks with personal stories and Native American legends. These talks are given at the Apgar, Many Glacier, Two Medicine, and Rising Sun Campgrounds. During July-August, the St. Mary Visitor Center also hosts weekly Native American dance troupes. For times, locations, and descriptions of the ranger programs offered, pick up the free "Ranger-led Activity Schedule" available at any of the park's visitors centers.

For information on ranger stations or programs and to download park brochures, contact **Park Service Headquarters** (406/888-7800, www.nps.gov/glac).

---

room, lounge, and pizzeria are open to nonguests. Stop in to warm yourself by the massive fireplace, check out the animal mounts that have decorated the place since its origins, or lounge lakeside on the veranda with a beverage.

There are many great hiking trails around the lake, including those to Fish Lake, Mount Brown Lookout, and the mellow Johns Lake Loop. Plenty of fish swim in the lake—17 varieties in all, mainly trout. Boat tours also depart from the lodge, as well as Red Bus Tours and ranger-led activities.

West Glacier Area

A bustling entrance to Glacier, West Glacier (population 227; elevation 3,220 ft/982 m) has the feeling of "last chance to get bug spray" and "first non-PB&J in a while." It is clearly not a destination but a portal, and a good place to find lodging, dining, and supplies in immediate proximity to the park.

The town itself grew up around the Belton Chalet, a lodge built by the Great Northern Railway in 1910, the same year

Glacier became a national park. The Belton, an arts and crafts-style gem, was the first permanent lodging on the west side of Glacier, and thanks to a painstaking restoration in 2000 and a wonderful restaurant, it remains one of the best accommodations in the area despite its proximity to both the road and the train tracks.

Bowman Lake

Some 32 miles (52 km) north of the west entrance to Glacier in the North Fork area, and only 30 miles (48 km) south of Canada, is Bowman Lake, another crystalline alpine gem ringed with mountains and forest. A long, bumpy ride is required to get here, and as a result it is never crowded. The density of mosquitoes tends to discourage visitors, too. But the 7-mile-long (11.3-km) lake is beautiful, and there is such a thing as bug spray. Boats are permitted, with restrictions on engines. Kayaks and canoes are a wonderful way to explore this photogenic setting. The lake is filled with fish, primarily kokanee and cutthroat trout, and

Scenic Point

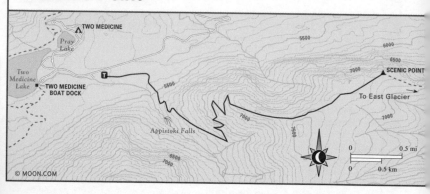

© MOON.COM

the fishing is legendary, particularly in late spring. There are plenty of worthwhile hikes from the area, including the arduous 13.1-mile (21.1-km) round-trip **Quartz Lakes Loop,** but be warned that this is the heart of grizzly country, and visitors should come prepared. Camping is available on a first-come, first-served basis at the primitive **Bowman Lake Campground** (48 sites, late May-mid-Sept., $15), where several of the trailheads can be accessed.

Adventure and Recreation

Hiking
East Glacier
Scenic Point
Distance: 7.4 miles (11.9 km) round-trip
Duration: 4 hours
Elevation gain: 2,124 feet (647 m)
Effort: moderate-strenuous
Trailhead: milepost 6.9 up Two Medicine Road

Scenic Point is one short climb with big scenery. The trail launches through a thick subalpine fir forest. A short side jaunt en route allows a peek at Appistoki Falls. As switchbacks line up like dominoes, stunted firs give way to silvery dead and twisted limber pines. Broaching the

ridge, the trail enters seemingly barren alpine tundra. Only alpine bluebells and pink mats of several-hundred-year-old moss campion cower in crags.

On the ridge, the trail traverses a north-facing slope; avoid the steep early-summer snowfield by climbing a worn path that goes above it before descending to Scenic Point. To reach the actual Scenic Point above the trail, cut off at the sign, stepping on rocks to avoid crushing fragile alpine plants. At the top, views plunge several thousand feet straight down to Lower Two Medicine Lake and across the plains. Return the way you came, or drop seven miles to East Glacier, passing outside the park boundary, where cow pies buzz with flies. The latter half of the Scenic Point-East Glacier trail requires a Blackfeet recreation permit ($10), available at the Two Medicine Ranger Station or Bear Track Travel Center (Exxon gas station) in East Glacier.

Aster Park
Distance: 3.8 miles (6.1 km) round-trip
Duration: 2 hours
Elevation gain: 610 feet (186 m)
Effort: easy
Trailhead: adjacent to Two Medicine boat dock

Beginning on the South Shore Trail, Aster Park is reached via a spur trail just past Aster Creek. About 1.2 miles

Two Medicine Lake Trails

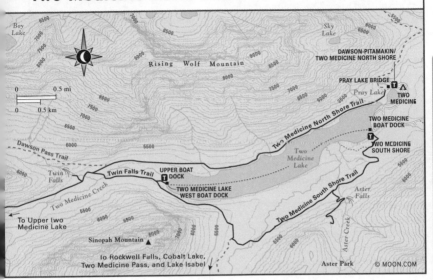

Boy Lake · Sky Lake · Rising Wolf Mountain · DAWSON-PITAMAKIN/ TWO MEDICINE NORTH SHORE · PRAY LAKE BRIDGE · Pray Lake · TWO MEDICINE · Two Medicine North Shore Trail · TWO MEDICINE BOAT DOCK · TWO MEDICINE SOUTH SHORE · Dawson Pass Trail · Two Medicine Lake · Twin Falls · Twin Falls Trail · UPPER BOAT DOCK · TWO MEDICINE LAKE WEST BOAT DOCK · Two Medicine Creek · Two Medicine South Shore Trail · Aster Falls · To Upper Two Medicine Lake · Aster Creek · Sinopah Mountain · To Rockwell Falls, Cobalt Lake, Two Medicine Pass, and Lake Isabel · Aster Park · © MOON.COM

southwest of the boat dock, turn left at the signed junction and follow the trail past Aster Falls as it switchbacks up to a flower-covered knoll. This overlook provides grand views of Two Medicine Lake and Rising Wolf.

Two Medicine Lake Loop, Twin Falls, and Upper Two Medicine Lake

Distance: 2-10.7 miles (3.2-17.2 km) round-trip
Duration: 1-5 hours
Elevation gain: 0-424 feet (0-129 m)
Effort: easy-moderate
Trailhead: North Shore Two Medicine Lake Trailhead at Pray Lake Bridge in Two Medicine Campground, South Shore Two Medicine Lake Trailhead near boat launch, Two Medicine Lake west boat dock

Two Medicine and Upper Two Medicine Lake are a set of subalpine lakes formed by the immense Two Medicine Glacier. As an added treat for hikers, the trail also takes in Twin Falls, a double flume of cascades. The North Shore and South Shore Trails connect at the west end of Two Medicine Lake to form the loop, a route that cuts through forest, avalanche chutes, huckleberry bushes, and meadows. The South Shore Trail takes in beaver ponds, a swinging bridge over Paradise Creek, and the precipitous slopes of Mount Sinopah, while the North Shore Trail trots along the base of Rising Wolf, the biggest peak in the area, and captures views of Pumpelly Pillar. A spur trail at the west end of the lake leads to Twin Falls and Upper Two Medicine Lake below Lone Walker Mountain. In early summer, water floods the upper lake's beach, leaving only a brushy shoreline. For lunch, help maintain the safety of those sleeping in the backcountry campground by sitting in the cooking area to eat.

To hike the Two Medicine Lake Loop, Twin Falls, and Upper Two Medicine Lake (10.7 miles), go either direction starting at the North Shore Trailhead or South Shore Trailhead, connecting the two trailheads with 0.8 mile of road walking. Other routes vary depending on starting trailheads, ending points, and whether or not you opt to use the Two

Medicine Lake boat as a shuttle. Taking the boat round-trip across the lake makes for the shortest hikes (2 miles round-trip for Twin Falls and 4.2 miles round-trip for Upper Two Medicine Lake). Hiking the North Shore Trail, Twin Falls, and Upper Two Medicine Lake to end at the west boat dock for a one-way shuttle (pay cash when boarding, $7 adults, half-price for children) across the lake makes for midsized hikes (4.6 miles for Twin Falls and 7.2 miles for Upper Two Medicine Lake). All trail junctions have signage, but maps help in clarifying routes.

St. Mary to Many Glacier
Apikuni Falls
Distance: 1.6 miles (2.6 km) round-trip
Duration: 1 hour
Elevation gain: 570 feet (174 m)
Effort: moderate
Trailhead: Grinnell Glacier interpretive site, 10.4 miles west on Many Glacier Road

Apikuni Falls springs from a hanging valley, which you can see from the trailhead. The short walk starts out across a flat meadow where wildflowers bloom thickly in July: geraniums, arrowleaf balsamroot, paintbrush, lupine, and stonecrop. But soon, the path steepens to climb to the cliffs between Mount Altyn and Apikuni Mountain, where the falls drop out of the basin above. Those with scrambling skills can climb a rough trail into the upper hanging valley.

Grinnell Glacier
Distance: 11 miles (17.7 km) round-trip
Duration: 6 hours
Elevation gain: 1,619 feet (493 m)
Effort: moderate-strenuous
Trailheads: on the south side of Many Glacier Hotel, at Swiftcurrent Picnic Area, or via the tour boat

In early summer, a large, steep snowdrift frequently bars the path into the upper basin until early July; check the trail status before hiking. The most accessible glacier in the park, Grinnell Glacier still requires stamina because most of its elevation gain packs within two miles.

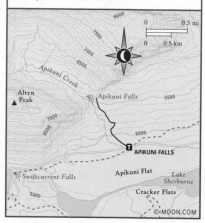

Many hikers take the boat shuttle, cutting the length to 7.8 miles round-trip, or just trimming 2.5 miles off the return. To hike the entire route from the picnic area, follow Swiftcurrent Lake's west shore to the boat dock. From Many Glacier Hotel, round the southern shore to meet up with the same dock. Bop over the short hill and hike around Lake Josephine's north shore.

Toward Josephine's west end, the Grinnell Glacier Trail diverges uphill. As the trail climbs through multicolored rock strata, Grinnell Lake's milky turquoise waters come into view below. Above, you'll spot Gem Glacier and Salamander Glacier, both shrunken to static snowfields, long before Grinnell Glacier appears. The trail ascends on a cliff stairway where a waterfall douses hikers before passing a rest stop with outhouses. A steep grunt up the moraine leads to a stunning view. Trot through the maze of paths crossing the bedrock to Upper Grinnell Lake's shore, but do not walk out on the glacier's ice, as it harbors deadly hidden crevasses.

Swiftcurrent Valley and Lookout
Distance: 3.6-16.2 miles (5.8-26.1 km) round-trip
Duration: 2-8 hours

Grinnell Glacier Trail

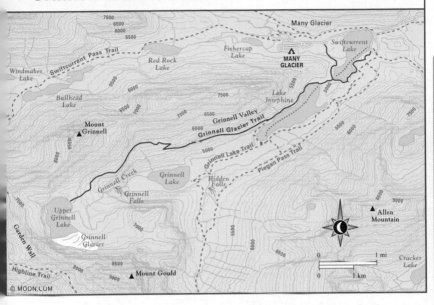

© MOON.COM

Elevation gain: 100-3,496 feet (30-1,066 m)

Effort: easy-strenuous

Trailhead: Swiftcurrent parking lot in Many Glacier

This popular trail leads to various destinations along a scenic path dotted with lakes, waterfalls, moose, glaciers, and wildflowers. The trail winds through pine trees and aspen groves as it rolls gently up to Red Rock Lake and Falls at 1.8 miles. At the top of the falls, a knoll provides a viewpoint to scan hillsides with binoculars for bears. The trail continues level through meadows rampant with Sitka valerian in July to Bullhead Lake at 3.9 miles. Scan scree slopes here for bighorn sheep.

From the lake, the trail switchbacks uphill. It cuts around a cliff face before reaching the pass at 6.6 miles. From here, Granite Park Chalet is 0.9 mile downhill. To reach the lookout, take the spur trail up 1.4 more miles of switchbacks (you'll lose count of them). The lookout surveys almost the entire park: glaciers, peaks, wild panoramas, and the plains. Many

Glacier Hotel looks minuscule. Enjoy the one-of-a-kind view from the outhouse. For a different descent, drop to The Loop to catch a shuttle.

Iceberg Lake

Distance: 10.4 miles (16.7 km) round-trip

Duration: 5 hours

Elevation gain: 1,193 feet (364 m)

Effort: moderate

Trailhead: behind Swiftcurrent Motor Inn cabins in Many Glacier

One of the top hikes in Glacier, the trail to Iceberg Lake begins with a short, steep jaunt straight uphill, with no time to warm up your muscles gradually. Within 0.4 mile you reach a junction. Take note of the directional sign here, and watch for it when you come down. On the return, some hikers zombie-walk right on past it.

From the junction, the trail maintains an easy railroad grade to the lake. Make noise on this trail, known for frequent bear sightings. Wildflowers line the trail in July: bear grass, bog orchids,

Swiftcurrent Valley and Iceberg Lake

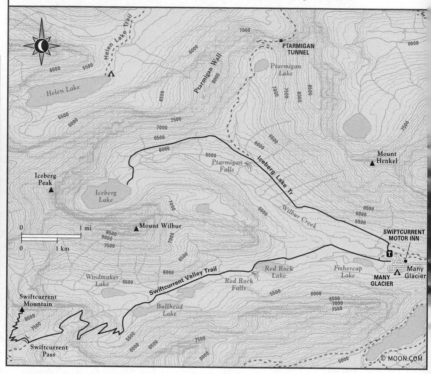

penstemon, and thimbleberry. One mile past the junction, the trail rounds a red argillite outcropping with views of the valley. As the trail swings north, it enters a pine and fir forest and crosses Ptarmigan Falls at 2.6 miles, a good break spot where aggressive ground squirrels will steal your snacks. Do not feed them; feeding only trains them to be more forceful. Just beyond the falls, the Ptarmigan Tunnel Trail veers right. Stay straight to swing west through multiple avalanche paths. After crossing a creek, the trail climbs the final bluff, where a view of stark icebergs against blue water unfolds. Brave hikers can dive into the lake, but be prepared to have the frigid water suck the air from your lungs.

Going-to-the-Sun Road
Trail of the Cedars and Avalanche Lake

Distance: 0.9-mile (1.4 km) loop; 6.1 miles (9.8 km) round-trip

Duration: 0.5-3 hours

Elevation gain: 0-477 feet (0-145 m)

Effort: easy-moderate

Trailhead: adjacent to Avalanche Campground and Picnic Area

With interpretive signs, the Trail of the Cedars boardwalk, reconstructed in 2018, guides walkers and wheelchairs on a loop that crosses two footbridges over Avalanche Creek. The route tours the lush rainforest, where fallen trees become nurse logs, fertile habitat for hemlocks and tiny foamflowers. Immense black cottonwoods furrowed with deep-cut bark and huge 500-year-old western red

Trail of the Cedars and Avalanche Lake

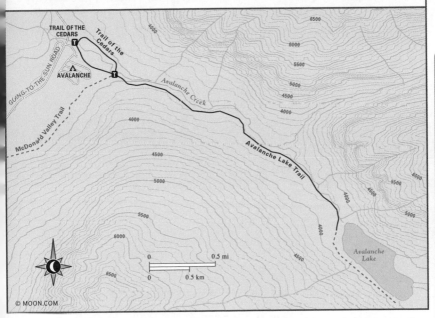

© MOON.COM

cedars dominate the forest. At Avalanche Gorge, the creek slices through red rocks. To finish the 0.9-mile loop, continue on the paved walkway past large burled cedars to return to the trailhead.

The trailhead to Avalanche Lake departs from the southeast end of Trail of the Cedars. Turn uphill for the short grunt to the top of the water-carved Avalanche Gorge. Be extremely careful: Too many fatal accidents have occurred from slipping. From the gorge, the trail climbs steadily through woods littered with glacial erratics. Some of these large boulders strewn when the glacier receded still retain scratch marks left from the ice. At the top, 1.9 miles from the trailhead, a cirque with steep cliffs and tumbling waterfalls cradles the lake. An additional 0.7-mile path goes to the lake's less-crowded head, where anglers find better fishing.

High season sees streams of people, some incredibly ill prepared, with no drinking water and inappropriate footwear like flip-flops or heels. Avoid midday crowds by hiking this trail earlier or later in the day, but make noise for bears.

★ Highline Trail and Granite Park Chalet

Distance: 7.4 miles (11.9 km) to Granite Park Chalet, 11.4 miles (18.4 km) to Loop
Duration: 5-6 hours
Elevation gain: 975 feet (297 m) up; 3,395 feet (1,035 m) down
Effort: strenuous
Trailhead: across Going-to-the-Sun Road from Logan Pass parking lot

Many first-time hikers stop every 10 feet to take photos on this hike, which scares severe acrophobes with its exposed thousand-foot drop-offs. The trail drops from Logan Pass through a cliff walk above the Going-to-the-Sun Road before crossing a flower land that gave the Garden Wall arête its name. At three miles, nearly all the elevation

Granite Park Chalet Trails

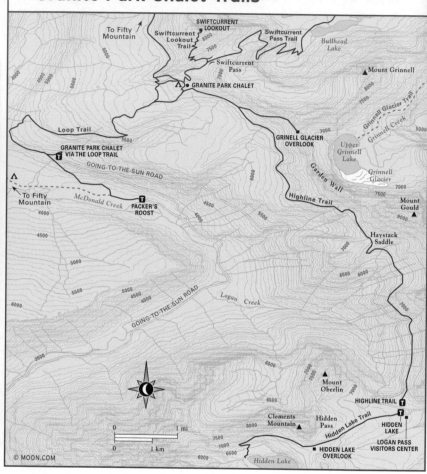

gain is packed into one climb: Haystack Saddle appears to be the top, but it is only halfway. After the high point, the trail drops and swings through several large bowls before passing Bear Valley to reach Granite Park Chalet atop a knoll at 6,680 feet.

En route, stronger hikers can add on side trails to Grinnell Glacier Overlook (1.6 steep miles round-trip) and Swiftcurrent Lookout (4.2 miles round-trip). To exit the area, some hikers opt

to hike out over Swiftcurrent Pass to Many Glacier (7.6 miles) and catch shuttles; backpackers continue on to Fifty Mountain (11.9 miles farther) and Goat Haunt (22.5 miles farther). Most day hikers head down The Loop Trail (4 miles) to catch the shuttle. Due to steep, snow-filled avalanche paths, the park service keeps the trailhead at Logan Pass closed usually into early July.

The chalet (July–early Sept.) does not have running water. Plan on purchasing

St. Mary Lake Trails

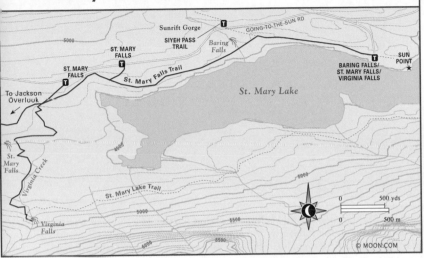

bottled water here, carrying your own, or filtering water from the campground stream below the chalet. Day hikers may also use the outdoor picnic tables or chalet dining room but do not have access to the kitchen. On a rainy day, a warm fire offers respite from the bluster and a chance to dry out. Sodas and candy bars are also sold.

Hidden Lake Overlook

Distance: 2.6 miles (4.2 km) round-trip to overlook, 5 miles (8 km) round-trip to lake
Duration: 2-4 hours
Elevation gain: 482 feet (147 m)
Effort: moderate
Trailhead: behind Logan Pass Visitor Center

Regardless of crowds, Hidden Lake Overlook is a spectacular hike. Avoid long lines of hikers by going shortly after sunrise or in the evening. The trail is often buried under feet of snow until mid-July or later, but tall poles mark the route. Once the trail melts out, a boardwalk climbs the first half through alpine meadows where fragile shooting stars and alpine laurel dot the landscape with pink. The trail ascends through argillite:

Look for evidence of mud-cracked and ripple-marked rocks from the ancient Belt Sea. Above, Clements Peak reveals various sea sediments in colorful layers.

The upper trail climbs past moraines, waterfalls, mountain goats, and bighorn sheep. At Hidden Pass on the Continental Divide, the trail reaches the platform overlooking the lake's blue waters. For ambitious hikers or anglers, the trail continues 1.2 miles down to the lake. Just remember: What drops 776 feet must come back up. After late September, bring ice cleats for walking the trail.

St. Mary and Virginia Falls

Distance: 2-3.4 miles (3.2-5.5 km) round-trip
Duration: 1-2 hours
Elevation gain: 216 feet (66 m)
Effort: easy
Trailhead: St. Mary Falls trailhead

In midsummer, the trail sees a constant stream of people, but the two falls are still gorgeous. Two trailheads depart from Going-to-the-Sun Road: The west trailhead descends from the shuttle stop, and the east trailhead launches from the vehicle parking lot. Both trails connect

Apgar Lookout

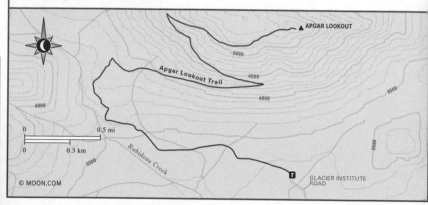

© MOON.COM

with the St. Mary Lake Trail leading to the falls. Between the trailheads and St. Mary Falls, the 2015 Reynolds Creek Fire burned the forest, but it opened up views of surrounding mountains and the St. Mary River. On hot days, hike this trail in the morning.

The trail drops one mile through several well-signed junctions en route to St. Mary Falls, where a wooden bridge crosses blue-green pools. From here, the trail switchbacks up 0.7 mile to Virginia Falls, a broad waterfall spewing mist. A short spur climbs to the base of Virginia Falls. Be wary of slippery rocks and strong, cold currents at both falls. Look for water ouzels (American dippers) that nest near waterfalls. Recognize the dark gray birds by their dipping action, up to 40 bends per minute.

Baring Falls

Distance: 0.6 or 1.2 miles (1 or 1.9 km) round-trip
Duration: 1 hour
Elevation gain: minimal, but 120 feet (37 m) back up to Sunrift Gorge trailhead
Effort: easy
Trailhead: Sunrift Gorge or Sun Point parking lot
From Sunrift Gorge, start by dropping south of the road bridge over Baring Creek. The 0.3-mile trail follows the creek down to the trail from Sun

Point. Turn right to reach Baring Falls (originally named Weasel Eyes by the Blackfeet, meaning "huckleberries").

From Sun Point, the 0.6-mile trail gradually descends to lake level where it crosses the creek below Baring Falls. The 2015 Reynolds Creek Fire burned the forest, but it opened up views of surrounding mountains and St. Mary Lake. On hot days, hike this trail in the morning.

West Glacier
Rocky Point

Distance: 1.4-1.6 miles (2.3-2.6 km) round-trip
Duration: 1 hour
Elevation gain: none
Effort: easy
Trailhead: Fish Creek Campground Loop D or the start of the Inside North Fork Road
Rocky Point is a short interpretive romp along Lake McDonald's north shore through the burn area of the 2003 Robert Fire and up a promontory. Places of heavy burn with slow regrowth alternate with lighter burn now clogged with lush greenery. Don't forget your camera: The view from Rocky Point looks up the lake toward the Continental Divide and grabs grand shots of Mount Jackson and Mount Edwards to the south. If the lake is calm, photos can capture stunning reflections. Snow leaves early and comes late to this

trail, making it good for spring and fall hiking. From the promontory, make a loop back on the Lake McDonald Trail.

Apgar Lookout
Distance: 7 miles (11.3 km) round-trip
Duration: 4 hours
Elevation gain: 1,868 feet (569 m)
Effort: moderate
Trailhead: end of Glacier Institute Road, 1.9 miles from Going-to-the-Sun Road
Directions: Take the first left after the west entrance station at the Glacier Institute sign. At the first fork, follow the sign to the horse barn and veer left, crossing over Quarter Circle Bridge. Drive to the road's terminus at the trailhead.

Beginning with a gentle walk, the trail soon climbs steeply toward the first of three long switchbacks (hike in the morning on hot days). As the trail ascends, some large burned sentinels stand as relics from the 2003 Robert Fire amid the thick growth of new lodgepoles. Snippets of views look down on the Middle Fork, Rubideau Basin, the railroad tracks, and West Glacier. Following the third switchback, the trail traverses the ridge, which has snow in June, to the rebuilt lookout. From this 5,236-foot aerie, partial views include the park's southern sector, Lake McDonald, and peaks of the Livingston Range. Park communication radio antennas clutter the summit, but at least they are clustered in one location.

Bicycling
East Glacier

There aren't many places in the country where you can hop on a bike, head to the nearest highway, and pedal through spectacular scenery in every direction. Although the inclines can be steep and the declines precipitous around East Glacier, the air is fresh and the mountain vistas unrivaled. The traffic—human and animal—needs to be minded.

For avid cyclists, it's possible to do a 137-mile (221-km) loop in and around the park: Head southwest from East Glacier on U.S. 2 to West Glacier, then over Going-to-the-Sun Road to St. Mary, then south on U.S. 89 and Highway 49 back to East Glacier. Remember that eastbound Going-to-the-Sun Road is closed to cyclists from Logan Creek to Logan Pass, 11am-4pm daily June 15-Labor Day, so plan accordingly. In the vicinity of East Glacier, biking to the Two Medicine Valley, 12 miles (19.3 km) northwest of town, is also a popular route.

The closest place from which to rent bicycles is the west side of the park, at Apgar Village, from **Glacier Outfitters** (196 Apgar Loop, 406/219-7466, www.goglacieroutfitters.com).

West Glacier

Biking in Glacier is not for the nonchalant. The climbs are treacherous, the edges precipitous, and the automobile traffic even worse. But the thrill of reaching the summit of Going-to-the-Sun Road, seeing how far you've come, soaking in the scenery, and whooshing back down again is unrivaled.

Still, as with any activity in Glacier, cyclists should be well aware of the conditions, restrictions, and potential hazards. Common sense prevails: Use helmets and reflectors; wear brightly colored and highly visible clothing; and watch for falling rocks, wildlife, and ice on the road. Bicycles are prohibited 11am-4pm daily June 15-Labor Day on the Going-to-the-Sun Road between Apgar Campground and Sprague Creek Campground. From Logan Creek to Logan Pass, eastbound (uphill) bicycle traffic is prohibited 11am-4pm daily June 15-Labor Day. It takes roughly 45 minutes to ride from Sprague Creek to Logan Creek, and three hours from Logan Creek to the summit of Logan Pass. Bicycles cannot be ridden on any of the hiking trails, other than on a few marked trails in Waterton Lakes National Park. For more information on restrictions and current road closures, check online at www.nps.gov/glac.

Bicycles can be rented at Apgar Village from **Glacier Outfitters** (196 Apgar Loop,

Waterton Lakes: Glacier's Canadian Sister

Just north of Glacier, across the Canadian border in the southwest corner of Alberta, lies Waterton Lakes National Park. Similar in terrain to Glacier, the park is much smaller (about 203 square miles compared to Glacier's 1,600 square miles) and houses a small town, Waterton Park, within its borders. Like its neighbor to the south, the stunning landscape of this park was formed by melting alpine glaciers more than 10,000 years ago and later shaped by floods, fires, wind, and its natural wildlife and flora.

Before European settlement, various nomadic groups of indigenous people passed through the area, gathering plants and hunting local wildlife. The most prominent in the area were the Kootenai, who eventually clashed with the Blackfeet that had followed the buffalo into Alberta and taken control of the plains. In 1858 the English explorer Thomas Blakiston was looking for a railroad pass through the Rockies. He encountered some members of the local Kootenai tribe, who directed him to a pass in the south. Traversing this path, he eventually came to an opening that looked on a chain of three lakes. He named the lakes after fellow British explorer and naturalist Charles Waterton, known to be quite eccentric. It became a national park in 1895, and the Great Northern Railway established the Prince of Wales Hotel in 1926, helping put the park on the map for tourists traveling from Glacier to Banff and Jasper in Alberta.

The star of Waterton's lakes is **Upper Waterton Lake,** situated on the U.S.-Canada border. It's the deepest lake in the Canadian Rockies and can be explored on a two-hour cruise that leaves from the Waterton marina and dips down into Montana before venturing back. If you have the time, you can disembark from the boat to follow the **Crypt Lake Trail,** considered one of the best hikes in Canada. Numerous trails around the lake lead past waterfalls, through valleys, and on to spectacular vistas.

Arguably one of the most photographed hotels in the world for its sublime setting, the **Prince of Wales Hotel** (Alberta 5, Waterton Park, 844/868-7474, www. glacierparkcollection.com) is a magnificent Swiss chalet-inspired lodge that overlooks the lake and the town below. Although pricey, it is a great place to stay to have the full Waterton experience. If a night's stay is not in your budget, try to stop in for high tea, which is served daily in the hotel lobby.

During the summer of 2017, two major wildfires roared through Glacier and Waterton Lakes National Parks. The Sprague Fire burned roughly 17,000 acres, primarily in Glacier's backcountry. The Kenow Fire burned more than 47,500 acres in Waterton Lakes, blackening entire valleys and altering the landscape for decades to come. The slopes on both sides of the Akamina Highway were burned and are visible to tourists. It's worth remembering that fire is a critical part of the ecosystem here; many species of trees rely on fire to reseed. So even though the scars are prominent, healthy regrowth is happening already and provides visitors a unique lens into the forces of nature here.

As you enter the town on the Waterton highway, the **Visitors Reception Centre** (403/859-5133) is on the right. It's open early May-mid-October and can provide you with plenty of information on the region. Construction of a new visitors center is expected to begin in 2019. During the off-season, the park's operations building (403/859-2224), located next to the visitors center, provides visitor information and assistance.

406/219-7466, www.goglacieroutfitters. com). They rent cruiser bikes ($12 for 2 hours, $22 for 4 hours, $42 for 24 hours), mountain bikes ($18 for 2 hours, $32 for 4 hours, $47 for 25 hours), hybrid road-mountain bikes ($18 for 2 hours, $32 for 4 hours, $47 for 24 hours), tandem bikes ($22 for 2 hours, $32 for 4 hours, $45 for 24 hours), kids' bikes ($16 for 2 hours, $26 for 4 hours, $36 for 24 hours), and even child trailers ($10 for 2 hours, $20 for 4 hours, $30 for 24 hours).

Horseback Riding

Guided horseback rides, from one hour to a full day, are available in good weather late May-mid-September at the corrals at Apgar, Lake McDonald, and Many Glacier from **Swan Mountain Outfitters** (406/387-4405 or 877/888-5557, www.swanmountainoutfitters.com), the only outfitter that can offer trail rides inside the park. Options include hour-long rides ($45), half-day trips ($125, 4-person minimum), and full-day trips ($225). Rates do not include gratuities, which are encouraged. Reservations are required.

For horseback riding outside the park on the Blackfeet Indian Reservation, **Glacier Gateway Trailrides** (MT-49, across from the Glacier Park Lodge, 406/226-4408, off-season 406/338-5560, $35-190 pp) offers excellent guided rides through magnificent country June-September. Trips range from one hour to full-day excursions; children must be at least seven years old. The guides are Native Americans, who offer a unique cultural perspective on places like Looking Glass and Two Medicine River Gorge.

Boating

Boats are permitted on **St. Mary Lake,** but you'll have to bring your own because there are no rentals on-site. There are 90-minute **tours** ($27.50 adults, $13.75 children 4-12, free for children under 4) available several times daily through the **Glacier Park Boat Company** (406/257-2426, www.glacierparkboats.com). The tours depart from the Rising Sun boat dock, 6 miles (9.7 km) inside the east entrance on Going-to-the-Sun Road, and offer views of various waterfalls, Sexton Glacier, and Wild Goose Island. A 15-minute walk to Baring Falls is also an option on the St. Mary Lake cruise. Twice daily, the cruises can be combined

Top to bottom: trail to Iceberg Lake; handhold on the most treacherous part of the Highline Trail; early morning at Swiftcurrent Lake.

with a guided hike to St. Mary Falls for a 3.5-hour outing.

Glacier Park Boat Company also offers excellent 45-minute cruises on **Two Medicine Lake.** These take place at least four times daily mid-June to early September. A 2.5-hour guided hike to Twin Falls can be added at no extra cost.

In the Many Glacier area, GPBC also provides a number of scenic cruises on **Swiftcurrent Lake** and **Lake Josephine.** There are up to seven trips daily during summer, and cruises can be combined with guided hikes or used as a shuttle for hiking trips. A highlight for many is seeing the Grinnell Glacier on a cruise across Lake Josephine.

For hour-long boat **tours** ($18.25 adults, $9.25 children 4-12, free for children under 4) on **Lake McDonald**—think sunset cocktail cruises in a historic wooden boat—GPBC is the ultimate resource.

Rowboats ($18/hour), **kayaks** ($15/hour), and **canoes** ($18/hour) are available to rent from GPBC at Apgar, Lake McDonald Lodge, Two Medicine, and Many Glacier.

Fishing

Because of the altitude in Glacier, the water is colder, and some of the lakes in the park are sterile. St. Mary Lake is not especially productive water. There are some rainbow trout, brook trout, whitefish, and bull trout in the lake for the patient angler. Shore fishing is possible, but the chances for catching increase significantly out in the deeper waters. St. Mary Lake can get rough quickly, with two- to three-foot swells, so keep a constant eye on the conditions.

In Many Glacier, presumably because of its proximity to the hotel and the road, the trout in crystal clear Swiftcurrent Lake see the most action, but they seem to have wised up. Brook trout in the 10-inch (25-cm) range are the most common catches here. Lake Josephine and **Grinnell Lake** have brook trout populations that

kayaking Lake McDonald

seem more willing to take the bait or go for flies.

There are some backcountry lakes worth hiking into if fishing is the goal. **Red Rock Lake,** located along Swiftcurrent Creek, for example, is accessible by a fairly level two-mile hike and holds plenty of brook trout in the 10- to 12-inch (25- to 30-cm) range. Dry-fly anglers will do best in the morning or evening, but will have to go deep in the afternoons.

While fishing permits or licenses are not necessary in Glacier National Park, it is imperative that anyone fishing abides by the regulations. A brochure can be picked up at any of the visitors centers or downloaded from the National Park Service website (www.nps.gov/glac).

Rafting

Although there is no rafting inside the park, a number of white-water outfitting services in West Glacier offer trips on the 87-mile (140-km) Middle Fork of

the Flathead River. The North Fork of the Flathead, which forms the western boundary of the park, can be rafted as well. **Glacier Raft Company** (106 Going-to-the-Sun Rd., West Glacier, 406/888-5454 or 800/235-6781, www.glacierraftco.com, half day from $61 adults, $51 children 12 and under, full day from $101 adults, $81 children) offers everything from half-day and dinner floats to multiday expeditions. The company caters to all floaters, from novices to adrenaline junkies. In addition, the company offers horseback riding excursions, fly-fishing, and kayaking.

Montana Raft Company (11970 U.S. 2, West Glacier, 406/387-5555 or 800/521-7238, www.glacierguides.com, all-inclusive half day from $61 adults, $51 children, full day from $99 adults, $76 children) is the sister company of Glacier Guides and has some of the most well-rounded and knowledgeable guides in the area. Group numbers tend to be smaller (9 in a boat as opposed to 14), and the company offers an expansive range of options including rafting and horseback riding, overnight adventures, inflatable kayak trips, family-friendly day trips, and scenic floats. Because of water conditions, in June the minimum age for rafters is eight; from July through the rest of the season, rafting is available to those ages six and up.

Another noteworthy outfitter offering rafting trips in the region is **Wild River Adventures** (11900 U.S. 2 E., 406/387-9453 or 800/700-7056, www.riverwild.com, half day from $58 adults, $48 children). All-day trips, including lunch, are $97 for adults and $77 for children. Minimum age for rafters in May and June is 12, and 6-year-olds and up can raft from July onward.

Helicopter Tours

If seeing the park from atop Going-to-the-Sun Road is not quite dramatic enough, consider a **Kruger Helicopter Tour** (11892 U.S. 2 E., West Glacier,

406/387-4565, www.krugerhelicopters. com, half-hour tours from $150/pp based on 4 people, 1-hour tours from $295/pp based on 4 people), which can give adventuresome visitors a bird's-eye view of Iceberg Lake and Gunsight Pass, the Chinese Wall, and more.

Cross-Country Skiing

When snow blankets the park, cross-country skiers and snowshoers find themselves in a winter paradise. Many of the hiking trails double as ski and snowshoe trails, but nothing is groomed, so keen and constant orientation is critical. The **Lower McDonald Creek** trailhead is just south of McDonald Creek Bridge, and the trail is 2-3 miles (3.2-4.8 km) round-trip of gentle, forested terrain that parallels the creek in some spots. Another fairly level but longer option is the **Rocky Point** trail, which is 6 miles (9.7 km) round-trip and rewards skiers with a phenomenal view of Lake McDonald. The trailhead can be found 0.2 mile (0.3 km) north of Fish Creek Campground. Farther north, toward Avalanche Campground, **McDonald Falls** (4 mi/6.4 km round-trip), **Sacred Dancing Cascades** (5.3 mi/8.5 km round-trip), and the **Avalanche Picnic Area** (11.6 mi/18.7 km round-trip) make excellent day trips.

Since many of the roads in the park are unplowed and impassable for cars in winter, they can make excellent ski trails. Going-to-the-Sun Road is one of the best, although because of avalanche danger, it can often be closed east of Avalanche Creek.

Although it's not in the park, one of the region's best-known and beloved areas for cross-country skiing is the **Izaak Walton Inn** (off U.S. 2, Essex, between East Glacier and West Glacier, 406/888-5700, www.izaakwaltoninn.com), which has repeatedly been named one of the best cross-country ski resorts in the Rockies. The resort boasts approximately 20 miles (32 km) of groomed trails, and its proximity to the park invites backcountry travel. Ski rentals are available, and a night or two at the inn will be something to remember.

Food

East Glacier Area

For a town with just over 300 year-round residents, East Glacier has a number of good restaurants that cater to Glacier-bound visitors. Often the best way to select a spot to eat is to walk around and see where the wait is shortest. **Serrano's Mexican Restaurant** (29 Dawson Ave., 406/226-9392, www.serranosmexican. com, 5pm-9pm daily May 1-Memorial Day and Labor Day-early Oct., 5pm-10pm daily Memorial Day-Labor Day, $11-20) is inside the oldest house in East Glacier. Nothing is old-fashioned, however, about the menu: There are classic and delicious Mexican favorites alongside local offerings that include Indian tacos and huckleberry carrot cake. A selection of American plates, including chicken, steaks, and burgers, is available too. The food here is good, and the atmosphere is quite festive. The fact that it's been in business for more than 25 years means something in this part of the world. As an aside, the on-site **Backpacker's Inn** offers nightly hostel-type lodging starting at $20 and private cabins starting at $50.

Two Medicine Grill (314 U.S. 2 E., 406/226-9227, www.seeglacier.com, 6:30am-9pm daily summer, 6:30am-8pm daily winter, breakfast $5-10, lunch $8-11, dinner $8-15) is a great spot for budget travelers. The menu has pretty standard fare for the region—bison burgers, homemade chili, chicken-fried steak—but the quality is excellent, and the staff are friendly and generous with advice and insights on the area. The huckleberry shakes are the stuff of legend, as is the double-crusted huckleberry pie.

Getting rave reviews from locals and tourists alike is **Summit Mountain Lodge Steakhouse** (16900 U.S. 2, 406/226-9319, www.summitmtnlodge.com, 5pm-9pm Tues.-Sun., $19-38), housed in an old train station with a beautiful outdoor dining area. You could eat dirt on a summer night, with a view like this, and be happy—but luckily, you don't have to. The food is marvelous and locally sourced whenever possible. There is a good wine list, and pairing suggestions are offered. Entrées include saltimbocca, grilled beef tenderloin, and wild prawns piccata, along with a variety of salads and pasta.

St. Mary to Many Glacier

Without a doubt, the fanciest (and priciest!) place to go for a meal in St. Mary is the **Snowgoose Grille** (844/868-7474, www.glacierparkcollection.com, 7am-10pm daily late May-late Sept., $18-40) in the St. Mary Village. This slightly modern take on the Western steak house offers porterhouse pork chop, bison stroganoff, and elk sausage gnocchi. There are also plenty of vegetarian options for both lunch and dinner. The adjacent **Curly Bear Café** is primarily a sandwich and ice-cream joint. Outside seating is available and highly desirable when the weather cooperates.

Two Dog Flats Grill (1380 Wisconsin Ave., 855/733-4522, www.glaciernationalparklodges.com, 6:30am-10am and 11am-10pm daily, $10-26) at the Rising Sun Motor Inn & Cabins is operated by Glacier National Park Lodges. It offers standard fare, from burgers and chicken to steak and pasta, and is open for three meals daily during the season. Basic boxed lunches are available with no substitutions.

The ★ **Park Café & Grocery** (U.S. 89 and Going-to-the-Sun Rd., 406/732-9979, www.parkcafe.us, 8am-7pm daily early June-mid-June, 7:30am-9pm June 20-Aug., 8am-7pm daily Sept. 1-mid-Sept., $14-22), in St. Mary, is staffed by people who know and really love Glacier National Park. The pies—nine flavors daily—are mouthwatering and worth

every mile on the trail you'll need to work them off. The food is mostly American, from steaks and fish to outrageous baked potatoes, and for the most part as healthy as it is inventive and delicious. There's also a fantastic gift store and grocery on-site. This place should not be missed!

Up the road in Babb is the ★ **Two Sisters Café** (U.S. 89, 4 mi/6.4 km north of St. Mary, 406/732-5535, www.twosistersofmontana.com, 11am-9pm daily June-Sept., $8-29), a colorful place that is worth the scenic drive along Lower St. Mary Lake. Although the decor is rather outrageous, the food is sublime—a hiker's dream come true. Try a Red Burger and a slice of homemade huckleberry pie.

For those not cooking their own supper over a fire pan in Many Glacier, there are only a few options. The **Ptarmigan Dining Room** (Many Glacier Hotel, 855/733-4522, www.glaciernationalparklodges.com, 6:30am-10am, 11:30am-2:30pm, and 5pm-9:30pm daily mid-June-mid-Sept., $20-44) offers such flavorful entrées as Rocky Mountain trout, a variety of salads, bison tenderloin, Alaska salmon, and more. Lighter fare, including appetizers, burgers, salads, and cocktails, is available in its **Swiss Lounge** (11:30am-10pm daily, drinks until 11pm, $11-21).

In the nearby Swiftcurrent Motor Inn & Cabins is a casual eatery, **'Nell's** (855/733-4522, www.glaciernationalparklodges.com, 6:30am-10am and 11am-10pm daily mid-June-mid-Sept., $10-21). It serves standard fare for three meals daily including pizza, pasta, and chicken, all of which can taste outstanding after a long day on the trail. Boxed lunches are available when ordered a day ahead.

West Glacier Area

Even if you are not planning to stay at the Belton Chalet, the hotel offers two distinct and rich dining experiences that are definitely worth a visit in this land of burgers and grilled cheese. ★ **The Belton Grill Dining Room** (12575 U.S. 2

E., 406/888-5000 or 888/235-8665, www. beltonchalet.com, 5pm-9pm daily summer, $22-41) provides an intimate, exquisite meal in the historic 1910 chalet. The menu changes seasonally, and chef Earl James offers innovative dishes incorporating the freshest ingredients from local Montana growers and the chalet's own Flathead Lake orchard. For dinner you could sample a Foie Gras Torchon appetizer, Wagyu sirloin strip, or pan-seared wild king salmon. For equally delicious lighter fare and a more moderately priced experience, you can visit the hotel's **Belton Tap Room** (3pm-9pm daily summer, $8-12), where you may choose to accompany a locally brewed Montana beer with pork belly sliders or a lamb burger.

The **Glacier Highland Restaurant** (U.S. 2, 406/888-5427, www.glacierhighland. com, 7:30am-10pm daily July-Aug., off-season days and hours vary, $13-33) is an authentic West Glacier diner experience. Located just before the entrance to the park and across from the Amtrak depot, this is an easy stop if you are craving a 5-ounce (142-g) burger with all the toppings and fresh-cut fries. Hearty homemade soups and a variety of delicious sweet treats, baked each day in the bakery, are also on offer.

For breakfast and lunch with outdoor seating options in Apgar Village, **Eddie's Café & Mercantile** (1 Fish Creek Rd., 406/888-5361, www.eddiescafegifts.com, 7am-9pm daily summer, $16-25) serves up excellent grub including steak and eggs, breakfast burritos, buffalo burgers, and fried chicken.

The closest restaurant to the entrance at West Glacier is the **West Glacier Restaurant** (200 Going-to-the-Sun Rd., 406/888-5359, 7am-9pm daily mid-May-Sept., $8-18). Set in a classic parkitecture-inspired building, the restaurant offers casual dining with homemade soups, burgers, sandwiches, and yummy baked goods. An attached bar has a selection of liquor, wine, and beer, not to mention

sports on satellite TV for those who are so inclined.

A long way down a dirt road in Glacier's North Fork Valley is a special off-the-grid spot that is worth every bump and then some. The remote and wonderful **Polebridge Mercantile** (265 Polebridge Loop, 406/888-5105, www. polebridgemercantile.com, 7am-9pm daily Memorial Day-Labor Day, 9am-6pm daily Labor Day-Thanksgiving and mid-Apr.-Memorial Day, 10am-5pm Fri.-Sun. Jan.-late Mar., $3.50-7.25) offers world-class baked goods—don't leave without at least a couple of huckleberry bear claws—sandwiches, soups, and other goodies in addition to groceries and gifts. Lodging is also available.

Accommodations

East Glacier Area

East Glacier has several small, kitschy motels that are ideal for a night or two before heading into the park, but they are not well suited for a week's stay. The standout alternative is the stately ★ **Glacier Park Lodge** (U.S. 2 and MT-49, 844/868-7474, www. glacierparkcollection.com, late May-late Sept., $159-499), which opened to guests in 1913. An Adirondack-style hotel commissioned by the Great Northern Railway, it was constructed of massive fir and cedar timbers, each weighing at least 15 tons. The local Blackfeet who watched the structure go up called it *omahkoyis,* or "big-tree lodge." The grounds are beautifully manicured—there's even a historic and very playable golf course in addition to a pitch-and-putt. The 161-room hotel offers fine and casual dining, a cocktail lounge, a gift shop, an outdoor swimming pool, and a day spa. The rooms are modest but comfortable. Travelers with children will appreciate the family rooms with multiple beds. Although the setting at the edge of East Glacier village is not quite as captivating, the Glacier

Park Lodge is certainly in the same class as the Lake McDonald Lodge and even the Old Faithful Lodge in Yellowstone National Park.

Slightly off the main drag is the tidy and comfortable **Mountain Pine Motel** (909 MT-49, 1 mi/1.6 km north of U.S. 2, 406/226-4403, www.mtnpine.com, May-Sept., $102-180), with 25 units and relatively modern amenities.

The **Whistling Swan Motel** (314 U.S. 2, 406/226-4412, www.seeglacier.com, $89-149 motel rooms, $169-249 cabins) is a long, skinny building that feels a bit like train cars—somewhat appropriate given that the Amtrak station is just across the street. The guest rooms are spotlessly clean and quite comfortable. Hosts Mark and Colleen are exceptionally hospitable and go out of their way to make every guest feel welcome and accommodated. This motel is also within easy walking distance of the local eateries and shops.

Another clean, comfortable lodging option right in town is the **Sears Motel** (1023 MT-49 N., 406/226-4432, June mid-Sept., $118-138). In addition to its 16 rooms, the motel also offers campsites for both tent campers and RVs.

The **East Glacier Motel & Cabins** (1107 MT-49, 406/226-5593, www.eastglaciermotel.com, June-July 1 $118-188, July 2-Aug. 15 $138-238) offers six motel units and 11 cabins at an excellent value.

On the east side of town, the cute, park-style cabins complete with kitchenettes, gas fireplaces, and covered front porches make **Traveler's Rest Lodge** (20987 U.S. 2, 406/226-9143 summer or 406/378-2414 winter, www.travelersrestlodge.net, Apr. 15-Oct. 1, $129-160) a great choice.

Two miles (3.2 km) west of town on what used to be a dude ranch is **Bison Creek Ranch** (20722 U.S. 2, 406/226-4482, www.bisoncreekranch.com, $89-140) a bed-and-breakfast offering simple sleeping cabins and larger A-frames. The same family has been pouring heart and soul into the ranch for more than 60

years, and it shows in every detail from the artwork to the meals to the housekeeping. The breakfasts—from cinnamon rolls and huckleberry pancakes to crepes—are excellent.

A few miles from town is **Summit Mountain Lodge** (16900 U.S. 2, 406/226-9319, www.summitmtnlodge.com, 5pm-9pm Tues.-Sun., from $159), which offers eight cabins with modern amenities. Single cabins have one queen bed and a full kitchenette. Double units have two queen beds and a living area. There are also family cabins ($285) that sleep six. The setting and the views are world-class. And the on-site steak house, housed in an old train station, is a special place for a memorable meal.

If you are willing to hike in to your accommodations, ★ **Granite Park Chalet** (888/345-2649, www.graniteparkchalet.com, from $108 pp, $80 each additional person, optional linen and bedding service $20 pp) is a fantastic option. The last of the railroad chalets to be built, Granite Park Chalet is a hiker's hostel geared toward do-it-yourselfers. The rooms are private; hikers prepare their own meals and, although linens can be ordered ahead of time, generally sleep in their own sleeping bags. The most popular trail in to Granite Park is the 7.6-mile (12.2-km) Highline Trail, accessed from Logan Pass. A shorter 4-mile (6.4-km) trail through burned country and with a steep 2,300-foot (701-m) climb can be accessed from the Going-to-the-Sun Road switchback known as The Loop.

St. Mary to Many Glacier

Although options abound in both St. Mary and Many Glacier for hotels, motels, and cabins, there are not many budget-friendly choices. The prices seem to reflect the scenery, which is spectacular, rather than the amenities, which can be quite modest. Campgrounds and RV parks are more common, but small cabins can be found as well. The **Cottages at Glacier**

(106 West Shore Dr., St. Mary, 855/684-3402, www.nationalparkreservations.com, late May-late Sept., from $250) offer views of St. Mary Lake and comfortable two-bedroom accommodations with a steep price tag. Still, for those who want a full kitchen, Wi-Fi, and satellite TV, these cottages are excellent. In nearby Babb, about 2 miles (3.2 km) north of St. Mary, the **Glacier Trailhead Cabins** (U.S. 89, 406/732-4143, www.glaciertrailheadcabins.com, mid-May-mid-Oct., $179-398) are clean, modern cabins in a quiet setting without TVs or phones. If you can get a cabin here, you will not be disappointed with the amenities, the location, or the rate. In business for more than 70 years, the **St. Mary Village** (U.S. 89 and Going-to-the-Sun Rd., 844/868-7474, www.glacierparkcollection.com, mid-June-late Sept., from $99) is a full resort with all the modern amenities. From tipis to cabins to luxury lodge rooms, this resort has 127 guest rooms among six facilities.

Adjacent to St. Mary Lake is the 1940s-era **Rising Sun Motor Inn & Cabins** (Going-to-the-Sun Rd., 855/733-4522, www.glaciernationalparklodges.com, mid-June-early Sept., $165-177), offering simple, clean, motel-style rooms and on-site dining.

In Many Glacier, the standout is clearly the ★ **Many Glacier Hotel** (855/753-4522, www.glaciernationalparklodges.com, mid-June-mid-Sept., $207-476), a historic Swiss chalet-style lodge built in 1915 by the Great Northern Railway. The hotel is right on the shore of Swiftcurrent Lake, and there is no limit to the natural beauty of the region or the number of ways in which to enjoy it. The hotel is being refurbished, wing by wing, but the rooms are still simple and charming; the steep prices speak more to the hotel's setting in the Many Glacier Valley than its amenities. There are no televisions in the rooms and the Wi-Fi is extremely limited. There is nightly entertainment and a wealth of activities that include boat cruises, ranger-led hikes, evening programs, Red Bus Tours, and horseback riding from the lodge.

Nearby, the **Swiftcurrent Motor Inn & Cabins** (855/753-4522, www.glaciernationalparklodges.com, mid-June-mid-Sept., $102-177) is decidedly less grandiose and accordingly less expensive. But this place also has a history; it was established as a tipi camp in 1911 by the Great Northern Railway. Three main lodgings are available: motel rooms, duplex-type cottages, and one-bedroom cabins without private baths. It has its own charm as a longtime stopping point for adventurers and road-trippers, and the location cannot be beat. For the price, it is an excellent place to stay.

West Glacier Area

The West Glacier area has a good selection of places to stay, but once inside the park, or even within view of it, accommodations do not come cheap. If you are on a tight budget, camping is the best option. The hotels listed are only open during the summer season, when Glacier is busiest. However, for avid cross-country skiers who want to take advantage of the park during the winter, the **Izaak Walton Inn** (off U.S. 2, Essex, between East Glacier and West Glacier, 406/888-5700, www.izaakwaltoninn.com, $159-409), a charming old railroad hotel that is in the National Register of Historic Places, is open year-round. In addition to homey rooms in the lodge, guests can select from unique accommodations including family cabins and restored railcars.

Also in Essex, 20 miles (32 km) from West Glacier and 35 miles (56 km) from East Glacier, is **Glacier Haven Inn & Healthy Haven Café** (14305 U.S. 2 E., 406/888-5720, www.glacierhaveninn.com, $99 cabins without bathrooms, $169-349 lodge rooms and cabins with full bath and kitchen), which offers clean, comfy accommodations in addition to great home-style cooking.

A reasonably priced motel in the West

Glacier area is the **Apgar Village Lodge & Cabins** (Lake View Dr., West Glacier, 406/888-5484 or 844/868-7474, www.glacierparkcollection.com, $82-323), 2 miles (3.2 km) east of West Glacier village at the south end of Lake McDonald. There are 28 cabins that sleep up to eight with Western decor, most with kitchens with stoves and refrigerators, and each with its own picnic table. Ask for a cabin on McDonald Creek; you can literally fish from your front door. There are also 20 modestly furnished, clean motel rooms, some overlooking the creek, with either a queen or two twin beds.

On the shores of Lake McDonald, the **Village Inn at Apgar** (1.3 mi/2.1 km from the entrance at West Glacier, 855/733-4522, www.glaciernationalparklodges.com, $171-279) is a quaint, 1950s motor inn that is listed in the National Register of Historic Places.

West Glacier Motel & Cabins (200 Going to the Sun Rd., West Glacier, 844/868-7474, www.glacierparkcollection.com, motel rooms from $129, cabins from $159) is divided between two properties—half the motel units are about 1 mile (1.6 km) from the park entrance in West Glacier, and the cabins and other motel units are on a secluded bluff that overlooks the Flathead River. It's a great value for the price and location. Pets are not allowed. The cabins on the bluff require a minimum stay of two nights and offer kitchenettes but no air-conditioning or television.

Also in West Glacier, just across the street from the Amtrak depot, is the **Glacier Highland Resort** (12555 U.S. 2 E., 406/888-5427, www.glacierhighland.com, May-Oct., $128-176), which offers 33 clean, simple rooms.

If you are willing to spend a bit more, there are two historic lodges that are worth a night's stay. **Lake McDonald Lodge** (Going-to-the-Sun Rd., 12 mi/19.3 km from West Glacier, 855/733-4522, www.glaciernationalparklodges.com, $113-364) was built in 1914 by the furrier

John Lewis and adheres to the Swiss chalet style of architecture. Though the lodge and cabins are showing their age, they still outshine the 1950s motor inn on-site. The 82-room lodge emanates rustic charm and still has personal touches, such as Lewis's hunting trophies displayed in the lobby. Built before there were roads running through Glacier, visitors arrived at the lodge by boat, and the hotel's original entrance faced the lake. Today most guests arrive by car, and the hotel is conveniently located off Going-to-the-Sun Road on the shore of Lake McDonald. Upon entering the lodge, visitors are struck by its warmth and charm. The spacious lobby is surrounded by balconies on three sides. Guests and visitors can enjoy sipping a cocktail on the sprawling veranda, a serene setting that affords a beautiful view of the lake. The guest rooms are rustic yet comfortable, and the location allows easy access to trailheads and boat tours. Fishing lessons and day trips by horseback are available and can be arranged by the hotel.

The most memorable stay in West Glacier is at the family-owned **★ Belton Chalet** (12575 U.S. 2 E., 406/888-5000 or 888/235-8665, www.beltonchalet.com, rooms $180-205, cottages $335) at the west entrance to the park. This was the first hotel built by the Great Northern Railway and dates to 1910. It was fully restored in 2000 and is a National Historic Landmark. Guests can experience a piece of history while enjoying modern amenities. All 25 guest rooms come with a queen bed and private bathroom and are beautifully furnished with antiques. The two cabins on the grounds each have three bedrooms to accommodate up to six people. Although the lodge is mostly closed during the winter season, the cabins are available to rent throughout the year. The hotel does not provide TVs, phones, or air-conditioning, as they can detract from the natural setting, but Wi-Fi is available at no charge. The lodge is immediately adjacent to both the highway and the train tracks, so silence is not possible. A fabulous restaurant on-site offers innovative and satisfying meals, and a fully stocked taproom specializes in Montana brews. You can enjoy a good book in the lobby's reading area, or curl up by the large stone fireplace. The incredibly friendly staff even offer wake-up calls for northern lights and bear sightings. Visitors looking for a bit of luxury, or relief for sore hiking muscles, will find a spa offering massages on-site. For an elegant vacation rental—complete with full kitchen, Wi-Fi, and flat-screen TV— the Belton's beautifully restored **Adobe House** is available off-site ($250-425 nightly with minimum stays required in high season and four-wheel drive necessary in low season).

Camping

Glacier has 13 front-country campgrounds with more than 1,000 sites, at least some of which are open May-mid-October. With the exception of St. Mary and Fish Creek, half the group sites at Apgar, and half the campsites at Many Glacier, all campgrounds are available on a first-come, first-served basis, with nightly fees ranging $10-23. You'll increase your chances of finding a site by showing up earlier in the day and scheduling your trip midweek rather than on the weekend. An excellent page on the National Park Service website (www. nps.gov/glac) shows updated availability at campsites across the park. For advance reservations at Fish Creek or St. Mary, contact the **National Park Reservation System** (877/444-6777, www.recreation. gov).

If your decision to camp is last-minute and you find yourself without such critical items as a tent or sleeping bag, **Glacier Outfitters** (196 Apgar Loop, 406/219-7466, www.goglacieroutfitters.com) can help with its stock of rentable items.

East Glacier Area

Less than 20 miles (32 km) from East Glacier are a couple of scenic and shady campgrounds. Set on the lake, **Two Medicine Campground** (mid-May-late Sept., $20), with 100 sites and 10 RV sites, is 13 miles (20.9 km) outside town in some of Glacier's most breathtaking wilderness. It is well developed with potable water and flush toilets, an amphitheater for nightly ranger presentations, and one of the original Great Northern Chalets, which has been converted into a camp store and gift shop. Outside the regular season, primitive camping ($10) is possible late September-late October. Shuttle service, boat tours, and Red Bus Tours are all available from the campground. Sites are available on a first-come, first-served basis, and hiking in the area is as limitless as it is sublime.

Farther north is a smaller (14 sites) and more secluded spot, **Cut Bank Campground** (June-Aug. 23, $10), accessed 5 miles (8 km) down a dirt road from U.S. 89. The campground has no water, so campers have to bring their own. Sites are available on a first-come, first-served basis, and day hikes in the area are top-notch. RVs are not recommended due to the nature of the road and the campground layout. Shuttles are only available from the highway.

St. Mary to Many Glacier

Two park campgrounds are available near the village of St. Mary. **St. Mary Campground** (www.recreation.gov, $23) has 148 sites, including 22 sites that can accommodate RVs and truck-trailer combinations up to 35 feet (10.7 m), as well as water and flush toilets. It is the park's largest campground, only 0.5 mile (0.8 km) from the St. Mary Visitor Center, and has limited shade but superb views. The regular season is late May-mid-September, but primitive camping ($10) is available early April-late May and mid-September-November. Winter camping is also possible December-March. Sites can be reserved up to six months in advance for June 1-the first Sunday in September online at www.recreation.gov.

The second St. Mary-area campground is **Rising Sun** (www.recreation.gov, mid-June-early-Sept., $20), which has 84 sites (with 10 sites for RVs), water, flush toilets, and showers. It is halfway along St. Mary Lake in the shadow of Red Eagle Mountain. Some sites are exposed, while others are tucked into the trees. All are available on a first-come, first-served basis.

Not far from the Many Glacier Hotel, the **Many Glacier Campground** ($23) has 109 sites, including 13 sites for RVs up to 35 feet (10.7 m), as well as water, flush toilets, and showers available at the nearby Swiftcurrent Motor Inn & Cabins. The regular season is late May-late September, but primitive camping ($10) is available late September-October. Half the sites can be reserved (www.recreation.gov) in advance mid-June-September 4, and the others fill up on a first-come, first-served basis. The views are phenomenal, and the access to hiking and boating is amazing. Arguably the most popular campground in the park, Many Glacier fills up early, so plan accordingly.

West Glacier Area

Apgar ($20) is the park's largest campground, with 194 sites. Not far from Apgar Village, campers will have easy access to the Apgar Visitor Center, gift shops, a camp store, and a casual restaurant. In the village, visitors can make arrangements for horseback riding, boat rentals, shuttle service, and Red Bus tours. The campground is set in the trees, giving shade and some privacy. Potable water is available, as are flush toilets and sinks with running water. Campers can walk to nearby Lake McDonald to take in the beautiful sunsets, and ranger programs are offered in the evening at the Apgar Amphitheater.

The second-largest campground in the park is **Fish Creek** ($23), with 178 sites, located 2.5 miles from Apgar Village. There are shade-giving trees in the campground and some of the sites offer limited views of Lake McDonald. Nightly ranger programs are available here. The campground has potable water, flush toilets, sinks with running water, and showers for registered campers.

Whitefish

Given a great boost when the train was rerouted from Kalispell in 1904, Whitefish (population 6,649; elevation 3,036 ft/925 m) grew up around Whitefish Mountain (long called Big Mountain) and the sport of skiing, and today is Montana's largest year-round resort community. Although Whitefish is clearly a ski town, it is also an art town, a gateway to Glacier, a summer hot spot, and a great place to find gourmet cuisine.

Getting to Whitefish

From **West Glacier,** Whitefish is 30 miles (48 km) west on U.S. 2, a 40-minute drive. From **Kalispell,** it's 15 miles (24 km) north on U.S. 93, a 25-minute drive.

Amtrak (500 Depot St., Whitefish) runs the **Empire Builder** from Chicago to Seattle with daily stops in Whitefish in each direction.

Getting Around

Glacier Taxi (406/250-3603, www. glaciertaxi.com, 24/7) covers all of Flathead County from Flathead Lake to Whitefish Mountain, Glacier National Park, Kalispell, and everything in between.

Entertainment and Events

Summer brings the **Downtown Farmers Market** (1 Central Ave., Whitefish, 406/407-5272, www. whitefishfarmersmarket.org, 5pm-7:30pm Tues. late May-late Sept.), which offers local produce and art, handmade crafts, prepared food, and a variety

Whitefish

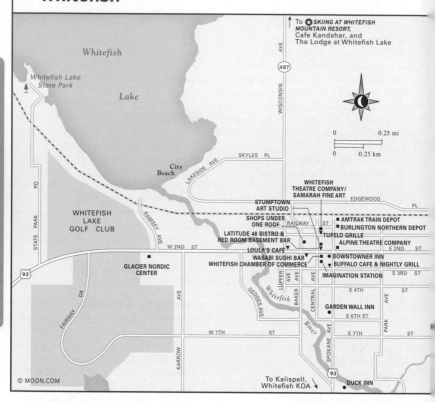

To **☆ SKIING AT WHITEFISH MOUNTAIN RESORT,** Cafe Kandahar, and The Lodge at Whitefish Lake

Whitefish Lake

Whitefish Lake State Park

Lake

City Beach

WHITEFISH LAKE GOLF CLUB

WHITEFISH THEATRE COMPANY/ SAMARAH FINE ART

STUMPTOWN ART STUDIO

SHOPS UNDER ONE ROOF

AMTRAK TRAIN DEPOT

BURLINGTON NORTHERN DEPOT

LATITUDE 48 BISTRO & RED ROOM BASEMENT BAR

TUPELO GRILLE

ALPINE THEATRE COMPANY

LOULA'S CAFE

WASABI SUSHI BAR

WHITEFISH CHAMBER OF COMMERCE

DOWNTOWNER INN

BUFFALO CAFE & NIGHTLY GRILL

GLACIER NORDIC CENTER

IMAGINATION STATION

GARDEN WALL INN

To Kalispell, Whitefish KOA

DUCK INN

© MOON.COM

of entertainment, often including live music.

Among the annual festivals celebrating local art, food, and culture are the **Whitefish Arts Festival** (504 Railway St., Whitefish, 406/862-5875, www. whitefishartsfestival.org), which is usually held the first weekend in July in Depot Park; the **Festival Amadeus** (600 2nd St., Whitefish, 406/407-7000, www. gscmusic.org), a weeklong classical music festival held in late July or August; and the **Huckleberry Days Art Festival** (Depot Park, Whitefish, 406/862-3501, www. whitefishchamber.org), held over three days in mid-August, which celebrates the juicy purple berry with music, entertainment, an art fair, and lots of family fun.

In mid-May, the annual **Feast Whitefish** (O'Shaughnessy Center, 1 Central Ave., Whitefish, across from the train station, 406/862-3501, www. feastwhitefish.com, $110) is the region's premier food event. It includes a weeklong dinner series with exquisite nightly meals by regional chefs, and a one-day distiller's fest (tickets from $30) that focuses on local vodkas, whiskeys, and other spirits by seven regional distilleries.

In winter, the area celebrates the snow with festivities like the **New Year's Eve Rockin' Rail Jam and Torchlight Parade** (Whitefish Mountain Resort, 406/862-2900, www.skiwhitefish.com) and the **Whitefish Winter Carnival** (www.

whitefishwintercarnival.com), a silly and fun event held annually in early February.

Despite its small size, Whitefish has a remarkably savvy theater scene, with offerings from both the **Alpine Theatre Project** (600 2nd St. E., 406/862-7469, www.atpwhitefish.org), a highly respected repertory theater company, and **Whitefish Theatre Company** (1 Central Ave., 406/862 5371, www. whitefishtheatreco.org), which offers eight community plays annually plus concerts, professional dance, improv performances, workshops, camps, and films.

Shopping

The streets of downtown Whitefish are filled with bars, restaurants, spas, and art galleries. Several galleries line Central Avenue, including **Stumptown Art Studio** (145 Central Ave., 406/862-5929, www. stumptownartstudio.org, 10am-6pm Mon.-Sat., noon-5pm Sun.), a marvelous gallery for buying, learning about, and even making art. **Samarah Fine Art** (100 Central Ave., 406/862-3339, www. samarahfineart.com,10am-6pm Mon.-Sat.) is a gallery that represents about 30 artists from across the state working in various traditional and contemporary media. Both galleries participate in the popular **Whitefish Gallery Nights** (www. whitefishgallerynights.org) the first Thursday evening of each month May-October. Thirteen galleries are involved, each sponsoring a different artist each night of the event. It's a great way to view art, meet the artists, sample good food, and experience the community.

The **Imagination Station Toys** (221 Central Ave., Whitefish, 406/862-5668, 9:30am-8pm Mon.-Sat., 11am-5pm Sun.) began about 20 years ago when the owners realized that they missed the toys of their youth. Their classic toy selection has grown over the years and is a lot of fun for adults and children alike. They also stock their store with the latest wooden toys from Europe, have a good selection of educational toys, and like to keep a lot of puzzles and board games on hand as well. Like a toy store for grown-ups, **The Shops Under One Roof** (205 Central Ave., Whitefish, 406/862-7253, 10am-5pm Mon.-Sat.) is a labyrinth of wonderful antiques and design shops.

If you have the time, a stop at **Kettle Care Organics** (3575 U.S. 93, Whitefish, 888/556-2316, www.kettlecare.com, 9am-6pm Mon.-Fri., 10am-3pm Sat.) is well worth the visit. This business is committed to producing fine all-natural body-care products while remaining conscious of its carbon footprint. The ingredients come from its certified organic farm and are created, packaged, and labeled for sale on-site. The store has a small showroom stocked with products; a trip to this store provides visitors an opportunity to see a successful homegrown green business in action.

Sports and Recreation
★ Skiing at Whitefish Mountain Resort

When it comes to skiing in Montana, it doesn't get much better than that at the **Whitefish Mountain Resort** (3840 Big Mountain Rd., 406/862-2900, www. skiwhitefish.com, full day $81 adults 19-64, $70 seniors 65-69 and teens 13-18, $41 juniors 7-12, free for ages 70 and over and 6 and under, half day $71 adults, $62 seniors and teens, $34 juniors), which offers 94 trails, 11 lifts, 2,353 feet (717 m) of vertical drop, and a 3.3-mile (5.3-km) run. When the snow conditions are just right, the trees all across the top of the mountain look like enormous snow monsters. It's magical—or terrifying, depending upon your point of view. This is a *big* mountain, with serious skiing and family fun at its best. The mountain stays open year-round for hiking, mountain biking, zip line tours, and an alpine slide, among other activities. In addition to offering regular 9am-4pm lift hours, it's also one of the few mountains in Montana that offers lighted night skiing ($23), 4pm-8:30pm.

Cross-Country Skiing

For cross-country skiers, fabulous groomed trails can be found locally at the **Glacier Nordic Center** (1200 U.S. 93 W., Whitefish, 406/862-9498, www.glaciernordicclub.com, $12 adults 18-69, $6 children 8-17, free for 70 and over and 7 and under) on the Whitefish Lake Golf Course. There are 15 kilometers of skate and classic trails on gently rolling terrain, and lighted night skiing on 4 kilometers of trails until 11pm. A Nordic shop (406/862-9498) on-site sells passes and rents gear for kids and adults by the half day, full day, or week. Lessons are available.

Hiking and Biking

Among the adventures at **Whitefish Mountain Resort** (3840 Big Mountain Rd., Whitefish, 406/862-2900, www.skiwhitefish.com, 8am-6pm daily mid-June-early Sept., Fri.-Sun. only through late Sept.) are serious mountain biking opportunities for the hard-core and not-so-hard-core, who might prefer to limit rides to downhill only. There are more than 30 miles (48 km) of lift-accessed ($39 adults full day, $28 adults 2 hours, $28 juniors full day, $23 juniors 2 hours) single-track and cross-country trails on the mountain. For hikers, the **Danny On Trail** winds 3.8 miles (6.1 km) from the base of the ski hill to the summit. The lift can be taken up or down to make the hike shorter and easier.

Golf

Public golf courses in Whitefish include the North and South Courses at the **Whitefish Lake Golf Club** (1200 U.S. 93 N., 406/862-5960, 406/862-4000 for tee times, www.golfwhitefish.com, $49-63 for 18 holes, $26-33 for 9 holes, $40 for 18 holes on the South Course after 2pm).

Food

Whitefish has a surprising number of excellent restaurants. One of the all-around best places to go for a hearty, delicious

Whitefish in winter is a skier's dream.

meal is the budget-friendly **Buffalo Café & Nightly Grill** (514 3rd St. E., 406/862-2833, www.buffalocafewhitefish.com, 7am-2pm and 5pm-9pm Mon.-Sat., 8am-2pm Sun., $12-25). From old-fashioned milk shakes and blueberry granola pancakes to Mexican specialties and baby back ribs, this local favorite has been mastering comfort food since the late 1970s. The service is both friendly and speedy.

When breakfast or pie (or any meal whatsoever) is on the docket, one should not overlook the incredible ★ **Loula's Café** (300 2nd St. E., 406/862-5614, www.whitefishrestaurant.com, 7am-3pm Sun.-Mon., 7am-3pm and 5pm-9:30pm Tues.-Sat., $11-22). Breakfast ($5.50-12.50) is everything from Chubby Yuppie Scrambles to Ski Bum Biscuits and Gravy, eggs Benedict, and breakfast burritos. Save room for pie. Lunch ($8.50-13) is a selection of mouthwatering burgers, sandwiches, soups, and salads. And pie. Don't forget the pie. Dinner ($10.50-22)

can be a more sophisticated affair with changing menus that pair specials with wine. And pie! If you happen to be in Loula's when the pies come out of the oven and you don't jump to buy at least one, you will regret it for the remainder of your trip. I'm not kidding. Eating a huckleberry cherry pie, straight from the box and still a bit warm, on the shores of Lake McDonald is a memory that will stay with you forever.

Although Montana is not known for its sushi, Whitefish residents could not live without **Wasabi Sushi Bar** (419 E. 2nd St., 406/863-9283, www.wasabimt.com, from 5pm daily May-Oct., from 5pm Mon.-Sat. Nov.-Apr., rolls $5-16), with classic nigiri and sashimi, a contemporary twist on sushi and tempura, and plenty of grill items that include steak, duck, scallops, fish tacos, and more.

While there are a handful of elegant high-end eateries in Whitefish, **Tupelo Grille** (17 Central Ave., 406/862-6136, www.tupelogrille.com, 5pm-10pm daily, lounge daily from 4pm, $18-42) is a unique choice with a wonderfully southern-inspired menu and an exceptional wine list. Just down the block is another gem: **Latitude 48 Bistro and Red Room Basement Bar** (147 Central Ave., 406/863-2323, www.latitude48bistro.com, 5pm-10pm daily, $7-32), an urban oasis with a phenomenal menu that offers small plates like seared beef tips and lamb sirloin, creative wood-fired pizzas, and substantial main courses in a fusion of traditional and contemporary trends.

For foodies looking for another unforgettable meal, **Café Kandahar** (3824 Big Mountain Rd., 406/862-6247, www.cafekandahar.com, 5:30pm-9:30pm daily mid-Dec.-late Mar. and mid-June-late Sept., market prices) on the ski hill cannot be over-touted. The menus change nightly, but in addition to the à la carte masterpieces, the chef always offers 5- and 7-course tasting menus and an 11-course degustation menu. Sample dishes include pork belly confit, Hudson

Valley foie gras, and elk roulade. But it is the way that chef Andy Blanton masterfully combines delicate flavors and exquisite ingredients that captivates diners. Make no mistake, this will be a pricey meal—but a phenomenal one.

Accommodations

Given its proximity to Whitefish Mountain, Whitefish Lake, and Glacier National Park, it's no surprise that Whitefish has an abundance of accommodations—but true to its resort-town vibe, beds don't come cheap. The largest and most diverse, without a doubt, is the **Whitefish Mountain Resort** (3840 Big Mountain Rd., 406/862-2900, www. skiwhitefish.com, $109-1,500), the resort community around Whitefish Mountain with eight different lodging options, 90 percent of which are condominiums that range from modest and economical guest rooms in the **Hibernation House** to palatial five-bedroom town houses. Rates are generally higher in winter, and particularly around holidays. Navigating the reservation system can be a feat, so practice patience and be clear about what you want and what your budget is.

Another sizable full-service resort, on the shores of Whitefish Lake and just over 1 mile (1.6 km) from downtown, is the ultra-appealing **Lodge at Whitefish Lake** (1380 Wisconsin Ave., 406/863-4000 or 877/887-4026, www. lodgeatwhitefishlake.com, $130-721). The lodge is pretty spectacular, and the rooms are all luxurious. The attached condos are sizable and great for larger groups, but somewhat less romantic. The immediate lake access is a disincentive to ever leave, and the on-site restaurants will keep you well fed and happy.

Smaller options for lodging in the town of Whitefish include the riverfront 15-room **Duck Inn** (1305 Columbia Ave., 406/862-3825 or 800/344-2377, www. duckinn.com, $199-289) and the charming five-bedroom **Garden Wall Inn** (504 Spokane Ave., 406/862-3440 or 888/530-1700, www.gardenwallinn.com, $155-395). Located in the heart of town, within easy walking distance to everything, the pet-friendly **Downtowner Inn** (2244 Spokane Ave., 406/862-2535 or 888/325-2535, downtownermotel.cc, $90-160) has basic but comfortable rooms.

Camping

By far the most economical accommodations in Whitefish are the campgrounds. There are a number of beautiful national forest campgrounds as well as two private campgrounds, including the **Whitefish KOA** (5121 U.S. 93 S., 2 mi/3.2 km south of Whitefish, 406/862-4242 or 800/562-8734, www.glacierparkkoa.com, mid-May-mid-Sept., $46-89 RV and tent sites, $99-205 cabins), which has every imaginable amenity. **Tally Lake** (913 Tally Lake Rd., 17 mi/27 km west of Whitefish, 406/646-1012, www.recreation.gov, late May-late Sept., from $18) is a gorgeous and popular spot with a nice campground. Closer to town, **Whitefish Lake State Park** (1615 E. Lakeshore Dr., 406/862-3991 or 406/751-4590, www. stateparks.mt.gov, year-round, water and showers available May-Sept., from $10) offers 25 waterfront tent and RV sites that go quickly at this beautiful, convenient spot.

Information

The **Whitefish Chamber of Commerce** (307 Spokane Ave., Whitefish, 406/862-3501, www.whitefishchamber.org, 9am-5pm Mon.-Fri.) is open year-round.

Kalispell

The town of Kalispell (population 22,761; elevation 2,956 ft/901 m) exists because of James Hill's Great Northern Railway and survives in spite of it. Freight and mercantile baron Charles Conrad founded the town of Kalispell when he convinced his friend Hill to run the railroad through it in 1891. By 1904, the Great Northern had abandoned its Kalispell route in favor of the more geographically amenable Whitefish line just 15 miles (24 km) to the north. The people of Kalispell were furious, but the town's economy survived thanks to Conrad's National Bank and the booming timber industry. Today it is still rather industrial—a nuts-and-bolts kind of town that serves as a natural supply and shopping center—and has some wonderful museums, parks, and an ideal location between Flathead Lake and Glacier National Park.

Getting to Kalispell

From **West Glacier,** Kalispell is 35 miles (56 km) southwest on U.S. 2 and MT-206, about a 50-minute drive. From **Whitefish,** it's 15 miles (24 km) south on U.S. 93, about a 25-minute drive.

Just south of Whitefish, Kalispell is the larger of the two cities and has commercial flights and bus service, along with taxi services.

The **Glacier Park International Airport** (FCA, 4170 U.S. 2 E., Kalispell, www.iflyglacier.com) is served by Delta, Alaska, United, and Allegiant. There are on-site car-rental counters for **Avis, Budget, Hertz,** and **National/Alamo; Dollar,** (406/892-0009, www.dollar.com), **Enterprise** (406/755-4848, www.enterprise.com), and **Thrifty** (406/257-7333, www.thrifty.com) are off-site but near the airport.

Greyhound (2075 U.S. 2 E., Kalispell, 406/755-7447) offers daily bus service in and out of Kalispell.

Getting Around

Eagle Transit (406/758-5728, http://flathead.mt.gov/eagle, 7am-7pm Mon.-Fri., $1) operates the buses in Kalispell. **Glacier Taxi** (406/250-3603, www.glaciertaxi.com, 24/7) covers all of Flathead County from Flathead Lake to Whitefish Mountain, Glacier National Park, Kalispell, and everything in between.

Sights
Conrad Mansion National Historic Site

Just a block from Woodland Park in Kalispell sits the palatial historic home of Charles Conrad, the founder of the city. The **Conrad Mansion** (330 Woodland Ave., Kalispell, 406/755-2166, www.conradmansion.com, 10am-5pm Wed.-Sun. mid-May-mid-June, 10am-5pm Tues.-Sun. mid-June-mid-Oct., $15 adults, $14 seniors 65 and over, $8 students 12-17, $6 children 11 and under) was completed in 1895 and designed by the renowned Spokane, Washington, architect Kirtland Cutter. The Conrads made sure that the residents of Kalispell felt some connection to the house: On Christmas Day of the year it was finished, the Conrad family invited people from around town who would otherwise have spent the holiday alone to share in their feast. The entire city was invited to a grand New Year's Eve ball a week later. Conrad himself had only lived in the house for seven years before his death at age 52. Over the years, Alicia Conrad hosted famous parties, including a Halloween gathering just after a fire had burned through the roof of the mansion. Alicia decorated the hole with Spanish moss, artificial bats, and volcanoes. After her death in 1923, the family continued to occupy the home until the mid-1960s. In 1974, his youngest daughter donated the residence to the city of Kalispell. The 26-room, nine-bedroom Norman-style mansion has been beautifully restored and is furnished with the

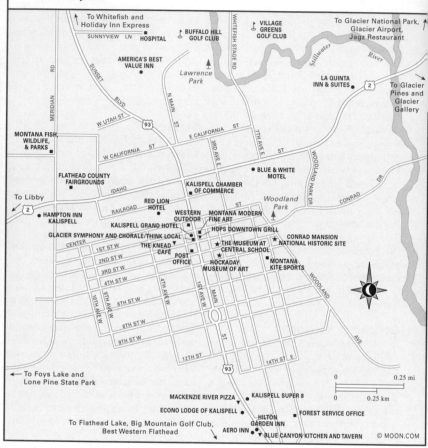

Kalispell

To Whitefish and
Holiday Inn Express

SUNNYVIEW LN
HOSPITAL
BUFFALO HILL
GOLF CLUB
VILLAGE
GREENS
GOLF CLUB

To Glacier National Park,
Glacier Airport,
Jagz Restaurant

AMERICA'S BEST
VALUE INN

*Lawrence
Park*

WHITEFISH STAGE RD

Stillwater

River

LA QUINTA
INN & SUITES

To Glacier
Pines and
Glacier
Gallery

MERIDIAN RD

SUNSET BLVD

W UTAH ST

N MAIN ST

E CALIFORNIA ST

3RD AVE E

7TH AVE E

ST

WOODLAND PARK DR

CONRAD DR

MONTANA FISH,
WILDLIFE,
& PARKS

W CALIFORNIA ST

ST

BLUE & WHITE
MOTEL

FLATHEAD COUNTY
FAIRGROUNDS

IDAHO

KALISPELL CHAMBER
OF COMMERCE

*Woodland
Park*

To Libby

RED LION
HOTEL

ST

CONRAD

RAILROAD

To Hampton Inn
Kalispell

WESTERN
OUTDOOR

MONTANA MODERN
FINE ART

KALISPELL GRAND HOTEL

HOPS DOWNTOWN GRILL

GLACIER SYMPHONY AND CHORALE/THINK LOCAL

CENTER

CONRAD MANSION
NATIONAL HISTORIC SITE

THE KNEAD
CAFÉ

THE MUSEUM AT
CENTRAL SCHOOL

1ST ST W

POST
OFFICE

HOCKADAY
MUSEUM OF ART

MONTANA
KITE SPORTS

2ND ST W

3RD ST W

4TH ST W

4TH AVE W

1ST AVE W

MAIN ST

WOODLAND AVE

10TH AVE W

8TH AVE W

6TH ST W

8TH ST W

9TH ST W

12TH ST W

14TH ST E

93

To Foys Lake and
Lone Pine State Park

MACKENZIE RIVER PIZZA

KALISPELL SUPER 8

ECONO LODGE OF KALISPELL

FOREST SERVICE OFFICE

To Flathead Lake, Big Mountain Golf Club,
Best Western Flathead

HILTON
GARDEN INN

AERO INN

BLUE CANYON KITCHEN AND TAVERN

| 0 | | 0.25 mi |
| 0 | | 0.25 km |

© MOON.COM

family's original furniture. There is also a large collection of family clothing and three generations of children's toys.

Hockaday Museum of Art

The **Hockaday Museum of Art** (302 2nd Ave. E., Kalispell, 406/755-5268, www. hockadaymuseum.org, 10am-5pm Tues.-Fri., 10am-4pm Sat., $5 adults, $4 seniors 60 and over, $2 college students, free for children K-12) was begun by local artists in the late 1960s, and today it is a well-established public museum known for showcasing some of the region's most important art and artists. Visitors will find works by T. J. Hileman, John Fery, and Charles M. Russell, among others. It has the largest collection of Glacier National Park art in the country and also a large permanent collection dedicated to the Blackfeet. Public tours of the museum are offered for free, with admission, on Thursday and Saturday at 10:30am. Hockaday hosts the **Arts in the Park** program each July, and the gift shop has a broad selection of original works, including jewelry, pottery, and prints by local artists.

The Museum at Central School

The Central School building was opened in 1894 and for more than 100 years housed different educational institutions. Slated for demolition in the early 1990s, the city of Kalispell instead invested more than $2 million renovating the historic building. Since 1999 it has been used by the Northwest Montana Historical Society, which oversees **The Museum at Central School** (124 2nd Ave. E., Kalispell, 406/756-8381, www.yourmuseum.org, 10am-5pm Mon.-Fri., 10am-2pm Sat. June-Aug., $5 adults, $4 seniors, free for children). The museum is dedicated to preserving the unique history of northwestern Montana and especially the history of Kalispell. Permanent exhibits include a historical examination of the Flathead Valley and the growth of the logging industry in Montana. On Thursdays 5pm-8pm late June-late August, live music, food vendors, arts and crafts, a farmers market, and a beer and wine garden converge on the grounds of the museum.

Entertainment and Events

With so much to do year-round in this part of the state, the calendar is always filled with seasonal events. In northwestern Montana, summertime means farmers markets, and a good one is the **Kalispell Farmers Market** (777 Grandview Dr., 406/881-4078, www.kalispellfarmersmarket.org, 9am-12:30pm Sat. early May-mid.-Oct.), held on the campus of Flathead Valley Community College.

Another market, which focuses on locally made arts and crafts, is the **Artists and Craftsmen of the Flathead Summer Outdoor Show** (920 S. Main St., Kalispell, 406/881-4288, www.artistsandcraftsmen. org), held over a weekend in the first part of July.

Perhaps the most anticipated event of the year is the **Northwest Montana Fair & Rodeo** (fairgrounds, 265 N. Meridian Rd., Kalispell, 406/758-5810, www. nwmtfair.com, from $32 adults, $20 children 6-12), usually held in mid-August and kicked off with a parade. The nearly weeklong event includes plenty of local agricultural exhibits, a carnival, three nights of professional rodeo, and a variety of entertainment, all of which attract visitors from across the region. For year-round entertainment, check out the **Glacier Symphony and Chorale** (69 N. Main St., Kalispell, 406/407-7000, www. gscmusic.org), which produces an interesting range of musical events.

Shopping

Western Outdoor (48 Main St., Kalispell, 406/756-5818 or 800/636-5818, www. westernod.com, 9am-6pm Mon.-Sat., 10:30am-4:30pm Sun. summer, 10am-6pm Mon.-Sat., 10:30am-4:30pm Sun. fall-spring) is one of the region's most popular shopping attractions. This Western goods store boasts more than 2,500 pairs of boots and close to 1,500 hats in every size, shape, and style imaginable. If you've always wanted real cowboy duds, the salespeople here are very attentive and will do their best to make sure you are outfitted properly.

Think Local (140 Main St., Kalispell, 406/260-4499, 10am-5:30pm Tues.-Sat., extended summer and holiday hours) showcases amazingly diverse works by 51 local artists including photographers, painters, rope and barnwood artists, and copper jewelers, all of them from Montana. A coffee shop in the back makes time spent browsing all the more enjoyable. A perfect winter shop in Kalispell is **Montana Kite Sports** (405 3rd Ave. E., 530/356-2758), which introduces the sports of "power kiting" and "ice boating" to the willing through gear sales and lessons. Hours here can change with the weather, so call ahead. For art lovers, Kalispell's **Montana Modern Fine Art** (127 S. Main St., 406/755-5321, www. montanamodernfineart.com, 11am-6pm Tues.-Sat.) is a rare opportunity to see phenomenal artworks and meet artists like Marshall Noice. He works in oils and pastels and captures the Western landscape in brilliant color and luscious form.

Sports and Recreation
Hiking and Biking

Just 4 miles (6.4 km) southwest of Kalispell, **Lone Pine State Park** (300 Lone Pine Rd., Kalispell, 406/755-2706, www.stateparks.mt.gov/lone-pine, $6/vehicle nonresidents) has a nature trail, 7.5 miles (12.1 km) of hiking and biking trails with scenic overlooks, and a year-round visitors center with flush toilets and a picnic shelter. A variety of programs—from yoga to full-moon hikes—are scheduled throughout the summer at the visitors center and picnic shelter. Young kids, ages 4-7, will be excited about the **Junior Ranger Club,** where they can learn about the natural world through activities and games.

Golf

Five public golf courses are in Kalispell, including the **Northern Pines Golf Club** (3230 U.S. 93 N., 406/751-1950, www.northernpinesgolfclub.com, $30-72 for 18 holes, $20-40 for 9 holes), the 36-hole **Buffalo Hill Golf Club** (1176 N. Main St., 888/342-6319, www.golfbuffalohill.com, $35-70 for 18 holes, $21-27 for 9 holes), and the **Village Greens Golf Club** (500 Palmer Dr., 406/752-4666, www.montanagolf.com, $45-55 for 18 holes, $27-32 for 9 holes).

Food

In keeping with the number of strip malls in town, Kalispell has an abundance of chain restaurants, many of them quite good, like **Mackenzie River Pizza** (2230 U.S. 93 S., 406/756-0060, www.mackenzieriverpizza.com, 11am-10pm daily, and 45 Treeline Rd., 406/756-3030, 11am-10pm Sun.-Thurs., 11am-11pm Fri.-Sat., $8-20.50), which serves pies from the traditional to the gourmet and rounds out the menu with a healthy selection of sandwiches, pasta dishes, salads,

and appetizers. Adjacent to the Hilton Garden Inn, **Blue Canyon Kitchen & Tavern** (1840 U.S. 93 S., 406/758-2583, www.bluecanyonrestaurant.com, 4pm-10pm Tues.-Sat., 4pm-9pm Sun.-Mon., $14-36) offers everything from flatbread and salads to bison shepherd's pie and elk meat loaf. It also offers half portions of many of the savory entrées, which is easier on the waistband and the wallet.

Some fantastic local restaurants also are well worth finding. **The Knead Café** (21 5th St. E., 406/752-8436 www.theknead.com, 8am-3pm Tues.-Sat., $8-15) is a great little Mediterranean-inspired breakfast and lunch joint that rightly calls itself a "spirited fusion of food, art, and music." An excellent choice for a gourmet dinner is the family-friendly **Jagz Restaurant** (3796 U.S. 2 E., 406/755-5303, www.jagzrestaurant.com, 4:30pm-9pm daily, $9-38), which serves a wide assortment of steaks, seafood, and pasta. **Hops Downtown Grill** (121 Main St., 406/755-7687, www.hopsmontana.com, 5pm-9pm Sun.-Thurs., 5pm-9:30pm Sat.-Sun., $10-19) is known for a wide selection of craft beer and gourmet burgers—from wild boar and buffalo to yak and American Kobe beef. Chicken, lasagna, ribs, and steak round out the menu.

Accommodations

Kalispell is definitely the region's best place to find an assortment of more budget-friendly chain hotels and motels, but prices can rise when the town is packed with travelers en route to or from Glacier or Flathead. Next to the airport, the **Aero Inn** (1830 U.S. 93 S., 406/755-3798 or 800/843-6114, www.aeroinn.com, $50-145) has 61 no-frills guest rooms and is reasonably priced. Another good value can be found at the 106-room pet-friendly **Blue & White Motel** (640 E. Idaho St., 406/755-4311 or 800/382-3577, www.blueandwhitemotel.com, $43-95), which, in addition to cool neon signage, has decent rooms, standard amenities, and a 24-hour restaurant next door (making it a favorite with truckers). Among the larger chain hotels and motels are **America's Best Value** (1550 U.S. 93 N., 406/756-3222, www.abvkalispell.com, $129-169), **Best Western Plus Flathead Lake Inn and Suites** (4824 U.S. 93 S., 406/857-2400 or 888/226-1003, www.bestwestern.com, $170-369), **Econo Lodge of Kalispell** (1680 U.S. 93 S., 406/752-3467 or 800/843-7301, www.choicehotels.com, $120-212), **Hampton Inn Kalispell** (1140 U.S. 2 W., 406/755-7900 or 800/426-7866, www.hamptoninn3.hilton.com, $179-354), the fairly glamorous-for-these-parts **Hilton Garden Inn** (1840 U.S. 93 S., 406/756-4500, www.hiltongardeninn3.hilton.com, $179-299), **Holiday Inn Express** (275 Treeline Rd., 406/755-7405, www.ihg.com, $160-270), **Kalispell Super 8** (1341 1st Ave. E., 406/203-1905, www.wyndhamhotels.com, $160-189), and **La Quinta Inn & Suites** (255 Montclair Dr., 406/257-5255 or 800/753-3757, www.lq.com, $166-224).

For a more historical experience, try the pet-friendly **Kalispell Grand Hotel** (100 Main St., 406/755-8100 or 800/858-7422, www.kalispellgrand.com, $75-183). This stately brick property is the last of eight hotels that once lined downtown. Less historic but reliable and pet-friendly, the **Red Lion Hotel** (20 N. Main St., 406/751-5050 or 800/733-5466, www.redlion.com, $209-329) is conveniently located next to the Kalispell Center Mall in the heart of downtown.

Camping

There are quite a few camping options, both public and private, around Kalispell, but nothing for tent campers in town. Among the largest full-service RV parks, and the only one with a heated swimming pool, is the shady and private **Glacier Pines** (120 Swan Mountain Dr., Kalispell, 406/752-2760, www.glacierpines.com, from $39 plus $2

pp), with 80 full-service sites, free Wi-Fi, a playground for small kids, horseshoes, and fire pits. A good primitive option for tent campers is the **Ashley Lake Campgrounds** (North Shore Rd., off Ashley Lake Rd., 17 mi/27.4 km west of Kalispell, 406/758-5204, www.fs.usda.gov, Memorial Day-Labor Day, no fees for day use or overnight camping), which offers 11 lakefront sites with no services other than a vault toilet.

Information and Services

The **Kalispell Chamber of Commerce** (406/758-2800, www.kalispellchamber.com, 8am-5pm Mon.-Fri.) and **Flathead Convention and Visitor Bureau** (406/756-9091, www.fcvb.org, 8:30am-4pm Mon.-Fri.) are housed in the historic Great Northern Depot building (15 Depot Park, Kalispell).

The **Flathead National Forest Headquarters** (650 Wolf Pack Way, Kalispell, 406/758-5208, www.fs.usda.gov/flathead, 8am-4:30pm Mon.-Fri.) has helpful information for campers and hikers.

Kalispell has the **Flathead County Library** (247 1st Ave. E., 406/758-5820, www.imagineiflibraries.org, 10am-8pm Mon.-Wed., 10am-6pm Thurs.-Fri., 10am-5pm Sat.), and the **main post office** (248 1st Ave. W., 800/275-8777, 9am-4pm Mon.-Fri.) is at the corner of 1st Avenue and 3rd Street.

The **Kalispell Regional Medical Center** (310 Sunnyview Ln., 406/752-5111, www.krh.org) has a 24-hour emergency room and is just north of downtown Kalispell. There are also several urgent care facilities in town, including **MedNorth Urgent Care** (2316 U.S. 93, 406/755-5661, www.mymednorth.com, 7:30am-7:30pm Mon.-Fri., 9am-3pm Sat.-Sun.) and **Family Health Care** (1287 Burns Way, 406/752-8120, www.mymednorth.com, 8am-6pm Mon.-Fri., 9am-2pm Sat.-Sun.).

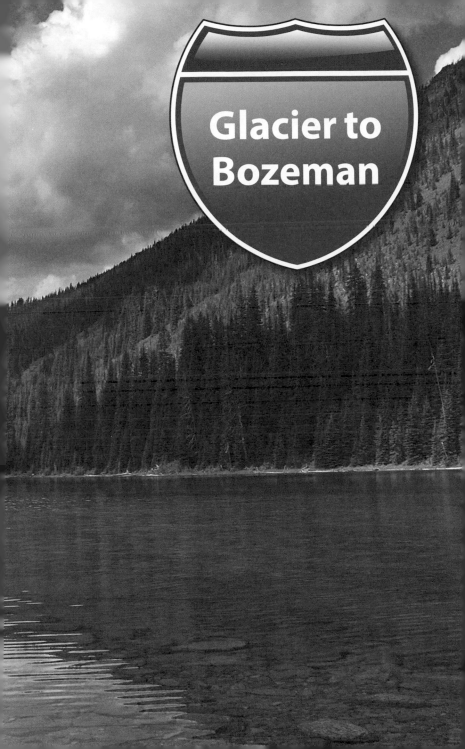

Glacier to Bozeman

Glacier to Bozeman

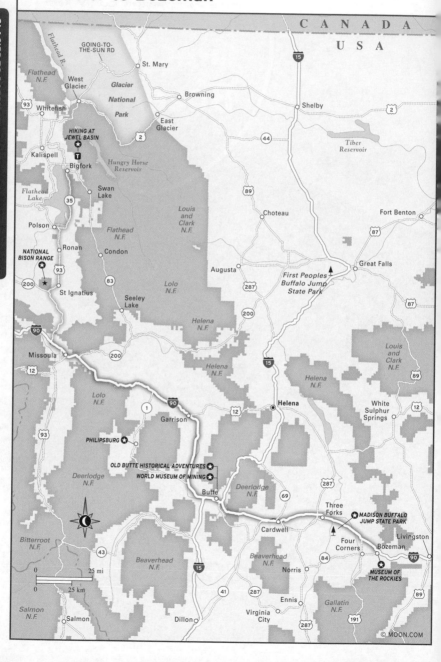

CANADA
USA

Flathead R.

GOING-TO-THE-SUN RD

St. Mary

Flathead N.F.

West Glacier

Whitefish

93

Browning

Shelby

2

Glacier National Park

East Glacier

HIKING AT JEWEL BASIN

Kalispell

Bigfork

2

44

Tiber Reservoir

Fort Benton

Hungry Horse Reservoir

89

Swan Lake

Choteau

87

Flathead Lake

Louis and Clark N.F.

Polson

Flathead N.F.

35

Ronan

Condon

NATIONAL BISON RANGE

93

83

Augusta

287

Great Falls

First Peoples Buffalo Jump State Park

87

St Ignatius

200

Lolo N.F.

Seeley Lake

Helena N.F.

200

90

Helena N.F.

Missoula

12

200

15

Louis and Clark N.F.

89

Lolo N.F.

1

Helena N.F.

White Sulphur Springs

12

Garrison

12

Helena

PHILIPSBURG

OLD BUTTE HISTORICAL ADVENTURES

WORLD MUSEUM OF MINING

Butte

287

Deerlodge N.F.

Deerlodge N.F.

69

Three Forks

MADISON BUFFALO JUMP STATE PARK

Bitterroot N.F.

Cardwell

Four Corners

Bozeman

Livingston

90

43

Beaverhead N.F.

Beaverhead N.F.

84

Norris

MUSEUM OF THE ROCKIES

41

287

Ennis

Gallatin N.F.

89

Virginia City

15

Salmon N.F.

Salmon

Dillon

287

191

0   25 mi
0   25 km

© MOON.COM

Highlights

★ **Hiking at Jewel Basin:** With 27 lakes, 35 miles (56 km) of trails, and no motorized vehicles or horses permitted, this is a hiker's paradise (page 244).

★ **National Bison Range:** On a low, rolling mountain near the Mission Mountains, some 400 bison wander as they did once on one of the country's oldest wildlife refuges (page 256).

★ **Philipsburg:** This fabulous mining town is experiencing a rebirth, with a couple of fantastic restaurants and a cool hotel (page 272).

★ **Old Butte Historical Adventures:** Spend some time with one of the passionate and knowledgeable guides here, where you'll see history both above and below the ground (page 275).

★ **World Museum of Mining:** This museum, built atop the Orphan Girl mine yard, is packed with artifacts from more than a century of hard-rock mining (page 277).

★ **Museum of the Rockies:** Renowned for its impressive dinosaur collection, this museum is home to 300,000 objects in permanent and traveling displays, a planetarium, and an outdoor living history farm (page 288).

★ **Madison Buffalo Jump State Park:** A hike on this park's cliff is both a lesson in Native American history and an exercise in solitude (page 290).

Whether you choose to travel along Flathead Lake and the Mission Valley to Missoula, or down the east side of the Mission Mountains through the Seeley-Swan Valley to Helena, this region of western Montana will put you amid lakes and towering forests, wonderful territory for hiking, boating, and exploring. The hard part is not deciding what you want to see, but what you are willing to miss.

With the largest freshwater lake in the western United States, and the wide-open space of the National Bison Range, the Flathead and Mission Valleys south of Glacier truly are God's country. Home to the lakeside towns of Bigfork and Polson, the Flathead Valley is situated west of the Continental Divide amid four mountain ranges. On the east side of the Mission Mountains is the Seeley-Swan Valley, with its single-lane highway, timeless lakeside resorts, and towering pine and fir forests.

Missoula is a university town and a real city by Montana standards, with plenty of places to get a great meal and a comfortable bed. But there's culture here too, along with nightlife, downtown shopping, and a miles-long walking path beside the river, connecting the University of Montana campus to downtown. Active travelers can keep up the pace with a hike up the M or an adventure in the nearby Rattlesnake National Recreation Area.

Farther east, two of the state's best-known mining camps, Helena and Butte, prospered and diversified, becoming a pair of Montana's most interesting and historically significant cities. Others, like Virginia City and Philipsburg, all but disappeared before rising again as well-maintained tourist attractions.

Indeed, history comes to life here, from the mines in and around Butte to the ghost towns above Philipsburg, and the cobblestone streets of Montana's capital city of Helena.

The area around Bozeman is a playground, bursting with mountains to climb, rivers to fish, and trails to hike. While the main draw is the natural splendor and recreational opportunities, Bozeman—home of Montana State University—is an increasingly sophisticated mountain town with a lively arts scene and plenty of culinary and shopping options.

Planning Your Time

About halfway between Yellowstone and Glacier, **Missoula** is a natural stopping point along both east-west I-90 and north-south U.S. 93. It's easier to get here by air than much of the state, but the city is also a great destination in itself. From boutique shopping and hip eateries near the **University of Montana,** to adventurous athletic pursuits in town and nearby, Missoula is Montana with an urban edge.

Between Missoula and Glacier, the stunning Flathead and Mission Valleys offer up plenty of history, remarkable wildlife refuges, and tiny but bustling villages lining the sandy shores of **Flathead Lake**—don't miss charming **Bigfork** with its galleries, eateries, and theater.

Butte is a fascinating destination, not so much for its present-day incarnation, which can be fairly described as a bit rowdy and somewhat bleak, but for its older glory: the remarkable architecture that still stands, the underground city that is just coming to light, and the mines that made Butte the "richest hill on earth" and one of the country's largest cities west of the Mississippi for nearly 50 years. Butte is a marvelous place to spend at least a day, and more if you are interested in mining or history.

Two Options for Glacier to Bozeman in Two Days

There's a choice to be made when you're traveling from Glacier to Bozeman. Do you want to go east or west of the Mission Mountains? Do you want to drive the interstate and visit Montana's bigger cities, or stick to the back roads and tiny towns? Depending on what has more appeal, here are two options.

From Bigfork to Bozeman, the **western route** through Missoula is about 300 miles (483 km) and about a 5-hour drive. The **eastern route** through the Seeley-Swan Valley is a little shorter at 273 miles (439 km) and about a 4-hour and 40-minute drive.

Option A: Western Route

DAY 1
Wherever you wake up, start your day with a morning hike into the **Jewel Basin;** Twin Lakes is a good bet. Then refuel with a hearty meal at **Echo Lake Café.** Drive through **Bigfork**—stop for a coffee or some shopping if you like—and then wind along the east shore of **Flathead Lake.** Make sure to stop and dip your toes in the water, and if it's cherry season, don't miss the chance to pick your own **Flathead cherries.**

Stop in to see the **St. Ignatius Mission** and then take a drive through the **National Bison Range.** If you manage to get to Ravalli by 3pm, stop for a fresh, still-warm donut at **Windmill Village Bakery.**

Continue on to **Missoula,** where you can enjoy a wood-fired pizza at **Biga's Pizza** and settle in for the night at **Goldsmith's Inn.**

DAY 2
In the morning, after breakfast at the inn or an espresso and a pastry from **Le Petit Outre,** walk along the **Riverfront Trail** in Missoula, and then hit I-90, heading eastward to **Butte.** In Butte, stop for a peanut burger and a shake at **Matt's Place** and visit the **World Museum of Mining** or the **Butte Under the Streets Tour.**

Continue on toward **Bozeman,** where you can grab dinner at **Blackbird Café** and settle in for the night at **The Lark.**

Option B: Eastern Route

DAY 1
From Bigfork, head southeast on MT-83 through the towering fir forests of the **Seeley-Swan Valley.** The lodges and cabins and little roadside restaurants are like something out of the 1940s or '50s.

Overnight at the magnificently situated **Holland Lake Lodge**—or the nearby **Holland Lake campground**—and take advantage of the hiking and swimming and boating from the lodge and campground. Enjoy dinner at the lodge and some stargazing.

DAY 2
In the morning, take a hike to **Holland Lake Falls** after a big breakfast and then continue south, past **Seeley Lake** and on to **Helena,** where you can enjoy lunch on the deck at **Karmadillos Southwestern Café,** and some shopping in the **Last Chance Gulch** before hitting the road for the last 90 minutes to Bozeman.

Best Restaurants

★ **Echo Lake Café, Bigfork:** This is the kind of place where you'll wait, happily, for generous portions of scrambles, crepes, and sandwiches, with homemade everything, from syrups and gravies to sauces and baked goods (page 245).

★ **Holland Lake Lodge, Condon:** Getting here is half the fun! Set on a gorgeous lake with trails in every direction, Holland Lake Lodge offers gourmet meals in an exquisite natural setting (page 248).

★ **Windmill Village Bakery, Ravalli:** Between Missoula and Glacier, this roadside bakery often has long lines for their made-to-order, enormous, and delicious donuts, which are iced while you watch and served warm (page 256).

★ **Scotty's Table, Missoula:** Located in the historic Wilma Theatre, this swanky little bistro serves up the best of regional farmers, growers, and producers (page 269).

★ **Biga Pizza, Missoula:** Innovative and made from scratch, everything here is cooked in the wood-fired oven, from award-winning pizzas—like prosciutto and fig, or sweet potato, bacon, and maple chipotle—to mouthwatering calzones (page 269).

★ **The Sweet Palace, Philipsburg:** Historic and huge, this is arguably the best candy shop in the state, with saltwater taffy, fudge, and chocolates made on-site, not to mention walls of nostalgic penny candy (page 274).

★ **Matt's Place, Butte:** Eating at the counter at this tiny 1940s diner with outstanding burgers, fresh fries, and the best milk shake you've ever had is a quintessential Butte experience (page 282).

★ **Uptown Café, Butte:** In the heart of the mining city, this spot balances white-tablecloth elegance, sophisticated flavors, and good old Butte hospitality for a memorable meal (page 282).

★ **Willow Creek Café and Saloon, Willow Creek:** Known for their mouthwatering ribs and chicken-fried chicken, this restaurant in the tiny town of Willow Creek is as charming as it is good (page 284).

★ **Star Bakery Restaurant, Nevada City:** First opened in 1863, this bakery serves wonderful, fresh baked goods and comfort foods for three hearty meals a day (page 286).

★ **Blackbird Kitchen, Bozeman:** Blackbird dishes up rustic Italian food—handmade pastas, wood-fired pizzas and inventive starters—made from locally produced ingredients in a warm, casual setting (page 297).

A host of other places in the region make great add-ons or stand-alone destinations. **Virginia City** and **Nevada City** are meticulously preserved ghost towns. Southeast of Missoula, **Philipsburg** is an ideal spot to enjoy a meal, get a good night's rest, and perhaps even catch a show.

With its fairly central location, ease of air or highway access, and abundance of accommodations, **Bozeman** is a superb launching point for the region. You could

Best Accommodations

★ **Goldsmith's Inn, Missoula:** In a lovely old home on the river that was at times the university president's residence, a fraternity house, and a laboratory, this inn offers comfortable, homey accommodations (page 270).

★ **The Broadway Hotel, Philipsburg:** With nine themed rooms in the heart of historic Philipsburg, the 1890 Broadway Hotel offers a comfortable stay with modern amenities and a fabulous breakfast (page 274).

★ **Copper King Mansion, Butte:** A stay at the charming and elegant Copper King, part museum and part bed-and-breakfast, is a delightful way to get to know the history of this mining city (page 283).

★ **Sacajawea Hotel, Three Forks:** A grand old hotel around which the town grew up, the updated Sacajawea is lovely and welcoming and boasts an outstanding restaurant (page 284).

★ **Nevada City Hotel & Cabins:** Overnighting in Nevada City in these rustic cabins and cozy Victorian-style rooms is like staying in an old-timey photograph (page 286).

★ **The Lark, Bozeman:** Local right down to the wonderful art on every wall, The Lark makes for an outstanding base camp for active, adventurous travelers (page 298).

★ **Element Bozeman:** Modern, sleek, and ideally situated in the heart of downtown Bozeman, Element is extremely comfortable and offers such amenities as cruiser bikes and a saltwater pool (page 298).

easily spend three days here, checking out the arts scene and nightlife and enjoying the spectacular recreational opportunities in every direction.

Bigfork

Arguably the most beautiful of the lakeside hamlets, year-round resort town Bigfork (population 4,270; elevation 2,979 ft/908 m) was named for its location along the fork of the Swan River. At the northeast corner of Flathead Lake, Bigfork has unlimited outdoor recreation opportunities, a handsome offering of live theater, art, fine dining, boutique shopping, and elegant accommodations. The feeling here is of an East Coast beach village 50 years ago—small, quaint, and lovely.

Getting to Bigfork

From **West Glacier,** Bigfork is 40 miles (64 km) south on U.S. 2 and MT-35, a drive of about an hour. From **Kalispell,** Bigfork is 20 miles (32 km) south on U.S. 93 and east on MT-82, a 25-minute drive.

From **Polson,** Bigfork is 35 miles (56 km) north on MT-35 (also known as the East Shore Route, as it parallels the eastern shore of Flathead Lake), a 45-minute drive.

Entertainment and Events

The repertory theater at **Bigfork Summer Playhouse** (526 Electric Ave., 406/837-4886, www.bigforksummerplayhouse.com, performances 8pm Mon.-Sat. plus occasional matinees 2pm Sun., mid-May-Labor Day, $26-30 adults, $22-26 seniors 65 and older, $17 children 10 and under) is a standout in the Northwest. For more

Cherry Picking

Picking fresh, sweet Flathead cherries, or just eating them, is an idyllic way to spend an afternoon. Several orchards dot the east side of the lake between Polson and Bigfork, so don't be shy about stopping at roadside stands to do a little taste-testing; in this valley, you can't go wrong. The primary harvest is late July through mid-August. The average season lasts just 7-10 days.

Try **Bowman Orchards** (19944 East Shore Rd./MT-35, 10 mi/16.1 km south of Bigfork at mile marker 21.5 on the east shore of Flathead, 406/982-3246, 9am-6pm daily), a family-owned business since 1921 that grows a variety of cherries and sells both the fresh fruit and a number of delicious cherry products.

Hockaday Orchards (45 Hockaday Ln., Lakeside, 406/844-3547, www. hockadayorchards.com, 8am-6pm daily as long as crop lasts) lets cherry lovers climb ladders to harvest their own crop. Bring your own bucket or box, as the cherries will get crushed in a bag. At just $1.25 per pound, you can afford to eat cherries all day long.

than 50 years the company has been staging award-winning productions of musical classics like *Fiddler on the Roof, Dirty Rotten Scoundrels,* and *Sugar Babies.* The contemporary theater is quite comfortable and roomy with 400 seats and air-conditioning. Also running all summer in Bigfork is the **Riverbend Concert Series** (Everit Slider Park, 406/837-5888, www.bigfork.org, 7pm Sun. late-June-late-Aug., $3 adults, $1 children), held every Sunday. The bring-your-own-seating concerts range from jazz to big band and light opera.

Sports and Recreation
★ Hiking at Jewel Basin
One of the best and most memorable places in the state to hike is **Jewel Basin** (Forest Rd. 5392, 10 mi/16.1 km northeast of Bigfork, 406/387-3800, www. fs.usda.gov), a wilderness area with high peaks, lush forests, 27 lakes, and 35 miles (56 km) of dedicated hiking trails. Camping is permitted, and the trails can be crowded on weekends. Some of the best day hikes include those into **Black Lake** (8 mi/12.9 km round-trip), the **Jewel Lakes** (9 mi/14.5 km round-trip), or the **Twin Lakes** (5 mi/8 km round-trip). The best map for the area is published by the Glacier National Park Conservancy (406/892-3250, www.glacier.org). Note

that grizzlies frequent the area, particularly in late summer when the huckleberries are ripe.

Boating
In Bigfork, you can rent ski boats, WaveRunners, kayaks, paddleboards, and pontoon boats from **Bigfork Outdoor Rentals** (110 Swan River Rd., 406/837-2498, www.bigforkoutdoorrentals.com) and have them delivered. At **Marina Cay Resort** (180 Vista Ln., 406/837-5861, www.marinacay.com), you can also rent a variety of watercraft, including fishing charters. For more information on Flathead Lake and the work being done to protect it, contact the nonprofit **Flathead Lakers** (406/883-1346, www. flatheadlakers.org).

Shopping
In tiny Bigfork, art is the thing, so stop in at a few galleries during your visit. You could cover the entire town, easily, in a day. Several artists have their own galleries in Bigfork to represent their work exclusively. Other galleries include **Collage Gallery** (573 Electric Ave., 406/837-0866, www.collagebigfork.com, 11am-5pm Mon.-Sat., noon-4pm Sun. May-Dec.), which offers rolling shows every month in addition to an eclectic and handsome collection of antiquities, books, Mexican

textiles, and works by deceased masters. The colorful and playful **ArtFusion** (471 Electric Ave., 406/837-3526, www.bigforkartfusion.com, 10am-5:30pm Mon.-Sat., 11am-5pm Sun.) represents more than 60 Montana artists including ceramicists, painters, jewelers, and photographers.

Persimmon Gallery (537 Electric Ave., 406/837-2288, www.persimmongallery.com) has a wonderful collection of more than 70 Montana and Northwest artists working in such media as jewelry, painting, mixed media, ceramics, glass, and fabric. One favorite is Judy Colvin, from St. Ignatius, who uses wool from the sheep raised on their ranch to make felted items that include gorgeous purses, scarves, wraps, hats, and wall hangings.

Food

If you cannot survive on cherries alone, there are a number of good restaurants concentrated around Bigfork. Steeped in local history, **Bigfork Inn** (604 Electric Ave., 406/837-6680, 4:30pm-midnight daily, $17-36) is a lovely spot for a hearty meal. Choose from specialties like smoked mixed grill, Haus or Gypsy Schnitzel, Crispy Country Inn Duck, or prime rib.

Flathead Lake Brewing Company (116 Holt Dr., 406/837-2004, www.flatheadlakebrewing.com, 11am-10pm daily, $13-18) serves casual but delicious fare—seared scallops with beet puree, braised pork shank, rib eye, housemade pizzas and pastas—in a festive environment.

For breakfast and lunch, the hands-down favorite in the Flathead Valley is the ★ **Echo Lake Café** (1195 MT-83, 406/837-1000, www.echolakecafe.com, 6:30am-2:30pm daily, $6-14), where everything is homemade and fabulous. Be prepared to wait in line with locals for a table.

Top to bottom: trail in Jewel Basin; Seeley Lake; Holland Lake.

A wonderful spot for breakfast, lunch, and prepared foods to go is **Vessel** (8265 MT-35, 406/837-7070, www.vesselbigfork. com, 7am-7pm Mon.-Fri., 8am-7pm Sat.-Sun., $5.50-8.50, pizzas $10-19), which serves excellent breakfast burritos, sandwiches, salads, soups—all of it made fresh daily—and take-and-bake pizzas. Their coffee bar and tea list are outstanding, too.

Accommodations

Luxuriousness and prices rise as you get closer to Bigfork. Depending on the size of your group, a vacation rental can be the most economical choice. In addition to listings on Airbnb, there are a few vacation rental companies in town, including **Bayside Property Management** (406/883-4313, www. rentalsinpolson.com) and **Flathead Lake Vacation Rentals** (406/883-3253, www. flatheadvacationrentals.com), which offers a variety of properties around the lake.

Five miles (8 km) south of Bigfork, the **Mountain Lake Lodge** (14735 Sylvan Dr., 406/837-3800 or 877/823-4923, www. mountainlakelodge.com, $139-295) is elegant and cozy with great vistas of the lake and plenty of amenities, including an outdoor infinity pool, a hot tub, a putting green, and a fire pit along with two restaurants on-site. Pets are welcome in some rooms for $20 per day per pet. Also south of town, in an idyllic setting just a short walk from the pebbled shores of Flathead Lake, is **Flathead Lake Resort** (14871 MT-35, 406/837-3333, www. flatheadlakeresort.com, $68-298), which offers modest accommodations from queen motel rooms to two-bedroom cabins, plus RV and tent sites. Just down the road is the funky **Islander Inn** (14729 Shore Acres Dr., 406/837-5472, www. sleepeatdrink.com, $75-197), which boasts colorful and cozy boutique-style bungalows, each designed to reflect various islands: Anguilla, Crete, Jamaica, Maui, Wild Horse, Zanzibar, or Bali. A gift shop, bakery, and restaurant are on the property, so you may not want to leave.

Right in town, and on the water, is the **Marina Cay Resort** (180 Vista Ln., 406/837-5861, www.marinacay.com, $109-545). The largest property in the vicinity, and the hub of water sports activities, Marina Cay boasts a number of accommodations, including condos and townhomes, as well as dining. The resort is within easy walking of the lake and the town's shops and restaurants.

For a phenomenal guest ranch experience, **Averill's Flathead Lake Lodge** (150 Flathead Lodge Rd., 406/837-4391, www. flatheadlakelodge, weeklong all-inclusive trips from $3,998 adults, $2,984 children 6-17, $1,675 children 3-5, $200 infants) is a historic family ranch set right on the water. From sailing to horseback riding, fly-fishing to mountain biking, this ranch is exceptional.

Camping

If you can get a tent site, camping is one of the best ways to stay as close to Flathead Lake as possible and truly enjoy the region. Among the most popular campgrounds is that at **Wayfarers State Park** (8600 MT-35, 0.5 mi/0.8 km south of Bigfork, 406/837-4196, www.stateparks. mt.gov/wayfarers, mid-Mar.-mid-Nov., $10-72). All state parks and their camping amenities can be seen online at www. stateparks.mt.gov.

Information and Services

The **Bigfork Area Chamber of Commerce and Visitor's Center** (Old Town Center, 8155 MT-35, 406/837-5888, www.bigfork. org, 9am-5pm Mon.-Fri., 10am-3pm Sat.-Sun. Memorial Day-Labor Day, 10am-2pm daily Labor Day-Memorial Day) is open to visitors on the east side of Flathead Lake.

Kalispell Regional Medical Center (310 Sunnyview Ln., Kalispell, 406/752-5111, www.krh.org) is 20 miles (32 km) north of Bigfork, just north of downtown Kalispell.

⏏ Detour: The Seeley-Swan Valley

Much quieter than Flathead and nestled in between the magnificent Mission and Swan mountain ranges, the Seeley-Swan Valley is a remarkable destination. Visitors feel like they are stepping back in time 50 years or more. There are unlikely to be any towns you've ever heard of in this valley, and no chain hotels, fast-food restaurants, or interstate highways. Instead you'll find pristine lakes and seemingly endless forests, wonderful old lodges, and timeless guest ranches. The communities in this valley—Swan Lake (pop. 113), Condon (pop. 351), and Seeley Lake (pop. 1,659)—are old timber camps that now cater to lake-loving summer crowds and outdoors enthusiasts, cross-country skiers, and snowmobilers.

This is a place to spend lazy lakeside days and cozy fireside evenings, and if lazy isn't your style, there are mountains in every direction for hiking as well as rivers and lakes for boating and fishing.

The 91-mile (147 km) stretch of Highway 83 through the Seeley-Swan Valley is the shortest route between Yellowstone and Glacier National Parks. The scenery and solitude make the trip worthwhile.

Getting to the Seeley-Swan Valley

The Seeley-Swan Valley is a 91-mile (147-km) corridor along Highway 83 between the Mission Mountains to the west and the Swan Mountains to the east.

From the north, U.S. 93 in Kalispell accesses Highway 82, which then turns into Highway 83. From Kalispell to Swan Lake, the distance is 35 miles (56 km), about a 40-minute drive. From Swan Lake to Seeley Lake, it's 57 miles (92 km) south, a one-hour drive.

From Missoula, Highway 200 leads to Highway 83. From Missoula to Seeley Lake, it's 55 miles (89 km), a one-hour drive.

Swan Lake

An hour's drive north of Seeley Lake and 16 miles (26 km) south of Bigfork is the quaint little village of Swan Lake (population 113; elevation 3,198 ft/975 m), on Highway 83 at the southern end of the lake of the same name. The area is a natural stopping point for migrating birds, making the Swan River National Wildlife Refuge a wonderful place for avid birders. The lake itself offers excellent fishing for northern pike, kokanee salmon, and rainbow trout. A few services are available in town, including lodging and dining options, but most people come to Swan Lake for recreation. There are 50 miles (81 km) of trails for cross-country skiers and many options for hiking.

Sports and Recreation

From Swan Lake, numerous lengthy trails get hikers and horseback riders into the Bob Marshall Wilderness Complex. The **Upper Holland Loop,** beginning from a trailhead on the north shore of Holland Lake, is a steep and rugged trail that climbs nearly 4,000 feet (1,219 m) over nearly 7 miles (11.3 km) or 13.3 miles (21.4 km) round-trip; it can be tackled on a well-planned full-day hike. The trail passes the Sapphire Lakes and Upper Holland Lake before descending again along Holland Creek. For maps and information, contact the **Swan Lake Ranger District** (200 Ranger Station Rd., off MT-35, Bigfork, 406/837-7500).

The **Swan River National Wildlife Refuge** (MT-83, 1 mi/1.6 km south of Swan Lake, 406/727-7400, www.fws.gov/refuge/swan_river) is nearly 1,800 acres of glacially carved grassy floodplain that provides habitat for more than 170 species of birds, including waterfowl, bald eagles, various types of hawks, owls, and songbirds. The bald eagles generally arrive in February, and visitors can often see eaglets fledging in mid-May. There are also plenty of other animals—moose, elk, beavers, bobcats, and the occasional grizzly bear—wandering through this quiet and undeveloped place. The refuge is closed for nesting season (Mar. 1-July 15), except for the viewing platforms.

Swan Mountain Outfitters (26356 Soup Creek Rd., on MT-83 between mile markers 64 and 65, 406/387-4405, www. swanmountainoutfitters.com) offers everything from two-hour trail rides ($70) in the national forest to daylong rides into Glacier ($255) to six-day pack fishing trips ($2,220/person). It also leads dinner rides, llama treks, and snowmobiling adventures in winter.

Food and Accommodations

The **Laughing Horse Lodge** (71284 MT-83, Swan Lake, 406/886-2080, www. laughinghorselodge.com, restaurant 5pm-9pm Wed.-Sun. May.-Dec., hours and days can vary, $14-38; lodge May-Dec., $126-495) is a wonderful place to eat, and you can stay here as well. Chef Kathleen cooks up everything from double-frenched pork chops to huckleberry peach pie. On the second and fourth Tuesday between late June and September, the lodge hosts a six-course tasting menu spotlighting cuisine and wines from around the globe. These nights are limited to 32 diners and sell out months in advance, so book ahead. The lodge is a cozy and fun bed-and-breakfast where pets are welcome and the activity menu is unlimited.

Camping

The **Swan Lake Campground** (MT-83, Swan Lake, 877/444-6777, www. recreation.gov, $18) is a Forest Service campground 0.5 mile (0.8 km) northwest of Swan Lake on Highway 83.

Condon

Just 27 miles (43 km) up Highway 83 from Seeley Lake is tiny Condon (population 351; elevation 3,785 ft/1,154 m), another gem in the string of lake towns between the Mission and Swan Ranges. Condon is surrounded by the Mission Mountains Wilderness Area to the west and the Bob Marshall Wilderness Complex to the east, making the region a favorite for outdoor recreation. Holland Lake is a gorgeous 400-acre lake with prime opportunities for fishing and boating.

Sports and Recreation

The stunning **Holland Lake** is the main attraction here and offers plenty of recreational opportunities, including boating, fishing, and swimming. The relatively easy and well-traveled **Holland Falls Trail** leads hikers on a 3-mile (4.8-km) round-trip hike to a waterfall. From the trailhead on Holland Lake Road just beyond the Holland Lake Campground, the trail skirts the north shore of the lake and climbs roughly 600 feet (183 m) before reaching the 40-foot (12.2-m) falls. There are natural seating areas for picnickers and waterfall gazers. The trail is often used by outfitters packing into Upper Holland Lake and the Bob Marshall Wilderness Complex.

Food and Accommodations

For a hearty meal, the **Hungry Bear Steakhouse** (6287 MT-83, between mile markers 38 and 39, 406/754-2240, 8am-9pm daily, $18-23) serves steak, seafood, and pizza with a full-service bar and kids' menu. Breakfast ($4.25-9) and lunch ($7-11) are served as well.

The **Swan Valley Cafe** (6798 MT-83, 406/754-3663, 8am-3pm Sat.-Thurs., 8am-8pm Fri. May-Nov., $6-21) is a great family-style restaurant with a six-page menu that is sure to please.

For a real culinary and visual treat, dine lakeside on gourmet fare at ★ **Holland Lake Lodge** (1947 Holland Lake Rd., 406/754-2282, www.hollandlakelodge. com, restaurant 8:30am-9:45am, noon-2pm, and 5:45pm-8:45pm daily mid-June-late Oct.; lodge cabins $320, lodge rooms $200). The beautiful inn serves breakfast ($6-12), lunch ($7-15), and dinner ($23-35) with entrées like gruyère egg bake, green chili burger with cheese and lodge salsa, and pecan-crusted pork tenderloin. Reservations are required, as hours can change depending on special events and guest occupancy. The exclusive lodge is the fanciest in the region. Its rates include phenomenal meals. Activity options at this lakefront idyll include hiking, canoeing, horseback riding, swimming, fishing float trips, and float plane excursions. The cabins are modest for the steep price, but the meals, scenery, and solitude more than make up for it.

Camping

The **Holland Lake Campground** (Holland Lake Rd., 406/646-1012, www.recreation. gov, Memorial Day-Labor Day, $18) has 40 sites, flush toilets, and lake access.

Seeley Lake

Seeley Lake (population 1,659; elevation 4,028 ft/1,228 m) is clearly a recreation town, and the lake itself is among the chain of lakes through which the Clearwater River flows. A resort town in the most classic sense—think rustic lodges and lakeside retreats with cabins dotting the forest—Seeley Lake is popular but relatively uncrowded. There are plenty of fish in the lake, including bass, kokanee salmon, bull trout, perch, and bluegills, in addition to year-round activities that include boating, hiking, excellent cross-country skiing, and snowmobiling.

Sports and Recreation

Boating

The **Clearwater Canoe Trail** is a 3.5-mile (5.6-km) stretch of flatwater that takes paddlers down the Clearwater River from north of the town of Seeley Lake and into the lake itself. Magnificent wildflowers, a variety of birds, and other wildlife are often seen along the way. A canoe trip takes 1-2 hours. A roughly 1-mile (1.6-km) hiking trail alongside the river leads paddlers back to the trailhead parking

lot. Canoes ($25 for 4 hours, $40 for 8 hours, $55 overnight) and other sporting equipment, including ski boats, pontoon boats, rafts, kayaks, paddleboards, and WaveRunners can be rented from **Rocky Mountain Adventure Gear** (3192 MT-83 S., 406/677-8300, www.rockymtngear. com, 9am-6pm daily).

Hiking and Biking

Among the most popular hiking trails in the region is the **Morrell Lake and Falls Trail,** a 5-mile (8-km) round-trip hike on relatively even terrain to a beautiful mountain lake and a series of towering cascades, the largest of which is 90 feet (27 m) high. From Seeley Lake, drive north less than 0.5 mile (0.8 km) to Morrell Creek Road (also known as Cottonwood Lakes Rd. or Forest Rd. 477). Turn right (east), drive 1.1 miles (1.8 km) to the junction of West Morrell Road, and turn left. Drive 5.6 miles (9 km) to another junction and turn right. Drive 0.7 mile (1.1 km) to the trailhead. The trail is well marked and follows the creek to a pond, Morrell Lake, and then the falls.

Near the western shore of the lake, a mile-long nature trail loops through **Girard Grove** and leads to what is thought to be the largest larch tree in the world. Known as **Gus,** the western larch species (also known as tamarack) is 163 feet (50 m) high, has a crown diameter of 34 feet (10.4 m), a circumference of 273 inches (693 cm), and is considered to be around 1,000 years old. Larch trees are special in that their needles turn gold in the fall and drop, meaning it's a faux evergreen that's actually a deciduous tree.

Mountain biking is permitted on a variety of Forest Service roads and trails, including a 14-mile (22.5 km) round-trip ride at the **Seeley Creek Nordic Ski Trails** (www.seeleylakenordic.org). From Highway 83, turn east onto Morrell Creek Road (also known as Cottonwood Lakes Rd. or Forest Rd. 477) and drive 1.1 miles (1.8 km) to the trailhead on the north side of the road. Bikes can be rented from **Rocky Mountain Adventure Gear** (3192 MT-83 S., 406/677-8300, www.rockymtngear.com, 9am-6pm daily, $20 for 4 hours, $30 for 8 hours, $40 overnight, $185 weekly). It also offers guide services for any kind of adventure you want to have.

For more information on Forest Service trails, contact the **Seeley Lake Ranger District** (3583 MT-83, 406/677-2233, www.fs.usda.gov).

Winter Recreation

Seeley Lake is a cross-country skier's paradise. Several of the local resorts, including the **Double Arrow Lodge** (301 Lodge Way, 2 mi/3.2 km south of Seeley Lake, 406/677-2777 or 800/468-0777, www.doublearrowresort.com), offer groomed ski trails. The cream of the crop in this region is the **Seeley Creek Nordic Ski Trails** (www.seeleylakenordic.org). This trail system has been under development since the 1970s, initially created from old logging camps and hilly logging roads, and has a degree of difficulty that resulted in the slogan, "Get good or eat wood." With 20 miles (32 km) of groomed classic and skate trails that can be combined to form some impressive routes, the area offers something for every ability level, and an annual 50-kilometer race is held the last Saturday in January. From Highway 83, turn east onto Morrell Creek Road (also known as Cottonwood Lakes Rd. or Forest Rd. 477) and drive 1.1 miles (1.8 km) to the trailhead on the north side of the road. Nearby are dogsled and snowmobile trails.

For backcountry skiers who want plenty of adventure with a side of luxury, **Yurtski** (406/721-1779, www.yurtski.com) offers a wide range of services. From extraordinary guided trips for newer skiers to gourmet-catered trips, self-service trips, or just shuttling gear, Carl and his team make use of their awesome backcountry yurts, local knowledge, and mad culinary skills.

Around Seeley Lake are more than 350 miles (565 km) of snowmobile trails. For information on specific trails and snowmobile-specific maps, contact the **Lolo National Forest** (3583 MT-83, 406/677-2233, www.fs.usda.gov/lolo). Snowmobiles, as well as snowshoe packages, snowbikes, ice fishing gear, and guided tours, are available at **Rocky Mountain Adventure Gear** (3192 MT-83 S., 406/677-8300, www.rockymtngear.com, 9am-6pm daily).

Food

In Seeley Lake, the local favorite is the lakefront **Lindey's Prime Steak House** (MT-83, 406/677-9229, 5pm-10pm daily May-Sept., 5pm-9pm daily Oct.-May, $23-31), where the steaks are of the same caliber as the great view. There is not much on the menu besides steak, but meat lovers will be exceedingly happy with this authentic Montana steak house. Another reliable spot for a meal in Seeley Lake almost any time of day is the **Filling Station Restaurant** (3189 MT-83, 406/677-2080, 11am-2am Mon.-Fri., 8am-2am Sat.-Sun., $7-12.50); the bar offers karaoke on Friday and Saturday nights.

The award-winning menu and wine list in the Double Arrow Resort's **Seasons Restaurant** (301 Lodge Way, 2 mi/3.2 km south of Seeley Lake, 406/677-2777, www.doublearrowresort.com/dining, $23-30) feature classic country cuisine—from rattlesnake and rabbit sausage to baby back ribs and bison tri-tip—in a welcoming and warm environment.

Accommodations

For the most part, the accommodations in the Seeley-Swan Valley are lovely and somewhat rustic. The **Double Arrow Resort** (301 Lodge Way, 2 mi/3.2 km south of Seeley Lake, 406/677-2777, www.doublearrowresort.com, cabins $100-800, main lodge rooms $110-165) is a handsome log lodge with history and character in a ranch-like setting. The accommodations are beautiful cabins and lodge rooms, all with private baths. A variety of activities, including fishing, golf, sleigh rides, horseback riding, and winter sports, can be arranged on-site. Another great old-school family resort in the area is **Tamaracks Resort** (3481 MT-83 N., 406/677-2433 or 800/477-7216, www.tamaracks.com, $145-450), which has 17 great old-school cabins that can accommodate up to 10 people. RV sites are also available as are boat rentals.

Seeley Lake Motor Lodge (3206 MT-83 N., 406/677-2335, www.seeleylakemotorlodge.com, $60-70 winter, $110-145 summer) is what good roadside motels used to be: comfortable, clean, and convenient.

Camping

With so much public forest and wilderness in the vicinity, the multitude of camping options in the area attracts large numbers of campers on summer weekends. **Placid Lake State Park** (5001 N. Placid Lake Rd., 406/542-5500, $14-28) has 40 sites, flush toilets, and drinking water; it is 3 miles (4.8 km) south of Seeley Lake on Highway 83, then 3 miles (4.8 km) west on a county road. **Salmon Lake State Park** (2329 MT-83, 5 mi/8 km south of Seeley Lake, 406/677-6804, May-Nov., $10-34) is another of the better options.

Polson

Polson feels like the kind of town where there is almost always a fair going on or some other reason to celebrate. Historically the economy has been based on lumber, steamboat trade, and ranching. Founded around a trading post at the southern end of Flathead Lake in 1880, the town was named for David Polson, a local rancher who married a Nez Perce woman and who played the fiddle at dances and powwows across the region. Settlement from 1910 greatly increased the size of the town, and when much of the state was losing population during the Great Depression, Polson actually doubled in size with farmers who came to try their luck with the Flathead Irrigation Project and people seeking work at the Kerr Dam construction project.

Today, Polson (population 4,777; elevation 2,931 ft/893 m) is a lakeside town, the heart of Montana's cherry-growing district, and the busiest town along Flathead Lake. Its proximity to the magnificent lake, the Flathead River, and the Mission Mountains makes Polson a natural playground.

Just over a dozen miles south of Polson, Ronan was settled in 1883 and provides excellent access to the Mission Mountains Wilderness Area and the Ninepipe and Pablo National Wildlife Refuge complex.

Getting to Polson

From **Bigfork,** Polson is 35 miles (56 km) south on U.S. 93 (also known as the East Shore Route), a 45-minute drive.

From **St. Ignatius,** Polson is 30 miles (48 km) north on U.S. 93, a 35-minute drive.

Sights
Miracle of America Museum

An eclectic little museum, to say the least, the **Miracle of America Museum** (36094 Memory Ln., 406/883-6804, www.miracleofamericamuseum.org, 9am-5pm daily, $6 adults, $3 children 2-12) likes to think of itself as the "Smithsonian of the West." Indeed, the founders were passionate collectors of Western artifacts, and the inspired museum is packed to the rafters with more than 100,000 objects including moonshine stills, antique motorcycles, entire buildings, and military paraphernalia. The museum is kid friendly, with coin-operated music machines and other paraphernalia children love. Behind the main building is the museum's Pioneer Village, which has 35 buildings spread across four acres. There's a helicopter to play in, a replica of Laura Ingalls Wilder's sod-roofed home, and a couple of kiddie trains that still operate.

Entertainment and Events

The biggest event of the year in Polson is probably the **Polson Main Street Flathead Cherry Festival** (Main St., 406/883-3667, www.flatheadcherryfestival.com). It has a fair-like environment and celebrates everything cherry, with pie-eating contests, seed-spitting contests, exhibitions, and entertainment throughout the weekend. The event is typically held the third weekend in July, and it is among the best ways to enjoy the phenomenal cherry harvest.

Sports and Recreation
Boating

Polson offers rafting opportunities on the warm, clear lower **Flathead River.** The only outfitter on the river, **Flathead Raft Company** (50362 U.S. 93 N., 406/883-5838 or 800/654-4359, www.flatheadraftco.com, full-day raft trips $80 adults, $65 children 6-12, full-day kayak trips $99 adults, $89 children 8-12, paddleboard rentals $30 half day), offers great scenic and white-water trips as well as white-water kayak instruction, river-boarding, or sea-kayaking trips on **Flathead Lake.**

A couple of outfits rent boats in Polson, including **Absolute Watersports Rentals** (303 U.S. 93, Somers, 406/883-3900) and the **Flathead Boat Company** (50230 U.S. 93 S., 406/883-0999, www.flatheadboatcompany.com, $250-350 for 4 hours).

Shopping

A good place to stop in Polson for some warm Montana bedding is **Three Dog Down** (48841 U.S. 93, 406/883-3696 or 800/364-3696, www.threedogdown.com, 9am-6pm daily), known in the region for custom-made comforters and pillows. Shopping here is a Montana experience—you can buy everything from soap to moccasins to saltwater taffy—and bargain hunters should know that singing

From an overlook near Polson, fog blankets Flathead Lake.

the "Star-Spangled Banner" will earn you a discount. A number of art galleries, gift shops, and jewelry stores are also in town.

Food

Lovers of all things pink will delight in the pinkaliciousness at **Betty's Diner** (49779 U.S. 93, 406/883-1717, www. bettysdiner.net, 7am-8pm Mon.-Sat., 7am-3pm Sun.). The goodness starts with breakfast ($6-11), including specialties for "kids and old farts." Lunch ($8-10) includes such classic diner favorites as burgers, cheesesteaks, patty melts, and other sandwiches. Dinner ($10.50-15) is everything from New York strip to shrimp baskets and chicken-fried steak.

For authentic Thai food, try **Hot Spot Thai** (50440 U.S. 93, 406/883-4444, 11:30am-2:30pm and 5pm-8pm daily, $10.50-13). It has a wonderful Thai chef and is open for lunch, dinner, and takeout. The spot doesn't have a liquor license, but diners can bring their own wine.

Lake City Bakery & Eatery (49493 U.S. 93, 406/883-5667, 7am-3pm daily, $7-12) is a wonderful spot for breakfast all day or lunch. The great old brick building was a grocery store in 1939. Everything is made from scratch.

For a great beer, try **Glacier Brewing Company** (6 10th Ave. E., 406/883-2595, www.glacierbrewing.com, 3pm-8pm Tues.-Sat.), a German-style alehouse serving its own impressive line of beer and homemade soda. Hours here change with the seasons and without advance notice, but are posted on the restaurant's Facebook page.

Accommodations

Plenty of choices for lodging exist in Polson and Bigfork, but a room with a view in these parts can get pretty expensive. Among the best bargains in the area is the rustic **Mission Mountain Resort** (3 minutes from Polson on MT-35, 406/883-1883, www.polsonmtresort.com, from $80-200 for 2 people, $10 each additional person), a collection of cabins and lodge rooms on 80 acres set back from the lake.

The waterfront **Best Western KwaTaqNuk Resort and Casino** (49708 U.S. 93 E., 406/883-3636 or 800/882-6363, www.kwataqnuk.com, $180-319), which is owned and operated by the Flathead Nation, has 107 guest rooms and an extensive menu of activities that includes lake cruises, boat rentals, fishing tours, and plenty of gaming at the on-site casino. Pets are permitted for a $20-per-night fee.

For standard pet-friendly accommodations right on the lake, try **America's Best Value Port Polson Inn** (49825 U.S. 93, 406/883-5385 or 800/654-0682, www. bestvalueinn.com, $112-124).

Camping

If you can get a tent site, camping is one of the best ways to stay as close to Flathead Lake as possible and truly enjoy the region. Among the most popular campgrounds are those at **Finley Point**

State Park (31543 S. Finley Point Rd., 11 mi/17.7 km north of Polson, then 4 mi/6.4 km west on County Rd., 406/887-2715, May-Sept., $10-72) and **Yellow Bay State Park** (23861 MT-35, 15 mi/24 km north of Polson at mile marker 17, 406/982-3034, mid-May-mid-Sept., $10-72). All state parks and their camping amenities can be seen online at www.stateparks.mt.gov.

Information and Services
The **Polson Chamber of Commerce** (418 Main St., 406/883-5969, www.polsonchamber.com, 10am-3pm Mon.-Fri., 10am-2pm Sat. Memorial Day-Labor Day, 10am-2pm Mon.-Fri. Labor Day-Memorial Day) is an excellent resource for the south end of the Flathead Valley.

Ronan
Named for the region's first Indian agent, Major Peter Ronan, who wrote the history of the Flathead people and was respected by them, the town of Ronan (population 2,016; elevation 3,048 ft/929 m) was once part of the Flathead Reservation before it was opened to sale and settlement in 1910.

Ronan's history is marked by tragedy and travesty. In 1912, a fire erupted in an automobile garage on a particularly windy afternoon. Within hours, the entire town lay in ruins. In June 1929, a robbery at the Ronan State Bank made a group of seven 20-something robbers $3,000 richer. They went on a spree of robberies across the state with police always a few steps behind. Eventually all but the ringleader were caught and either killed during the pursuit or sent to prison. A woman who accompanied them, known dramatically as "the woman in white," was eventually found murdered in a Helena brothel.

Today, Ronan is known for its proximity to two of the state's most beautiful

wildlife refuges: the Ninepipe National Wildlife Refuge and, farther south, the National Bison Range.

Ninepipe National Wildlife Refuge
Five miles (8 km) south of Ronan and just north of the National Bison Range on land of the Confederated Salish and Kootenai Tribes, the **Ninepipe National Wildlife Refuge** (www.fws.gov/refuge/nine-pipe) is a waterfowl preserve. Established in 1921, these wetlands are at the base of the Mission Mountains and situated around a large reservoir. The marshlands are difficult to walk through, but good bird-watching is possible from the road that runs along the reservoir. The refuge is situated on a popular migratory path for numerous birds, including mallards, gadwalls, great blue herons, and swans. It has become an important breeding and resting area for the Flathead Valley Canada goose population. The refuge is closed during waterfowl hunting season (fall) and the nesting season (spring).

Ninepipes Museum of Early Montana
The **Ninepipes Museum of Early Montana** (69316 U.S. 93, Charlo, 406/644-3435, www.ninepipesmuseum.org, 9am-5pm Mon.-Sat. Mar.-Oct., $7 adults, $6 seniors and veterans, $5 students, $3 children 6-12, group rates available) is halfway between Missoula and Kalispell next to the Ninepipe waterfowl refuge. It documents daily life on the Flathead Reservation over the last 100-plus years and even includes a complete replica of a Native American camp. In addition to Native American life, the history of early trappers, miners, loggers, and ranchers is on display, including photos, artwork, costumes, and artifacts from people in these different walks of life.

St. Ignatius

The oldest town on the Flathead Reservation, and among the oldest settlements in the state, St. Ignatius (population 824; elevation 2,939 ft/896 m) is the site of the St. Ignatius Mission, built in 1854 by Jesuit priest Adrian Hoecken, who moved from Washington State to be closer to the indigenous people he wanted to reach. The town grew quickly as nearly 1,000 Native Americans resettled near the mission, and in 1864 a group of nuns added schools and a hospital to the community.

The building considered to be the oldest in the state, constructed in 1846, is at Fort Connah, just 6 miles (9.7 km) north of St. Ignatius on U.S. 93. It is all that remains of the last trading post built in the United States by the Hudson's Bay Company. The post was in operation until 1871.

Getting to St. Ignatius

From **Polson,** St. Ignatius is 30 miles (48 km) south on U.S. 93, a 35-minute drive. From **Missoula,** St. Ignatius is 40 miles (64 km) north on U.S. 93, a 45-minute drive.

Sights
St. Ignatius Mission

The beloved redbrick chapel standing today on the **St. Ignatius Mission** (300 Bear Track Ave., 406/745-2768, 9am-7pm daily summer, 9am-5pm daily winter, mass 9am Sun., free, donations accepted) was built in the 1890s, but the mission itself was settled as early as 1854 by Jesuit priest Adrian Hoecken and hundreds of Native Americans who set up camp near him. In 1864, a group of nuns from Montreal, the Sisters of Providence,

Top to bottom: Ninepipe National Wildlife Refuge; bison on the National Bison Range; kayaking on Brennan's Wave in downtown Missoula.

came to the mission to open a boarding school for girls, a hospital, and eventually, with the help of Ursuline nuns, an orphanage, a kindergarten, and a school for boys. At its peak in the mid-1890s, some 320 children attended school at the mission. The school was burned to the ground in 1919 and never reopened. There is a dark history of child abuse that is not acknowledged at the site. Court records and newspaper clippings from as recently as 2018 show that Jesuit nuns and priests at the mission were perpetrating terrible crimes against the children they were supposed to be caring for.

The brick chapel was completed in 1894 with 58 original murals painted by Joseph Carignano, who worked in the kitchen and as a handyman for the mission. Carignano taught himself to paint and managed to complete the frescoes in only 14 months despite working on them only when he wasn't doing his primary job. The paintings tell the life story of St. Ignatius Loyola. Restoration of the murals began in the summer of 2018. Because of plaster's sensitivity to temperature, restoration can only take place during the summer. Church officials hope the restoration will be completed by 2020.

In addition to the chapel, a small museum and gift shop can be found in the log house that was the original residence of the Sisters of Providence.

★ National Bison Range

Established in 1908 when the population of bison across North America had dropped from upward of 30 million animals down to just a few hundred, the **National Bison Range** (58355 Bison Range Rd., 406/644-2211, www.fws.gov, gate hours 6:30am-10pm daily summer, exact hours vary depending on sunlight, year-round, $5/vehicle May-Oct.) is one of the oldest animal refuges in the country and well worth a visit. Located off Highway 212 in Moiese, the refuge comprises 18,500 acres and is home to around

400 bison, not to mention white-tailed and mule deer, bighorn sheep, pronghorn, and elk.

There are two driving routes: The year-round West Loop and Prairie Drive is a short 5-mile (8-km) tour that takes about 30 minutes; the other, Red Sleep Mountain Drive, is a 17-mile (27-km) one-way loop that climbs about 2,000 feet (610 m) and takes close to two hours. The longer route, open in summer, is incredibly scenic and definitely worth the time. The roads through the refuge are gravel; no bicycles or motorcycles are permitted on them, but parking is available at the **visitors center** (9am-5pm daily). Several short hiking trails leave from the day-use area as well as from Red Sleep Mountain Drive.

Before beginning your tour, stop in at the visitors center for informative displays, knowledgeable park rangers, and a large relief map of the refuge marked with small lights indicating where bison can likely be seen that day.

Shopping

The **Four Winds Indian Trading Post** (U.S. 93, 3 mi/4.8 km north of St. Ignatius, 406/745-4336, www.fourwindsindiantradingpost.com, 10am-6pm daily summer, noon-5pm daily winter) is the oldest operating Indian trading post in the state. Opened in 1870, the Four Winds has long supplied local Native Americans with a variety of wares, including beads, face paint, animal hides, and dance bells. The store is authentic and sells traditional Native American crafts alongside history books and made-in-Montana products.

Food and Accommodations

Ten minutes south of St. Ignatius, in the tiny town of Ravalli, is ★ **Windmill Village Bakery** (26715 U.S. 93, 406/745-2270, www.windmillvillagebakery.com, 7am-3pm Tues.-Sat. Apr.-Oct.), a pastry lover's paradise. There is often a line (in the middle of nowhere!) for the

Powwows

Drumming is an important component of powwows.

There is some debate as to how powwows got their name. Some argue it comes from the word *pa-wa,* the Pawnee word for "to eat." Others suggest the word descends from the Algonquin word *pauau,* which suggests a gathering of people for celebration. Either way, powwows are a time for gathering, celebrating, and honoring traditions. Many contemporary powwows include dancing, singing and drumming contests, encampments, feasting, parades, and more.

When you're attending a powwow as a spectator, remember that your role is to be a respectful observer. Photographs are often allowed, unless the announcer says otherwise, but it's always a good idea to ask before you snap a picture. Be sure not to use a flash in a dancer's face. Don't enter the dance floor unless you are invited to do so. Be mindful that food booths, raffle ticket sales, and art and crafts booths are often needed to defray the costs of the powwow, so support them when you can. Be patient and don't expect all the events to start when the program says they will.

One of the most important events on the Flathead Reservation is the annual **Fourth of July Powwow** (888/835-8766, www.arleepowwow.com) at Arlee. The celebration has played out each year since 1898 with camping, competition dancing, drumming and singing, traditional games, and a host of food and arts and crafts vendors. Though the U.S government ban on "Indian doings" in the 19th and 20th centuries forbade such celebrations, Native Americans held the event on the Fourth of July so that the Army would see it as a patriotic display.

The **People's Center Annual Powwow** (53253 U.S. 93, Pablo, 406/675-0160) is held the third Saturday in August in nearby Pablo. Not a competition, like many powwows, at this celebration dancers and drum groups are gifted honorariums. There are also booths selling beadwork, local art and food.

glazed doughnuts, which are made as you watch and served warm. They are big as a child's head; you won't eat more than one. And next time you're in Montana, you'll drive hours out of your way to have another one.

There are a handful of places to stay in the vicinity of St. Ignatius, including the no-frills, roadside **Sunset Motel** (333 Mountain View Dr., 406/745-3900, $74-111).

The **Bear Spirit Lodge B&B** (38712 St. Mary's Lake Rd., 406/745-3089, www. bearspiritlodge.com, $119-122) is a cozy place in a phenomenal setting, and the hosts, Ann and Great Bear, are beyond compare. Take a sauna or a hot tub under the starry skies, and you will never want to leave this welcoming place.

About 12 miles (19.3 km) up the road in Charlo is **Ninepipes Lodge** (69286 MT-93, 406/644-2588, www.ninepipeslodge. com, $94-183), set against the backdrop of the Mission Mountains and adjacent to the Ninepipes Reservoir. It's a full-service resort with a great restaurant, **Allentown Restaurant** (breakfast $7-13, lunch $9-15, dinner $15-27), serving steaks, pasta, seafood, and salads. On warm nights, eat outside on the deck overlooking the kettle pond with unrivaled mountain views.

Missoula

Given its site at the hub of five river valleys—the Jocko and Blackfoot Rivers to the north, the upper and lower Clark Fork east and west of the city, and the Bitterroot to the south—Missoula's long-time status as an important trade center makes perfect sense. About halfway between Yellowstone and Glacier National Parks, Missoula (population 72,364; elevation 3,200 ft/975 m) is on the way to just about everywhere in this part of the state and a natural stopping point for visitors to the region.

In addition to its history of logging and paper milling, the other defining element of the city—the University of Montana—keeps Missoula young, vibrant, and relatively liberal. Perhaps because the school is best known for its creative writing, art, drama, and dance programs, Missoula is decidedly arts-oriented.

In addition to its proximity to both the Flathead and Bitterroot Valleys, Missoula offers outdoors enthusiasts abundant options right in town—hike the "M" on Mount Sentinel or hang glide off it, kayak the Clark Fork or bike along its shores. There is world-class fishing on a number

of rivers, hot-potting (the art of getting to and swimming in natural hot springs), mountain biking, and no end of places to hike.

Getting to Missoula
Air
Just 4 miles (6.4 km) northwest of the university, **Missoula International Airport** (MSO, 5225 U.S. 10 W., 406/728-4381, www.flymissoula.com) is served by Alaska, Allegiant, American, Delta, Frontier, and United. On the first floor of the terminal are **Alamo, Avis, Budget, Enterprise, National, Thrifty,** and **Hertz** car-rental agencies. **Dollar** has shuttles to and from the airport. Most hotels offer free shuttle service to and from the airport; the **Airport Shuttle** (406/543-9416 or 406/880-7433, www.msoshuttle.com) also provides transportation into town.

Driving
I-90 runs directly through Missoula, making it an easy destination by car. Missoula is 40 miles (64 km) south of **St. Ignatius** on U.S. 93, a drive of roughly 45 minutes.

From **Butte,** Missoula is 120 miles (193 km) northwest on I-90, a drive of about one hour and 45 minutes. Missoula is 200 miles (320 km) northwest of **Bozeman** on I-90, about a three-hour drive.

Bus
The **Greyhound** bus station (1660 W. Broadway, 406/549-2339) has several buses in and out of town daily.

Getting Around
The **Mountain Line** (406/721-3333, www. mountainline.com, 6am-8:45pm Mon.-Fri., 9am-6pm Sat., free) is the free municipal bus service; the city has worked hard to make this a zero-fare public transportation system.

For taxi service, call **Yellow Cab** (406/543-6644, www.yellowcabmissoula. com) or **Green Taxi** (406/728-8294), which only uses hybrid cars.

Missoula

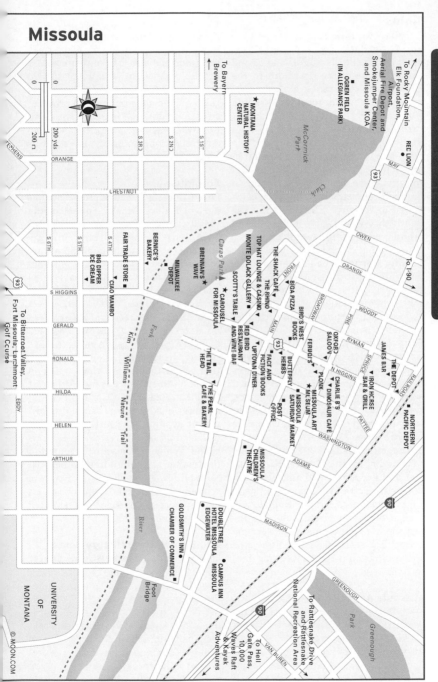

To Rocky Mountain
Elk Foundation,
Airport,
Aerial Fire Depot and
Smokejumper Center,
and Missoula KOA

RED LION

MAY

93

OWEN

To I-90

ORANGE

WOODY

BROADWAY

PINE

RYMAN

JAMES BAR

THE DEPOT

IRON HORSE
BAR & GRILL

SPRUCE

OXFORD
SALOON

N HIGGINS

CHARLIE B'S

DINOSAUR CAFE

FERIDI'S

PLONK

MISSOULA ART
MUSEUM

BUTTERFLY
HERBS

FACT AND
FICTION BOOKS

MISSOULA
SATURDAY MARKET

POST
OFFICE

WASHINGTON

PATTEE

RAILROAD

NORTHERN
PACIFIC DEPOT

BIRD'S NEST
BOOKS

BIGA PIZZA

THE RHINO

THE SHACK CAFE

FRONT

MAIN

93

RED BIRD
RESTAURANT
AND WINE BAR

UPTOWN DINER

THE TRAIL
HEAD

THE PEARL
CAFE & BAKERY

MISSOULA
CHILDREN'S
THEATRE

ADAMS

MADISON

90

GOLDSMITH'S INN
CHAMBER OF COMMERCE

DOUBLETREE
HOTEL MISSOULA
EDGEWATER

CAMPUS INN
MISSOULA

90

VAN BUREN

GREENOUGH

Greenough
Park

To Rattlesnake Drive
and Rattlesnake
National Recreation Area

To Hell
Gate Pass,
10,000
Waves Raft
& Kayak
Adventures

UNIVERSITY
OF
MONTANA

© MOON.COM

To Bitterroot Valley,
Fort Missoula, Larchmont
Golf Course

Foot
Bridge

River

Williams

Kim

Nature Trail

Clark Fork River

Caras Park

MONTE DOLACK GALLERY

TOP HAT LOUNGE & CASINO

BERNICE'S
BAKERY

BRENNAN'S
WAVE

MILWAUKEE
DEPOT

SCOTTY'S TABLE

CAROUSEL
FOR MISSOULA

FAIR TRADE STORE

BIG DIPPER
ICE CREAM

CIAO MAMBO

S HIGGINS

GERALD

RONALD

HILDA

HELEN

ARTHUR

EDDY

93

S 6TH

S 5TH

S 4TH

S 5TH

S 3RD

S 2ND

S 1ST

TOHENS

CHESTNUT

ORANGE

McCormick
Park

Club

MONTANA
NATURAL HISTORY
CENTER

OGREN FIELD
(IN ALLEGIANCE PARK)

To Bayern
Brewery

0   200 yds
0   200 m

Sights
Carousel for Missoula and Caras Park

Aside from being a beautiful hand-carved carousel, one of the first built in the United States since the Great Depression, what makes the **Carousel for Missoula** (101 Carousel Dr., 406/549-8382, http://carouselformissoula.com, 11am-7pm daily June-Aug., 11am-5:30pm daily Sept.-May, $2.25 adults, $0.75 children under 16, $1.50 adult with child on lap) so sweet is the way in which it came to be. Local cabinetmaker Chuck Kaparich vowed to the city of Missoula in 1991 that if they would "give it a home and promise no one will ever take it apart," he would build a carousel by hand. As a child, Kaparich had spent summer days in Butte at the Columbia Gardens riding the carousel. For four years, he carved ponies, taught others to carve, and worked to restore and piece together the more than 16,000 pieces of an antique carousel frame he had purchased. The town raised funds and collectively contributed more than 100,000 volunteer hours. In May 1995 the carousel opened with 38 ponies, three replacement ponies, two chariots, 14 gargoyles, and the largest band organ in continuous use in the United States.

The jewel-box building opens to the surrounding green of **Caras Park** in summer and keeps the cold and wind out during the rest of the year. A fantastic adjacent play area, **Dragon Hollow,** was built with the same remarkable volunteerism over a substantially shorter time period. The entire playground was constructed by volunteers in just nine days in 2001.

Missoula Art Museum

With the tagline "Free Expression Free Admission," the **Missoula Art Museum** (MAM, 335 N. Pattee St., 406/728-0447, www.missoulaartmuseum.org, 10am-5pm Tues.-Sat., free) honors the past and celebrates the future. The building itself represents such a marriage, brilliantly combining a 110-year-old Carnegie library with a contemporary glass, steel, and wood addition. The museum has six exhibition spaces that host 20-25 solo and group exhibitions annually, most of them quite contemporary and provocative. Don't miss the museum's own impressive Contemporary American Indian Art Collection, among the largest of its kind in the country.

Fort Missoula

Originally established to protect settlers against Indian attacks, **Fort Missoula** (3400 Captain Rawn Way, 406/728-3476, www.fortmissoulamuseum.org, 10am-5pm Mon.-Sat., noon-5pm Sun. Memorial Day-Labor Day, noon-5pm Tues.-Sun. Labor Day-Memorial Day, $4 adults, $2 students, $3 seniors, $10 family, free for children under 6) was never used for its intended purpose. When no attacks occurred, the fort was used to house the African American 25th Infantry in 1888 and as an alien detention center for Italian Americans and Japanese Americans during World War II. The museum houses exhibits about the fort's history as well as rotating historical exhibits. The fort grounds, for which admission is free, are open year-round. While the museum is housed in the fort's original buildings, other historic buildings, including a one-room schoolhouse, an 1860s church, and a homesteader cabin, have been relocated to the grounds.

Montana Natural History Center

The **Montana Natural History Center** (120 Hickory St., 406/327-0405, www.montananaturalist.org, 9am-5pm Mon.-Fri., noon-4pm Sat., $3 adults, $1 children 4-18, free for children under 4) is one block south of McCormick Park. Originally housed on the University of Montana's campus, the center was created by educators who wanted to work with schools and the public to help nurture an understanding and appreciation of nature. It offers workshops, including children's activities, as well as field trips and evening lectures conducted by local scientists and naturalists. To see what is being offered on specific dates, look under "Community Activities" on the website.

University of Montana

The **University of Montana** (32 Campus Dr., 406/243-0211, www.umt.edu) was founded in 1895 at the base of Mount Sentinel. To secure Missoula as the site of the state's university, city leaders bribed state legislators with 5 gallons (18.9 liters) of whiskey, a case of beer, a case of wine, and 350 cigars. Regardless of its shady beginnings, the university has flourished into a well-respected liberal arts institution with a top-notch football team, a broad interest in the performing arts, a well-known creative writing program, and an ability to produce numerous Fulbright and Rhodes scholars each year.

The university has a fun campus to explore. **University Center,** on the east side of the campus almost directly under the M on the hillside, is the hub of campus life. Wander in to grab a bite at the food court, or peruse the well-stocked bookstore. To find out what lectures, plays, concerts, or other entertainment is happening on campus, visit the website (http://events.umt.edu).

Rocky Mountain Elk Foundation Visitor Center

Strengthening the view that hunters are often the most resolute conservationists, the **Rocky Mountain Elk Foundation Visitor Center** (5705 Grant Creek Rd., 406/523-4500 or 800/225-5355, www.rmef.org, 8am-5pm Mon.-Fri., 10am-5pm Sat. Jan.-Apr., 8am-6pm Mon.-Fri., 9am-6pm Sat.-Sun. May-Dec., free) has protected and enhanced millions of acres of wildlife habitat across North America since its humble origins in 1984. The center does an impressive job of putting the elk in the context of a wide range of wildlife and emphasizing the importance of habitat conservation. A favorite among hunters due to its wealth of trophy mounts, the visitors center is like a natural history museum, and in addition to a pleasant wooded walking trail on the property's 22 acres, there are some great kid-friendly interactive exhibits and wildlife conservation films. Tours can be arranged by emailing in advance, and free youth seminars are held monthly on such subjects as fire, archery, big game, and horns versus antlers.

Aerial Fire Depot and Smokejumper Center

Sharing space with the largest smokejumper training base in the country, the **Aerial Fire Depot and Smokejumper Center** (5765 W. Broadway, 0.5 mi/0.8 km west of the Missoula airport, 406/329-4934, www.smokejumpers.com, 8:30am-5pm daily Memorial Day-Labor Day, by appointment Labor Day-Memorial Day, free admission, free tours daily in summer) is a fascinating place for those interested in wildfires and the firefighters who parachute in to battle them. There is a memorial to those killed on duty and a replica of a 1930s fire lookout; visitors on the 45-minute tour have access to the smokejumper loft where the jumpers work when they are not fighting fires.

Brennan's Wave

Although there is no street address, everyone in Missoula knows exactly where Brennan's Wave is. Located on the Clark Fork River, right next to Caras Park, this engineered white-water masterpiece was built in honor of Brennan Guth, a Missoula native and world-class kayaker who perished in 2001 while paddling in Chile. Brennan's Wave hosts big competitions—the 2010 U.S. Freestyle Kayaking Championship brought 200 competitors to town and thousands of spectators—and plenty of everyday paddlers looking for a thrill. The banks are always lined with enthusiastic spectators, and the Wave is a popular gathering spot whenever the river is not covered by ice.

Entertainment and Events
Nightlife

Home to college students and artists, there is no shortage of watering holes in Missoula, and a brief walk will take you to establishments that are pulsing with activity. Microbrew enthusiasts will enjoy **Bayern Brewing's Edelweiss Bistro** (1507 Montana St., 406/721-1482, www.bayernbrewery.com, 11am-8pm Mon.-Sat.), which always has six of its beers available along with its own coffee blends and a small but delectable sampling of German food, including sausages, meats, cheeses, and pretzels. The beer garden is a great place to relax in summer, and brewery tours are available by appointment. The **Kettle House Brewing Co.** (313 N. 1st St. W. and 602 Myrtle St., 406/728-1660, www.kettlehouse.com, noon-8pm daily, growlers to-go sold until 9pm) is the home of the famous Cold Smoke Scotch Ale and has two locations for visitors to sample excellent local brews.

For more of a late-night scene, try tried-and-true favorites like **The Rhino** (158 Ryman St., 406/721-6061, 11am-2am Mon.-Sat., noon-2am Sun.), with more than 50 beers on tap; **Feruqi's** (318 N. Higgins Ave., 406/728-8799, 4pm-2am Mon.-Sat., 7pm-2am Sun.), an intimate spot known for its martinis and setting in a historic building; or the **Oxford Saloon** (337 N. Higgins Ave., 406/549-0117, www.the-oxford.com, 24 hours daily), which dates back to the 1880s and still offers live poker nightly at 8pm. Though it no longer serves brains and eggs, the Oxford still makes a pretty tasty Garbage Omelet.

Charlie B's (428 N. Higgins Ave., 406/549-3589, 11am-2am daily) is a longtime favorite and has a reputation for hard drinking that starts early in the day. The adjacent **Dinosaur Café** (428 N. Higgins Ave., 406/721-3808, 11am-10pm Mon.-Thurs., 11am-11pm Fri.-Sat.) offers inexpensive and excellent Cajun food—think po'boys, gumbo, and éttoufée—to go with your booze.

Complete with a Hunter S. Thompson quote etched on the outside of the building, **James Bar** (127 W. Alder St., 406/721-8158, 11am-2am daily) is a classy joint for cocktails and good, local cuisine—including elk, bison, lobster, and lamb sliders—instead of standard bar fare.

Music lovers will do well at the **Top Hat Lounge & Casino** (134 W. Front St., 406/830-4640, www.logjampresents.com, 11:30am-10pm Mon.-Wed., 11:30am-2am Thurs.-Sat.), which has been bringing live music of every genre to Missoula since 1952. The place can pack in 700 bodies, and the tapas-style menu does not disappoint. A bit mellower and far more upscale is **Plonk** (322 N. Higgins Ave., 406/926-1791, www.plonkwine.com, 11:30am-2am Tues.-Sat., 4pm-2am Sun.-Mon.), which pairs exquisite wine, inspired cocktails, and elegant food with eclectic music. Too pricey for the average college student, Plonk tends to appeal to an older crowd.

Festivals and Events
Weekly Summer Events

With an active, outdoorsy, and independent population, Missoula hosts a number of weekly events during summer that encourage everything from outdoor dining to art appreciation. **First Friday Gallery Night** (406/532-3240) is held 5pm-8pm on the first Friday of every month. Some 15-20 galleries open their doors, often to display new exhibitions, and they provide complimentary hors d'oeuvres and refreshments to art strollers. **Out to Lunch** (406/543-4238, www.missouladowntown.com, 11am-2pm Wed. June-Aug.) in Caras Park is a riverside performing arts picnic for the whole city, with talented local musicians and more than 20 food vendors. Also in Caras Park and run by the Missoula Downtown Association, **Downtown ToNight** (406/543-4238,

Montana Wineries

Since 1984, when Tom Campbell Jr. and his father first started experimenting with growing grapes along the shores of Flathead Lake, in prime Montana cherry territory, several other wineries have sprouted across the state, primarily in the western region. Many have disappeared after hard winters and rough economies, but a handful are proving that Montana vintners have what it takes. Though many vintners buy grapes from out of state, there are several growers among them, including a few that opt for unconventional but delicious base fruits like cherries, huckleberries, chokecherries, apples, pears, currants, and rhubarb.

♦ **Glacier Sun Winery & Tasting Room** (3250 U.S. 2 E., Kalispell, 406/257-8886, www.glaciersunwinery.com, 8am-5pm Mon.-Fri.) grew out of the idea of a small, roadside fruit and veggie stand. Today the winery still sells fruits, veggies, and pre-pared foods, but also produces 18 varietals from locally grown fruits and regionally grown grapes.

♦ **Mission Mountain Winery** (82420 U.S. 93, Dayton, 406/849-5524, www.missionmountainwinery.com, tastings 10am-5pm daily May-Oct., 10am-6pm daily July-Aug., $5 tasting fee) is the state's first bonded winery and produces more than 6,500 cases annually of more than 10 different award-winning varietals. Its vineyards grow the grapes for its highly regarded pinot noir, pinot gris, and small amounts of riesling, chardonnay, and gewürztraminer. The tasting fee is waived with purchase of a bottle.

♦ **Ten Spoon Vineyard and Winery** (4175 Rattlesnake Dr., Missoula, 877/549-8703, www.tenspoon.com, tastings by appointment) is among the fastest-growing wineries in the state and has a marvelous origin story. Owner Connie Poten bought some pastureland in the Rattlesnake Valley outside Missoula to protect the rapidly disappearing open space. She met Andy Sponseller on a local preservation campaign, and their shared love of wine led to the backbreaking work that built the vineyard and set the stage for their subsequent success with varietals including Moonlight pinot noir, Ranger Rider Red, Blind Curve sauvignon blanc, Flathead cherry dry, Farm Dog Red, and Fat Cat.

♦ **Hidden Legend Winery** (1345 U.S. 93 N., Ste. 5, Victor, 406/363-6323, www.hiddenlegendwinery.com, tours and tastings 11am-6pm Tues.-Sat.) in the Bitterroot Valley specializes in honey-based mead with Montana twists like chokecherry and elderberry.

♦ **Trapper Peak Winery** (75 Cattail Ln., Darby, 406/821-1964, tours and tastings by appointment), also in the Bitterroot Valley, produces an affordable selection of cabernet sauvignon, petite sirah, merlot, cabernet franc, and muscat using California grapes.

♦ **Tongue River Winery** (99 Morning Star Ln., Miles City, 406/853-1028, www.tongueriverwinery.com, 8am-6pm Mon.-Sat., 2pm-7pm Sun.) is the only winery in southeastern Montana. It offers an expansive list of award-winning wines, and tours of both the vineyard and winery can be arranged.

www.missouladowntown.com, 5:30pm-8:30pm Thurs. June-Aug.) features live music, food vendors, and a beverage garden.

Known as the Garden City, Missoula boasts three fabulous farmers markets, including the **Clark Fork Market** (under the Higgins St. Bridge in downtown, 406/396-0593, www.clarkforkmarket.com, 8am-1pm Sat. May-Sept., 9am-1pm Oct.), which offers an abundance of local produce, meat, and other products, including hot prepared food. There is live music 10am-12:30pm, and plenty of parking is available. The **Missoula Farmers Market** (Circle Square, north end of Higgins Ave., 406/274-3042, www.missoulafarmersmarket.com, 8am-12:30pm Sat. May-Oct., 5:30pm-7pm Tues. June 19-Sept.) features more than 100 vendors of fresh local produce, flowers, eggs, honey, and more. The **Missoula People's Market** (E. Pine St. between Higgins Ave. and Pattee St., 406/830-3216, www.missoulapeoplesmarket.org, 9am-1pm Sat. May-Sept.) has prepared food and features art and crafts by local artisans.

Shopping
Gifts and Art
The Fair Trade Store (519 S. Higgins Ave., 406/543-3955, 10am-6pm Mon.-Sat., noon-4pm Sun.) is operated by the Jeannette Rankin Peace Center and promotes equitable and fair partnerships between producers and distributors of goods. There is a distinctive and colorful selection of merchandise from around the globe, including textiles, pottery, silver, and handmade cards.

In addition to being Missoula's oldest espresso bar, **Butterfly Herbs** (232 N. Higgins Ave., 406/728-8780, www.butterflyherbs.com, 7am-7pm daily) is a fun and eclectic gift shop. It sells whole herbs, teas, coffee, and spices in bulk as well as soaps, handmade jewelry, candles, and other decorative goods.

Rockin Rudy's (237 Blaine St., 406/542-0077, www.rockinrudys.com, 9am-9pm Mon.-Sat., 11am-6pm Sun.) uses as a tagline, "A place. Sort of." More than just a place, Rockin Rudy's is *the* place in Missoula for music, posters, cards, gag gifts, jewelry, and on and on. Big and random, this place is part of Missoula culture.

One of the most recognizable artists in the region, Monte Dolack shows his work and that of his partner, Mary Beth Percival, at **Monte Dolack Gallery** (139 W. Front St., 406/549-3248, www.dolack.com, by appt. only). The artists travel frequently, which is reflected in their primarily nature-based, often whimsical and witty works, which include tranquil watercolors and vivid posters.

Bookstores
In a famously literary town, **Fact and Fiction Books** (220 N. Higgins Ave., 406/721-2881, www.factandfictionbooks.com, 10am-6pm Mon.-Fri., 10am-5pm Sat., noon-4pm Sun.) is a Missoula institution and a good place to learn about local culture and regional authors.

For used, rare, and out-of-print books, **The Bird's Nest** (219 N. Higgins Ave., 406/721-1125, 10am-4pm Tues.-Sat.) is a real find, right across the street from Fact and Fiction.

Outdoor Gear
The Trail Head (221 E. Front St., 406/543-6966, www.trailheadmontana.net, 9:30am-8pm Mon.-Fri., 9am-6pm Sat., 11am-6pm Sun.) is a part of the Missoula community and thrives by knowing the area as well as its activities and specific conditions. Trail Head staff participate regularly in volunteer efforts to preserve and enhance recreational opportunities in the region. The store has fantastic gear for nearly every activity in the area, including skiing, boating, camping, and climbing. Since 1974, great adventures have started here.

Montana's Literary Treasure

Few states can boast a nearly 1,200-page, 5-pound (2.3-kg) tome dedicated to the remarkable literature that has come from and defined the state. (The state's "Big Sky" moniker even came courtesy of A. B. Guthrie Jr.'s classic 1947 novel *The Big Sky*.) Montana's literary anthology, *The Last Best Place*, was published in 1988, and the state's literary status only continues to grow. This may partly be attributed to poet and professor Richard Hugo, who directed the University of Montana's renowned creative writing program from 1964 until his death in 1982. The less prosaic might ascribe the inordinate number of well-known authors and poets to things like the light, space, and quality of life here, or the long, cold winters and limited distractions. Among the state's best-known writers are Wallace Stegner, Norman Maclean, Maile Meloy, Bill Kittredge, Sandra Alcosser, James Welch, Rick Bass, Tom McGuane, Annick Smith, Ivan Doig, Mary Clearman Blew, Richard Ford, Judy Blunt, David Quammen, and Susan Henderson.

Montana's literary heritage is very much alive in Missoula, where one of the area's softball teams goes by the name "The Montana Review of Books," which once had an outfield lineup with 12 published novels among them. The city boasts some fabulous independent bookstores that promote and often host local writers, including **Fact and Fiction** (220 N. Higgins Ave., 406/721-2881). But the literary spirit is perhaps most alive in any number of watering holes, some more savory than others. **Charlie B's** (428 N. Higgins Ave.), a favorite haunt of the late James Crumley, has no sign, tinted windows, and a big wooden door. Crumley was also a regular at **The Depot** (201 Railroad St. W.). During his tenure at the University of Montana, Bill Kittredge and plenty of creative writing students frequented **Diamond Jim's Eastgate Casino and Lounge** (900 E. Broadway) just over the Van Buren footbridge from campus. **The Rhino** (158 Ryman St.) was identifiable in Jeff Hull's short stories and his 2005 novel. Probably the best-known among Missoula's thirsty literary geniuses, Dick Hugo often wrote about bars—**The Dixon Bar** (MT-200, Dixon), which is, for the moment anyway, a bar and grill; **Trixi's Antler Saloon** (MT-200, Ovando); and more famously, the **Milltown Union Bar** (11 Main St., Milltown), which is now the Milltown Moose Lodge, home to the fraternal Moose club, and is virtually unrecognizable.

Sports and Recreation

Rattlesnake National Recreation Area and Wilderness

Less than 5 miles (8 km) north of town, the 60,000-acre **Rattlesnake National Recreation Area and Wilderness** (406/329-3814, www.fs.usda.gov) is fed by some 50 creeks and has 30 lakes, waterfalls, and many miles of trails, some of which lead up to McLeod Peak, the highest spot in the area at 8,620 feet (2,627 m). The area is a dream for hikers, runners, mountain bikers, campers, cross-country skiers, and anglers; it is home to deer, elk, coyotes, mountain goats, bighorn sheep, black bears, and more than 40 species of birds in spring and fall. Camping is permitted anywhere beyond the 3-mile (4.8-km) radius from the Rattlesnake's main trailhead.

To get to the area from Missoula, take the I-90 Van Buren Street exit at the east end of town and travel 4.5 miles (7.2 km) north on Rattlesnake Drive.

Hiking and Biking

Hugely popular with walkers, runners, and bikers, the flat **Clark Fork Riverfront Trail** (www.ci.missoula.mt.us/2209/Riverfront-Trails) is 3.8 miles (6.1 km) long and provides access to **Caras Park, Bess Reed Park,** and **Kiwanis Park** on the river's north bank and **McCormick Park, Clark Fork Natural Park, John Toole Park,** the **University of Montana River Bowl,** and **Jacob's Island Park** on the south bank. The trail, graveled in places and paved in others, connects to a number of other intersecting trails and runs on both the north and south sides of the Clark Fork River. It is easily accessible throughout town, but the most abundant parking can be found at Caras Park near the Carousel for Missoula. The trail on the river's north side is about 0.5 mile (0.8 km) longer than that on the south side.

The Clark Fork Riverfront Trail connects to the 2.5-mile (4-km) **Kim Williams Nature Trail,** a converted railroad bed near the base of Mount Sentinel (where you can hike the M) that winds through a 134-acre natural area in Hellgate Canyon. The trail is wide and level, and it is open to pedestrians, equestrians, and cyclists. It's also frequented by wildlife, so keep your eyes open. The trail runs through Hellgate Canyon and connects to the Deer Creek-Pattee Canyon Loop. The trail can be accessed easily from Jacob's Island Park near the Van Buren Pedestrian Bridge. Leashed dogs are welcome on all of Missoula's trails.

M Trail on Mount Sentinel

For a bird's-eye view of the city, hike up the **M Trail on Mount Sentinel.** It is a popular trail, so there will likely be others huffing and puffing up the hill with you. There are 13 switchbacks on the west-facing slope, and the views over Missoula and the Bitterroot Valley at sunset are worth the sweat.

Skiing

Twenty minutes north of Missoula, **Snowbowl** (1700 Snowbowl Rd., 406/549-9777 or 800/728-2695, www. montanasnowbowl.com, $50 adults full day or $45 half day, $47 students and seniors full day or $45 half day, $24 children 6-12 full or half day, free for children under 6) is a nice little ski hill with an average of 300 inches (762 cm) of snow annually, 2,600 feet (793 m) of vertical drop, and a run that covers 3

miles (4.8 km). In summer, the mountain is open Friday-Sunday late June-mid-September for mountain biking, disc golf, and diggler, which is a cross between mountain biking and snowboarding (rentals available).

There is no shortage of cross-country ski trails around Missoula. One unique destination is the **Garnet Resource Area** (406/329-3914, www.garnetghosttown. net), with 50 miles (81 km) of trails in a ghost town. In summer, hiking and mountain biking are popular. To get to Garnet, follow Highway 200 east of town and turn south at the Garnet Range Road, located between mile markers 22 and 23, about 30 miles (48 km) east of Missoula. Follow the range road approximately 12 miles (19.3 km) to the parking area. The road is closed January-April, when access is limited to snowshoers, cross-country skiers, and snowmobilers.

There are also more than 150 miles (242 km) of cross-country ski trails in the **Lolo National Forest** (406/329-3814 or 866/377-8642, www.fs.usda.gov/lolo).

Fishing

While access to the Clark Fork River right in town is easy, the river is still recovering from decades of pollution. Better bets are the Bitterroot River, the Blackfoot River, and Rock Creek. One guiding outfit that does them all is **Classic Journey Outfitters** (877/327-7878, www. montanaflyfishingguide.com, $575 full-day float, $425 half-day float, multiday trips with lodging available). Owner Joe Cummings grew up fishing on a ranch in nearby Stevensville and left to play professional football. But his heart has always been where the big, wild trout are. He and his guides fish year-round, have a passion for dry flies, and know the area backward and forward. Another guide who is a phenomenal naturalist in addition to being a world-class fishing instructor is Tom Jenni of **Tom Jenni's Reel Montana** (406/539-6610 or 866/885-6065, www.tomjenni.com). Jenni grew up in

Free Flight in Missoula

While it makes some people crazy, for others the combination of wind and mountains in Missoula means **hang gliding** and **paragliding.** It's not uncommon to see these colorful oversize-kite contraptions launching off Mount Sentinel and soaring over the city. But what goes up must come down, and when Bill Johnson (widely considered to have been the first hang gliding pilot in the state) landed on top of the university field-house in the 1970s, reports of a plane crash swiftly clogged the emergency services switchboard. When the fire department arrived, Johnson had broken down his glider, packed it neatly in a bag, and even asked the firefighters for help getting down. The firefighters were too busy scanning the scene for a crashed plane to realize that they were aiding Johnson in his getaway.

The sports took hold in the state in the 1970s when gear was cheap and mostly homemade. Mount Sentinel, the United States Hang Gliding and Paragliding Association's longest-running site, offers unique sea breeze-like winds most summer evenings, allowing pilots to soar the sky for hours at a time. By October 2006 the number of launches off Mount Sentinel gave pause to Missoula's air traffic controllers, who feared a plane-versus-glider crash, and the area was closed to flight for nearly a year. The state's hang glider pilots joined with people in Missoula who appreciated the life and color that the sport brought to town, and in July 2007 Mount Sentinel opened again to hang gliding and paragliding. **Glide Missoula** (www.glidemissoula.org), the local free flight club, operates the local sites and is actively working to secure launch sites in the valley.

Local pilot Casey Bedell from **Blackbird Paragliding** (530/545-0268, http://blackbirdparagliding.com) keeps the sports of hang gliding and paragliding alive with his own gravity-defying flights as well as lessons and tandem flights ($199) for the curious. On a windy day in Missoula, there may not be a more memorable way to see the city and the valleys around it.

Missoula and has been fishing its rivers for more than 30 years.

Boating and Water Sports

With five rivers in the vicinity, Missoula is a boater's town. There is even an artificial practice wave, Brennan's Wave, right in town for kayakers to play safely in. **10,000 Waves Raft & Kayak Adventures** (131 E. Main St., 406/549-6670 or 800/537-8315, www.10000-waves.com) offers everything from scenic rafting to white-water adventures, sit-on-top kayaks, and kayak instruction on numerous sections of the Blackfoot and Clark Fork Rivers. There are also overnight trips ($595 adults, $565 children 5-12) and gourmet dinner trips ($115 adults, $90 children 5-12), plus half-day trips ($70 adults, $50 children 5-12) and full-day trips ($85 adults, $65 children 5-12) on the Blackfoot River. Another local outfitter that specializes in all things white-water is **Zoo Town Surfers** (3067 Fleet St. in Missoula, or river headquarters 5077 Old U.S. 10 W., Alberton, 406/546-0370, www.zootownsurfers.com). It offers scenic and white-water rafting trips, kayak clinics, and stand-up paddleboarding experiences on local lakes and rivers.

Golf

Although there are a couple of nine-hole courses in town including **University of Montana Golf Course** (515 South Ave. E., 406/728-8629, $17 for 9 holes, $30 for 18) and **Linda Vista Public Golf Course** (4915 Lower Miller Creek Rd., 406/251-3655, $15 for 9 holes, $20 for 18), the only 18-hole public course in Missoula is the **Larchmont Golf Course** (3200 Old Fort Rd., 406/721-4416, $34 for 18 holes on foot, carts $18-36).

Horseback Riding

Less than 30 minutes south of Missoula in Lolo, amazing trail ride experiences can be had at **Dunrovin Ranch** (5001 Expedition Dr., 406/273-7745, www.dunrovinranchmontana.com), where the emphasis is on community, education, science, and the arts. Animals are at the center of the experience here and make every visit remarkable, from the family of smooth-gaited Tennessee walking horses to "diva donkeys," beloved dogs, and ospreys and other wild animals that call the ranch home. Though Dunrovin offers lodging and the full guest ranch experience, it also offers riding opportunities for nonguests. Corral sessions ($50) are great for children as young as three, and give new riders the opportunity to start slow. Trail rides off the ranch are available to anyone older than eight, ranging from one hour ($80 pp) or two hours ($115 pp) to half-day (4-6 hours, $160 pp) and full-day (6-9 hours, $260 pp) excursions. Rides might climb up to magnificent mountain views or travel along and across the river or through lush forests, and private rides can be arranged as well. Dunrovin Ranch also offers a historical ride perfect for history buffs and mountain men wannabes.

Food

Missoula's dining scene offers more cultural diversity than much of the rest of the state, with plenty of sushi and Thai offerings, but its strong suit is still fresh Rocky Mountain cuisine. Among the best is **Red Bird Restaurant and Wine Bar** (111 N. Higgins Ave., Ste. 100, 406/549-2906, www.redbirdrestaurant.com, 5pm-10pm Tues.-Sat., $13-41), an elegant little bistro in a historic hotel building. Everything is fresh, creative, and made on the premises, including steaks, seafood, pasta, and

Top to bottom: hiking the M Trail on Mount Sentinel; skiing at Snowbowl; Victorian flair in Philipsburg.

soups. For a dress-up-and-hit-the-town evening, this is a wonderful spot.

Serving American bistro fare with a global twist, ★ **Scotty's Table** (131 S. Higgins Ave., 406/549-2790, www. scottystable.net, 11:30am-2:30pm and 5pm-9pm Tues.-Fri., 9am-2pm and 5pm-9pm Sat.-Sun., $26-32) is an upscale dining spot for the whole family. The gourmet kids' menu was inspired by the chef's own child. The main menu's entrées include mouthwatering cioppino and local pork confit, but the appetizers are enchanting—try the fried risotto known as arancini, walnut-encrusted blue cheese cakes, mussels and fries, or the charcuterie plate; you might not even make it to the main course.

For a creative take on Italian food, **Ciao Mambo** (541 S. Higgins Ave., 406/543-0377, www.ciaomambo.com, 5pm-10pm daily, $7-32), a Montana-started franchise, serves up everything from Italian nachos and fried mozzarella balls to wood-fired pizza, pasta, and steaks.

The **Pearl Café & Bakery** (231 E. Front St., 406/541-0231, www.pearlcafe. us, 5pm-9pm Mon.-Sat., $14-32) boasts "country fare with an urban flair." The cuisine is creative, fresh, and absolutely gorgeous. From rabbit with red wine mushroom sauce to classic filet mignon, the Pearl is indeed a standout.

For the best local pizza, you can't beat the wood-fired offerings from ★ **Biga Pizza** (241 W. Main St., 406/728-2579, www.bigapizza.com, 11am-3pm and 5pm-9:30pm Mon.-Thurs., 11am-3pm and 5pm-10pm Fri., 5pm-10pm Sat., pizzas $10-20). From the simple house pie with garlic oil, tomato sauce, fresh basil, and fresh mozzarella to the caramelized goat cheese and the house-made fennel marmalade with local bacon, its combinations are nothing short of mouthwatering. Gluten-free crusts are available too, as are calzones and antipasti.

A thriving brewpub in Missoula, the **Iron Horse Bar & Grill** (501 N. Higgins Ave., 406/728-8866, www. ironhorsebrewpub.com, 11am-2am daily, $12-22) is set in the old train depot. The place is always hopping, and terrific outdoor seating is available when the weather permits. The menu is extensive, serving up everything from ahi tuna to nachos to spicy tandoori chicken, salads, burgers, and small plates.

A community favorite since 1949 and serving three meals a day in a classic Pontiac-Oldsmobile dealership setting, **The Shack Café** (222 W. Main St., 406/549-9903, www.theshackcafe.com, 7am-3pm Mon.-Wed., 7am-9pm Thurs.-Sun. $11-20) specializes in food grown and raised locally. Don't miss the huckleberry pancakes for breakfast; it may be the best breakfast in town. Lunch includes hefty sandwiches, and dinner entrées range from sandwiches and salads to Mexican fare and pasta.

For a quick and scrumptious bite with a killer cup of coffee, try **Bernice's Bakery** (190 S. 3rd St. W., 406/728-1358, www.bernicesbakerymt.com, 6am-8pm daily, sandwiches $6-10), a real-butter and from-scratch kind of place featuring high-quality organic ingredients, menus that change daily, and sheer artistry in everything it does. The staff support a strong coffeehouse vibe and a commendable commitment to community. If you leave without indulging your sweet tooth, you've made an enormous mistake. **Caffè Dolce** (500 Brooks St., 406/830-3055, www.caffedolce.com, 8am-3pm Mon., 8am-9pm Tues.-Sat., 9am-2pm Sun., $15-29) offers fresh, healthy, and utterly delicious fare for breakfast, lunch, and dinner. The pasta is homemade, the wine list is enormous and fabulous, and the traditional Italian coffee service goes from morning until evening. There's also a location at **Southgate Mall** (2901 Brooks St., 406/830-3055, 8am-9pm Mon.-Fri., 9am-9pm Sat., 10am-6pm Sun.). Yet another spot for divine bread and pastries in Missoula is **Le Petit Outre** (129 S. 4th St. W., 406/543-3311, www.lepetitoutre. com, 7am-6pm daily, $3-12). They serve outstanding croissants, scones, *canelé*, breads, and various sweet and savory delights. Naturally, they have excellent coffee and espresso.

If you're just starting your Montana adventure, you'll need to get in shape for all the ice-cream offerings. A great place to start is **Big Dipper Ice Cream** (631 S. Higgins Ave., 406/543-5722, www. bigdippericecream.com, $3-8), which has unexpected but out-of-this-world flavors like cardamom, El Salvador coffee, Mexican chocolate, and mango habanero sorbet in addition to the lip-smacking classics. Don't miss daily special flavors like cotton candy, Thai peanut curry (really), and Elvis (peanut butter, banana, chocolate chip, chocolate, and bacon). During summer, the walk-up window is open 11am-11pm daily. Hours vary the rest of the year, so call ahead.

Accommodations

As one of Montana's bigger cities, Missoula has plenty of lodging options. This is not a town of boutique hotels; this is where you'll find chain hotels, independent motels, and some charming bed-and-breakfasts. The old-school independent motels line much of East and West Broadway, while some of the newer chain hotels can be found on Reserve Street. Among the well-known and well-maintained chains in town are the **C'Mon Inn Hotel & Suites** (2775 Expo Parkway, 406/543-4600 or 888/989-5569, www.cmoninn.com, $140-230), **Courtyard by Marriott** (4559 N. Reserve St., 406/549-5260, www.marriott.com, $169-247), the pet-friendly **Econo Lodge** (4953 N. Reserve St., 406/542-7550, www.choicehotels.com, $81-112), **Hilton Garden Inn Missoula** (3720 N. Reserve St., 406/532-5300 or 877/782-9444, www.hiltongardeninn3.hilton. com, $149-313), **Holiday Inn Express & Suites** (150 Expressway Blvd., 406/830-3100 or 800/315-2605, www.hiexpress. com, $142-198), and **La Quinta** (5059 N. Reserve St., 406/549-9000 or 800/753-3757, www.laquintamissoula. com, $134-189).

In the heart of Missoula on the banks of the Clark Fork River is the pet-friendly **Doubletree by Hilton Missoula Edgewater** (100 Madison St., 406/728-3100 or 800/222-8733, www. missoulaedgewater.doubletree.com, $154-413), an enormous hotel with all the amenities.

A couple of medium-size hotels offering good value near the university and downtown, respectively, are **Campus Inn Missoula** (744 E. Broadway, 406/549-5134 or 800/232-8013, www. campusinnmissoula.com, $77-227) and **Red Lion** (700 W. Broadway, 406/728-3300 or 800/733-5466, www.redlion.com/ missoula, $92-173).

A few miles from downtown is the quiet, comfortable, and pet-friendly **Best Western Plus Grant Creek Inn** (5280 Grant Creek Rd., 406/543-0700 or 800/780-7234, www.bestwestern.com, $146-259). Kids will love the indoor-outdoor heated pool. But for avid swimmers, the only hotel to consider in Missoula is **Wingate by Wyndham** (5252 Airway Blvd., 406/541-8000 or 866/832-8000, www.wingatemissoula.com, $129-269), which boasts extremely clean and comfortable rooms with an indoor water park that will delight little ones with a kiddie pool, froggy slide, and mushroom waterfall. Bigger kids will like the three-story waterslides.

As a university town with some beautiful old homes, Missoula has an abundance of appealing B&Bs. One of the best, and right on the river, is a vast 1911 home built for the University of Montana's president. Since then, the home has been a fraternity house, a lab, and an office. But now it is the wonderful ★ **Goldsmith's Inn** (803 E. Front St., 406/728-1585, www.missoulabedandbreakfast.com, $139-202), a charming turn-of-the-20th-century bed-and-breakfast within easy walking distance of the university and downtown. Much smaller but equally inviting is the dog-friendly **Blossom's Bed & Breakfast** (1114 Poplar St., 406/721-4690, www.blossomsbnb.com, $150-195), a 1910 Craftsman gem not far from the trails of the Rattlesnake Recreation Area and Wilderness. Nestled on a mountainside outside of town is **Blue Mountain Bed & Breakfast** (6980 Deadman Gulch Rd., 406/251-4457 or 877/251-4457, www.bluemountainbb.com, $150-186), a tranquil spot where you can explore nature and even bring your own horse. By far the most dramatic B&B in town is the pet-friendly, four-room **Gibson Mansion** (823 39th St., 406/251-1345 or 866/251-1345, www.gibsonmansion.com, $179-324, $40 for one dog, $60 for two dogs), designed and built in 1903 by architect A. J. Gibson, who was responsible for many of the buildings on the university campus. The period details are spot-on, the gardens exquisite, and the breakfasts decadent.

Twenty minutes north of Missoula is the **Gelandesprung Lodge at Snowbowl** (1700 Snowbowl Rd., 406/549-9777, www.montanasnowbowl.com, from $44 shared bath, $56 private bath, $88 two-room suite), a European-style lodge right on the mountain and open throughout the ski season and on weekends in summer. Rates are announced seasonally, so call ahead or check online.

At the other end of the spectrum is an ultraluxe experience that will thin your wallet considerably. The **Resort at Paws Up** (40060 Paws Up Rd., 406/244-5200, luxury tents $980-1,670/night for 2 people) in Greenough, about 32 miles (52 km) east of Missoula, is among the most glamorous spots in the state. There are luxury homes and luxury tents that are unimaginably elegant, with heated floors, electricity, king-size feather beds, a dining pavilion with your own personal chef, a camping butler, and nightly bonfires with s'mores. This is camping fit for a high-maintenance king. The food is exquisite, as is the spa, and the activities and adventures are limitless.

Camping

There are only a handful of private campgrounds in Missoula, but the **Lolo National Forest** (406/329-3750, www.fs.usda.gov/lolo) has a wide range of campsites in beautiful settings, among them Lolo Creek, Ninemile, and Rock Creek. Camping is also permitted in certain sections of the **Rattlesnake National Recreation Area and Wilderness** (406/329-3814) beyond a 3-mile (4.8-km) radius from the main trailhead.

For in-town convenience with RV-specific sites, try the **Missoula KOA** (3450 Tina Ave., 406/549-0881 or 800/562-5366, www.missoulakoa.com, year-round, $35-44 tents, $44-79 RVs, $65-153 cabins). The tree-lined property offers 200 RV and tent sites in addition to amenities like a heated pool, two hot tubs, bike rentals, mini golf, free Wi-Fi, nightly ice cream, and a café that serves breakfast daily in summer. Another great option for Yogi and Boo-Boo fans is the award-winning **Jellystone Park** (9900 Jellystone Ave., 800/318-9644, www.campjellystonemt.com, $36 tents, $47 RVs, $66 cabins), which offers an expansive menu of amenities including air-conditioned cabins, heated swimming pool, playground, mini golf, game room, and nightly visits with Yogi. Offering nice, shady sites just outside of town is the Good Sam-recognized **Jim and Mary's RV Park** (9800 U.S. 93 N., 406/549-4416, www.jimandmarys.com, RV sites $49, including water, sewer, electric, cable TV, and Wi-Fi).

Information and Services

The **Missoula Chamber of Commerce** (825 E. Front St., 406/543-6623, www.missoulachamber.com, 8am-5pm Mon.-Fri.) and **Destination Missoula** (101 E. Main St., 800/526-3465 for travel consultation, www.destinationmissoula.org) are both great sources of information for visitors.

The **U.S. Forest Service** (26 Fort Missoula Rd., 406/329-3511) and the

Montana Department of Fish, Wildlife and Parks (3201 Spurgin Rd., 406/542-5500, 8am-5pm Mon.-Fri.) offices offer good information about hiking, camping, and fishing in the national forests.

The main hospitals are **St. Patrick's** (500 W. Broadway, 406/543-7271) and **Community Medical Center** (2827 Fort Missoula Rd., 406/728-4100), both of which have 24-hour emergency rooms. There are several walk-in urgent care facilities in town. The **CostCare Family Practice Walk-In Clinic** (2819 Great Northern Loop, 406/541-3046, www. costcare.com, 8:30am-5pm Mon.-Fri., 9am-2pm Sat.-Sun.) has several locations and expanded hours, including weekends.

★ Detour: Philipsburg

The little town of Philipsburg (population 920; elevation 5,280 ft/1,609 m) is something of a hidden gem. Off the main drag but right on the Pintler Scenic Route, also known as Highway 1, P-burg, as it is known locally, is an 1890s silver-mining town. Surrounded by mountains—the Pintler Range to the south, the Sapphire Mountains to the west, and the Flint Range to the east—Philipsburg is populated by a beautiful collection of brightly painted Victorian brick buildings that have been brought back from the dead—the state's oldest operating school, jail, and theater are all here—by an exceedingly proud and active local population, many of whom are transplants from faraway places. There is a wonderfully restored hotel, a couple of great restaurants, a fantastic brewery, a candy store straight out of your childhood dreams, and many other reasons to come to Philipsburg and stay awhile. Like all mining towns in these parts, P-burg has seen its own rise and fall. The ups and down are immortalized in a poignant poem by Richard Hugo titled "Degrees of Gray in Philipsburg." Before you go, look it up.

Getting to Philipsburg

From **Missoula,** Philipsburg is 75 miles (121 km) southeast on I-90 and MT-1, an 80-minute drive. From **Butte,** it's 55 miles (89 km) northwest on I-90 and MT-1, a one-hour drive.

Sights

The **Opera House Theatre** (140 S. Sansome St., 406/859-0013, www. operahousetheatre.com) was built in 1896, complete with a sod basement, elaborate dressing rooms, and indoor plumbing. Countless performers played the stage here for throngs of culture-hungry miners. In 1919 the elegant boxes were removed to make way for sound equipment, and the theater continued to attract a wide range of entertainers. It is still undergoing an extensive restoration that started in the late 1990s. This is the oldest continually operating theater in the state, with one of the youngest theater companies, the **Opera House Theatre Company** ($20 adults, $10 children 15 and under), performing live theater and vaudeville shows to much fanfare every summer. Inside, look for five original backdrops painted by Charlie Russell contemporary Edgar S. Paxson.

Granite Ghost Town State Park

Just northeast of town, off Highway 1 near mile marker 36, is a marked but rough dirt road that leads 4 miles (6.4 km) up the mountain to **Granite Ghost Town State Park** (347 Granite Rd., 406/287-3541, www.stateparks.mt.gov, dawn-dusk daily May-Sept., $6/vehicle nonresidents), once the site of one of the world's richest silver-mining districts. Today it's a fascinating and entirely abandoned ghost town.

Granite's first silver strike came in 1865 at the hands of Hector Horton. In the fall of 1872, the Granite mine was established, then relocated in 1875. But when the mine failed to produce anything of substance, a telegram was sent from mine owners on the East Coast that it should be shut down; the telegram was fatefully delayed. As foreman Charles D. McClure prepared to give his workers the bad news, the miners struck silver ore that would produce 1,700 ounces (48,194 g) of silver to the ton, yielding $40 million. Because of the great demand for silver by the U.S. government for coinage, the population of Granite swelled to more than 3,000 almost overnight with miners in pursuit of the $4-per-shift wages. The town grew on the steep mountainside with a two-level main street and many buildings on stilts. Local establishments included the usual abundance of saloons, brothels, and churches, but there was also a sophisticated reading room, bathhouse, and toboggan run that zoomed 2,000 vertical feet (610 m) down the mountain to Philipsburg.

Two mines ran full-bore, making Montana the country's largest silver producer until 1893, when Congress voted to end silver purchases, leading to a rapid mass exodus from Granite. The barely staffed mines eventually merged and produced a modest supply of silver for another decade or so until they flooded in 1915. A 1958 fire demolished what was left of the buildings. Today the town is like a graveyard, filled with brick foundations, rusting equipment, and the faded memories of Montana's biggest silver boom.

By far the most scenic—if somewhat hair-raising—way to get from Philipsburg's Flint Creek Valley to the Bitterroot Valley south of Missoula is by way of **Skalkaho Pass,** a largely graveled 50-mile (81-km) high-mountain road. Highway 38 heads up through the thickly forested Sapphire Mountains 6 miles (9.7 km) south of P-burg and brings adventurous drivers down 3 miles (4.8 km) south of Hamilton. The road is primitive, not for trailers or the faint of heart (particularly driving east, which puts cars along

some pretty precipitous cliffs), seasonal, and well worthwhile.

Skalkaho Pass was long used as a trail by Native Americans traveling between the valleys. A more permanent road was built in 1924 to connect the mining areas around Philipsburg with the agricultural resources in the Bitterroot. There are two campgrounds along the road as well as the spectacular **Skalkaho Falls.** The summit is at 7,260 feet (2,213 m), and the region is home to an abundance of wildlife, including moose, elk, deer, black bears, and mountain goats. Though not well traveled due to its altitude and spotty road conditions, the area does offer incredible recreation opportunities, including hiking, mountain biking, cross-country skiing, and snowmobiling on the plentiful trails.

Sports and Recreation

With all the rivers and lakes in this region—Rock Creek, the Clark Fork, Blackfoot, and Bitterroot Rivers, and more—there are plenty of good places to wet a line. You can get geared up in Philipsburg at **Flint Creek Outdoors** (116 W. Broadway, 406/859-9500, www.blackfootriver.com, 9am-6pm daily summer, 10am-5pm Fri.-Sun. fall-spring), a fishing aficionado's version of The Sweet Palace across the street. The owners of Flint Creek also offer guided fishing trips as **Blackfoot River Outfitters** (from $460 for half-day floats, from $510 for all-day floats for single angler). Once you're geared up, head out to **Rock Creek,** a gorgeous 29-mile (47-km) stream known for its late-May-early-June salmonfly hatch, 15 miles (24 km) west of town. The creek, which looks and fishes more like a river, is chockablock with rainbow, cutthroat, and brown trout. You'll likely be wade fishing here, and although the Rock Creek Road is bumpy and winding, and the fish tend to be a bit smaller than they are closer to the confluence with the Clark Fork River, the access is broad and the anglers are fewer than on other stretches.

Food

Visitors to Philipsburg are advised to arrive in town with an empty belly; the town has a couple of great places to eat. The first stop should always be at ★ **The Sweet Palace** (109 E. Broadway, 406/859-3353, www.sweetpalace.com, 10am-6pm Sun.-Fri. June-Aug., 10am-5pm Sun.-Fri. Sept.-May), itself a Victorian confection. The store is all nostalgia and sugar, and it is certainly among the best candy shops in the state.

The **Doe Brothers Restaurant** (120 E. Broadway, 406/859-6676, 11am-6pm daily, $8-17) is a malt shop in its most classic form, housed in a faithfully restored 1887 drugstore. The counter is lined with sweetheart chairs, and the tables come with boards for chess and checkers. The owners, transplants from North Carolina, have lovingly intertwined some of their own family history with that of Philipsburg. The service is beyond compare, and the food is terrific. The homemade bread is dusted with sugar, the ice cream is all Montana-made, and the entrées—ranging from mouthwatering buffalo burgers and elk stew to Butte-style pasties, crab cakes, and specials like teriyaki salmon—are large and savory. Don't miss the onion rings, which are served hanging on little stands, or the beer-battered fried pickles. And whatever you do, don't forgo dessert.

The **UpNSmokin BBQ House** (127 E. Broadway, 406/240-1616, www.upnsmokin.com, 11am-8pm daily, $10-15) serves up mouthwatering small-batch applewood-smoked barbecue—from brisket and prime rib to pulled pork ribs, sausage, and chicken—for true aficionados. If you need a delicious, easy-on-the-palate craft beer to wash down the succulent barbecue, head over to **Philipsburg Brewing Company** (101 W. Broadway, 406/859-2739, www.philipsburgbrew.

com, 10am-8pm daily) for a pint or a growler. Opened in 2012 in a stunning Victorian building, the bar even boasts a copper plate, cooled with glycol lines, so that mugs set on the bar never get warm. Not unlike the dance floors on springs that Philipsburg was once known for, this is P-burg technology at its best.

Accommodations

For such a tiny town, P-burg has no shortage of wonderful and unique accommodations, with nary a chain hotel to be found.

The front-runner in town is ★ **The Broadway Hotel** (103 W. Broadway, 406/859-8000, www.broadwaymontana.com, $85-170), a cozy hotel with individually themed guest rooms in a beautifully restored 1890 building. There are only nine guest rooms and a couple of cabins, so book early. Some of the rooms are pet friendly, but you'll need to announce Fido well in advance to guarantee his accommodations. Guests enjoy amenities that include a continental breakfast, a coffee bar, ample common areas, wireless Internet, and a local library. TVs and DVD players are in every room.

The newest hotel in town is also the oldest: **The Kaiser House Lodging** (203 E. Broadway, 406/859-2004, www.kaiserhouselodging.com, $94-180). Completed in 1881, the building was a fine restaurant and hotel. The basement was a game room, where high-stakes billiards and cards were played. The place has been beautifully restored, and each of the five rooms has historical charm and modern amenities including telephone, satellite TV, free Wi-Fi, and air-conditioning. The morning breakfasts are a treat.

Nestled creekside along the Skalkaho Pass Road is the ultra-swanky **Ranch at Rock Creek** (79 Carriage House Ln., off MT-38, 877/786-1545, www.theranchatrockcreek.com, $900-1,700 pp/night all-inclusive), which offers an unmatched setting, exquisite service and amenities, and extraordinary accommodations including riverfront cabins, glamorous wall tents, rooms in a converted hayloft, and a five-bedroom riverfront home. Luxury is infused in every detail.

Information

A good source of information on the local area is the **Philipsburg Chamber of Commerce** (109 E. Broadway, 406/859-3388, www.philipsburgmt.com, 9am-5pm Sun.-Fri.).

Butte

Everyone in Montana is (or should be) rooting for Butte. Once the cosmopolitan and urban moneymaking center of the state, Butte (population 34,553; elevation 5,700 ft/1,737 m) today is beat-up and a little bleak; "rough around the edges" is putting it mildly. The most far-reaching and present reminder of its former glory, other than the open-pit mining scars that rend the entire valley, are the car license plates that start with 1, Butte's rank in population when motor vehicles showed up on the scene.

Despite its diminished status, Butte is a remarkable place with the most compelling and diverse history in the state as well as an infrastructure of fabulous old buildings that are just waiting for a renaissance. In fact, Butte is among the largest registered National Historic Landmark Districts in the country, with more than 4,000 historic structures. There is more culture here than just about anywhere in Montana, and there are some marvelous establishments for dining and imbibing.

A weekend in Butte gives visitors an incredible opportunity to learn about Montana's past and see firsthand what happens to a place when all of its natural resources are exploited as quickly as possible. Indeed, there is something of *The Lorax* in Butte, and something of *The*

Giving Tree. But no copper king or corporation can rob this place of its fascinating past and modern-day spirit. And no one is willing to rule out a renaissance—least of all the citizens of Butte.

Getting to Butte
Air
The **Bert Mooney Airport** (BTM, 101 Airport Rd., 406/494-3771, www.butteairport.com) in Butte is served by Delta and Alpine Air Express, with daily direct flights to and from Salt Lake City, Billings, Bozeman, and Helena. NetJets also serves the airport. The car-rental agencies at the airport are **Avis, Budget, Enterprise,** and **Hertz.**

Driving
Butte is 120 miles (193 km) southeast of **Missoula** on I-90, a drive of about two hours.

From **Bozeman,** Butte is 85 miles (137 km) west on I-90, about a 90-minute drive. From **Helena,** it's 70 miles (113 km) south on I-15, a drive of one hour and 15 minutes.

Bus
Bus service from **Greyhound** and **Rimrock Stages** (406/723-3287) is available at 1324 Harrison Avenue.

Getting Around
The Butte-Silver Bow Transit System (406/497-6515, www.buttebus.org, free) offers bus service 6:45am-6:15pm Monday-Friday, with shorter hours on Saturday. You can pick up a bus schedule at the public library or download a copy online. **Mining City Taxi** (406/723-6511) offers service 24 hours every day.

Sights
★ Old Butte Historical Adventures
If you only have one day to spend in Butte, plan to attend one of the walking tours put on by **Old Butte Historical Adventures** (117 N. Main St., 406/498-3424, http://buttetour.info, scheduled

Butte

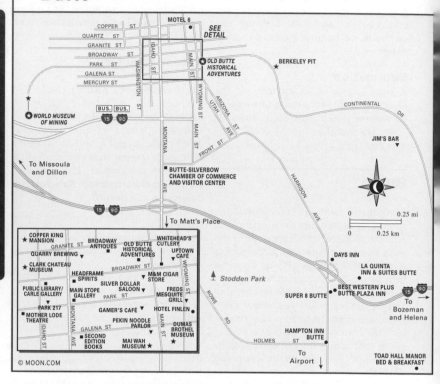

SEE DETAIL

© MOON.COM

tours 10am-2pm Mon.-Sat., by reservation only Sun. Apr.-Oct., by reservation only Nov.-Mar., $20 adults, $17.50 seniors, military, and students with ID, $10 children 5-11). It offers a variety of walking tours of Butte's underground city, complete with a speakeasy, a barbershop, and an old city jail. Other tours stay aboveground and visit the gorgeous Finlen Hotel, an old brothel, and the Mai Wah Museum in Chinatown. Ghost tours, labor history tours, and ethnic culture walking tours can also be arranged. What makes these tours so compelling, other than the mind-blowing history, is the passion and knowledge of the guides—you may just fall in love with Butte. Reservations are strongly recommended.

Berkeley Pit

The transition from underground mining to pit mining in Butte began in 1955. The first open-pit mine dug in pursuit of copper, the **Berkeley Pit** (east end of Park St., 406/723-3177, www.pitwatch. org, 9am-5pm daily Mar.-Nov., $2 to access the viewing stand, $1 children) swallowed several of the underground mines along with entire neighborhoods as the Anaconda Company dug deeper and wider for smaller amounts of copper. The ore mined at the Berkeley Pit, for example, was roughly 0.75 percent copper, compared to the original Marcus Daly ore, which was 30 percent copper.

In 1982, because of steadily falling copper prices, the Berkeley Pit was shut down. With it, the pumps from the nearby Kelley Mine, which had kept the pit dry for nearly 30 years, were shut down as well. The mines under the city and the pit itself immediately started to fill with water bearing the same acidity levels as lemon juice or cola. The water depth today surpasses 5,346 feet (1,629 m) and continues to climb—though more slowly than expected—with 2.6 million gallons (9.8 million liters) flooding in every day. The water itself is highly toxic and appears various shades of brown, blue, green, and red, depending on the concentration of chemicals and subsequent chemical reactions.

In 1994, the EPA established a "critical water level" of 5,410 feet (1,649 m), stipulating that when the water in the pit reaches that level, it could seep into Silver Bow Creek or the alluvial groundwater aquifer and contaminate the region's water supply. The government requires the parties responsible for treating the groundwater to pump and treat the water before it reaches that level, or incur fines of $25,000 per day. Current projections predict the water will reach critical level in 2023.

In November 1995, a flock of snow geese landed in the Berkeley Pit; fog and snow kept them from flying off, and after several days 342 birds were found dead in the water. Since then, a program has discouraged migrating birds from landing on the pit water. In November 2016, more snow geese landed in the pit in a single day than often do in an entire year. Crews employed a number of ways to encourage the birds to leave after a short rest—fireworks, bird wailers, drones—but several thousand stayed for a few days and, sadly, perished as a result.

One curious creature that managed to live in and around the pit for years was a dog known by miners as "The Auditor." He greeted workers daily for 17 years but never came close enough for anyone to touch. He was a white (OK, gray) dog with dreadlocks that dragged on the ground. The miners built him a shanty and left food and water; they pointed to The Auditor as proof that there were indeed things able to withstand the toxicity of the Superfund site. The pit's unofficial mascot died in 2003, but not before the community raised enough money to commission a bronze statue of the mangy mutt, which is on display at the pit viewing stand.

Our Lady of the Rockies

High atop the crest of the Continental Divide is **Our Lady of the Rockies** (tours leave from 3100 Harrison Ave., 406/782-1221, www.ourladyoftherockies.net, 10am and 2pm daily weather permitting, gift shop 9am-5pm daily June-Oct., $16 adults, $14 seniors, clergy, and military, $12 children 13-17, $8 children 5-12, $2 children under 5), a 90-foot (27-m) statue of the Virgin Mary meant to watch over this predominantly Catholic town. Between 1979 and 1985, the statue was built and erected entirely by volunteers, many of them miners who had lost their jobs when the Berkeley Pit, Butte's last operating mine, closed down. Bob O'Bill, who worked for the Anaconda Mining Company for years, vowed that if his wife recovered from illness, he would hoist a statue of the Virgin Mary on the East Ridge overlooking the city. When the final piece was set in place by helicopter, Butte came to a screeching halt to watch in proud silence. Indeed, the statue is a reflection of this city's indomitable spirit. The roughly 2.5-hour tours leave from the gift shop on Harrison Avenue and include a trip inside the metal sculpture.

★ World Museum of Mining

Off West Park Road, across from the Montana Tech campus, is the **World Museum of Mining** (155 Mining Museum Rd., 406/723-7211, www.miningmuseum.org, 9am-6pm daily Apr.-Oct., $8.50 adults, $7.50 seniors 65 and over, $5 students 5-17, free for children under 5), which sits on the now-defunct Orphan Girl mine yard. It houses numerous

large-scale exhibits, and the mine yard is filled with a variety of equipment covering a century of use, including smelter cars, ore carts, and trucks. When you purchase your entry ticket to the museum, you may also want to buy a ticket for the **underground mine tours** that take place three times a day at 10:30am, 12:30pm, and 3pm. Visitors to the underground mine wear hard hats, cap lamps, and battery belts and descend 65 feet (19.8 m) into the mine. The tours are led by former mine workers who tell their personal stories. They also explain how equipment was used and how the ore was mined and removed from the pit. Combined tickets can be purchased for the museum and the underground tour at the 65-foot level ($17 adults, $14 seniors 65 and over, $10 students 4-17, no children under 4) or at the 100-foot level ($21 adults, $18 seniors 65 and over, $15 students 6-17, no children under 6).

A highlight of the museum is its **Hell Roarin' Gulch,** a full-scale, authentic reproduction of an 1890s mining town. There are 50 buildings on the site, 15 of which are original historic buildings that have been relocated to the museum. Visit a bank, general store, school, and Chinese herbalist whose shelves are stocked with original herbs and medicines. The buildings have been painstakingly re-created using as many antiques and original materials as possible. There's also a rock and mineral room in the museum that will delight rock hounds and a remarkable doll and dollhouse collection.

Copper King Mansion

The **Copper King Mansion** (219 W. Granite St., 406/782-7580, www. thecopperkingmansion.com, tours 10am-4pm daily May-Sept., by appointment Oct.-Apr., $10 adults, $5 children) is both a museum and bed-and-breakfast ($105-150). Guided tours show off this 34-room

Top to bottom: view of Butte; World Museum of Mining; the historic Hotel Finlen.

Victorian home built in 1898 for the infamous King of Copper, William Andrews Clark. Considered one of the wealthiest men in the world in his day, Clark could easily afford to import all the material for the house's construction as well as the European artisans needed to do the work. The cost to construct the mansion is estimated at around $500,000, which represents one half-day's wages for Clark at the peak of his career. His personal fortune is thought to have exceeded $50 million by 1900. Each room has a fresco painted on its ceiling by artists personally commissioned by Clark. There is elaborate woodwork throughout the house, including the fireplaces, bookcases, and stairways. Tiffany stained glass windows and magnificent chandeliers enhance the elegance. It is an exquisite way to truly appreciate the wealth in this city around the turn of the 20th century.

Clark Chateau Museum

W. A. Clark's son, Charles, also commissioned a house in 1898. The **Clark Chateau Museum** (321 W. Broadway, 406/565-5600, www.clarkchatcaubutte. wordpress.com, noon-4pm Thurs.-Sun. May-mid-Sept., tours at 1pm and 3pm, by appointment fall-spring, $10 guided tour, $7 general admission, free for children 10 and under, discounts for students, seniors, and military) is a replica of a chateau Charles had admired in France. Today the house is a period museum and Butte's community arts center. Up the gorgeous spiral staircase to the 2nd and 3rd floors is the museum's permanent collection, dedicated to showcasing the diverse cultural and ethnic heritage of the city. Two galleries offer current shows, and the exhibits change over the course of the season. Tours can be arranged off-season by emailing clarkchateau@gmail. com.

Dumas Brothel Museum

Butte also happens to be home to "America's longest-running house of prostitution." The Dumas Brothel was the center of Butte's red-light district back in its mining heyday. Opened in 1890, it only closed its doors in 1982. The brothel reopened as the **Dumas Brothel Museum** (45 E. Mercury St., 406/530-7878, 11:30am-5:30pm Wed.-Sun., $10 admission, children 5 and under free with adult, discounts available for military, seniors, students, and groups), allowing visitors to get a glimpse into the seedier side of the city's history. At its height, the brothel used all 43 rooms and was open 24 hours a day to cater to the miners, who worked around the clock. There were even underground tunnels that led to other downtown buildings, providing secret entry for some of its more distinguished clientele. Since the building was actually constructed to serve as a brothel, it has some unique design elements, including windows lining the hallway. The rooms themselves, known as "cribs," are small enough to hold a bed and not much more. Naturally, the brothel is rife with ghost stories, including the tale of Madame Elenor Knott, who agreed to run away with her married lover in 1955. When he didn't show up for their rendezvous, Elenor took her own life. Her ghost is often reported, and even photographed, in the building. The museum was purchased in 2012 by Travis Eskelsen and Michael Piche, who committed themselves to its preservation and restoration. Tragically, Piche died in 2018. Eskelsen will continue his work in restoring the museum. Always call before visiting, since the restoration process often requires closures, and museum hours change regularly depending on the number of visitors. This is a labor of love in every way imaginable, like so much of Butte's restoration. Be patient and flexible—it's worth it.

Mai Wah Museum

The **Mai Wah Museum** (17 W. Mercury St., 406/723-3231 or 406/565-1826 off-season, www.maiwah.org, 10am-4pm

Tues.-Sat. June-Sept., $5 adults, $3 children under 12) is dedicated to documenting and preserving Butte's Chinese heritage. By 1910, Butte's Chinatown had more than 2,000 Chinese residents, and the 1914 directory listed 62 Chinese businesses that included gambling parlors, noodle shops, herbalists, and grocery stores. The permanent exhibit tells the story of Chinese immigrants to the city who came in search of lucrative jobs in the mining industry 1860-1940. It houses exhibits containing photos, artifacts, and interpretive materials. The museum is in the Wah Chong Tai and Mai Wah buildings, just off China Alley, the heart of Butte's Chinatown. Originally the buildings were a mercantile store and noodle shop that historically served as meeting places and a major point of social interaction for the Chinese immigrant community.

Entertainment and Events
Nightlife

Like a puckish teenager, Butte's reputation has always preceded it. This is a scrappy town where no one likes to back down. Even the most elegant older women love to tell of carrying pearl-handled revolvers every time they traveled into or through Butte. It's a fighting town, which means Butte is a drinking town.

Butte has numerous bars, many of them good ones, with the best being the **M&M Cigar Store** (9 N. Main St., 406/530-6020 or 406/299-3998, 24 hours daily), witness to Butte's glory days from a front-row seat. Opened in 1890, the M&M remained unlocked for more than 100 years. There was once a bowling alley in the basement, a dining and drinking room on the 1st floor, and a gambling lounge upstairs. The cigars were added during Prohibition as a polite show of compliance, but the liquor was never locked up. In a 1970 *Esquire* article, Jack Kerouac wrote a poignant description of a late night spent at the M&M, summing

it up: "It was the end of my quest for an ideal bar." The M&M fell on hard times over the years and had to close down for a short period, but it reopened in 2005 with a beautiful restoration and the same spirit it has always had. So far, the doors have not been locked again since.

The **Silver Dollar Saloon** (133 S. Main St., 406/782-7367, 4pm-2am daily) is another legendary Butte watering hole, established on the border between Chinatown and the red-light district. The adjacent building was both a brothel and a boardinghouse for Chinese laborers. One of the hubs of the city's St. Patrick's Day festivities, the Silver Dollar is known for its live music offerings.

For a more family-friendly place with outstanding beer, try **Quarry Brewing Company** (124 W. Broadway St., 406/723-0245, www.wedig.beer, 3pm-8pm Mon.-Fri., 1pm-8pm Sat., 1pm-6pm Sun.) in the old Grand Hotel. Its five different German-style beers are brewed on-site, and kids will appreciate the play area, free popcorn, and homemade root beer and orange cream soda.

Jim's Bar (2720 Elm St., 406/782-3431, 3pm-2am Sun.-Thurs. 2pm-2am Fri.-Sat.) is kind of a biker bar, with plenty of fun and rowdy events such as biker rodeos and beach volleyball. Closing hours here are dependent on the number of customers.

The Arts

For a selection of contemporary gems, try **Main Stope Gallery** (8 S. Montana St., 406/723-9195, www.mainstopegallery.com, 10am-5pm Tues.-Sat.), which sells pottery, paintings, photography, and other fine art by contemporary Montana artists. Located on the 3rd floor of the Butte public library, the **Carle Gallery** (226 W. Broadway, 406/723-3361, www.buttepubliclibrary.info, 10am-5pm Mon. and Fri.-Sat., 10am-8pm Tues.-Thurs.) pays tribute to Butte artist John Carle, known for his paintings of the city's buildings and people, and hosts monthly shows. The gallery also hosts rotating exhibits from the World Museum of Mining and Mai Wah Museum.

Mother Lode Theatre

Seeing an event at the **Mother Lode Theatre** (316 W. Park St., 406/723-3602, http://buttearts.org) is an event in itself. Built entirely with private funds by the Masons in 1923 as the 1,200-seat Temple Theatre, the glorious building was converted into a movie house during the Depression. As the mines were abandoned, so was the theater. In the 1980s, the only other theater in town was condemned and razed. True to form in Butte, people made it a priority to restore the building; the only more pressing project at the time was a complete overhaul of the city's water system. The Butte Center for the Performing Arts formed as a nonprofit organization to raise the funds necessary and oversee the construction work. The Masons donated the building to the city, and $3 million was raised for the overhaul, completed in 1996. A 106-seat children's theater known as the Orphan Girl Theatre (named for a mine in Butte) was added in 1997 thanks to another big donation.

Today, the Mother Lode provides performance space for the Butte Symphony, Montana Repertory Theatre, Missoula Children's Theatre, traveling Broadway productions, concerts, and numerous other events and organizations.

Silver Bow Drive In

Since 1977, the **Silver Bow Drive In** (116054 S. Buxton Rd., 406/782-8095, www.silverbowdrivein.com, spring-early-Sept., $6 adults, $4 children 3-11, cash only) has been an absolute classic. There really isn't a better way to see a movie under the Big Sky. Two screens allow for a capacity of nearly 500 cars. Don't bring food with you—a concession stand (that until 1973 was at a drive-in theater in Deer Lodge) serves great popcorn and other goodies including Tombstone pizza and ice cream. The audio can be found on your FM dial, or a few portable radios are available to rent for those without a working car radio or who want to sit outside. This is old-timey goodness.

Shopping

Once home to 100,000 people and a number of copper kings, it's no surprise that Butte offers plenty of antiques shopping in the historic uptown. Several antiques stores are located in the area bounded by Main, Montana, Granite, and Galena Streets. **Broadway Antiques** (45 W. Broadway St., 406/723-4270, 10am-5pm Tues.-Sat.) is packed with trinkets and treasures. Not exactly an antiques store, but more of an antique, **Whitehead's Cutlery** (73 E. Park St., 406/723-9188, www.whiteheadscutlery.com, 11am-5pm Mon.-Sat.) was founded in 1890 and is considered to be the oldest continuously operated family-owned small business in the state. Its founder, Joseph Whitehead, made his living by traveling to mining camps in the region selling and sharpening knives. His first grinder in Butte was powered by a St. Bernard that ran on a treadmill to run the wheel. While his own line of products expanded from knives to include straight razors, barber supplies, and hockey and figure skates, Joseph's son Edward collected knives and swords from around the world. The impressive collection is on display and worth a visit. Another Butte treasure is **Second Edition Books** (112 S. Montana St., 406/723-5108, www.secondeditionbooks.com, 9:30am-5:30pm Mon.-Sat.), a second-generation, family-run used bookstore. In addition to a great selection of Butte books, both common and rare, Second Edition Books carries a nice selection of books on Montana, mining, engineering, geology, Yellowstone, and Glacier. There is also a children's section.

If you lack space in your suitcase for antique treasures and have a taste for spirits, stop into **Headframe Spirits** (21 Montana St., 406/299-2886, www.

headframespirits.com, 10am-8pm daily), founded in 2010 but steeped in Butte history. You can sip and sample the Neversweat Bourbon Whiskey, Destroying Angel Whiskey, Anselmo Gin, High Ore Vodka, and Orphan Girl Bourbon Cream Liquor. Tours of the distillery are offered Thursday at 5pm, Friday at 4pm, Saturday at 2:30pm and 4:30pm, and Sunday in July only at 2pm. Or you can skip the tour and relax with a cocktail in the tasting room. It's really a fitting way to spend an afternoon in Butte.

Food

No other Montana town can match the culinary history and culture of Butte. The Butte pasty, inspired by the Cornish dish, is a flaky pastry filled with meat and potatoes for the ultimate miner's lunch; when in Butte, it is the thing to try. The **Gamer's Café** (15 W. Park St., 406/723-5453, 7am-2pm Mon.-Sat., $3-9) is a quaint little spot, founded in 1905, that feels like an old ice-cream parlor. There are no irritating keno machines, despite the name (those are next door in the casino), and the home-cooked food is excellent. Breakfast is served all day, and lunches include homemade soups, burgers, and sandwiches. Still, this is Butte, and you've got to try a pasty: The ones here are made with New York steak from Montana beef and potatoes grown just down the road in Twin Bridges. Don't miss the apple dumpling for dessert, warm with a scoop of ice cream.

For a rare treat and a step back in time, head to ★ **Matt's Place** (2339 Placer St., 406/782-8049, 11:30am-6:30pm Tues.-Sat. first Mon. in Mar.-week before Christmas, $5-10). Open since 1930 and run by only two families in all that time, Matt's is famous for nut burgers (topped with ground peanuts and mayonnaise) and pork chop sandwiches, both of which ought to be washed down with one of its world-class milk shakes; the ice cream is made daily on-site. The place only seats 18 at a counter, so you'll likely make some new friends. Although not exactly healthy, a meal at Matt's is a unique, delicious, and entirely worthwhile experience.

Another fun and historic establishment is the **Pekin Noodle Parlor** (117 Main St., 406/782-2217, 5pm-10:30pm Sun.-Mon. and Wed.-Thurs., 5pm-3am Fri.-Sat., $6-17), Butte's oldest Chinese restaurant, open since 1911. The place is casual and utterly authentic with private booths hidden behind curtains. Everything is the color of a Creamsicle. Reading the menu is a lesson in history, and an evening in the parlor is time well spent. Hours can vary depending on the number of customers, so call ahead.

The locals love **Fred's Mesquite Grill** (205 S. Arizona St., 406/723-4440, 11am-8pm daily, $8-30), a casual place with ample outdoor seating and the best ribs and kebabs in town. Fred was a salty character with a heart of gold and had a penchant for motorcycles and great food. Though he died in 2007, his legacy is still alive—and delicious.

Long considered the best restaurant in Butte, the ★ **Uptown Café** (47 E. Broadway, 406/723-4735, www.uptowncafe.com, 11am-2pm and 5pm-9pm Mon.-Fri., 5pm-9pm Sat.-Sun., $13-37) is a gourmet restaurant with sophisticated style and plenty of Butte spirit. The creative and mouthwatering dinner menu offers pasta, beef, poultry, and seafood entrées, and daily changing specials are posted online. If you want to believe the renaissance in Butte is imminent, enjoy a meal at the Uptown Café.

A decidedly interesting place for upscale dining, craft cocktails, and excellent wine in Butte is **Park 217** (217 W. Park St., 406/299-3570, www.park217.com, 5pm-close Tues.-Sat., wine bar from 4pm, $15-33), which opened in 2015. Housed in a restored hotel with an exposed granite foundation and wood accents, the below-street-level restaurant has a metropolitan ambience and harkens back to the days when much of Butte's nightlife happened beneath the streets. The menu features excellent steaks and seafood and changes regularly to make the most of fresh, seasonal ingredients. The wine bar features an impressive wine list that spans the globe, plus spirits and craft beers.

Accommodations

Although Butte has quite an assortment of nice chain-type hotels, there are a couple of places that will have significantly more appeal to those caught up in the saga of Butte's past and present. William Andrews Clark's ★ **Copper King Mansion** (219 W. Granite St., 406/782-7580, www.thecopperkingmansion.com, $105-150) is also a bed-and-breakfast. Accommodations range from the butler's room to the Clarks' master bedroom. Because it is a functioning museum, check-in is at 4pm and guests must check out by 9am to accommodate the tour schedule. Guided tours are free for guests, and a full breakfast is served in the formal dining room.

In the heart of uptown Butte is another fantastic old building striving to achieve its former glory. **Hotel Finlen** (100 E. Broadway, 406/723-5461 or 800/729-5461, www.finlen.com, $84-116) was built in 1924 on the site of the old McDermott Hotel, one of the grandest in the Northwest. Modeled after the Astor Hotel in New York City, the Finlen is a nine-story Second Empire building with a copper-shingled roof. Over the years, Hotel Finlen was visited by Charles Lindberg, Harry Truman, John F. Kennedy, and Richard Nixon. As is true of all of Butte, Hotel Finlen fell into disrepair and neglect as the mining economy dried up. The Taras family purchased the hotel in 1979 and has worked hard to restore the lobby and mezzanine, both of which are more beautiful than ever. The 30 guest rooms are basic, and the 25 guest rooms in the motor inn are dated; still, there is history here, and with some luck, a future.

For classic charm on the lush grounds of the Butte Country Club, **Toad Hall Manor Bed & Breakfast** (1 Green Ln., 406/494-2625 or 866/443-8623, www.toadhallmanor.com, $130-185) is an excellent choice. From a goblet of sherry or port upon arrival to feather beds, Jacuzzi tubs, and decadent breakfasts, Toad Hall Manor offers classic B&B style.

Information and Services

The front of the **Butte-Silver Bow Chamber of Commerce and Visitor Information Center** (1000 George St., 406/723-3177 or 800/735-6814, www.buttechamber.org, 8am-6pm Mon.-Sat, 9am-4pm Sun. summer, 10am-5pm Mon. and Fri.-Sat. winter) is stocked with brochures, pamphlets, and tour information; in back, you can usually find a helpful chamber employee to answer questions. A terrific Butte online resource is www.butteamerica.com.

The emergency room at **St. James Hospital** (400 S. Clark St., 406/723-2627) is open 24 hours every day. Butte has walk-in medical facilities, including **St. James Rocky Mountain Clinic** (435 S. Crystal St., #300, 406/496-3600, 8am-5pm Mon.-Fri.) and **Express Care** (435 S. Crystal St., #200, 406/723-6889, 8am-5:30pm Mon.-Fri.).

Three Forks

Named for the three rivers that form the headwaters of the Missouri River, Three Forks (population 1,944; elevation 4,075 ft/1,242 m) was put on the map by Lewis and Clark in 1805. The town is rich in fur trapping and trading history and equally distinguished today by a tightly knit community and a mild climate that locals refer to as the "banana belt."

The **Three Forks Rodeo** is held annually the third weekend in July at the fairgrounds and includes a parade, two nights of rodeo, plenty of food, and entertainment. The town's **Christmas Stroll** is to what every small town should aspire: the crowning of a Christmas King and

Queen, fireworks, horse-drawn wagon rides, a community cookie exchange, and s'mores around the bonfire.

For a historical treat, the ★ **Sacajawea Hotel** (5 N. Main St., 406/285-6515, www.sacajaweahotel.com, $150-254) is one-of-a-kind. Lovingly restored in 2010 by the Folkvord family, local farmers who own the enormously successful Wheat Montana Bakeries, the Sac is a historic gem. There are 29 charming and comfortable rooms, some of which are pet friendly, ranging from full beds to kings. The amenities are pretty plush and the food is sensational. Visit the Sac for a meal, or just a cocktail, at **Pompey's Grill** (4:30pm-9pm Mon.-Thurs., 4:30pm-10pm Fri.-Sat., 4pm-9pm Sun., $18-46).

Six miles (9.7 km) south of Three Forks, the small community of **Willow Creek** (population 210; elevation 4,153 ft/1,266 m) has plenty of charm. The creek that runs through town was originally named Philosopher's River by William Clark, but the town wisely renamed it and the town for the willows that grow along the banks. The town's half-dozen artists organize the **Willow Creek Art Walks** the third Friday of each month June-August. A local gallery not to be missed is **Aunt Dofe's Hall of Recent Memory** (102 Main St., 406/285-6996, www.auntdofe.com, hours vary), which supports the work of contemporary local artists. Across the street, the ★ **Willow Creek Café and Saloon** (21 N. Main St., 406/285-3698, noon-10pm Mon., 4am-10pm Tues.-Fri., 11am-10pm Sat.-Sun., $9.50-29) draws diners from far and wide for its quaint ambience and savory cuisine, including the best ribs in the valley, maybe the whole state. You can't go wrong with the daily specials—everything is made from scratch. And if you can time your dinner on a night when **Montana Rose** is playing, you're in for a real treat.

Nevada City is a beautifully restored ghost town.

◈ Detour: Virginia City and Nevada City

Another 75 miles (121 km) southeast of Butte are Virginia City and Nevada City, two thriving ghost towns left over from Montana's glorious gold-mining era. In May 1863, a party of six prospectors left Bannack after a string of bad luck. While they set up camp for the night along Alder Creek, the men discovered what would become one of the richest gold deposits in North America. Nine camps grew up along the creek almost overnight, the largest of which would be named Virginia City.

Within a year, the town had upward of 10,000 residents and became the first territorial capital. It was also the site of the state's first newspaper, the first public school, and the first Masonic lodge. The town's history is intertwined with the Vigilantes of Montana, the group that would hang Sheriff Henry Plummer, among others, in 1864.

By 1875, much of the mining activity in the region had abated, and Virginia City's population had dwindled to less than 800. Over the years, as new technologies developed, including the mining dredges, the area was mined over and over for traces of what might be left. Still, between 1863 and 1889, some $90 million worth of gold had been extracted from the region. Today, that amount of gold would be worth $40 billion.

In 1961, Virginia City was designated a National Historic Landmark and protected as an important historic site. Since then, many of the buildings have been restored to function as shops, restaurants, and a hotel. The display of artifacts in both Virginia City and Nevada City constitutes the largest collection of Old West memorabilia outside the Smithsonian. The population of 198 people works hard to re-create the atmosphere of Virginia City at its peak.

There are **train rides** on a 1910 locomotive between the cities, and an abundance of living history exhibits scattered around the sites. Plenty of services—accommodations and restaurants—are available for visitors who plan to stay.

Entertainment and Events

Throughout the summer, nightly cabaret entertainment at **Brewery Follies at Gilbert Brewery** and nightly 19th-century melodrama courtesy of the **Virginia City Players at the Opera House** entertain visitors.

For more than six decades, the illustrious **Virginia City Players** (338 W. Wallace St., Virginia City, 406/843-5312 or 800/829-2969, ext. 2, www.virginiacityplayers.com, 4pm Tues.-Thurs., 7pm Fri.-Sat., 2pm Sat.-Sun., times can vary year to year so check the website or call ahead, $20 adults, $18 college students, seniors, and military, $12 children 17 and under) have been entertaining the crowds at the Virginia City Opera House with turn-of-the-20th-century-style melodrama and variety acts. They generally offer three shows over the course of the summer season and also play silent movies on one of only two operating photoplayers in the world. Reservations are strongly encouraged.

For more outlandish theater and comedy geared strictly to adults, the **Brewery Follies** (200 E. Cover St., Virginia City, 800/829-2969, ext. 3, www.breweryfollies. net, 8pm Tues.-Wed., 4pm and 8pm Thurs.-Mon. Memorial Day weekend-Sept., $20) at the Old H. S. Gilbert Brewery offers the unique setting of a restored 1864 brewery with bawdy entertainment and excellent microbrews.

Food and Accommodations

This is not plain burger-and-fries country (although the beef in southwestern Montana is notably good). There is fine dining at **Wells Fargo Steakhouse** (314 W. Wallace St., Virginia City, 406/843-5556, 5pm-10pm Tues.-Sun. mid-May-mid-Sept., $18-35), a stately building with tall tin ceilings and a grand horseshoe bar. In addition to gourmet cuisine like crispy cumin-crusted chicken, seared duck breast with brown ale glacé, and, of course, mouthwatering steaks, the Wells Fargo often hosts live music in its ballroom-size dining room.

The ★ **Star Bakery Restaurant** (1576 U.S. 287, Nevada City, 406/843-5777, www.aldergulchaccommodations. com, 7am-7pm Thurs.-Mon. Memorial Day-Labor Day, $15-30) has been serving delicious and hearty meals since 1863 when it was a hot spot with miners. Today the clientele is more family-oriented, and the menu has plenty to appeal to everyone, including homemade sandwiches, beer-battered shrimp, and sodas from the early-1900s soda fountain. The restaurant is known for its fried pickles, so you might want to indulge. The emporium offers quick sugary goodies like ice cream, fudge, and penny candy, too.

For a historical lodging experience, the **Fairweather Inn** (305 W. Wallace St., Virginia City, 406/843-5377 or 800/829-2969, ext. 4, www. aldergulchaccommodations.com, June-mid-Sept., $120-164) is a building from 1863 with plenty of charm. There are 14 guest rooms, six of which have en suite baths; the others share facilities. Don't expect to find a bed larger than a double in this property. The ★ **Nevada City Hotel & Cabins** (1578 U.S. 287, Nevada City, booking 855/377-6823, or 406/843-5377 or 800/829-2969, ext. 4, mid-May-late Sept., $120-175) has a more rustic exterior with slightly more elegant interiors. All the guest rooms have private baths, and two Victorian suites have their own balconies. The cabins are true sod-roofed pioneer cabins that have been updated with comfortable accommodations and modern amenities. Both hotels offer ideal access to all the sights in Virginia City and Nevada City plus some local discounts.

Information and Services

The **Virginia City Chamber** (406/843-5555 or 800/829-2969, www.virginiacity. com) does not have a physical address but provides information by phone and on its website. The **Montana Heritage Commission** (300 W. Wallace St., Virginia City, 406/843-5247, www. montanaheritagecommission.mt.gov, summer) is a good source of information because it manages most of the sights in Virginia City and Nevada City.

Visitor services are available at four staffed areas throughout summer: **Virginia City Depot Visitors Information Center, Virginia City Depot Gift Store, Nevada City Open Air Museum,** and the **Alder Gulch Shortline Railroad.** More information is available from the Montana Heritage Commission (406/843-5247, www.montanaheritagecommission. mt.gov).

Cell service is not available in Virginia City or Nevada City.

Bozeman

With Montana State University anchoring it and a geographical setting that has always appealed to outdoors enthusiasts and nature lovers, over the last 25 years Bozeman (population 45,250; elevation 4,820 ft/1,469 m) has grown from a cow town to a town of wine bars and art. The historic downtown is the heart of the community and attracts locals for numerous special events. There are a number of excellent restaurants and bars that appeal to everyone from broke and thirsty students to whiskey and wine connoisseurs. A handful of galleries and some unique shops round out downtown's offerings.

Although the city is expanding exponentially and always on the list of Montana's fastest-growing cities, and Gallatin County (which encompasses the geography of Gallatin Valley) was ranked the fastest-growing county of its size in the United States in 2018, the original draw—nature—is still intact. Bridger Bowl and Big Sky are two excellent alpine skiing destinations nearby. The Gallatin, Madison, and Yellowstone Rivers, three blue-ribbon trout streams, are also nearby, in addition to numerous smaller streams. And there are literally hundreds of hiking and biking trails, enough to satisfy the most hard-core enthusiast.

Getting to Bozeman
Air
Bozeman Yellowstone International Airport (BZN, 406/388-8321, www.bozemanairport.com) is 8 miles (12.9 km) northwest of downtown Bozeman in the nearby town of Belgrade. Delta, Alaska, American, Allegiant, Frontier, Jet Blue, and United all offer daily nonstop service to and from major U.S. cities, including Salt Lake City, Minneapolis, Seattle, Atlanta, Chicago, and Denver. Seasonal nonstop flights serve Houston, Las Vegas, Los Angeles, New York, Phoenix, Portland, and San Francisco.

Driving
Off I-90, Bozeman is easily accessible by car. It is 85 miles (137 km) east of **Butte** on I-90, about a 90-minute drive.

From **Butte,** Bozeman is 90 miles (145 km) southeast on I-90, a 1.5-hour drive. From **Helena,** it's 100 miles (161 km) southeast on U.S. 287 and I-90, a drive of about 1 hour and 40 minutes.

Bus
Greyhound travels to almost 40 towns and cities in Montana from the bus depot (1205 E. Main St., 612/499-3468, 10am-3pm daily).

Getting Around
From the airport, the Best Western, Comfort Inn, and Hampton Inn offer shuttle service. A number of car-rental agencies are at the airport too; the car-rental center is located next to the baggage claim. **Alamo, Avis, Budget, Enterprise, Dollar, Hertz, Thrifty,** and **National** have on-site counters.

The only ground transportation provider within the terminal, **Karst Stage** (406/556-3540 or 800/287-4759, www.karststage.com), offers daily bus service in winter to Big Sky ($54 one-way with two-fare minimum, $82 round-trip) and West Yellowstone ($178 pp round-trip, or $98 pp one-way). Shuttles are by reservation only in non-winter months.

Greater Valley Taxi (406/388-9999 or 406/587-6303, www.greatervalleytaxi.com) has a courtesy phone next to the baggage claim area. Rides into Bozeman cost $3.50 per mile plus a $6.00 pickup fee. Each additional passenger is $5. It is also a good option for getting around town while you are in Bozeman. **Shuttle to Big Sky & Taxi** (406/995-4895 or 888/454-5667, www.bigskytaxi.com) provides private van and SUV transportation to, from, and around Big Sky. **Uber** (www.uber.com) also serves the Bozeman area.

Sights

★ Museum of the Rockies

Best known for its paleontology exhibit curated by dinosaur guru Jack Horner, **Museum of the Rockies** (600 W. Kagy Blvd., 406/994-2251, www. museumoftherockies.org, 8am-6pm daily Memorial Day-Labor Day, 9am-5pm Mon.-Sat., noon-5pm Sun. Labor Day-Memorial Day, $14.50 adults, $13.50 seniors 65 and over, $10 MSU students with ID, $9.50 children 5-17, free for children 4 and under) is a fantastic resource for the entire state. The museum tackles 500 million years of history (no small feat) with permanent exhibits that reflect Native American culture, 19th-to 20th-century regional history, an outdoor living history farm (open only in summer), a planetarium, and, of course, the dinosaurs.

The Siebel Dinosaur Complex includes hundreds of important fossils and an array of impressive life-size reproductions. The traveling exhibitions vary widely—think the villas of Oplontis near Pompeii, guitars, *National Geographic*'s 50 greatest photos, and even chocolate—but typically offer excellent contrast to the permanent exhibits.

The Martin Children's Discovery Center upstairs offers a great place for preschool and elementary schoolchildren to play in hands-on Yellowstone exhibits. They can camp in a tent, listen for the eruption of Old Faithful (beware—it's loud, surprising, and often scary for little ones), recline in an eagle's nest, cook up a feast in a log cabin, fish for magnetic fish, and dress up as a park ranger or firefighter. For kids with vivid imaginations, this may be the highlight of the museum. In addition, the museum offers several engaging classes for children as young as infants and excellent day camps for elementary-age kids.

The gift shop is outstanding and includes a great selection of local jewelry, science-oriented toys, art, books, and even candy.

Some argue that the admission fees are too steep, particularly if you come when there is no traveling exhibit, but on a rainy day in Bozeman, the museum can provide hours of compelling exploration. Additionally, admission provides unlimited access for two consecutive days.

Downtown Bozeman

Historic downtown Bozeman is interesting architecturally and compelling culturally. It is without a doubt the heart and soul of the city, and more often than not it is the gathering point for Bozeman's most celebrated events, including **Bite of Bozeman, Music on Main, Crazy Days,** various parades, and **Christmas Stroll.** Businesses have faced some stiff competition from big-box stores on the perimeter of town, and there is significant turnover in retail and restaurants, but local residents support downtown in meaningful ways, even starting a petition campaign to fight to keep staple businesses, like the Owenhouse Ace Hardware, on Main Street. For a list of businesses and a calendar of weekly, annual, and special events that really showcase Main Street, visit www.downtownbozeman.org.

Gallatin History Museum

Touted as the place "where history and Main Street meet," the **Gallatin History Museum** (317 W. Main St., 406/522-8122, www.gallatinhistorymuseum.org, 11am-5pm Tues.-Sat. Memorial Day-Labor Day, 11am-4pm Tues.-Sat. Labor Day-Memorial Day, $7.50 adults, free for children under 12, school groups, and researchers) is operated by the Gallatin Historical Society in Bozeman's 1911 county jail building. The museum shared space with the prisoners 1979-1982 before the current jail was completed. It boasts a comprehensive permanent collection of items that reflect Bozeman's early history, including an authentic 1870s homesteader's cabin, an agricultural room, substantial historical photographs, and a sheriff's room that houses plenty of artifacts and

Bozeman

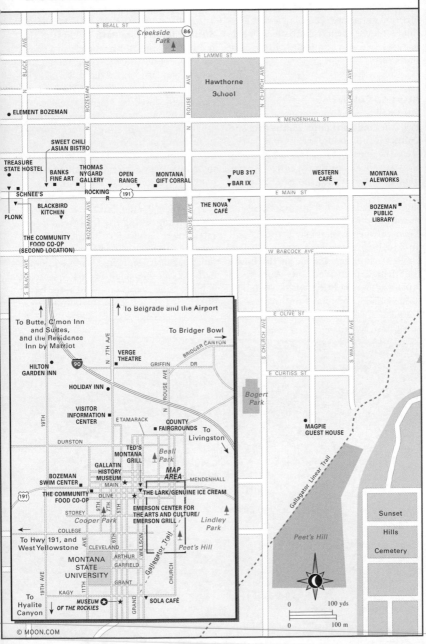

© MOON.COM

exhibits related to crime and punishment in the Old West. The Silsby Fire Engine, a top-of-the-line engine when it was manufactured in the late 1800s, is a favorite exhibit for kids. The museum offers weekly lectures, free with admission, throughout the summer.

Emerson Center for the Arts and Culture

Operated as an elementary school 1918-1991, the **Emerson Center for the Arts and Culture** (111 S. Grand Ave., 406/587-9797, www.theemerson.org), or The Emerson, as it is more commonly called, is the nucleus of Bozeman's robust arts scene. More than 30 studios, galleries, boutiques, and art-related businesses reside in the building in addition to Crawford Theater, one of the best in town, and an excellent restaurant, the Emerson Grill. In summer, **Lunch on the Lawn** (11:30am-1:30pm Wed. July-Aug., free) is a Bozeman tradition with live music, food vendors, and lots of smiling faces.

★ Madison Buffalo Jump State Park

Farther afield—closer to Three Forks—but well worth the visit is **Madison Buffalo Jump State Park** (6990 Buffalo Jump Rd., 7 mi/11.3 km south of Logan off I-90, 406/994-4042, www.stateparks. mt.gov, sunrise-sunset daily, $6/vehicle nonresidents, $4/walk-in, bicycle, bus passenger). Used by Native Americans some 2,000 years ago (and as recently as 200 years ago), long before horses were brought to North America, buffalo jumps are a testament to human ingenuity. A small, covered interpretive display explains how Native Americans persuaded bison up the hill and off the cliff to their deaths, but the real lesson comes from hiking the trail (watch for rattlesnakes and cacti, both of which love the sun here) and exploring the site independently. Tipi rings can be identified, as can eagle-catching pits. Splinters of bison bone have been found at the base of the cliff. Aside from the compelling

Bozeman is a fast-growing college town.

history of the area and the magnificent views from the top, the park's location limits traffic, and you are likely to have the place to yourself.

Entertainment and Events
Nightlife

In downtown Bozeman, **Plonk** (29 E. Main St., 406/587-2170, www.plonkwine. com, 11:30am-2am daily) is an elegant wine bar as known for its tapas and desserts—start with the cheese board or ploughman's platter and finish with the chef's chocolate board for dessert—as for its remarkably global selection of more than 600 wines. The atmosphere is a captivating integration of 100-year-old architecture, contemporary original works of art, minimalist urban design, and an eclectic collection of well-played vinyl records. In the summertime, the crowd spills outside to a handful of sidewalk tables. In a mostly family-friendly town, this is one establishment that does not welcome children or babies.

Also downtown, **Bar IX** (311 E. Main St., 406/551-2185, www.bar-ix.com, 2pm-2am Mon.-Fri., 11am-2am Sat.-Sun.) is both industrial and rustic, and it's usually hopping. Its happy hour specials and Bucket Nights are well known locally. Appealing to Bozeman's athletic crowd, **Pub 317** (321 E. Main St., 406/582-8898, www.pub317.com, 11am-2am daily) is one of the few bars that hosts running races. Twice each year, the Irish pub sponsors 10Ks or half-marathons that end back at the bar. There's usually live Irish music on Sunday, live bluegrass on Tuesday, and trivia nights on Wednesday. An ideal spot for a gourmet Montana meal or just a mean cocktail, **Open Range** (241 E. Main St., 406/404-1940, www. openrangemt.com, dining 5pm-10pm daily, drink service 10pm-close daily) is an upscale favorite.

Popular with the college (and alumni) crowds is the **Rocking R Bar** (211 E. Main St., 406/587-9355, www.rockingrbar.com, 11am-2am daily), a favorite hangout since the 1940s.

Theater

For a relatively small Rocky Mountain town, Bozeman has a decent number of theater offerings. The best is certainly **Broad Comedy** (406/522-7623, www. broadcomedy.com), which produces irreverent and side-splitting satire by a female cast (and geared to mature audiences only). The company has achieved global recognition and plenty of YouTube followers. If you are in town when the company is performing, be there. Broad Comedy was also the founder of (and still runs) the highly respected and always full Camp Equinox, an incredible summertime theatre experience for kids.

Verge Theater (2304 N. 7th Ave., 406/587-0737, www.vergetheater.com) has been around for more than 20 years (until 2013 as Equinox Theatre Company) and produces eclectic and original shows, many of which are hilariously funny. The company produces eight main stage shows each year and six children's matinees. It is also home to the region's only full-time improv comedy troupe.

One of the state's most beloved troupes, **Montana Shakespeare in the Parks** (www.shakespeareintheparks.org) is based out of Montana State University and travels all over the state bringing fantastic, outdoor (when weather permits), and free Shakespearean theater to parks and even cow pastures around the Northern Rockies in small, underserved communities. The company, which travels to do school workshops in the off-season, has been bringing the Bard to the people since 1973. Bill Pullman is one of the company's most famous alumni. You can always catch a glimpse of them at Bozeman's Sweet Pea Festival, but going to see them anywhere in Montana or Wyoming is worth doing.

Music

Thanks to the eager audiences provided by the university, Bozeman also has a lively and impressive music scene. **Intermountain Opera Bozeman** (104 E. Main St., Ste. 101, 406/587-2889, www. intermountainopera.org) has been producing two professional shows annually since 1978. The shows feature world-class performers and conductors with a local chorus and orchestra and are staged at the **Willson Auditorium** (404 W. Main St., 406/587-2889) in the spring and fall. The **Bozeman Symphony Orchestra and Symphonic Choir** (406/585-9774, www. bozemansymphony.org) presents a number of performances each season, starting in September, that range from late Renaissance pieces through the 20th century. It also performs annually with the Montana Ballet Company in *The Nutcracker*. **Vootie Productions** (406/586-1922, www.vootie.com) brings outstanding performers to town regularly.

Live from the Divide (627 E. Peach St., www.livefromthedivide.com, show dates vary, tickets from $20) is an independently produced hour-long public radio program celebrating the songwriters of American roots music. Tickets are sold to 50 lucky music lovers who get to sit in on the taping. Check the calendar online for the next show.

Festivals and Events

Although Bozeman residents joke about the "nine months of winter and three months of houseguests," people take summertime recreation very seriously, and the town of Bozeman (www. downtownbozeman.org) has created numerous ways to celebrate outside as much as possible. Residents and visitors gather on the lawn at the Emerson Center for the Arts and Culture for **Lunch on the Lawn** (11:30am-1:30pm Wed. July-Aug., free), a concert series that attracts 100-200 people and an interesting mix of food vendors. **Music on Main** (6:30pm-8:30pm Thurs. July-Aug., free) is an opportunity for folks to gather downtown on closed-off streets and enjoy live music, food vendors, and early-evening

activities for kids. On the second Friday of every month June-September, art lovers gather for the **Downtown Bozeman Art Walk** (406/586-4008, 6pm-8pm), an opportunity to stroll through the galleries downtown, sipping wine and tasting hors d'oeuvres along the way. Another summer event, **Crazy Days** (downtown, 406/586-4008), is a price-slashing shopping extravaganza that happens each year the third weekend in July.

Bozeman also boasts two fabulous **farmers markets.** The original is the **Bogert Farmers' Market** (S. Church Ave., www.bogertfarmersmarket.org, 5pm-8pm Tues.), held in Bogert Park. It includes everything from produce, arts, and crafts to gourmet food trucks, entertainment, and activities (like reverse bungee jumping and rock climbing for kids). The park is packed, so plan to stay in immediate contact with little ones; for a more relaxing evening, bring a blanket and park yourself away from the masses. A larger market, the **Gallatin Valley Farmers' Market** (901 N. Black Ave., 406/388-6701, ext. 101, www. gallatinvalleyfarmersmarket.com, 9am-noon Sat. mid-June-early Sept.), runs at the Gallatin County Fairgrounds.

Shopping

Like most regional hubs in Montana, Bozeman offers an abundance of shopping opportunities for every taste and budget level. Major stores include Target and Costco on North 19th Avenue as well as Walmart and Murdoch's Ranch & Home Supply on North 7th Avenue. **Downtown Bozeman** (www. downtownbozeman.org), however, is by far the best place to go for unique items and pure charm.

The **Country Bookshelf** (28 W. Main St., 406/587-0166, www. countrybookshelf.com, 9am-7pm Mon.-Fri., 9am-6pm Sat., 10am-5pm Sun.) is Bozeman's most beloved bookstore and the state's largest independent bookstore. It is especially geared to local and

Downtown Bozeman offers excellent strolling, shopping, and dining.

regional authors, many of whom are willing to show their affection for the place with readings and book signings. On the same block is **Vargo's Jazz City & Books** (6 W. Main St., 406/587-5383, 9:30am-7pm Mon.-Fri., 10am-6pm Sat., 11am-5pm Sun.), an excellent place to get lost. The shop specializes in slightly more obscure books, CDs, and vinyl, both new and used.

For marvelous gifts and cards, there are three excellent boutiques downtown. **Perspectives** (424 E. Main St., 406/522-7125, www.perspectivesmt.com, 10am-5:30pm Mon.-Sat.) offers an adorable selection of baby clothes, shoes, and gifts in addition to distinctive bags, cards, stationery, and jewelry. Touted as a shop "for the everyday celebration," **HeyDay** (7 W. Main St., 406/586-5589, www.heydaybozeman.com, 10am-7pm Mon.-Sat., 10am-5pm Sun.) specializes in timeless home decor and elegant gifts. From gardening to personal grooming, cooking, and entertaining, this stylish little shop is sure to make you smile. For gifts that could only come from Montana, **Montana Gift Corral** (237 E. Main St., 406/585-8625, www.giftcorral.com, 9am-8pm Mon.-Fri., 9am-6pm Sat., 10am-5pm Sun.) is the place to go.

Hunters and outdoors enthusiasts will find top-of-the-line shopping in downtown Bozeman. Occupying two beautifully restored 1903 storefronts is an outstanding local shoe store and something of a Bozeman institution, **Schnee's** (35 E. Main St., 406/587-0981, www.schnees.com, 8am-8pm Mon.-Fri., 9am-6pm Sat., 10am-5pm Sun.). It sells everything from locally made bombproof hunting boots to a selection of very hip street shoes and sandals. It also sells clothes and accessories, leather bags, and hunting and fishing gear, and takes its 100 percent satisfaction guarantee very seriously.

Bozeman has a number of notable art galleries. **Thomas Nygard Gallery** (133 E. Main St., 406/586-3636, www.

nygardgallery.com, 9am-5pm Mon.-Fri.) specializes in Western, wildlife, and sports art. Just down the street, **A. Banks Gallery** (127 E. Main St., 406/586-1000, www.abanksgallery.com, 10am-5:30pm Mon.-Fri., 10am-4:30pm Sat., noon-4pm Sun.) displays an outstanding collection of American, Western, and sports art. **Visions West Contemporary** (34 W. Main St., 406/522-9946, www.visionswestcontemporary.com, 10am-5:30pm Mon.-Wed., 10am-6pm Thurs.-Sat.) is a dynamic space that focuses on contemporary artists in the West.

Bozeman's most significant shopping event is **Crazy Days** (downtown Bozeman, 406/586-4008), an annual event held on the third weekend in July. Merchants reduce their inventory prices by up to 75 percent and put much of it out on the street. Early birds are the winners here; it's not uncommon to see several brand-new pairs of last year's skis being carried away by happy new owners.

Sports and Recreation
Hiking

Many of Montana's cities and towns have constructed an enormous letter on a mountain or hill nearby. Bozeman's B has faded away over time, but the **M** (for Montana State University) is one of the community's favorite, and often most crowded, hiking spots. Accessed from a small parking lot on the west side of Bridger Drive, just past and across the road from the Bozeman Fish Technology Center, the M is hard to miss and well worth the hike. There is a steep route up (20-30 minutes) or a longer, gentler route (45 minutes-1 hour), making mix-and-match loops a possibility. The diehards can follow the trail 21 miles (34 km) to the **Fairy Lake Campground** near the end of Bridger Canyon.

South of town is another excellent recreation area, **Hyalite Canyon** (south on S. 19th Ave. to Hyalite Canyon Rd.), one of the most popular in the state. There are excellent opportunities for boating on the reservoir, fishing in Hyalite Creek, and hiking on the various trails, including the stunning **Palisades Falls** trail, which is paved for wheelchair access. Other recreational opportunities include mountain biking, ice climbing, and backcountry skiing in winter.

Skiing

One of only two nonprofit ski areas in Montana, **Bridger Bowl** (15795 Bridger Canyon Rd., 406/587-2111, www.bridgerbowl.com, 9am-4pm daily during ski season, full day $63 adults, $35 seniors, $25 children 7-12, free for children 6 and under and seniors 80 and over) is only 16 miles (26 km) north of Bozeman and offers 2,000 acres of exceptional terrain and first-class facilities for about half of what you would pay at Aspen or Vail. Multiday tickets and ski school options are available, and there are 75 marked trails and eight lifts to get you on the mountain, including **Schlasman's,** which summits the ridge, an area long known as an "earn your turns" mecca. Though the area is hugely popular with locals and a seat in the cafeteria can be hard to find at lunchtime, lift lines are rarely longer than 10-15 people. In the summer, trails are open to hikers and mountain bikers.

In downtown Bozeman, **Lindley Park** (E. Main St. and Buttonwood Ave.) offers extensive groomed cross-country ski trails courtesy of the Bridger Ski Foundation. The best place to park is the northwest parking lot of Bozeman Deaconess Hospital (915 Highland Blvd.). Season passes can be purchased online (www.bridgerskifoundation.org, $50 individual, $100 family), or donations can be made in the boxes at the various trailheads.

The 18-hole golf course at **Bridger Creek** (2710 McIlhattan Rd., 406/586-2333, www.bridgercreek.com) is also

Top to bottom: view from the trail to the M; skiers at Bridger Bowl; Hyalite Canyon, a popular recreation spot.

groomed for skiers in the winter. Buttons can be purchased at a variety of locations in town, including **Bangtail Bike & Ski** (137 E. Main St., 406/587-4905, www.bangtailbikes.com), an excellent cycle and Nordic ski shop that also rents cross-country skis. During winter, the **Bridger Ski Foundation** (www.bridgerskifoundation.org) grooms miles of trails that bring out racers and novices alike to make tracks around the city's hospital.

Fishing

Bozeman is a trout lover's paradise, with several blue-ribbon streams nearby. The **Gallatin, Jefferson,** and **Madison Rivers** flow through the valley, forming the headwaters of the Missouri River in aptly named Three Forks (31 mi/50 km west of Bozeman on I-90). Al Gadoury of **6X Outfitters** (406/586-3806, www.6xoutfitters.com, wade or float trips $500 for 1-2 people, $600 for 3-4 people, $40-120 private-water rod fee) is widely considered to be among the region's best outfitters, particularly when it comes to spring creeks and private water. As an aside, his shore lunches (think grilled moose burgers) are second to none.

Other local outfitters can offer excellent advice and guide services. **The River's Edge** (2012 N. 7th Ave., 406/586-5373, www.theriversedge.com, 8am-6pm daily) is one of Bozeman's oldest and most venerated. **Montana Troutfitters** (1716 W. Main St., 406/587-4707, www.troutfitters.com, 7am-7pm daily) has been guiding fly-fishing excursions since 1978 and offers excellent online fishing reports. **Yellow Dog Flyfishing Adventures** (406/585-8657 or 888/777-5060, www.yellowdogflyfishing.com) offers first-class trips in the region and mind-blowing fishing adventures around the world.

Golf

There are three private golf courses in and around Bozeman (Valley View Golf Club, Riverside Country Club, and Black Bull Run Golf Club), and two that are open to the public. The 18-hole **Bridger Creek Golf Course** (2710 McIlhattan Rd., 406/586-2333, www.bridgercreek.com, weekdays $21 for 9 holes and $34 for 18 holes, weekends and holidays $23 for 9 holes and $36 for 18 holes) offers 6,511 yards (5,954 m) of golf from the longest tees for a par of 71. Special family nights are ideal for little ones just picking up the game, and novice nights provide a non-stressful atmosphere for new players. Its camp offerings for kids and its group and private lessons for anyone are highly rated. **Cottonwood Hills Golf Course** (8955 River Rd., 406/587-1118, www.cottonwoodhills.com) offers a 9-hole, 1,181-yard (1,080-m) par-3 course ($10 adults, $8 children 6-12) as well as an 18-hole, 6,751-yard (6,173-m) course with a par of 70 ($24 for 9 holes, $44 for 18 holes).

Food

After traveling through rural Montana, Bozeman seems like a food lover's mecca. With everything from sushi to tapas, the town affords diners much more than the burgers and steaks for which the state is so well known (although there is an outstanding selection of those as well).

The **Community Food Co-op** (908 W. Main St., 406/587-4039, www.bozo.coop, 7:30am-10pm Mon.-Sat., 8am-10pm Sun., deli counter 8am-8pm daily) is a cornerstone of the community, and its **downtown branch** (44 E. Main St., 406/922-2667, 7:30am-8pm Mon.-Sat., 8am-8pm Sun.) is not only convenient but also offers an excellent hot bar, salad bar, and sandwich and smoothie counter. Everything the Co-op does—gourmet and often locally produced groceries, mouthwatering prepared foods, and a primo coffee shop, juice bar, and bakery—is done brilliantly. The homemade soups are excellent, as is the salad bar and just about everything in the sprawling deli case. Exotic hot lunches and dinners are often available at prices that cannot be matched elsewhere.

Just down the block, the super-casual and family-friendly **Naked Noodle** (27 S. Willson Ave., 406/585-4501, 11am-9:30pm Mon.-Tues. and Thurs.-Sat., 11am-9pm Sun., $8.25-14.25) dishes up pasta that is cooked and topped to order as you stand watch. The hearty salads—such as Korean beef—are excellent too.

Another spot for fresh, creative cuisine is right across the street from the Museum of the Rockies. **Sola Café** (290 W. Kagy Ave., 406/922-7652, www.solacafe.com, 7am-8pm Mon.-Thurs., 7am-4pm Sat.-Sun., $5-15) is a good place for salads, panini, soups, sandwiches, daily entrée specials, and an assortment of fresh-baked goodies. Sola is also a full-service coffee bar. Online and text ordering along with a drive-through window make gourmet takeout dinners a great option.

Right downtown and worth noting is **Ted's Montana Grill** (105 W. Main St., 406/587-6000, www.tedsmontanagrill.com, 11am-10pm Sun.-Thurs., 11am-11pm Fri.-Sat., $11-36) in the historic Baxter hotel. It is the flagship restaurant of local part-time resident and unequivocal philanthropist and land steward Ted Turner. Everything is made from scratch, and each meat cut is available in bison or beef. The apple cobbler is extremely good.

For excellent (but pricey!) Asian food, **Sweet Chili Asian Bistro** (101 E. Main St., 406/582-1188, www.sweetchilibistro.com, 11am-9pm Mon.-Thurs., 11am-9:30pm Fri.-Sat., noon-9pm Sun., $15-27) serves up an extensive menu of fresh and flavorful Asian cuisine along with sushi and a full bar. The room is dimly lit with red lights, lending some romantic ambience. This is still Bozeman though, and any restaurant is fairly casual.

★ **Blackbird Kitchen** (140 E. Main St., 406/586-0010, www.blackbirdkitchen.com, 5pm-9pm Mon.-Thurs., 5pm-9:30pm Fri.-Sat., $12-30) is a tiny little spot that is usually standing room only.

From the kale salad to the Willow Spring lamb chop, the wood-fired pizza, and handmade pasta, the country Italian flavors are sensational. The wine list is extensive, and if you leave without sampling the chocolate *budino* (pudding) sprinkled with sea salt and drizzled with olive oil, you've made a mistake.

On the east end of town, **Montana Ale Works** (611 E. Main St., 406/587-7700, www.montanaaleworks.com, 4pm-10pm Sun.-Thurs., 4pm-11pm Fri.-Sat., bar until midnight daily, $10.50-24) combines a hip eatery with an extremely popular smoke-free bar and pool lounge. The menu offers inventive takes on Western staples like burgers and steaks, and the atmosphere, in a beautifully rehabbed 100-year-old railroad warehouse, is energetic and suitable for everyone from toddlers to grandparents; it can be loud at any time of the week, so a separate dining room is a good option for those with noise issues.

As Bozeman has evolved from its ranching and agricultural heritage, many of the classic diners have been lost to trendier eateries, but the **Western Café** (443 E. Main St., 406/587-0436, 6am-2pm daily, $6-12) has stood the test of time. It's an old-timers' classic for breakfast and lunch, including its famed chicken-fried steak and cinnamon rolls.

For a more upscale breakfast or lunch option downtown, **The Nova Café** (312 E. Main St., 406/587-3973, www.thenovacafe.com, 7am-2pm daily, $6.50-13.25) is considered the best breakfast place in town. The café uses fresh, healthy ingredients and gets almost everything—from meats and produce to salsa—locally. The service and the food are consistently outstanding.

A few steps off Main Street, tucked into the Emerson Center for the Arts and Culture, the **Emerson Grill** (111 S. Grand Ave., 406/586-5247, 5pm-9pm Mon.-Thurs., 5pm-10pm Sat.-Sun., $15-43) is a perfect spot for a bite. With walls the color of acorn squash and high-backed wooden booths that recall a 100-year-old schoolhouse, this northern Italian restaurant offers a warm, intimate ambience and excellent, uncomplicated food. The flatbread pizzettes—one of the Grill's signature dishes—are especially good (try the pear, white sauce, caramelized onions, and gorgonzola version), and the extensive boutique-style wine list boasts descriptions like "Sophia Loren in a glass."

A great spot for gourmet wood-fired pizza is **Pizza Campania** (1285 N. Rouse Ave., 406/404-1270, 11am-9:30pm Mon.-Fri., 4pm-9:30pm Sat.-Sun., $10-16). Toppings include such delicacies as fennel sausage, fig preserves, goat gorgonzola, and brie. The restaurant also serves great salads and desserts, and opens up to the outside with a glass garage-style door. Patio diners can sit by the fire with a great bottle of wine.

Two breakfast and lunch places specializing in delicious farm-to-table fare are **The Farmer's Daughters Café** (510 N. 7th Ave., 406/404-7999, www.farmersdaughtersbzn.com, 7am-3:30pm daily, $7-11), which dishes up everything from salmon toast and chia pudding bowls to pastries and smoothies; and **Feed Cafe** (1530 W. Main St., 406/219-2630, www.feedcafebozeman.com, 7am-2pm daily, $6.50-12.50), which has a larger menu and features fantastic breakfast sandwiches, omelets, *shakshuka,* house-made pastries, and much more. Both have excellent coffee and espresso, but The Farmer's Daughters also offers wine, beer, and champagne.

Accommodations

For a long time, Bozeman's accommodations were lacking in charm for a town with seemingly sophisticated tastes. That has changed with the addition of two terrific contemporary hotels. And for those willing to look, there are numerous and diverse offerings, from roadside motels to upscale chains, cozy vacation rentals, and, farther afield, a historical gem.

★ **The Lark** (122 W. Main St., 866/464-1000, www.larkbozeman.com, $187-349) considers itself a base camp and works hard at getting guests out of its modern, art-filled rooms and into the wilds of Bozeman and its surrounds. A map room helps with planning, and motel employees are called guides. Still, your time inside The Lark will be a pleasure with 38 unique rooms, each filled with work by local artists and craftspeople. Kids will love the bunk room, and everyone will appreciate the heart-of-downtown location, which is within walking distance to everywhere. Look out for the **Genuine Ice Cream** (www.genuineicecream.com) truck just outside the hotel, dishing up handmade ice cream in flavors like fresh mint chip, matcha green tea, honey lavender, and Nutella crunch.

A modern property in downtown Bozeman with a decidedly Scandinavian feel is ★ **Element Bozeman** (25 E. Mendenhall St., 406/582-4972, www.elementbozeman.com, from $234), a Starwood Hotel. Just a block off Main Street, this high-rise (for Bozeman, anyway) hotel has spacious rooms, a complimentary breakfast bar, evening reception, and fully stocked kitchenettes, as well as a patio grill, an indoor pool, a fitness center, and bikes to borrow.

Another new and swanky little motel is on the less-than-scenic North 7th Avenue: **RSVP Motel** (510 N. 7th Ave., 406/404-7999, www.rsvpmotel.com, $129-294). In what was once a run-of-the-mill roadside motel, RSVP is chic, comfortable, and undeniably hip, even for Bozeman. The owners have decked out the beautiful rooms with furnishings and art from their world travels. There's a little pool and a fantastic on-site restaurant, The Farmer's Daughters Café. Plus the staff is eager to curate your Bozeman visit and can make any arrangements.

Offering an ideal location right downtown, and the cheapest rooms anywhere, the **Treasure State Hostel** (27 E. Main St., 406/624-6244, www.treasurestatehostel.

com, dorm bed from $28, private room from $38) is a find in Bozeman. Just 20 minutes from Bridger Bowl and an hour from Big Sky, the hostel is popular with skiers in winter.

The **Magpie Guest House** (323 S. Wallace Ave., 406/585-8223, www.magpiegh.com, $160-175) offers charming accommodations for up to four people in an ideal downtown location, sandwiched between the library and Peet's Hill, with all the comforts of home.

At the 19th Street exit on I-90, visitors will find the extremely comfortable all-suites **Residence Inn by Marriott** (6195 E. Valley Center Rd., 406/522-1535, www.marriott.com, from $179) with 115 suites. The hotel offers a hot breakfast each morning and social hours Monday-Thursday. Other reliable chain hotels in the area include **C'Mon Inn Hotel & Suites** (6139 E. Valley Center Rd., 406/587-3555 or 866/782-2717, www.cmoninn.com, from $150), the upscale **Hilton Garden Inn** (2032 Commerce Way, 406/582-9900, http://hiltongardeninn3.hilton.com, $189-316) on the northwest side of town, and the older but well-maintained **Holiday Inn** (5 E. Baxter Ln., 406/587-4561 or 800/315-2621, www.holidayinn.com, from $121). **Travelodge** (1200 E. Main St., 406/586-8534, www.wyndhamhotels.com, from $149) is a hotel at the east end of downtown, not far from the interstate, with clean, spacious rooms.

Bozeman Cottage Vacation Rentals (406/580-3223, www.bozemancottage.com) offers a broad array of properties to meet individual preferences for location, price, size, and style—from a lodge near Bridger Bowl to downtown cottages and riverfront cabins. There are plenty of pet-friendly offerings, and last-minute bargains can be had for those inclined to wing it. **Mountain Home** (406/586-4589 or 800/550-4589, www.mountain-home.com) has an excellent array of vacation rentals in and around Bozeman and across southwestern Montana.

Information and Services

A good place for information, travel services, and maps is the **Bozeman Chamber of Commerce** (2000 Commerce Way, southeast corner of N. 19th St. and Baxter Ln., 406/586-5421 or 800/228-4224, www.bozemancvb.com, 8am-5pm Mon.-Fri.). The chamber also staffs a **visitors center** at Bozeman Yellowstone International Airport, which offers the same assortment of information, brochures, and maps as at the chamber. Downtown shoppers can find an abundance of information at the **Downtown Bozeman Visitor Center** (222 E. Main St., 406/586-4008).

The **main post office** (2201 Baxter Ln. at 19th St., 8:30am-5pm Mon.-Fri., 9am-1pm Sat.) offers a 24 hour automated postal service that accepts major credit and debit cards. The old post office still operates downtown at 32 East Babcock Street, one block south of Main Street.

Bozeman Deaconess Hospital (915 Highland Blvd., 406/585-5000, www.bozemanhealth.org) has a 24-hour emergency room. Another option is **Bozeman Urgent Care Center** (1006 W. Main St., Ste. E, 406/414-4800, 8am-7pm Mon.-Fri., 9am-5pm Sat.-Sun.).

Essentials

Getting There

Getting to Bozeman
Car
Off I-90, Bozeman is easily accessible by car. It is 142 miles (229 km) west of **Billings,** 202 miles (320 km) southeast of **Missoula,** and 85 miles (137 km) east of **Butte.** The driving distances are slightly farther from Wyoming: **Jackson** is 215 miles (345 km) south and **Cody** is 214 miles (345 km) southeast of Bozeman.

Car and RV Rental
A number of car-rental agencies are at the airport; the car-rental center is located next to the baggage claim. **Alamo, Avis, Budget, Enterprise, Dollar, Hertz, Thrifty,** and **National** have on-site counters.

There are a handful of places in Bozeman where RVs can be rented, including **Cruise America RV Rental** (80675b Gallatin Rd., 800/671-8042 or 406/624-0424, www.cruiseamerica.com), **Blacksford** (at the Bozeman Yellowstone Airport, 406/763-6395, www.blacksford.com), and **C&T Motorhome Rentals** (31908 E. Frontage Rd., 406/587-8610 or 406/587-0351, www.ctrvrentals.com).

Air
Bozeman Yellowstone International Airport (BZN, 406/388-8321, www.bozemanairport.com) is 8 miles (12.9 km) northwest of downtown Bozeman in the nearby town of Belgrade. Delta, Alaska, American, Allegiant, Frontier, JetBlue, and United all offer daily nonstop service to and from major U.S. cities, including Salt Lake City, Minneapolis, Seattle, Atlanta, Chicago, and Denver. Seasonal nonstop flights serve Houston, Las Vegas, Los Angeles, New York, Phoenix, Portland, and San Francisco.

Bus
Greyhound travels to almost 40 towns and cities in Montana from the **bus depot**

(1205 E. Main St., 612/499-3468, 10am-3pm daily).

Getting to Billings
Car
As the largest city in Montana, Billings is an easy driving destination. It's along I-90 and I-94 begins just outside the town. Billings is 142 miles (229 km) east of **Bozeman** and 60 miles (97 km) northeast of **Red Lodge.** In Wyoming, **Cody** is 106 miles (171 km) away.

Car and RV Rental
At the Billings airport, **Enterprise, Thrifty, Dollar, Hertz, Alamo, Avis, Budget,** and **National** have on-site car-rental counters.

In Billings, RVs can be rented at **Cruise America RV Rental** (720 Central Ave., 800/671-8042 or 800/549-2301, www.cruiseamerica.com) and **Happy Campers Travel Trailer & RV Rentals** (2110 1st Ave. N., 800/598-0241 www.montanahappycampers.com).

Air
Billings Logan International Airport (BIL, 1901 Terminal Cir., 406/247-8609, www.flybillings.com) is situated atop the rimrocks off I-90 at the 27th Street exit. Delta, United, Allegiant, Alaska Airlines, American, and Cape Air offer regular flights.

If you arrive early at the airport or have some time to spare before you are picked up, visit the **Peter Yegen Jr. Yellowstone County Museum** (1950 Terminal Cir., 406/256-6811, www.pyjrycm.org, 10:30am-5pm Mon.-Fri., 10:30am-3pm Sat., free). Once outside the terminal, follow the road around the west parking lot; the museum is on the right before the airport exit. The museum has artifacts and exhibits highlighting the history of the northern plains from early Native American influence through westward expansion and mining up to the 1950s. There's even a two-headed calf! The museum's deck provides a splendid view of the city below.

Bus
The **Greyhound bus terminal and ticket offices** (1830 4th Ave. N., 406/245-5117, www.greyhound.com) are open 24 hours a day year-round.

Getting to Jackson Hole
Car
The major routes into Jackson Hole—including U.S. 89/191/287 from Yellowstone and Grand Teton National Parks, U.S. 26/287 from the east, Highway 22 from the west over Teton Pass, and U.S. 189/191/89 from the south—can all experience weather closures in the winter, particularly over Teton Pass. There is no car traffic in the southern portion of Yellowstone during the winter. For Wyoming road reports, call 800/WYO-ROAD (800/996-7623, www.wyoroad.info).

Jackson is roughly 240 miles (385 km) south of **Bozeman,** 177 miles (280 km) southwest of **Cody** through Yellowstone National Park, and 275 miles (445 km) northeast of Salt Lake City. Keep in mind that while distances through the national parks may be shorter in actual mileage, the time is often extended by lower speed limits, traffic congestion, and animal jams. In addition, most of the park roads are closed in winter, and car travel is not possible between Bozeman and Jackson or between Cody and Jackson. Driving distances around the parks increase significantly.

Car and RV Rental
The airport has on-site car rentals from **Alamo, National, Hertz,** and **Enterprise. Avis/Budget, Dollar,** and **Thrifty** are available off-site.

In Jackson, RVs can be rented from individuals (like VBRO, but for RVs) on **Outdoorsy.com** (www.outdoorsy.com). High-end campervans are available for rent from **Moterra Campervans** (2950 Big Trail Dr., 307/200-7220, www.gomoterra.com).

Air
The only airport within a national park, **Jackson Hole Airport** (JAC, 1250 E. Airport Rd., Jackson, 307/733-7682, www.jacksonholeairport.com) is served by American, Delta, United, and Frontier. The schedules change seasonally but include regular flights from Salt Lake City, Denver, Seattle, Chicago, Minneapolis, Dallas, Houston, Phoenix, San Francisco, and Los Angeles.

Bus
The Driver Provider (800/700-2687, http://driverprovider.com) and **Alltrans** (307/733-3135 or 800/443-6133, www.jacksonholealltrans.com) provide various shuttles and tour options. Shuttles can also be arranged through **Jackson Hole Shuttle** (307/200-1400, www.jhshuttle.com).

The nearest **Greyhound** stop is in Idaho Falls, Idaho, about 100 miles west of Jackson.

Getting to Missoula
Car
I-90 runs directly through Missoula, making it an easy destination by car. Missoula is 115 miles (185 km) west of **Helena** and the same south of **Kalispell,** 120 miles (193 km) northwest of **Butte,** and about 200 miles (320 km) northwest of **Bozeman.**

Car and RV Rental
On the 1st floor of the airport are **Alamo, Avis, Budget, Enterprise, National, Thrifty,** and **Hertz** car-rental agencies. **Dollar** has shuttles to and from the airport.

RVs can be rented at **Cruise America RV Rental** (12787 US-93 in Lolo, 800/671-8042 or 406/273-4994, www.cruiseamerica.com). Custom VW Westfalia vans can be rented at the Missoula International Airport from **Dragonfly**

Vans (406/552-2980, www.dragoflyvans.com).

Air

Just 4 miles (6.4 km) northwest of the University of Montana campus, **Missoula International Airport** (MSO, 5225 U.S. 10 W., 406/728-4381, www.flymissoula.com) is served by Alaska, Allegiant, American, Delta, Frontier, and United. Most hotels offer free shuttle service to and from the airport; the **Airport Shuttle** (406/543-9416 or 406/880-7433, www.msoshuttle.com) also provides transportation into town.

Bus

The **Greyhound bus station** (1660 W. Broadway, 406/549-2339) has several buses into and out of town daily.

Getting to Great Falls
Car

Great Falls is situated directly off I-15, allowing easy access by car. It is 218 miles (355 km) northwest of **Billings,** 186 miles (300 km) north of **Bozeman,** 155 miles (250 km) northeast of **Butte,** and approximately 90 miles (145 km) from **Helena** (to the south).

Car and RV Rental

The airport's on-site car-rental companies are **Alamo, Avis, Enterprise, Hertz,** and **National. Budget** also offers car-rental services off-site with shuttles to and from the airport.

In Great Falls, RVs can be rented at **Gardner's RVs** (3928 Tri Hill Frontage Rd., 406/454-0777, www.gardnerrv.com).

Air

The **Great Falls International Airport** (GTF, 2800 Terminal Dr., 406/727-3404,

www.flygtf.com) is southwest of the city. It is served by Alaska Airlines, Allegiant, Delta, and United.

Bus or Train

Greyhound Bus Lines (326 1st Ave. S., 406/453-5261, www.greyhound.com) offers service to other major towns and cities in Montana.

Getting to Kalispell
Car

Kalispell is easily accessible by car. It's 115 miles (185 km) north of **Missoula** at the junction of U.S. 2 and U.S. 93. From **Whitefish,** Kalispell is 15 miles (24 km) south on U.S. 93, a 25-minute drive.

Car and RV Rental

There are on-site car-rental counters for **Avis, Budget, Hertz,** and **National/Alamo. Dollar** (406/892-0009, www.dollar.com), **Enterprise** (406/755-4848, www.enterprise.com), and **Thrifty** (406/257-7333, www.thrifty.com) are off-site but near the airport.

In Great Falls, RVs can be rented at **Gardner's RVs** (3100 U.S. 93 S., 406/752-7683, www.gardnerrv.com).

Air

The **Glacier Park International Airport** (FCA, 4170 U.S. 2 E., Kalispell, www.iflyglacier.com) is served by Delta, Alaska, United, and Allegiant.

Bus or Train

Greyhound (2075 Hwy 2 E., 406/755-7447) offers daily bus service in and out of Kalispell.

Amtrak (500 Depot St., Whitefish) runs the **Empire Builder** from Chicago to Seattle with daily stops in Whitefish in each direction.

Road Rules

Driving Rules

Rental cars are available at the major airports. If you plan on renting a car, it's a good idea to reserve one well in advance. Unless you will be driving entirely on paved roads, which is doubtful, a high-clearance or all-wheel-drive vehicle is a good idea. Many Forest Service campgrounds are located along gravel roads, and anytime you venture off the beaten path, you're bound to encounter some type of gravel or dirt road. In the winter, all-wheel drive is a must. And be aware that rock chips on the windshield are common occurrences at any time of year. Make sure your insurance will cover it, or consider paying for added insurance from the car-rental agency.

Car-rental agencies serving the region include **Alamo** (800/227-7368, www.alamo.com), **Avis** (800/352-7900, www.avis.com), **Budget** (800/527-0700, www.budget.com), **Enterprise** (800/261-7331, www.enterprise.com), **Dollar** (800/800-5252, www.dollar.com), **Hertz** (800/654-3131, www.hertz.com), **Thrifty** (800/847-4389, www.thrifty.com), and **National** (888/868-6204, www.national-car.com).

Distances between settlements can be great in this region. As a rule of thumb, planning ahead is critical. Don't wait until your gas light is on to fill up your tank, and make sure your spare is inflated. Carrying emergency gear is recommended. A sleeping bag, headlamp, and some food are the bare minimum for winter travel. Rest areas—even on major highways and interstates—can be hundreds of miles apart. Most major towns and cities have reliable mechanics and car dealerships, but don't expect to find parts for your old Porsche roadster in very many places.

In general, the **speed limit** is 80 mph on interstates and 70 mph on most two-lane highways, although it can vary quite a bit depending on location and time of day. Many two-lane roads have numerous turnouts, where slower-moving vehicles can pull over and let cars pass. Locals are used to driving faster on these roads, so if you're getting tailgated, just pull over and let them go by. Increasingly, passing lanes are being incorporated into many state highways, particularly on roads over mountain passes. Be aware that Montana has a "move over law" which requires drivers to slow down and change lanes for stopped emergency or maintenance vehicles. Courtesy would suggest you do the same for any vehicle stopped alongside the road.

Travel Maps

Free road maps can be found at visitors centers and rest areas, while an excellent supplement is the **Delorme Gazetteer series** (www.delorme.com), available at bookstores and in many gas stations. These oversize companions are a must for those venturing off the beaten path, as they include topographic data, Forest Service roads and trails, camping and hiking information, fishing areas, scenic drives, and more. Sporting goods stores offer more specialized maps, from national forests and wilderness areas to Bureau of Land Management lands and mile-by-mile river guides. The free road maps you get when you enter the national parks are sufficient to use during your stay.

Traveling by Bike

This region has many options for those cycling through. Numerous back roads and accessible campgrounds make for some fun trips, but be prepared for long-distance rides and not much company. Both the Wyoming and Montana transportation websites (www.wyoroad.info, www.mdt.mt.gov/travinfo) offer excellent information for cyclists. You can order a **Montana Bicycle Touring Packet** online, as well as download maps and road grade information from each site. In Wyoming,

Montana License Plates

You wouldn't know it just by driving around, but Montana's license plates have provided an interesting look at the state's population trends since the first plate was produced in 1914. In the 1930s, the state added a number to the left side of the plate that corresponded to county population—the number 1 was for the county with the highest population, and 56 was for the lowest. If you correlate these with the city that is the county seat, you get a snapshot of the state's population history—and you can tell where people are from just by looking at their plates. In lieu of road-trip bingo, a fun game is to see how many plates you can identify while driving around.

When the list for the license plate was created, Silver Bow County was the largest in the state, as Butte—with a population of just under 40,000 people—was a thriving city, booming with the economic flush of mining. Great Falls was number 2, Billings was 3, and Missoula 4. Libby—in northwest Lincoln County—came in last at number 56. In 1930 the total population of the state was just 537,606; the population of Billings was a mere 16,280, and the state capital, Helena, had just under 12,000 residents.

Over the past 80-plus years, the state motor vehicle department has left the number and corresponding counties the same. That is, a car with a number 1 is still from Butte-Silver Bow County, and a truck with a number 56 is from the Libby area. However, the population snapshot paints a dramatically different picture these days. While Butte has lost nearly 7,000 people since 1930, other cities have seen significant increases, leaving Butte now the sixth-largest city in Montana. Billings is the largest city, with more than 110,000 residents, and Missoula has moved up to number 2 with more than 72,000 people.

If the state did change the numbers for the license plate, Butte-Silver Bow would now be 8, and the top five counties would be Yellowstone (Billings), Missoula, Gallatin (Bozeman), Flathead (Kalispell), and Cascade (Great Falls). Lincoln County, now with more than 19,000 residents, jumped more dramatically than any other. It's moved from last place (56) to 10th largest since 1930. The least populated county in Montana is Petroleum County in eastern Montana, with 523 people spread across more than 1,600 square miles (4,144 sq km). It is the third-least-populated county in the continental United States. Generally, western Montana is growing in population and eastern Montana is shrinking, except for areas impacted by the oil boom in neighboring North Dakota. Also, transplants tend to settle in larger, more urban centers where service-related jobs are typically abundant.

Why aren't the numbers on the plates being changed? Montana drivers have a certain amount of pride regarding their heritage, and the numbers hark back to a different era. Newcomers may not pay much attention to it, but old-timers and natives certainly do. The numbers are part of the state's cultural history—something nobody wants to change anytime soon.

information can also be found on www.cyclingwyoming.org.

Road Conditions and Closures

In general, interstates and major highways are in good condition across the region, although short summers mean road construction can be expected at any time of the day—or night, in some cases. State highways are often narrow and winding, not compatible with drowsy or inattentive drivers. Wildlife is a concern on any road, particularly at twilight and dark, and fallen rocks can be a problem in mountainous areas. For Wyoming road conditions, the **Wyoming Department of Transportation** (888/996-7623, www.wyoroad.info) has a wealth of information. Montana information can be found through the **Montana Department of Transportation** (800/226-7623, www.mdt.mt.gov/travinfo).

Winter Travel

Winter driving in Montana and Wyoming takes special care, focus, and—at times—lots of caffeine. Roads can be rendered impassable in a matter of minutes by snow and wind, and mountain passes are especially susceptible to fast-changing conditions. Because of the area covered, it may take a while before snowplows clear the roads. And be extremely cautious when driving behind or toward a snowplow, as visibility can be diminished to nothing. Be aware that because of wildlife, salt is rarely used on roads in Montana and Wyoming. Instead, the roads are graveled to provide better traction in icy conditions. Loose gravel often translates into cracked or chipped windshields, so drive with caution, and never get too close to a graveling truck.

Snow tires are a must in many places, and carrying emergency supplies is strongly recommended. A good emergency kit includes a shovel, a first-aid kit, jumper cables, a flashlight, signal flares, extra clothing, some food, water, a tow strap, and a sleeping bag. Don't rely on your cell phone to save you—although service is improving, there are many dead zones across the region.

Both states' transportation websites (www.wyoroad.info, www.mdt.mt.gov/travinfo) have links to current and projected weather patterns, and toll-free information numbers are updated regularly. It's a good idea to carry these numbers in your car. Occasionally weather information can be found on the AM band of your car radio—you'll notice signs along roads indicating when this is possible.

National Park Passes

With three of the country's most popular national parks located in Montana and Wyoming, this is where many visitors begin and end their journey. **Glacier National Park** (www.nps.gov/glac) falls entirely within Montana. Although most of **Yellowstone National Park** (www.nps.gov/yell) is in Wyoming, three of the park's entrances are found in Montana. Just south of Yellowstone in Wyoming is **Grand Teton National Park** (www.nps.gov/grte). Each park offers a different type of beauty, from Glacier's receding namesakes and high-alpine scenery to the majestic peaks of the Tetons and Yellowstone's striking geothermal features and abundant wildlife. Visitors will find a variety of accommodations in the parks, including rustic cabins, grand lodges, and tent and RV campgrounds. Popular activities include hiking, boating, fishing, and wildlife-viewing. Informational visitors centers and museums are sited in each park and offer excellent resources for history buffs.

The entrance fee in the summer for each park is $35 for automobiles, which is valid for seven days. An America the Beautiful national parks and federal recreation lands annual pass, which permits entrance to more than 2,000 federal recreation sites, costs $80. Campground and other lodging fees are extra. Annual passes for any of the three parks are available for $70.

There are two passes available for U.S. citizens and permanent residents who are 62 years or older. The lifetime pass costs $80. The annual pass costs $20. The Senior Pass offers discounts on some campsites, RV sites, and guided tours.

Each state also has numerous national monuments, historic sites, trails, and recreation areas that fall within the national park system. Consult the National Park Service website (www.nps.gov) for more information on these areas.

Travel Tips

Canadian Crossings and Customs

Of the many roads that cross into Canada from Montana, only three border crossings are open 24 hours, year-round. U.S. 93 (Roosville) and I-15 (Sweetgrass) are the busiest, while the remote crossing near Raymond on Highway 16 sees much less traffic. U.S. citizens are now required to carry passports when crossing into Canada; Canadians entering the United States must have a passport, a NEXUS card, an Enhanced Driver's License (EDL), or Enhanced Identification Card (EIC). Citizens of other countries must show their passports and appropriate visas and may be asked to prove that they have sufficient funds for their length of stay. U.S. citizens returning to the United States by air must present a U.S. passport.

When heading north into Canada, travelers age 21 and older can import, duty-free, a maximum of 40 ounces (1.2 liters) of liquor or 24 12-ounce (0.4 liter) cans of beer or ale into the country as personal luggage. Up to 50 cigars and 200 cigarettes may be allowed entry duty-free for those age 18 or over. U.S. visitors spending more than 48 hours in Canada may bring $400 worth of duty-free goods back with them, or $200 if staying less than 48 hours. If you're carrying more than $10,000, you'll need to declare the amount. Handguns can't be taken into Canada, although hunting rifles are allowed. Bear spray and hunting knives are also prohibited.

Tourist Information

Both states have excellent information available for those interested in traveling to the region. Most chambers of commerce and visitors centers (listed for each town in this book) are good sources when driving around, but the online sites are where you should start your research. For Wyoming, visit **Wyoming Tourism**

(307/777-7777, www.travelwyoming.com) for the latest information. You can check out the various towns, attractions, and events, as well as order a **free vacation guide.**

For Montana, the **Montana Office of Tourism** (800/847-4868, www.visitmt. com) is the state's official tourism organization for vacation information and to order the annual free **Montana Guidebook.** Montana has divided the state into six different tourism regions, and specific booklets are available for each one.

Communications and Media
Cell Phones

Although Montana and Wyoming may be remote, cell phone coverage is overall very good and getting better each year. That being said, rural and mountainous areas may have spotty coverage. Indeed, check the storefronts in some of the smaller towns in the region (I'm looking at you, Augusta), and you'll see that cell phone service is just being brought to the area. Verizon is the main carrier, although AT&T is increasingly available.

Internet Access

Many coffee shops and public libraries have computers available for Internet use, and most larger towns have business centers with computers and fax machines.

High-speed Internet connections are generally available, but the service is often slower and more problematic compared to larger metropolitan areas. Wireless Internet is frequently offered at coffee shops, libraries, hotels, and other public places.

Media

USA Today is the one national newspaper that can be found throughout the region, and *The Wall Street Journal* is also popular. If you want a national newspaper like *The New York Times* or *The Washington Post,* many towns still have smaller newspaper and magazine stores, but you may get a copy that is a few days old at best. Large grocery stores typically have regional dailies. In Montana, the larger dailies are the *Missoulian,* the *Great Falls Tribune,* the *Montana Standard, Helena Independent Record,* and the *Billings Gazette,* although every small town seems to have at least a weekly newspaper, which can be a great source of information on local events and attractions. Other Montana publications to look out for include the *Lively Times* (www.lively-times.com), a monthly statewide guide to entertainment. The *Montana Quarterly* and *Big Sky Journal* are excellent literary reads and feature well-written articles about the Treasure State and the Greater Yellowstone area.

In Wyoming, the larger daily newspapers include the *Casper Star-Tribune* (the only statewide newspaper), the *Wyoming Tribune Eagle* in Cheyenne, and the *Laramie Boomerang.* Other popular papers include the weekly *Jackson Hole News & Guide* and Worland's *Northern Wyoming Daily News.* Other Wyoming publications to watch for include *Wyoming Magazine* (www.wyoming-magazine.com), which focuses on travel and adventure in the state, and *Wyoming Lifestyle Magazine* (www.wyolifestyle.com).

One of best sources of local and national news is **National Public Radio,** which can be heard in even the smallest of towns in both states. **Montana Public Radio** covers western Montana (www.mtpr.org), while **Yellowstone Public Radio** (www.ypr.org) covers the rest of the state as well as northern Wyoming. **Wyoming Public Radio** (www.wyoming-publicradio.net) also covers much of the state.

Food

One thing is certain: This is meat-and-potatoes country, which can be great for those craving a good steak, as you can find one in almost every town. Locally raised beef can be found on the menus of many restaurants, and bison is becoming increasingly popular as well. If you haven't had it, it's highly recommended, and beef lovers will generally enjoy bison. A good bison burger or tenderloin is hard to beat, but if you are asked how you like it cooked, never ask for anything more than medium. Wild-game dishes, mostly elk and venison, are also found at finer establishments, with pheasant and other regional game occasionally on the menu. If you enjoy trying new fare, this can be an exciting option.

With all the meat on the menu, you would think that vegetarians would be out of luck when dining out, but surprisingly, options abound, especially at higher-end restaurants. The "eat local" campaigns are in full swing out West, and many of the best restaurants get as much of their food as possible from local and regional growers. Despite the region being seriously landlocked, seafood is no longer necessarily a bad idea. Fresh seafood is flown in from Hawaii or Seattle daily in many places, and it is generally pretty good. Yes, there are even fresh sushi bars in Montana and Wyoming, and some are darn tasty. Innovative cuisine can be found in every major town, but certainly Jackson, Bozeman, Bigfork, Whitefish, Missoula, and Billings stand out.

Does either state have a well-known meal? Well, not really. Montana is famous for its huckleberries and Flathead cherries, so a good pie or milk shake is a must. Pasties in Butte are considered indispensable regional cuisine, and Rocky Mountain oysters (calf testicles) are usually breaded and fried—not exactly gourmet, and not exactly popular or necessarily worth trying. Delicious Indian tacos load the ingredients onto fry bread, and good Mexican and Chinese restaurants can be found throughout the region. Other regional specialties in both states include wild game, chicken-fried steak, chili, and trout.

You'll also see the standard fast-food

establishments, especially near the interstates, but avoid these and try a local restaurant instead. You'll find the best food at the most random of places—and it will certainly be a more interesting culinary and cultural experience. And remember, folks out here are friendly—if you stop and ask someone about the best place in town, they will happily point you in the right direction and will probably know the owner.

If you are traveling the back roads and small towns and get tired of ordinary bar-type food (burgers, burgers, and more burgers), consider a quest to find the best chicken-fried steak or the best piece of pie. Sometimes a personal challenge can relieve the boredom of limited options. Plus, who doesn't want an excuse to eat homemade pie for breakfast, lunch, and dinner?

Accommodations

Because Montana and Wyoming are both big destinations for visitors, it's no surprise that a wide variety of lodging options are available, from standard hotels and motels to luxury resorts and guest ranches. Generally speaking, all lodging is more expensive in the summer (except for those nearby ski resorts), and rooms fill rapidly—advance reservations are a must, especially around special events like Cheyenne's Frontier Days or Bozeman's Sweet Pea Festival. Rooms, cabins, and even campgrounds in the national parks fill up several months—if not longer—in advance. Shoulder seasons (spring and fall) offer reduced rates and thin crowds, while rooms at the ski resort lodges fill up fast in the winter but may be wide open during the summer.

Most larger towns have numerous choices for chain motels, which are typically clustered around the interstate exits. Gateway towns to Yellowstone and Grand Teton National Parks also have chain hotels, as well as a number of mom-and-pop motels sprinkled around town. Travelers used to standard hotels will be happy with these choices, but those who seek a unique experience will want to try some of the smaller boutique hotels located in towns in both states. It just depends on whether you would rather stay in the usual Super 8 or sleep in a room that once accommodated Ernest Hemingway or Annie Oakley. An excellent resource is **Historic Hotels of the Rockies** (www.historic-hotels.com).

There are a number of bed-and-breakfasts in Montana and Wyoming, most of which are in the higher-traffic tourist areas. Many are located on the banks of a river or nestled in the pine trees and often make great escapes from the busier hotel atmosphere. A fairly comprehensive listing can be found at **BnBFinder** (www.bnbfinder.com). Very few hostels exist in Montana and Wyoming, but **Hostels.com** (www.hostels.com) has a list of what might be available.

Guest ranches range from traditional horse-and-cowboy dude ranches to luxury "glamping" (a portmanteau of *glamorous* and *camping*) resorts that offer spa services and high-end cuisine. Two excellent resources for those seeking a real Western working vacation are the **Montana Dude Ranchers' Association** (888/284-4133, www.montanadra.com) and the **Wyoming Dude Ranchers' Association** (www.wyomingdra.com). Many of these are focused on horseback riding, fly-fishing, and family activities and often booked in weeklong blocks. In the winter, many of these ranches offer cross-country skiing, snowshoeing, or dogsledding.

Higher-end guest ranches are becoming very popular in Montana and Wyoming, offering guests a chance to experience a more rustic atmosphere with upscale amenities. These are typically set in remote locations with beautiful surroundings and are private, in some cases gated from public access. Typically these are the priciest accommodations, ranging

Historic Hotels Beyond Park Boundaries

So much is written about the glorious hotels inside the parks that have not only shaped the visitor experience for more than 100 years, but gave rise to a unique form of architecture known as "parkitecture." The Old Faithful Inn, Jenny Lake Lodge, and Lake McDonald Lodge are outstanding examples. Because securing lodging at these beautiful old hotels can be challenging and expensive, we've come up with a list of lovely historic hotels outside the parks.

Yellowstone National Park

◆ Just 30 minutes north of Yellowstone, in the mountains of **Paradise Valley, Chico Hot Springs** dates back to old mining days. It is one of the region's favorite resorts thanks to its cozy rooms, outstanding dining, natural hot springs pools, abundance of year-round activities, something of a Hollywood vibe, and even its resident ghost.

◆ The **Pollard Hotel** in lively downtown **Red Lodge** is a redbrick beauty dating back to 1893. It has hosted such legendary guests as Calamity Jane and Buffalo Bill in its stately rooms and suites.

Grand Teton National Park

◆ Not only does the **Triangle X Ranch** sit inside the boundaries of the park for the most extraordinary setting imaginable, but the ranch lodge is the original Turner family home. Its cabins housed valley families for generations before providing cozy accommodations for guests.

◆ **The Wort Hotel** in downtown **Jackson Hole** was opened as a glamorous lodging place in 1941, but its origins go back farther to its use as a corral and livery stable. Today, the elegant hotel is in the National Register of Historic Places and continues to be the heart of this town.

Glacier National Park

◆ **Belton Chalet** is an iconic lodge just outside the park in **West Glacier.** Built by the Great Northern Railroad, as were so many of Glacier's glorious buildings, the hotel opened in 1910 and underwent an award-winning restoration in 1999.

◆ Built in 1939 by the Great Northern Railroad as lodging for its workers, the Tudor Revival **Izaak Walton Inn** in **Essex** is about halfway between the entrances at East and West Glacier. Charming rooms are set in the old lodge, as well as in cabooses, luxury railcars, cabins, and an old schoolhouse.

from several hundred to $1,000 and more per night.

Cabins and other vacation rentals are becoming increasingly popular, as many travelers are looking for that Western cabin experience. These can range from rustic—just beds, no plumbing—to luxurious—down comforters, a rock fireplace—and are perhaps the best way to stay. Sites like **Airbnb** (www.airbnb.com) and **VRBO** (www.vrbo.com) offer private homes and cabins for rent, while many resorts provide nightly cabin rentals. For Forest Service cabins—which can be quite primitive but are set in phenomenal locations—travelers can check availability and make reservations at www.recreation.gov.

Plenty of RV and tent camping sites in Montana and Wyoming are available for those on the road. From national forest campgrounds to large private RV resorts, there is something for everyone. RV campers will find private campgrounds in most towns, and most national forest campgrounds have room for all but the longest RVs. It's generally legal to camp on national forest land, unless you see a sign indicating that overnight camping isn't allowed. For something closer to backcountry experience without hoofing it, drive on a Forest Service road until you find a nice campsite, pull over, and set up camp. Not only is it often scenic, it's also free.

Access for Travelers with Disabilities

For the most part, Montana and Wyoming comply with state and federal guidelines for handicapped access. Most hotels offer accessible rooms, and the national parks and even some state parks feature accessible trails. However, it's important to remember that many parts of both states are rural, and some features may be outdated, less accessible, or nonexistent.

Women Traveling Alone

Overall, Montana and Wyoming can be exciting for a woman traveling alone. For the most part, the West is full of independent and strong women, and you won't seem out of place in most areas. Outgoing and talkative women—as well as men—will feel right at home. Folks are pretty friendly and accommodating around these parts, and in general they like to meet people from other places. Of course, there is always the occasional weirdo, so if a place or a person makes you uncomfortable, the best thing to do is leave. Use the same precautions and common sense that you would at home. And it's worth noting that bear spray can be just as effective on a creepy dude as it is on a curious grizzly.

LGBTIQ Travelers

It's safe to say that many people in Montana and Wyoming are socially conservative, and same-sex public displays of affection are not very common. You shouldn't necessarily anticipate discrimination or hostility if you are LGBTIQ, but you'll want to be aware of your surroundings. You might not think much of expressing yourself at a back-road Montana or Wyoming bar, but you never know what the group in the corner is thinking. Sadly, this is where Matthew Shepard was brutally murdered in 1998 for no other reason than because he was gay. Montana and Wyoming still have a long way to go in terms of recognizing and celebrating alternative lifestyles. In general, "don't ask, don't tell" is the safest policy to assume when traveling here.

That being said, there are thriving—although often underground—gay communities in many Montana and Wyoming towns, particularly college towns like Missoula, Bozeman, and Laramie. Two excellent resources for LGBTIQ travelers are the **Western Montana LGBT Community Center** (406/543-2224, www.gaymontana.org) and the **University of Wyoming's Rainbow Resource Center** (307/766-3478, www.uwyo.edu/RRC).

Death in Yellowstone

Death in Yellowstone opens with a 1970 editorial from the *Billings Gazette,* its first line a gut punch: "A child has died in a particularly horrible fashion in Yellowstone Park." It goes on to describe the child's death in a hot spring and highlight the prospect of other deaths in the park, "from less rare incidents such as bear maulings." The editorial urges visitors to respect the wildness of the place. It ends simply: "The park is raw nature. And it can kill."

The book is *Death in Yellowstone: Accidents and Foolhardiness in the First National Park,* written by park historian Lee H. Whittlesey in 1995, and with a second edition out in 2014, it continues to be the best-selling book in the park. *Death in Yellowstone* is broken into chapters by the kinds of deaths met by more than 300 Yellowstone visitors since 1870, including death in hot water, deaths from poisonous plants, deaths by bears and other animals, deaths from poisonous gas, from falls, from fires, and lightning, from falling rocks and murder, among many others. It's morbid pulp, and we can't get enough of it.

In June of 2016, Colin Nathaniel Scott, 23, slipped and fell into a superheated acidic mud pot in the Back Basin area of the Norris Geyser Basin. He and his sister had wandered 225 yards off the boardwalk when the accident happened. She was filming on her phone as her brother fell to his death. Rangers arrived quickly and found a few of his personal items but could not recover the body due to a lightning storm. When they returned the next day, because of the heat and acidity of the water—a scientific borehole test measured water temperatures up to 459 degrees Fahrenheit, and a pH equal to battery acid—there were no remains to recover. Scott is one of more than 20 people who have met their ends in the geothermal features in the park.

Whittlesey gets into the gory details of so many of the park deaths. There was David Allen Kirwan, who dove headfirst into a hot spring to save his friend's dog. He made it out of the water, and was heard saying, "That was a stupid thing I did," as his skin was peeling away from his body, his eyes burned white. There was Dick Rock, a well-known poacher, who was gored by a bison in 1902, in front of a slew of onlookers. The bison repeatedly threw Rock's body into the air, ripping all the clothes from his body and leaving the corpse with 29 horn holes. Then there was Harry Walker who, in 1972, camped illegally with a friend near Grand Geyser and left food strewn around their site. Early one morning, they surprised a grizzly who had come for the food. Walker was dragged away. When the rangers found his body the next day, a quarter of it had been eaten by the bear. Walker died of suffocation from trauma to his trachea and rangers noted that his entire pelvic area was missing. No, Whittlesey does not skimp on the details.

The common denominator in almost all the stories—besides making for riveting, if macabre, reading—is not bad luck or bad timing, but bad judgement. Most of the hundreds of deaths in the book could have been avoided with common sense and a respect for the power of nature. *Death in Yellowstone* is a collection of absorbing and cautionary tales, reminding us that this is not Disney World, that Yellowstone is a place of beauty and wildness, a place that both deserves and demands respect. No wonder Whittlesey chose Shakespeare and a line from *A Midsummer Night's Dream* for the book's epigraph: "What fools these mortals be!"

Health and Safety

While medical services and health care in many of the larger Montana and Wyoming towns are excellent—and in some cases on par with bigger cities—it's important to remember that when traveling around, you'll mostly likely be far away from emergency medical services. Rural and mountainous highways are especially troublesome, as cell phone coverage can be spotty. Most small towns have a local clinic, and services are available in the national parks. Refer to specific areas of the text for emergency numbers, and remember that calling 911 doesn't always work in many rural areas.

In general, **weather, altitude,** and **insect bites** pose the greatest risk traveling here. The summer sun can get extremely hot, and it is easy to get dehydrated, so make sure to drink plenty of water during the day. Hiking—and just walking, for some people—can be a strenuous activity as the altitude increases. It's best to carry plenty of food and water, and take your time getting to your destination. Always let someone know where you are going and when you plan to be back. The earliest and most obvious sign of altitude-related health problems is a headache, and the best remedy is drinking water and moving to a lower elevation if possible.

The common insect nuisances are mosquitoes and ticks. Montana and Wyoming mosquitoes rarely carry diseases, but they can be annoying at certain times during the summer. While West Nile virus is becoming an increasing threat to livestock across the West, human infection is less common. Still, it's a good idea to carry bug repellent with DEET, especially when hiking or camping near water. Ticks can pose a small threat of Rocky Mountain fever or Lyme disease, and they seem to have become more pervasive in the last 10 years or so. It's a good idea to check every part of your skin after a day of hiking or fishing outdoors—places where you might encounter underbrush, dense trees, and grassy meadows. If you find a tick with its head stuck in your skin, pull gently with tweezers or your fingers until the tick works its way out. Don't forget to check your pets too.

A common backcountry ill is **giardia,** sometimes called "beaver fever," a microscopic parasite that lives in mountain streams and can wreak havoc in your intestinal tract. Avoid drinking unfiltered or untreated water directly from streams, rivers, springs, or lakes. Carry a water filter or water-purifying tablets (iodine or similar products), and you'll have nothing to worry about.

If you're camping or staying in a cabin, **hantavirus** can be a concern. Hantavirus is a potentially fatal disease caused by contact with rodent droppings, particularly those of deer mice. Symptoms include fever, muscle aches, coughing, and difficulty breathing. Campers should avoid sleeping on bare ground, and you should avoid cabins if you see signs of rodents. For more information, visit the Centers for Disease Control and Prevention (www.cdc.gov).

Winter poses different types of health concerns, namely **hypothermia** and **frostbite.** If you or someone in your party shows any signs of hypothermia—uncontrollable shivering, slurred speech, loss of coordination—get them out of the wind and inside immediately. If you're camping, a dry sleeping bag is your best bet. It's a good idea to dress in layers, avoid cotton clothing, always bring a hat, and—most important—make good decisions *before* you put yourself in a situation where you could be stranded in the wind and cold. If you're outside in the winter, a sign of frostbite is the whitening and hardening of the skin. The best way to warm the affected area is with other skin, but avoid warming it too quickly because thawing can be quite painful.

Weather

The old saying is a tad cliché but none-theless often true: If you don't like the weather in Montana or Wyoming, just wait five minutes. What this means to the traveler is that weather in this part of the West can change dramatically in an unbelievably short amount of time. In the summer, extreme heat can dehydrate the human body rapidly, and in the win-ter, extreme cold can render your body useless in a matter of minutes. Sudden changes in the weather can happen at any time of the year in mountainous areas. It can snow, sleet, hail, and rain at a mo-ment's notice. If you're heading into the backcountry or getting ready for a three-day river float, check the forecast, but don't rely on it; plan for the worst with extra gear and plenty of food and water.

In general, Montana and Wyoming have a semiarid climate. There is enough moisture at certain times of the year, but summers are typically dry and warm, with July-August being the hottest months. Mountainous areas see heavy snowfall during the winter (to the de-light of skiers), while the eastern part of both states can seem downright desert-like much of the year.

Wildlife

Although many people visit Montana and Wyoming for the abundant wild-life, with so much human interaction, safety is a real concern. A general rule of thumb is *never* to approach wildlife, no matter what the situation. It's just a bad idea, and each year people are hurt or killed because they ignore this basic rule. Not only are they putting them-selves in harm's way, but they are often precipitating imminent doom for the ani-mal as well. The old adage, "A fed bear is a dead bear," can be applied universally to wildlife. The problem of humans get-ting too close to animals, particularly in Yellowstone National Park, gets plenty of coverage these days on YouTube and the evening news. Do not become a cautionary lesson for other travelers; keep your distance from wildlife. Period.

Safety in Bear Country

Grizzly bears and black bears live in many parts of Montana and Wyoming, and although encounters are rare, it is necessary to learn what to do in case it happens to you. It is also important to know how to avoid the situation in the first place. No method is absolutely fool-proof, but with caution and attentiveness you can avoid most of the common mis-takes that lead to bear encounters.

When out in the backcountry, it's the unexpected bear encounter you really want to avoid. The best way to do this is to let the bears know you are present. Make noise in areas of dense cover and blind spots on hiking or biking trails. Immediately move away from any animal carcass you come across, as there may be a bear nearby protecting it. Avoid hiking or biking in the early morning or at dusk, and travel in larger groups; the more of you there are hiking together, the more likely a bear will sense you and move away. Making noise is a great way to let bears know you are near, and in most cases they will be long gone before you have the chance to get a glimpse of them. Be aware that dogs can provoke bears and bring them right to you. And, of course, never leave food out.

If you're camping in an area frequented by bears, look for bear signs (waste, over-turned rocks, decimated fallen timber, claw marks and hair on trees) around the campsite. Because bears are attracted to all kinds of odors—food, toothpaste, soap, deodorant—your cooking, eating, and food storage area should be at least 50 yards (45.7 m) from your tent. It's tempt-ing to bring tasty items like sausage, ham, tuna, and bacon with you, but these smell good to bears too. Freeze-dried foods are your best bet. Store foods in airtight bags and be sure to hang all food at least 12-15 feet (3.7-4.6 m) off the ground and away from tree trunks. Some designated campsites have bear storage containers or food storage poles.

Carrying **pepper spray** (sold in most sporting goods stores, but it's worth noting that at the Grizzly and Wolf Discovery Center in West Yellowstone, you can buy bear spray at cost) is a must in bear country, and it has been proven useful in fending off bear attacks. These sprays only work at close range (10-30 feet/3-9.1 m) and can quickly dissipate in the wind or sometimes blow back in your face. Carry the spray in a holster or on a belt across your chest for easy access. It's important to note that these spray canisters are not allowed on commercial airplanes, they expire after a certain date, and they should not be left in a very hot place like a closed car. Also, test your container every now and then in light or no wind to make sure it works.

If you happen to encounter a bear, and it notices you, try not to panic or make any sudden moves. Do not run—bears can run more than 40 mph in short bursts—and do not try to climb a tree. Make yourself visible by moving out into the open so the bear can identify you. Avoid direct eye contact with the bear; talking in a low voice may convince the animal that you are human. If the bear is sniffing the air or standing on its hind legs, it's most likely trying to identify you. If it's woofing and posturing, this could be a challenge. Stand your ground if the bear charges; most charges are bluffs, where the bear will stop short and wander away.

If a grizzly does charge and knocks you to the ground, curl up in the fetal position with your hands wrapped behind your neck and your elbows tucked over your face. Keeping your backpack on may offer some protection. Remain as still as possible, as bears will often only sniff or nip you and leave. This is considered playing "active dead." If the bear rolls you over, as it will likely try to do, roll yourself back over on your stomach and keep your neck as protected as possible. Remain on the ground until you know the bear has vacated the area.

In general, black bears are more common and seem to have more interaction with people. In many places they can be a nuisance—getting into garbage, breaking into homes—but don't think that they are not dangerous. Black bears will generally try to avoid you and are easily scared away, but if you encounter an attacking or aggressive bear, this usually means it views you as food. In this case, most experts recommend fighting back with whatever means possible: large rocks or sticks, yelling, and shouting.

It's a rare event when a bear attacks sleeping campers in tents at night, as tragically happened at the Soda Butte campground near Cooke City in July 2010, but if you find yourself in that situation, defend yourself as aggressively as you can. In these circumstances, bears are viewing you as prey and may give up if you fight back. Never play dead in this case, and to thwart off an attack, always keep pepper spray and a flashlight handy.

Before you go into the backcountry, brush up on your **bear identification.** You can't tell what kind of bear you see by its color alone. Grizzlies are often larger and have a trademark hump at the top of their neck. Grizzlies also have more of a dish-shaped face profile, compared to a straighter profile of black bears.

Other Wildlife

Although bears get the majority of the press, there are other animals that you need to be aware of when traveling around Montana and Wyoming. **Moose** are huge animals that are prone to sudden charges when surprised, especially females traveling with young. If you travel through Yellowstone National Park, you'll encounter numerous **bison,** large animals with sharp horns.

Although it may be tempting to walk up to them, avoid doing so. While they are not vicious, bison can charge if provoked and have maimed and even killed visitors in the past. Statistically, bison injure more people in Yellowstone than any other animal. Be aware that these lumbering beasts can sprint the length of a football field in six seconds and can leap a 6-foot (1.8-m) fence. Likewise, **elk** in the park can seem downright docile, but it's important to remember not to approach them.

Mountain lions generally keep a low profile, but as humans encroach on their habitat, encounters are becoming more frequent in the West. Most attacks have been on unattended children, and they rarely target adults. If you happen to find yourself in a situation with a mountain lion, be aggressive and fight back if necessary, or throw rocks and sticks to try to make it go away.

Rattlesnakes can be found in the central and eastern parts of Montana and Wyoming, especially in the drier prairies. Rattlesnake bites are rarely fatal (less than 4 percent when antivenin is used in time), and the snakes generally avoid humans. Be careful where you step when hiking around these areas, and pay attention if children are with you. If you surprise or step on a rattlesnake—chances are you'll hear its trademark rattle before you do—it may coil and strike. Any bite from a rattlesnake should be regarded as a life-threatening medical emergency that requires immediate hospital treatment by trained professionals.

With all of the incredible wildlife-viewing opportunities around Montana and Wyoming, it can be easy for some people to get complacent when taking pictures or hiking around. Treat all wildlife with respect and care, and never feed or approach any type of wild animal. If you are lucky enough to see many of these critters, observe them in their natural habitat and then carry on.

The last thing you want is to become a statistic.

Resources

Suggested Reading
History
Clayton, John. *Wonderlandscape: Yellowstone National Park and the Evolution of an American Cultural Icon.* New York: Pegasus Books, 2017. Using iconic figures—including painters, naturalists, and entrepreneurs—as the storytelling mechanisms, John Clayton paints a fascinating cultural picture of the park.

Guthrie, C. W. *Glacier National Park, The First 100 Years.* Helena, MT: Farcountry Press, 2008. A marvelous volume compiled to celebrate the park's centennial in 2010, this book features exquisite photos and artwork in addition to compelling history.

Righter, Robert W. *Crucible for Conservation: The Struggle for Grand Teton National Park.* Moose, WY: Grand Teton Natural History Association, 1982. This gripping history makes one grateful that things worked out the way they did.

Saunders, Richard L., editor. *A Yellowstone Reader: The National Park in Folklore, Popular Fiction, and Verse.* Salt Lake City: University of Utah Press, 2003. This volume offers a core sample of historical literature that spans the late 19th century through the 1980s.

Natural History
Johnsgard, Paul A., and Thomas D. Mangelsen. *Yellowstone Wildlife: Ecology and Natural History of the Greater Yellowstone Ecosystem.* Boulder: University Press of Colorado,

2013. With stunning images by Mangelsen and detailed natural histories of the animals that call the park home, this is an outstanding book for wildlife lovers.

Murie, Margaret, and Olaus Johan Murie. *Wapiti Wilderness.* Boulder: University Press of Colorado, 1985. A magnificent read by two of the region's now deceased but beloved conservationists, the chapters alternate between his work studying elk and her descriptions of their fascinating life together.

Phillips, Michael K., and Douglas W. Smith. *The Wolves of Yellowstone.* Stillwater, MN: Voyageur Press, 1996. Rife with fabulous color photos and intimate details by the two men who oversaw the project, this book tells the story of the wolves' reintroduction to Yellowstone in 1995.

Recreation

Arthur, Jean. *Top Trails: Glacier National Park: Must-Do Hikes for Everyone.* Birmingham, AL: Wilderness Press, 2014. Writer and storyteller Jean Arthur has been hiking Glacier for 30 years—often in the company of rangers, historians and Blackfeet guides—making her book equal parts trail guide and cultural history.

Nystrom, Andrew Dean, and Bradley Mayhew. *Top Trails Yellowstone & Grand Teton National Parks: 46 Must-Do Hikes for Everyone.* Birmingham, AL: Wilderness Press, 2017. A National Outdoor Book Award winner, this guide covers wonderful hikes from 0.5-mile (0.8-km) jaunts to 30-mile (48-km) treks by an author who lived in the park and hiked every trail at least once.

Watters, Ron. *Winter Tales and Trails: Skiing, Snowshoeing and Snowboarding in Idaho, the Grand Tetons and Yellowstone National Park.* Pocatello, ID: Great Rift Press, 1997. Both a classic and a necessity for winter adventurers, this guide blends advice with great stories. You'll wish Ron were along for the trip.

Internet Resources

Montana Fish, Wildlife & Parks
www.fwp.mt.gov
This official state site is useful for finding state parks, fishing and hunting information, and other recreational opportunities.

Montana Office of Tourism
www.visitmt.com
Searchable by region and town, places to go, things to do, and a variety of other user-friendly options, the website is superbly organized and easy to navigate.

Montana Traveler Updates
www.mdt.mt.gov/travinfo
The best resource for up-to-date road information comes courtesy of the Montana Department of Transportation.

National Park Service
www.nps.gov
The NPS website is helpful for making plans to visit any of the national parks.

Recreation.gov
www.recreation.gov
This government-run site allows visitors to make reservations at public campgrounds.

U.S. Forest Service
www.fs.fed.us
The Forest Service's website is helpful for pursuing recreational opportunities—including multiuse trails, campgrounds, and cabin rentals—throughout Montana and Wyoming.

Wyoming State Parks, Historic Sites, and Trails
www.wyoparks.state.wy.us
Useful information on parks, recreation, and historic preservation.

Wyoming Travel and Tourism
www.travelwyoming.com
The state's comprehensive offering for visitors, this is a great place to find information on towns, accommodations, travel ideas and itineraries, shopping, and dining.

Wyoming Travel Information
www.wyoroad.info
Up-to-date road information provided by the Wyoming Department of Transportation.

Wyoming Game and Fish Department
http://wgfd.wyo.gov
The website offers much of what visitors need to know about fishing and hunting in the state.

RESOURCES

Index

LIST OF MAPS

PHOTO CREDITS

ACADIA
NATIONAL PARK
HILARY NANGLE

ARCHES & CANYONLANDS
NATIONAL PARKS
W. C. McRAE & JUDY JEWELL

BANFF
NATIONAL PARK
ANDREW HEMPSTEAD

DEATH VALLEY
NATIONAL PARK
JENNA BLOUGH

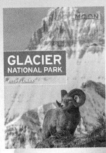

GLACIER
NATIONAL PARK
BECKY LOMAX

GRAND
CANYON
KATHLEEN BRYANT

GREAT SMOKY
MOUNTAINS
NATIONAL PARK
JASON FRYE

MOUNT RUSHMORE
& THE BLACK HILLS
Including the Badlands
LAURAL A. BIDWELL

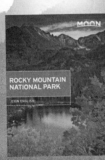

ROCKY MOUNTAIN
NATIONAL PARK
ERIN ENGLISH

YELLOWSTONE
& GRAND TETON
INCLUDING JACKSON HOLE
BECKY LOMAX

YOSEMITE
SEQUOIA &
KINGS CANYON
ANN MARIE BROWN

ZION &
BRYCE
Including Arches, Canyonlands,
Capitol Reef, Grand Staircase-
Escalante & Moab
W. C. McRAE & JUDY JEWELL

In these books:

- Full coverage of gateway cities and towns
- Itineraries from one day to multiple weeks
- Advice on where to stay (or camp) in and
  around the parks

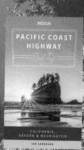

MAP SYMBOLS

═════	Expressway	○	City/Town	ⓘ	Information Center	⚑	Park
─────	Primary Road	◉	State Capital	🅿	Parking Area	⛳	Golf Course
─────	Secondary Road	⊛	National Capital	⛪	Church	✚	Unique Feature
═ ═ ═	Unpaved Road	✪	Highlight	🍇	Winery/Vineyard	🌊	Waterfall
----------	Trail	★	Point of Interest	🚩	Trailhead	▲	Camping
··········	Ferry	•	Accommodation	Ⓣ	Train Station	▲	Mountain
◄━━━►	Railroad	▼	Restaurant/Bar	✈	Airport	⛷	Ski Area
▩▩▩	Pedestrian Walkway	■	Other Location	✈	Airfield	〰	Glacier
▥▥▥	Stairs						

CONVERSION TABLES

$^\circ$C = ($^\circ$F − 32) / 1.8
$^\circ$F = ($^\circ$C × 1.8) + 32
1 inch = 2.54 centimeters (cm)
1 foot = 0.304 meters (m)
1 yard = 0.914 meters
1 mile = 1.6093 kilometers (km)
1 km = 0.6214 miles
1 fathom = 1.8288 m
1 chain = 20.1168 m
1 furlong = 201.168 m
1 acre = 0.4047 hectares
1 sq km = 100 hectares
1 sq mile = 2.59 square km
1 ounce = 28.35 grams
1 pound = 0.4536 kilograms
1 short ton = 0.90718 metric ton
1 short ton = 2,000 pounds
1 long ton = 1.016 metric tons
1 long ton = 2,240 pounds
1 metric ton = 1,000 kilograms
1 quart = 0.94635 liters
1 US gallon = 3.7854 liters
1 Imperial gallon = 4.5459 liters
1 nautical mile = 1.852 km

MOON YELLOWSTONE TO GLACIER NATIONAL PARK ROAD TRIP

Avalon Travel
Hachette Book Group
1700 Fourth Street
Berkeley, CA 94710, USA
www.moon.com

Editor: Leah Gordon
Acquiring Editor: Nikki Ioakimedes
Series Manager: Sabrina Young
Copy Editor: Brett Keener
Production and Graphics Coordinator:
  Darren Alessi
Cover Design: Erin Seaward-Hiatt
Interior Design: Darren Alessi
Moon Logo: Tim McGrath
Map Editor: Kat Bennett
Cartographers: Brian Shotwell, Karin Dahl,
  Erin Greb
Indexer: Rachel Kuhn

ISBN-13: 9781640490963

Printing History
1st Edition — December 2019
5 4 3 2 1

Front cover photo: Glacier National Park
© stellalevi\Getty Images

Printed in China by RR Donnelley